Contents

Acknowledgments

First thanks go to my brother, Christopher Severin, who gave me as a Christmas gift the *second* volume of Virginia Woolf's *Diary*. Thus began a journey of great fascination and reward. Anne Olivier Bell, whose wise and witty editing of Woolf's 1915 to 1941 diaries sets the standard for such work, has been generosity itself through my labors. In 2001, she allowed me to interview her regarding her work in the very room it was done. She then kindly drove me to see Charleston. Quentin Bell, before his death, also promptly and fully answered all my letter queries regarding his aunt Virginia and her diaries. My thanks go, too, to Andrew McNeillie, who took time during the 2001 Woolf conference in Wales to tell me about his own "heady" days as assistant editor of the 1920 to 1941 diaries in that "visually stunning Sussex country." In 2003 scholar Sybil Oldfield continued their largesse. She drove me through Lewes, Sussex; took me to the bridge overlooking the River Ouse near the Woolf's Rodmell home on what was a cold, overcast April day; and even boosted me up onto the Monk's House wall so I could see into the garden.

Stateside, many others have also aided this work. My great thanks go to Gay Talese, the pioneer in artful nonfiction, who has been my strongest supporter since 1983—and particularly supportive of this book. Nancy Price, the novelist and poet, endured reading the (much) longer version of this book; she even ironed pages that had become bent in the mail. Poet Kathleen Kelly also leant her wise counsel throughout the process—particularly in finding the work's shape. Woolf biographer Panthea Reid read two drafts of this volume, which has profited greatly from her thorough and helpful advice. In the 1990s, I also had the honor of giving programs in Iowa and Colorado with pianist Gary Arvin and mezzo-soprano Julie Simpson. I introduced Woolf and her diary, and they then performed with great artistry Dominick Argento's Pulitzer Prize-winning song cycle "From the Diary of Virginia Woolf."

I also am indebted to the Henry W. and Albert A. Berg Collection of English and American Literature in the New York Public Library and to its curators for many hours of congenial work with Woolf's manuscripts. My gratitude goes as well to Dorothy Sheridan, Head of Special Collections at the University of Sussex Library, for allowing me to work with the Monk's House papers. I also wish to express gratitude to the International Virginia Woolf Society, whose members are so welcoming of papers and essays, and especially to Woolf scholar Mark Hussey, who shared his thoughts regarding several chapters of this book. Shannon McCarthy, assistant editor at the University Press of Florida, for the past months has been a model of efficiency—and of grace.

My work with Woolf's diaries and the (many) diaries she read has received support from several arms of the University of Northern Iowa. I thank the Graduate College and the College of Humanities and Fine Arts for grants and leaves in support of the work. My special thanks to Rosemary Meany, Linda Berneking, and others in the Rod Library, who helped me locate and retrieve many obscure diaries. A final persistent thank you to John Lounsberry, who anchors all my days.

Abbreviations

AML	*A Moment's Liberty: The Shorter Diary*. Abr. and ed. Anne Olivier Bell.
CH	*Carlyle's House and Other Sketches* [Woolf's 1909 Diary]. Ed. David Bradshaw.
CM	*Charleston Magazine*
CR	*The Common Reader*. 2 vols.
D	*The Diary of Virginia Woolf*. Ed. Anne Olivier Bell. 5 vols.
E	*The Essays of Virginia Woolf*. Eds. Andrew McNeillie and Stuart N. Clarke. 6 vols.
G&R	*Granite and Rainbow*
L	*The Letters of Virginia Woolf*. Eds. Nigel Nicolson and Joanne Trautmann. 6 vols.
MOB	*Moments of Being*. Ed. Jeanne Schulkind.
PA	*A Passionate Apprentice: The Early Journals 1897–1909*. Ed. Mitchell A. Leaska.
RN	*Virginia Woolf's Reading Notebooks*. Ed. Brenda Silver.
SF	*The Complete Shorter Fiction of Virginia Woolf*. Ed. Susan Dick.
TG	*Three Guineas*

Introduction

A *masterpiece. One of the great diaries of the world.*

So declared Quentin Bell, Virginia Woolf's nephew, of her heart-stopping, boundary-stretching diary that serves as a doorway to her fiction and non-fiction. Woolf's diary is her longest, her longest sustained, and her last work to reach the public. Diary scholar Harriet Blodgett calls it "a high point in English diary-keeping" and "a remarkable social document."[1]

Woolf begins her first extant diary at age fourteen in 1897, and her final entry comes at the age of fifty-nine, four days before her suicide in March 1941. Thirty-eight handwritten diary volumes are safeguarded today in the United States and England. Together they offer some 2,312 entries and 770,000 words—more words than any one of her novels.

Like a hidden gold mine, this diary reached readers in tantalizing segments across a half-century: from 1953 to 2003. As each vein of the mother lode appeared, it has been carefully scoured for Woolf's references to her works or to the talented friends and family members who made up her storied Bloomsbury Group; scoured, too, for the wider circle of notables, including George Bernard Shaw, Vita Sackville-West, T. S. Eliot, and Ethel Smyth, who came to want to know her. The diaries have been sifted, too, for Woolf's views on a range of subjects—from art to war. What remains now is to understand the diary as a *diary*: Woolf's development as a diarist and her place among, and legacy to, the worldwide community of diarists she so greatly valued and admired.

However, challenges abound. Diaries are still *"terra incognita,"* French diary theorist Philippe Lejeune reminded us in 2004 (76). I will argue in this book that this fact made the diary particularly attractive to Woolf. Furthermore, as Lejeune also points out, "There is no such thing as a typical diarist" (154). Woolf's diary itself shifts form radically—particularly across her first two decades as a diarist explored in this book. How to sort through and say something meaningful about such a variegated mass?

My answer is to offer close readings of each of her first twelve diary books—something never as yet attempted. Woolf took great care with her diary books throughout her life. In the early years she created and bound the books herself. She treats her 1903 diary as a book with "chapters" and even makes a table of contents. She remarks at the start of her 1918 diary: "There's no reason after all why one should expect special events for the first page of a new book; still one does," revealing that she thought of each book as a discrete aesthetic unit—yet part of the enlarging whole (*D* 1: 99). Following her line, I treat each of her twelve early diaries (1) as a work of art itself; (2) as it relates to her other early diaries; and (3) as it intersects with her public works (letters and published essays, reviews, fiction, and nonfiction). This method lays bare Woolf's development as a diarist, and, an extra dividend, as a public writer as well. We see—more clearly than ever before—*how* she becomes the writer so widely revered today.

In the following pages, I challenge several long-standing views of Woolf's diaries. Mitchell Leaska, who published Woolf's first seven diary books in 1990 under the title *A Passionate Apprentice: The Early Journals 1897–1909*, declared that Woolf first offers her "artistic credo" in her 1908 Italian diary (xxvi). I argue here that she articulates her aesthetic much earlier, starting at age seventeen in her 1899 Warboys diary. I also offer a more nuanced reading of Woolf's newly discovered 1909 diary which has been treated as bitter and even as anti-Semitic since 2002 when it was found in a desk drawer in Wales.

I call, too, for reconsideration of the pervading view that Woolf's diary-writing breaks into two parts: her "apprentice" years from 1897 to 1909, and the remainder of her diary-writing (1915 to 1941). The six volumes of Woolf's published diary create this view. During an interview of Andrew McNeillie, the assistant editor of Woolf's 1920 to 1941 diaries, I asked why Anne Olivier Bell, who painstakingly edited the essential five-volume 1915 to 1941 *Diary of Virginia Woolf*, chose to begin with Woolf's 1915 diary rather than with the earlier diaries. McNeillie believes the Bells thought of the early volumes as "something apart"—as different from the diaries that unfold from 1915 on. One can understand this view: the first seven diaries are extraordinarily various, but so are the five diaries that follow. Close study of the diary books themselves reveals that Woolf's diary-keeping falls into *three* stages: her experimental early diaries from 1897 to mid-1918 (treated in this book); her mature, spare modernist diaries from 1919 to 1929; and a final diary flowering from 1930 to her death during which she wrote many more diary entries per year than in the 1920s and read more diaries of others as well.

This book also conveys a final new insight: the crucial role of *other* diaries in Woolf's creative life. Woolf was more steeped in diary literature than any other well-known diarist before her—and likely even since. In the 1600s Samuel Pepys and John Evelyn admired each other and visited in each other's homes. However, we have no sign either man told the other he kept a diary, much less—heaven forefend!—that they *exchanged* diary books with each other, or with Lady Anne Clifford, who began her own diary in 1603. James Boswell is often dubbed "Pepys's son" for the insatiable curiosity he shares with his putative pater, wedded to unabashed delight in recording his own vices and peccadilloes. But Boswell could never have read his "father's" prose, for Pepys's diary did not see print until 1825—thirty years after Boswell's death. Fanny Burney was alive in 1825—a spry seventy-three—and likely read Pepys's wildly popular diaries. By then, however, she had been penning her own ebullient diaries for more than fifty years and hardly needed Pepys to show her how to write a lively diary entry. Woolf read all five of these important British diaries and sixty-one other diaries that can be tracked. (She unquestionably read more.)

She read Walter Scott's and Fanny Burney's diaries before starting her first surviving diary at age fourteen. Scott and Burney are rightly called her *diaristic* father and mother. At fifteen, she found refuge in Pepys's diaries in the days before her half-sister, Stella, wed. Young Virginia called her "dear Pepys . . . the only calm thing in the house" (*PA* 66). At age twenty-one, she read Boswell's *Journal of a Tour to the Hebrides with Samuel Johnson* and praised it at length in her own pivotal 1903 diary. She would return to these four major British diarists again and again throughout her life.[2] Woolf did more, though, than just *read* diaries across her days. She wrote reviews of diaries and journals as well as lively essays that entered imaginatively into other diary worlds ("Fanny Burney's Half-Sister," "Dr. Burney's Evening Party," "Gas at Abbotsford").

Her taste in diaries ran to the eclectic. She read the diaries of governesses and Eton masters, country parsons and city curates, literary lawyers and doctors, printers and politicians, artists and aristocrats. She savored the diaries of other writers: Emerson, Tolstoy, Chekhov, Stendhal, the Goncourt brothers, de Maupassant, Jules Renard, André Gide, Jonathan Swift, Boswell, Burney, Scott, William Allingham, Dorothy Wordsworth, Mary Berry, George Eliot, Mary Coleridge, Katharine Bradley and Edith Cooper ("Michael Field"), Beatrice Webb, and Katherine Mansfield. Twenty-five of the sixty-six traceable diaries Woolf read were written by (or in defense of) women and served as one source of her deep knowledge of women's lives. Women's diaries, I believe, greatly aided Woolf's own writing path. How reassuring it must have been for the self-described painfully shy and nervous fourteen-year-old to know that excruciating shyness and lifelong "fidgets" did not keep Fanny Burney from becoming "the mother" of English fiction, as Woolf twice called her (*MOB* 105; *E* 2: 314; *E* 3: 337).

From 1908 to 1910, as she worked on her own first novel, Woolf read diaries written by, or in defense of, four Regency women: *The Journal of Elizabeth Lady Holland (1791–1811)*; Lady Charlotte Bury's *Diary of a Lady-in-Waiting* (published in her own defense and to spur sympathy for the maligned Princess Caroline of Wales); and physician Charles Meryon's six volumes of Boswellian diaries which preserve the brilliant talk and exploits of Lady Hester Stanhope. Woolf's reviews reveal the lessons she drew from these diaries: if a woman wished to be remembered, she must be convention-breaking—and courageous.

In 1910, Woolf read published excerpts from Mary Coleridge's diary, a more recent foremother. She found there a kindred spirit, one who savored fantasy and relished change, one who wrote: "I go to bed as feminine as Ophelia, fiery, enthusiastic, ready to go to the stake for some righteous cause. I get up the very next morning, almost as masculine as Falstaff, grumbling at Family Prayers" (221). Was this an early seed for *Orlando*? Woolf found in Coleridge a writer with an eye on women—in literature and in life. In writer Mary (Seton) Berry's *Journals*, likely read in 1915 or early 1916, Woolf found an even more fiery voice for women than Coleridge's and the whole kernel of *A Room of One's Own*.

Woolf's experience as an avid diary reader must have differed seismically from that of most of us who read *her* diary. We've likely read Anne Frank's diary in early consolidated or later unexpurgated form. A bit of Pepys and Boswell perhaps? Woolf's diary, maybe another diary, and (of course) our own. Since, with one exception, the sixty-six traceable diaries Woolf read were English language or European diaries from 1603 to her present time, to open a new diary must have been for Woolf like resuming an historical narrative, with every chance of meeting familiar events and even personages from other diaries, but now with new details or from another point of view. If Woolf's mind was an historical mural, each diary offered foreground or background and often entirely new tableaus.

Similarly, when she opened her own diary in the morning or in a quiet moment after tea, she was adding her own strokes to the universal painting. She was joining the commonwealth of diarists whose work not only refreshed her but also meant literally for her *life*. In the following pages I explore not only Woolf's own early diaries but also fifteen key diaries she read through 1918 that helped shape the writer she became. One feels on a treasure hunt, for again and again one meets passages that turn up transformed in Woolf's later published works. Woolf herself understood the, perhaps unusually intense, role reading played in her work. "I ransack public libraries," she told her 1921 diary, "& find them full of sunk treasure" (*D* 2: 126). Woolf biographer Hermione Lee suggests that Woolf's mind was "full of echoes": "A great mass of reading finds its way into her prose, and what strikes one most is the exuberant and careful way in which she works through influences towards her own tone of voice" (405, 166). By following Woolf's diary-reading, we see the raw items as they enter the "compost heap" (as she called her diary) to undergo the extraordinary transmutation into art.

⌇

Woolf creates a diary more structurally experimental than any of the diaries she read. In its protean, ever-stretching form, her diary must be a primary stop for those who love or who study diaries—often one and the same. Lejeune in 2005 found himself "struck by the creative resources" within the diary form: "Extremely easy, extremely difficult. Perhaps, for anyone who takes this challenge seriously, a new frontier" (186). In Woolf's first two decades as a diarist, not one of her diaries resembles another. She begins conventionally enough at age fourteen, trying to keep a daily journal in a small brown leather diary with a lock and key. Entries begin to falter in October as they do the few other times she tries a daily diary, for she was by temperament one of our great *periodic diarists*. In her first two decades, she experiments with dated entries and undated entries and entries that collect several dates ("Saturday 3, Sunday 4, Monday 5 November"; "Sunday, Monday, Tuesday, & Wednesday; Wednesday being the 12th of December"). She tries titled *essay-entries*, some dated, some not, and diaries of special scope. Her first 1905 diary, for instance, focuses narrowly on marking her first success as a professional writer. Entries wither in early May, but in the late summer she constructs a new larger diary and turns inward for the ghostly, haunted Cornwall diary. She then turns outward and keeps two *travel diaries*: the Great Britain travel diary of 1906 to 1908 and the Continental travel diary of 1906 to 1909. "I begin to distrust description," she writes in Italy in her 1908 diary (*PA* 384). *Places* turn to *portraits* in her newly found 1909 diary. In fact, place and décor telegraph character ("Carlyle's House," "Cambridge," "Hampstead") in the style of Henry James.

A five-year gap then yawns, the longest in Woolf's diary history. In 1915, the now married Virginia Woolf weaves portrait and place, event and thought, together into a richly colored *life diary* tapestry. Illness ends this diary after only six weeks. Two-and-a-half years later, she writes herself back into the world with a very different diary: her succinct, staccato Asheham House natural history diary. After sixty-seven days she adds a city diary to this country diary, and from October 1917 to October 1918, her most intense period of diary-writing, she keeps *two* diaries, writing in *both* diaries on seventeen days. In the fall of 1917, she reads the Goncourt brothers' collaborative diary which spurs her to try a joint diary that year and the next with her husband, Leonard Woolf. (The effort fails.)

In 1918, as my volume ends, Woolf has used her diaries—and others' diaries—to write herself back from illness. Her 1918 diaries both reach out and coalesce. We leave her ready to launch her mature, spare (modernist) diary style. Even then, she does not cease her diary stretch. "[D]oes my style remain fixed?" she ponders. "To my mind it changes always. But no one notices. Nor can I give it a name myself" (*D* 2: 94).

Did Woolf's vast diary reading spur her experiments? Only, I believe, in part. She certainly met the full range of ingenious formats through which humans have shared their diaries. She read single and multi-volume diaries, daily diaries and periodic. She read life diaries, travel diaries, war diaries, and diaries of illness. She read *journal-letters* such as Swift's famed *Journal to Stella*; the eponymous "letters and diaries of"; and memoirs launched, closed, or peppered throughout with diary entries. She read memoirs drawn from notebooks and scrapbooks such as Lady Dorothy Nevill's. She warmed to collaborative diaries like the Goncourt brothers' or the aunt and niece who wrote their joint diary under the name "Michael Field."

A diary's pull for Woolf may have been its versatility, its blank-faced malleability. Nevertheless, I am inclined to think her morphing journal grew mostly from her worldview and resulting literary aesthetic—shaped, as she jibed, "by my own queer, difficult nervous system" (*D* 3: 39). "Life" (the world) for Woolf was of essence *change*: "different shades & degrees of light—melting & mixing infinitely," as she wrote at seventeen in her 1899 diary (*PA* 156). To record a day's expedition was to freeze it, to solidify in words what at the time was more fluid. To describe the next expedition in the same way not only bored Woolf but also would be false to the experience that was, by definition, different in subtle or substantive ways. As Christine Froula has suggested, "the difficulty of writing renews itself every day, not because other people have written but because time, the world, continue to unfold past every act of writing" (133).

Woolf's ceaseless drive to stay "fluid" explains two traits that have annoyed some readers and surprised others. Woolf receives more rebuke than most artists for her sensitivity to criticism. However, censure, particularly through the early years, literally could stall her, send her into creative chill. The rapidly written diary helped her keep fluid. In it, in fact, she invents her "quick change" tactic in the 1920s as a way to keep in motion in other works to avoid creative stall. Similarly, the wish to escape rigidity or hardening explains what seems Woolf's inordinate diary obsession with old age, starting as early as her 1918 diary at age thirty-five.

Woolf by nature was a highly fluid, richly fecund writer. In her 1926 diary she speaks of "the suggestive power of every sight & word," and in her 1924 diary she describes "things churning up in my mind & so making a perpetual pageant, which is to me my happiness" (D 3: 104; D 2: 315). Metaphors begin to tumble from her pen, bounteously—one often extending another. She will shift her form or her position. As a result, a diary with a limited cast of players pursuing an endless round of teas, parties, and talks manages, in Woolf's hands, to stay incredibly fresh.

The diary seems fresh, as well, because of its swift, spontaneous prose. Woolf's diary belongs with that cream of diaries that are not only delicious but unrevisedly so. Most of the diaries touted as among the great diaries of the world are also works that have reached us carefully edited and revised: Samuel Pepys's diary, James Boswell's, Fanny Burney's—even young Anne Frank's. From the start Woolf followed her diary mentor, Sir Walter Scott, in penning her diary "*hab nab at a venture*": as an exercise in rapid unrevised freewriting (Lockhart 8: 251). Only in her third decade as a diarist, when she became more reflective on her diary habit, did she allow that this method aided her professional prose, for it gave her regular practice in the direct pounce: on subject, thought, and word.

Speed also allowed her to ambush her unconscious. Diary writing "loosens the ligaments," she told her diary in 1919 and again in 1924 in the context, interestingly, of telling the truth of women's friendship (D 1: 266; D 2: 320). The "advantage of the method," she observed in 1919, "is that it sweeps up accidentally several stray matters which I should exclude if I hesitated, but which are the diamonds of the dustheap" (D 1: 234). To write with spontaneous ease was, for Woolf, one sign of genius. English poet Christina Rossetti, Woolf told her 1918 diary, "wrote very easily; in a spontaneous childlike kind of way one imagines, as is the case generally with a true gift" (D 1: 179). Each time Woolf opened her diary, therefore, served as both test—and testament—that she wrote with an incandescent pen.

Across Woolf's early diaries we watch her slowly turn into an exquisite diary portraitist. Some readers believe that Woolf's diary portraits alone secure her place as the "Shakespeare of the diary genre," as diary scholar Anna Jackson both states and then steps back from calling her ("Towards a Poetics of the Diary" 259). Should it surprise us that Woolf pens striking diary portraits? Her older sister, the artist Vanessa Bell, painted portraits, as did Duncan Grant and Roger Fry. Portraiture was one of those inexhaustible Bloomsbury topics. Why wouldn't the jealous younger sister try her hand? Woolf uses the term "sketchbook" for several of her diaries,[3] and as late as 1930, she writes at age forty-eight:

> I will obediently, like a student in the art school—sketch Sir George [Duckworth, her abusive half-brother]. First his jowl: it is of the finest semi-transparent flesh; so that one longs to slice it, as it rests, infinitely tender, upon his collar. Otherwise he is as tight as a drum. One expects his trousers to split as he sits down. This he does slowly & rises with difficulty. Still some sentiment begins to form misty between us. He speaks of "Mother." I daresay finds in me some shadowy likeness—well—& then he is not now in a position to do me harm. (*D* 3: 293)

As the above suggests, a typical mature Woolf diary portrait is acutely observed, insightfully probed, often wickedly funny, and for all these reasons revelatory and memorable. Much of the humor in Woolf's diary portraits stems from the Stephen children's penchant from the earliest days to see themselves and others as animals, fish, and fowl—in short, to thrust the human back into nature. Virginia was called "the Goat"; Vanessa "dolphin"; cousin Madge Vaughan "toad"; art student Katherine Cox "bruin"; tall doting Violet Dickinson "wallaby"; Leonard and Virginia interchangeably "marmot" and "mandrill"; and Vita Sackville-West "creature" to Virginia's "Potto" (a lemur). Even in her first diary, in her miniature or snapshot phase, Virginia writes that Miss Florence May "looked like a poor green melancholy poll parrot" at her pianoforte recital, while Aunt Dorothea Stephen is "as fat as a grampus" (*PA* 59–60, 105). At age seventeen, Virginia offers her first "type": a Stephen. Her important 1903 diary begins with admiring portraits of "theorizing women": "An Afternoon with the Pagans" and a sketch of her Greek teacher "Miss Case" (*PA* 185, 182). Portraits dominate the newly found 1909 diary. From the Goncourt brothers' journals Woolf learns in 1917 that a diary can capture an entire literary scene. She launches into diary portraits of the Bloomsbury Group and the 1917 Club. In 1918, as my volume comes to a close, we see signs of the highly self-conscious and penetrating portraitist soon to come.

Seeking truth, Woolf tends to paint balanced portraits. If, when angered, she fires off a withering portrait, she often will pause and recall her subject's virtues. In general, Woolf liked people and was curious about them. Throughout her diary she will use portraits of others to explore her own conflicts. Only when a "hate my kind" revulsion enters the diary do we sense illness in the wings.

⌇

Woolf's diary *is* a writer's diary. Leonard Woolf was right about that, but it is much more. Few diaries capture the creative process as fully as Woolf's. In her early diaries we see her psychological tricks to induce prose. Artists, particularly, have valued her diary. "I think every writer should buy and keep a copy of this book; what emerges from it is salutary," English poet, playwright, and novelist Rumer Godden wrote in 1953 when the diary's first (abridged) version appeared (1). W. H. Auden observed that he had "never read any book that conveyed more truthfully what a writer's life is like, what are its worries, its rewards, its day-by-day routine" (99). He closes his review by suggesting that Woolf's diary holds up a standard: "I cannot imagine a time, however bleak, or a writer, whatever his school, when and for whom her devotion to her art, her industry, her severity with herself—above all, her passionate love, not only or chiefly for the big moments of life but also for its daily humdrum 'sausage-and-haddock' details—will not remain an example that is at once an inspiration and a judge" (103–4).

American composer Dominick Argento also felt the power of the 1953 *Diary*. His song cycle "From the Diary of Virginia Woolf" won a Pulitzer Prize in 1975 and has introduced Woolf's diary to musicians and music lovers across the world. "The text I originally planned to use for this song-cycle was a series of excerpts from Virginia Woolf's novel, *The Waves*," Argento explained. "Needing clarification about Mrs. Woolf's intentions at certain points, I consulted her recently published *Diaries*. A quick survey of these convinced me that the *Diaries* would yield far more musical potential than my initial idea. The only problem was deciding which of the thousands of entries to use" (Album notes).

Finally, one must ask: would Woolf's other works—her fiction, essays, biographies, and journalism—exist without her diary? These works unfurl always in tandem with the diary. Woolf describes her diary, curiously, as a kind of intermediate stage between the unconscious and the public world: it was not "writing," she insisted, but something else (*D* 2: 179). But of course it was writing, but writing of a special sort. Beyond its blank-faced versatility, the diary suited other facets of her evolving aesthetic. As Lejeune noted in 2007, a diary is "a force of opposition and renewal" (209). The diarist opposes oblivion: life is renewed in each record and in all future re-readings. Furthermore, a diary "challenges classical aesthetic models by introducing fragmentation, repetition, and especially its unfinished quality as dynamic sources of inspiration" (209). It "taps into a new type of relationship between author and reader, with a more active role for the reader" (209). In her diary Woolf could explore these inviting traits, which came to characterize her modernist works.

Woolf's own words reveal she thought diary-writing one path to immortality. "Should you wish to make sure that your birthday will be celebrated three hundred years hence, your best course is undoubtedly to keep a diary," begins her 1920 commemorative essay on John Evelyn's diary (*CR* 1: 78). Of Pepys she writes two years before: "the very fact that he kept a diary seems to make him one of ourselves" (*E* 2: 235).

The greatest diaries, I have come to believe, spring from the greatest need. In the case of gifted, complex minds, like Woolf's, a diary comes to serve multiple roles. Diary pen strokes soothed Woolf—like her half-sister Stella's hands. In the diary, she could confide, write out her "fidgets," and "medicine" her jealousy or despair. She could plan her public works—and also practice them in her diary. The diary served as a compost heap, or a reservoir for her flooding thoughts. She used it to store praise but, in time, to turn fiercely from ego. She wanted her diary for more than herself and her precious art. She wished to capture the world and to stay time through her pen.

In the end, one faces the paradox of diaries. Diaries are among the most fragile of literary forms. Often multivolume like Woolf's, parts easily can be lost. A diary's fate, furthermore, often rides on the diarist's descendants: this has meant wholesale destruction, ripped out pages, crossings-out, or, worse yet, rewritten passages. Vulnerable at the diarist's death, in life the diary, paradoxically, often is the stable bridge through the diarist's chaotic days. The diary is the life raft. So it was for André Gide who wrote regularly in *his* diary, "I cling to you in the face of death." So it was for Virginia Woolf. Diaries, for her, meant *life*. In the following pages, which trace Woolf's first twelve diaries, we watch her seize life repeatedly and become the writer we know.

1

Early Diary Influences

The word "influence" comes from the Latin *influere*, meaning "to flow in." This chapter reveals how early others' diaries flow through Virginia Woolf's young mind, and shape not only her soon-to-be-started diary but also her future public prose. At age fourteen she finds her diary parents—important literary parents—in Sir Walter Scott and Fanny Burney. She adopts all her diary's stylistic traits from Scott's diary—and other aesthetic views as well. In his many-sidedness he serves as a vital model and mentor. Burney, whom Woolf calls the "mother of English fiction," reinforces many of Scott's diary traits, but Burney also takes note of women in her diary and provides young Virginia with a way of seeing she will use throughout her life. Woolf's uncanny parallels with Burney and her haunting interaction with this diary mother are explored here at length.

At age fifteen, Woolf reads Samuel Pepys's celebrated diary, another London Nobody (like Burney) who becomes famous through his pen. Pepys models busy London success—and diary success across the ages. Six months later, as Virginia considers college for herself, she reads *Extracts from the Letters and Journals of William Cory*, the poet, beloved master of Eton and fellow of King's College, Cambridge. His *Journals* describe English male public school and university life: she sees what she is missing. Cory offers compensations, however: detritus for the compost heap Woolf will transform into art.

The influx of influence begins. The young girl's skillful use of these early diary sources impresses. Samuel Johnson writes of "the salutary influence of example" (170). Like all influences, the diaries the teenager reads prompt, foster, dispose, nourish, and embolden her in certain ways; more than anything, they set her in motion.

Virginia Woolf's 1897 Diary

"We have all started to keep a record of the new year—Nessa, Adrian and I." These, the first words to reach us from Virginia Stephen, diarist, suggest she thought of diaries as plural as well as single: as a concert of human voices. This start should be recalled as her lifelong play with other diaries unfurls.

A diary affirms the fourteen-year-old's place in a journal-writing family. Her father keeps a diary, as did her grandmother Stephen, her Quaker aunt (Caroline Stephen), and her older cousin, Katherine Stephen. Stella Duckworth, Virginia's twenty-seven-year-old half-sister and now substitute mother, also keeps a diary, and Thoby, her much-admired older brother, keeps a notebook "with careful observations and drawings of birds and animals" (Lee 223). Now the other Stephen children at home will keep diaries too.

Diary-writing, in short, probably does not seem at all remarkable to the young girl; rather, it is a practice most family members pursue. Although by her fifteenth birthday, January 25, 1897, she is well launched in her small brown leather diary with its lock and key, she receives another diary as a gift from her cousin Mia. Diary *giving*, in fact, may have been a family custom, for in May Virginia buys a diary for her half-brother, George Duckworth, and purchases another diary as a birthday gift for her older sister, Vanessa. The quality and character of a diary book matter to the young diarist, for after only a week of diary-keeping, Virginia writes that her own leather diary "must and shall survive Nessas[1] Collins and Renshaw. It has a key, and beautiful boards, and is much superior" (*PA* 10). Writing—especially diary writing—forges a bond with her older sister. "Nessa drew at the 'Oak Davenport' which holds all our paper now and is very nice," Virginia writes January 22, "and I wrote on a table beside her" (*PA* 19).

Diary-writing links Virginia to older and busier family members, but it also allows her to vent private rebellions and chart her own course. As diary scholar Elizabeth Podnieks writes, the very act of diary-keeping "registers concern and respect for one's self, life, feelings, and experiences" (65). Podnieks joins Adrienne Rich, Harriet Blodgett, Judy Simons, Deborah Martinson, Joanne Campbell Tidwell, and others in finding the diary a particularly attractive form for females, for here may be found "a private persona . . . often at odds with the public image of feminine propriety" (Simons 202). The 1897 diary reveals just such a persona, for it documents a tension between the growing social claims on the teenager and her own move toward social, religious, intellectual, and literary independence.

The 1897 diary shows the young girl's dislike of Victorian rites and the anguish social pressures gave. "Ida [Milman] has asked us to tea there tomorrow—No way out of it—," Virginia despairs February 3 (*PA* 29). The next day's entry records the result: "Had a long dreary tea with the Milmans, dances were discussed afterwards, in which Miss Jan [Virginia's nickname] did not take much interest—" (*PA* 29). Fifteen days later, "Poor Miss Jan utterly lost her wits" at the Stillmans, causing her to record her "conviction that what ever talents Miss Jan may have, she does not possess the one qualifying her to shine in good society" (*PA* 39).

Beyond dreary social pulls, Virginia found herself witness to the marriage plot—even pressed into service as its enabler. Her diary records her recoil. Stella marries in April; in May, cousin Adeline becomes engaged to the composer Ralph Vaughan Williams; eighteen-year-old Vanessa "comes out" in June; and Virginia herself is "forced" to wear "stays" (*PA* 64). One can picture other fifteen-year-olds caught up in the romance of engagements, weddings, balls, and ball gowns.[2] Virginia's anxiety at being placed in the role of Stella's chaperone, her recoil from the "dreadful idea" of being a bridesmaid, and her impatient disdain for the "dratted never-to-be-finished evening dress" (*PA* 50, 98) might be read by some as revealing a reluctance to leave the nursery and embrace adult sexuality (or heterosexuality). Others may find her response entirely age appropriate. The intensity of her resistance suggests these demands interfere with something more vital underway.

For the fifteen-year-old resists more than social rites; she shows independence on religion as well. From the start, the diary is kept in concert with other work. About this time Virginia is writing a now-lost work she describes in her 1929 diary as "a long picturesque essay upon the Christian religion, I think; called Religio Laici, I believe, proving that man has need of a God; but the God was described in process of change" (*D* 3: 271). As writer-scholar Louise DeSalvo has wryly noted, arguing for humanity's "need of a God" in the household of the author of *An Agnostic's Apology and Other Essays* reveals the adolescent's independent thought (*Impact* 243). It also lays her claim to the family legacy of religious writing as well as diary-keeping. On February 24 Virginia tells her diary that "father has given me Essays in Ecclesiastical Biography, which will do for me for some time" (*PA* 42). These essays were by her grandfather, Sir James Stephen.

On March 28, Virginia joins family members at the Church at St Mary Abbots to hear Stella's marriage banns. Her diary reveals not only her Emily Dickinson-like resistance to conventional religious acts (and use of the word "chorister") but also early signs of her eye, ear, and wit:

> A little black gentleman showed us into seats at the top of the church. Soon music and singing began, the row in front of us rose, and behind a wheezy old lady began to follow the choristers in a toothless tuneless whistle—so on for the rest of the performance. At certain parts we stood, then sat, and finally knelt—this I refused to do. . . . In the middle the banns of John Waller Hills and Stella Duckworth along with several others were read, and no one pronounced any reasons why etc. etc. . . . We had a sermon from a new pastor—he said we shall never hear the beloved voice again, alluding to the departed vicar—the old ladies snuffled and sobbed—Finished Sterling. (*PA* 61)

"Sterling" was Thomas Carlyle's *The Life of Sterling*, one of the huge number of books Virginia "devoured" across this year (*PA* 95). The speed at which the young girl reads offers one of the earliest signs of her genius. The biographies and histories, essays, novels, plays, and poems she reads forge an intellectual and literary world far more invigorating than Aunt Minna's "stream of gossip" and other social shallows (*PA* 88). Thus, while the external social "whirlpool" is captured in full force in the 1897 diary, Virginia simultaneously tallies the enlarging intellectual and literary sphere that will replace it (*PA* 98).

Other people's diaries particularly supply this alternative community, this vision of other lives. For one who is to become herself a great diarist, Woolf could hardly have begun better, for during these early teenage years she reads the diaries of Sir Walter Scott, Fanny Burney, Samuel Pepys, and William Johnson Cory.

Sir Walter Scott's "Gurnal"

"*As I walked by myself / I talked to my self / And thus my self said to me,*" Sir Walter Scott begins his diary in 1825. Virginia likely reads this diary even before age fifteen when her father gives her John Lockhart's ten-volume *Memoirs of the Life of Sir Walter Scott* as a birthday gift. She boasts in her diary February 21, 1897: "I managed to finish the 7th volume of Scott, to begin and finish the 8th volume and to begin the ninth volume. This is partly explained by the amount of Diary in the 8th, which I have just read, so that I skipped it, but it was a most wonderful feat nevertheless" (*PA* 40). When, precisely, she "just read" Scott's diary I cannot say. That she does not list his diary separately among other books tallied in her journal suggests she may have read it before 1897. Louise DeSalvo notes that in 1896 Leslie Stephen was at work on his own life of Scott for the *Dictionary of National Biography* (*Impact* 219). He likely drew on Scott's diary for his entry and might have recommended the work to his daughter. The Scottish writer had been a favorite of Virginia's mother as well. "For Scott [mother] had a passion," Woolf recalled in her 1939 memoir "A Sketch of the Past": "for a birthday present she chose all the works of Scott which her father gave her in the first edition" (*MOB* 86).

One can never gauge a book's precise impact on its reader—which facets of Scott's journal might have impressed young Virginia enough to shape her own views and work. Nevertheless, signs of the volume's influence abound. Scott's first diary resembles the very diary she begins to keep. "I have a handsome locked volume, such as might serve for a lady's Album," Scott writes in his first entry, November 20, 1825.[3] From him she may have drawn her habit of beginning diaries with the place of composition: "Warboys. August 4 [1899]" akin to "Edinburgh—November 20, 1825." Scott often uses initials in place of names and he regularly employs ampersands—traits Virginia's diary also apes. In his opening entry he credits Byron's diary as providing the method he will follow: "throwing out all pretence to regularity and order, and marking down events just as they occurred to recollection" (Lockhart 8: 108). Virginia follows this practice as well, and in later years she often alludes to Byron as offering the "loose" and expansive style she seeks in her diary, essays, and fiction.[4]

Scott extols rapid writing repeatedly in his diary—thus the initials and the ampersands—and he swears he "will not blot out what I have once written here" (Lockhart 8: 281). Young Virginia adopts these diary practices as well. Scott favors speed for the vigor and spontaneity it gives his work—his fiction and poetry as well as his diary. "I am sensible," he tells his diary, "that if there be anything good about my poetry or prose either, it is a hurried frankness of composition" (Lockhart 8: 370). Earlier he remarks that he has been "often amused with the critics distinguishing some passages as particularly laboured, when the pen passed over the whole as fast as it could move . . . . This *hab nab at a venture* is a perilous style, I grant, but I cannot help it. . . . It is the difference between a written oration and one bursting from the unpremeditated exertions of the speaker, which have always something the air of enthusiasm and inspiration. I would not have young authors imitate my carelessness, however" (Lockhart 8: 251). Scott also uses speed to keep doubt at bay. "It is only when I dally with what I am about, look back, and aside, instead of keeping my eyes straight forward, that I feel those cold sinkings of the heart," he observes (Lockhart 8: 186). Speed becomes one of several diary tricks Woolf will use to hasten prose.

Scott thus voices in his journal several aesthetic views Woolf adopts for her own diary (and general literary) aesthetic. He offers the figure of sketch versus finished picture she will later elaborate as well.[5] From Scott, too, she may have drawn her notion of her diary as a compost heap, a great desk or catch-all, for he writes that he intends his work *Chronicles of the Cannongate* "as an *olla podrida* [stew pot], into which any odds and ends of narrative or description may be thrown" (Lockhart 8: 346). In such condition, he notes, "I wrote easily."

Scott read voraciously as a youth and adored history—the path Virginia now will take. She finds in his diary a fellow Briton who writes novels, but also essays and reviews for the major publications of his time. (He, of course, writes poetry as well.) His is a writer's diary, used to plan and to comment on his work-in-progress and on other writers as well.[6] He offers the younger diarist astute views on women writers. On March 14, 1826, for instance, he (famously) writes of Jane Austen: "That young lady had a talent for describing the involvements, and feelings, and characters of ordinary life, which is to me the most wonderful I ever met with. The Big Bow-wow strain I can do myself like any now going; but the exquisite touch, which renders ordinary commonplace things and characters interesting, from the truth of the description and the sentiment, is denied to me. What a pity such a gifted creature died so early!" (Lockhart 8: 292–93).

Two weeks later Scott again uses his diary as a reading notebook: "Reading at intervals a novel called Granby, one of the class that aspire to describe the actual current of society, whose colors are so evanescent, that it is difficult to fix them on the canvass. . . . The women do this better: Edgeworth, Ferrier, Austen, have all given portraits of real society, far superior to anything man, vain man, has produced of the like nature" (Lockhart 8: 314). These passages may have encouraged young Virginia to believe she, too, might describe "the involvements, and feelings, and characters of ordinary life" and capture the "current" and "evanescent" colors of society. "What a strange scene if the surge of conversation could suddenly ebb like the tide, and show us the state of people's real minds!" Scott exclaimed (Lockhart 8: 167).

Scott's "Gurnal" may have impressed forever on Virginia Stephen the merits of diary-keeping. "I have all my life regretted that I did not keep a regular Journal," he begins his diary at age fifty-four. "I have myself lost recollection of much that was interesting; and I have deprived my family of some curious information by not carrying this resolution into effect" (Lockhart 8: 108). These words stress family as well as personal gains from diary-keeping. In introducing Scott's diary into his biography, Lockhart describes Scott "riding with Johnny Ballantyne and [himself] round the deserted halls of the ancient family of Riddell, and remarking how much it increased the wonder of their ruin that the late Baronet had 'kept day-book and ledger as regularly as any *cheesemonger in the Grassmarket*'" (8: 99).

Beyond stylistic traits and support of diary-keeping itself, Scott's diary words on his youth may have heartened the younger diarist. "What a life mine has been!" he exclaims, "—half educated, almost wholly neglected, or left to myself; stuffing my head with most nonsensical trash, and undervalued by most of my companions for a time" (Lockhart 8: 161). Was that not Virginia's life at this moment—half educated, almost wholly neglected? "[I]n my teens," he writes, "I used to fly from company to indulge in visions and airy castles of my own" (Lockhart 8: 313). She might have seen herself also in the following diary passage and reflected on Scott's link of "involuntary passions" to "warm imagination"—she of the broken umbrellas and moments "furious and tantrumical" (*PA* 73, 69). Scott writes:

What a detestable feeling this fluttering of the heart is! I know it is nothing organic, and that it is entirely nervous; but the sickening effects of it are dispiriting to a degree. Is it the body brings it on the mind, or the mind that inflicts upon the body? I cannot tell; but it is a severe price to pay for the *Fata Morgana* with which Fancy sometimes amuses men of warm imagination. . . . In youth this complaint used to throw me into involuntary passions of causeless tears. But I will drive it away in the country by exercise. (Lockhart 8: 291)

The country—and country exercise—become vital to Woolf, as soon we will see.[7]

Scott's diary offers a further view of illness that Woolf, too, will embrace. "I do think illness if not too painful unseals the mental-eye & renders the talents more acute," he writes in 1827 (Anderson 318). Scott also claims the outsider role for himself which might have offered Virginia some consolation for her social unease. "What is called great society, of which I have seen a good deal in my day," he writes in 1827, "is now amusing to me, because from age and indifference I have lost the habit of considering myself as a part of it, and have only the feelings of looking on as a spectator of the scene" (Lockhart 9:164). As John Patten notes, Scott exhibited a many-sidedness akin to Shakespeare's (146). His journal, like Woolf's, becomes "the crowning glory of his life" (Patten 17).

Several readers have tasked Woolf with diary reserve, undeservedly, I be-lieve.[8] She may have drawn some reserve from her diary "father." She found in Scott's diary not only admissions of "involuntary passions" but also a model of diaristic (and daily) restraint. As DeSalvo writes, "Reading [in Lockhart's biography] about the life of a successful literary figure who had his share of dif-ficulties no doubt provided Woolf with a role model, and probably also an emo-tional education" ("1897" 88). The year Scott begins his diary turns into a year of distress. He loses his fortune in January 1826; his wife of twenty-nine years dies in May; and fears for his ailing grandson rarely leave his mind. In his diary Scott rejects emotional display as debilitating and spurs himself on. "I hate red eyes and blowing of noses," he writes when his favorite daughter, Sophia, departs for London. "*Agere et pati Romanum est.* Of all schools, commend me to the Stoics. We cannot indeed overcome our affections, nor ought we if we could, but we may repress them within due bounds, and avoid coaxing them to make fools of those who should be their masters" (Lockhart 8: 138). At the loss of his wife he writes, "I will not yield to the barren sense of hopelessness which struggles to invade me," and a month later: "everybody has his own mode of expressing interest, and mine is stoical even in bitterest grief" (Lockhart 8: 334, 372).

Scott remains a signal influence throughout Woolf's life. We have been slow, however, to see that his diaries are perhaps as important to her as his novels. Several commentators have explored Woolf's use of Scott's novel *The Antiquary* in her 1927 novel *To the Lighthouse*. In a letter to Violet Dickinson, dated pro-visionally 1902, Virginia asks Dickinson if she would like to see that volume of Lockhart's *Life of Sir Walter Scott* that includes his "diary of a voyage to the lighthouses on the Scottish coast" (*L* #42, 1: 49). Scott mingles with Woolf's re-creation of her father in *To the Lighthouse*: we might read that novel as her imaginative reprise of Scott's lighthouse voyage as well.[9]

In 1932 Woolf expresses delight when Hugh Walpole dedicates his book *The Waverly Pageant* to her, and in 1933 she writes to him that "It struck me today on my walk, that I like Scott's diaries better than all but three or four of his novels" (*L* #2784, 5: 219). Toward the close of her life, she still remembers Scott the dia-rist. "Why not write about Scott's diaries, so bring in the immortal novels?" she asks her 1938 diary, suggestively (*D* 5: 138). Two months later she confesses to Ethel Smyth that she has "glutted [her] passion for Scott on his tomb" during a visit to the Dryburgh ruins (*L* #3408, 6: 247). And she makes good on her wish to write on his diaries, for she publishes in January 1940 "Gas at Abbotsford," an essay that interacts with—in fact, elaborates and reinvigorates—admired Scott diary scenes.

Fanny Burney's Diary

If Sir Walter Scott serves as young Virginia's diary *father*, his contemporary, Fanny Burney, looms large as her diary *mother*. Burney lived nearer to Virginia than the Scottish writer: in fact, her diary shows her rise from London "Nobody" to celebrated author. As with Scott's journal, I cannot say precisely when Woolf first reads Burney's diary. In "A Sketch of the Past," written in 1939, Woolf links Burney's diary to the "winter of [the] engagement" of Stella and Jack Hills; that is, to the winter of 1896/1897 (*MOB* 105). Because Virginia does not list Burney's diary with other books read in 1897, one is tempted to place the winter reading in 1896. "It was to me like a ruby; the love I detected that winter of their engagement," Woolf wrote in 1939: "It springs from the ecstasy I felt, in my covert, behind the folding doors of the Hyde Park Gate drawing room. I sat there, shielded, being half insane with shyness and nervousness; reading Fanny Burney's diary; and feeling come over me intermittent waves of very strong emotion—rage sometimes; how often I was enraged by father then!—love, or the reflection of love, too. It was bodiless; a light; an ecstasy. But also extraordinarily enduring" (*MOB* 105).

That Burney's diary figures in an ecstatic, enduring feeling should bear full weight. Woolf twice calls Burney the "mother" of English fiction (*E* 2: 314; *E* 3: 337). Because she reads Burney's diary soon after losing her own mother at age thirteen, Virginia may have seized on Burney as a surrogate (literary) mother. The uncanny parallels between the Burney and Stephen households could hardly have been lost on young Virginia: the mother's early death; the adored but demanding (in fact, enraging) father; the mix of half-brothers and sisters; the beloved sister Susanna ("my heart's earliest darling") who also kept a diary.[10] The Burneys were also a diary-writing family.[11]

In 1939, Woolf confesses to "being half insane with shyness and nervousness" as an early teen "reading Fanny Burney's diary." How reassuring it must have been to read of another's nerves and "untamable shyness" and to find these traits did not foreclose success (*Diary and Letters of Madame D'Arblay* 3: 282). Woolf mentions Burney's shyness in both her 1929 essay "Dr. Burney's Evening Party" and her 1930 essay "Fanny Burney's Half-Sister" (*CR* 2: 99; *G&R* 193). She likely borrows the term "fidgets" from Burney's diary—an important word in her own diary—although Scott uses the term as well.[12] At age nineteen Burney writes of performing a play for guests at her home: "I can, in general, get by heart with the utmost facility; but I was so much fidgetted, that my head seemed to turn round, and I scarse knew what I was about" (*Early Diary* 1: 129).

Of her trip to meet Dr. Johnson and Hester Thrale following the success of *Evelina*, twenty-six-year-old Burney confesses, "I was really in the fidgets from thinking what my reception might be," and even after the triumph of her third novel, *Camilla*, she reports that the royal princesses "made a thousand inquiries about my book, and . . . how I stood as to fright and fidget" (*Diary and Letters of Madame D'Arblay* 1: 76; 3: 108). The word "fidgets" first appears in Woolf's 1897 diary; however, not in connection with the diarist but with Stella, who in February wishes to see a woman doctor "about her [own] fidgets" (*PA* 43). Five months later, however, only four days before Stella's death, Virginia confesses, "At night I had the fidgets very badly, & [Stella] sat with me till 11.30—stroking me till they went" (*PA* 114). As she grows as a diarist, Woolf will acknowledge that "writing out the fidgets" is one of many diary uses; diary strokes, one might say, replace Stella's soothing hands.

Burney's shyness and "fidgets" made her acutely sensitive to her works' reception—a trait Woolf also will share. Historian Thomas Macaulay writes that when Burney's first novel, *Evelina*, appeared, "Poor Fanny was sick with terror, and durst hardly stir out of doors" (*Diary and Letters of Madame D'Arblay* 1: xxv). According to diary scholar Judy Simons, Burney "writes the same story— of panic and survival—again and again as she goes through her life" (201–2). Did young Virginia internalize this "story" behind the folding screen? And would it always sustain her?

Beyond the family parallels and the shyness and the fidgets, young Virginia could find much more to identify with in Burney's diary. Burney's passion for books surely registered; in fact, it may have fueled Virginia's race through her father's stacks. Both young girls read hungrily in their fathers' extensive libraries. At age seventeen, the future Madame d'Arblay teaches herself French "for the sake of its bewitching authors—for I shall never want to speak it" (*Early Diary* 1: 102). At age nineteen Fanny gushes, "I have a most prodigious enthusiasm for authors" (*Early Diary* 1: 176).

Virginia shares, too, Burney's prodigious passion for the pen. In her early diaries Burney explains that she writes her plays, novels, and diary in "the children's play-room" two flights up—a setting comparable to Virginia's 1897 nursery (*Early Diary* 1: lxxxv–lxxxvi). Later in life, Woolf escapes to her writing lodge at the end of the Monk's House garden, re-creating Burney's practice at Lynn. In her 1929 essay "Dr. Burney's Evening Party," Woolf notes that Burney "was immensely susceptible to the power of words" and describes Burney stealing off to write in London, "as she had stolen to the cabin [at the end of the garden] at Lynn," confiding to her diary, "I cannot any longer resist what I find to be irresistible, the pleasure of popping down my thoughts from time to time upon paper" (*CR* 2: 98, 101). Burney's full diary sentence is revealing, for she writes: "I burnt all [my writing] up to my 15th year—thinking I grew too old for scribbling nonsense, but as I am less young, I grow, I fear, less wise, for I cannot any longer resist what I find to be irresistible, the pleasure of popping down my thoughts from time to time upon paper" (*Early Diary* 1: 314). "Scribbling," like "the fidgets," becomes a useful term for Woolf. "Scribbling" minimizes writing—makes it less formidable.

Upon her joyful return to her father's home following her five-year exile as Second Keeper of the (Queen's) Robes at George III's court, Burney exults that "in this season of leisure and comfort, the spirit of composition proves active. The day is never long enough, and I could employ two pens almost incessantly, in merely scribbling what will not be repressed" (*Diary and Letters of Madame D'Arblay* 2: 430). Here Burney reveals another gift Woolf later will show: spontaneous invention. In her final days at Windsor Burney pays tribute to this faculty: "The power of composition has to me indeed proved a solace, a blessing! When incapable of all else, that [power], unsolicited, unthought of, has presented itself to my solitary leisure, and beguiled me of myself" (*Diary and Letters of Madame D'Arblay* 2: 402).

How easily young Virginia might have identified with this mother of English fiction. Burney was near-sighted by all accounts—including her own—but it hardly dimmed her powers of observation, powers Woolf notes admiringly in 1929 (*Early Diary* 1: 211; *CR* 2: 101). When Burney was fifteen, Mr. Seaton calls her "The silent, observant Miss Fanny" (*Diary and Letters of Madame D'Arblay* 3: 450). At age thirty-nine, at the close of a day at the famous Warren Hastings trial, Burney asserts in her diary, "I have the faces of all them, most certainly, in full mental possession; and the figures of many whose names I know not are so familiar now to my eyes, that should I chance hereafter to meet them, I shall be apt to take them for old acquaintances" (*Diary and Letters of Madame D'Arblay* 2: 444).

"[T]he quickest observation," Woolf admires in "Dr. Burney's Evening Party"; "the most retentive memory" (*CR* 2: 101). Burney's powers of recall likely surpassed Woolf's. Across her diary, Burney reprises conversations—often switching to dramatic dialogue, turning journal into play (*Early Diary* 1: 34–38; 2: 94–97, 103–8; *Diary and Letters of Madame D'Arblay* 1: 95–97, 99–100, 104–8, 117–20, 130–31, 140, 226, 241; 3: 177–78). Woolf will do this herself in her 1918, 1923, and later diaries. In fact, when Woolf challenges herself to recall talk in her diaries, she may be recalling these Burney diary feats—as well as James Boswell's. Diary editor Ellis remarks of Fanny's first dialogue (with Mr. Seaton) entered into her diary at age sixteen: "This passage is particularly interesting as giving the first example of her extraordinary power of retaining protracted conversations unmarked by any special brilliancy, or novelty of thought" (*Early Diary* 1: 39). We can understand why King George III hastens to hear Burney's reports of the Hastings trial when she explains in her diary that "The words may be given to the eye, but the impression they make can only be conveyed by the ear; and I came back so eagerly interested, that my memory was not more stored with the very words than my voice with the intonations of all that had passed" (*Diary and Letters of Madame D'Arblay* 2: 395).

Burney's memory for talk helps make her a "character-monger"—as Dr. Johnson called her (*Early Diary* 1: vii). I believe Woolf was thinking back through this mother in becoming a brilliant diary portraitist. Burney's diary portraits are highly self-conscious. By age twenty-five her private diary has long become a journal-letter shared with her beloved sister Susanna, family friend Samuel Crisp, and others.[13] She writes in it of Sir Herbert Packington: "As you have the satisfaction of knowing him, I must deny myself the pleasure of describing his person, which otherwise I should think well worth description for its excellent ugliness. He is, however, very good-natured, extremely civil, and uncommonly hospitable" (*Early Diary* 2: 199–200). Negative brush strokes countered with positive will become an habitual Woolf diary gesture too.

Burney can capture a subject succinctly: "In the afternoon we had also Mr. Wallace, the attorney general, a most squat and squab looking man" (*Diary and Letters of Madame D'Arblay* 1: 205). She also relishes longer portraits. Her portrait of Miss W___ is especially droll: "She is short, thick-set, fat, clumsy, clunch, and heavy.... I would fain give you a specimen of the conversation that you might laugh too; but, unless I could *paint* her, and shew you, at the same time, the extreme vacancy of her countenance, and give you some idea of the *drone* of her voice and of her unmeaning manner,—I could hope for no success at all equal to my wishes, or to the subject" (*Early Diary* 2: 202, 203).

In 1777, Mr. Crisp wrote to Fanny: "'tis true your [journal] letter was an excellent one; full of excellent portraits, as like, and as strongly painted as Sir J[oshua]. Reynolds's" (*Early Diary* 2: 160). Macaulay seconded this praise, noting Burney's "quickness in catching every odd peculiarity of character and manner; the skill in grouping; the humour, often richly comic, sometimes even farcical" (*Diary and Letters of Madame D'Arblay* 1: xxiii). Burney herself offered counsel on portraits. "Humour springing from mere dress, or habits, or phraseology, is quickly obsolete," she writes at age thirty-seven; "when it sinks deeper, and dives into character, it may live *for ever*" (*Diary and Letters of Madame D'Arblay* 2: 350).

Burney's diary captures character and talk, scenes and historical drama. When she is only twenty-three, Mr. Crisp acknowledges, "You have learn'd from that R[ogue] your father (by so long serving as his amanuensis, I suppose) to make your descriptions alive" (*Early Diary* 2: 101). Macaulay declares that Burney's diary account of King George III's illness "contains much excellent narrative and description, and will, we think, be more valued by the historians of a future age than any equal portion of Pepys' or Evelyn's 'Diaries'" (*Diary and Letters of Madame D'Arblay* 1: xxxviii). W. C. Ward, the editor of *The Diary and Letters of Madame D'Arblay*, declares that Burney's 1792–93 record "must be pronounced, from the historical point of view, one of the most valuable in the 'Diary' [for] it gives us authentic glimpses of some of the actors" in the French Revolution (3: 11).

Although in its final (much edited) form, Burney's diary differs from Woolf's more Scott-like spontaneous and unrevised diary, it also reinforced many of Scott's diary traits. "I have a thousand things to write, too many to observe method, and therefore I shall commit them as they occur," Burney writes at age twenty (*Early Diary* 1: 213). At twenty-five, she shows the poise fifty-seven-year-old Woolf will model at the start of "A Sketch of the Past." "March is almost over—and not a word have I bestowed upon my Journal!" Burney wails. "n'importe—I shall now whisk on to the present time, mentioning whatever occurs to me promiscuously."[14] Mr. Crisp at least twice urges speed to Fanny as the best tack for her "journalizing." "Dash away whatever comes uppermost," he tells her; "the sudden sallies of imagination, clap'd down on paper, just as they arise, are worth folios" (*Early Diary* 1: 268).

He urges her to value "trifles" as well. Twenty-two-year-old Burney protests his sharing her journal-letters with his sisters, calling them "trifling stuff." "You cannot but know *that trifling, that negligence, that even incorrectness*, now and then in familiar epistolary writing, is the very soul of genius and ease; and that if your letters were to be fine-labour'd compositions that smelt of *the lamp*, I had as lieve they [traveled elsewhere]," Crisp admonishes her.[15] Forty years later, Burney gives similar advice to her son, Alexander: "your expressions upon its view lose much of their effect by being overstrained, *recherchés*, and designing to be pathetic. We never touch others, my dear Alex, where we study to show we are touched ourselves. I beg you, when you write to me, to let your pen paint your thoughts as they rise, not as you seek or labour to embellish them. . . . Be natural, my dear boy, and you will be sure to please your mother without wasting your time" (*Diary and Letters of Madame D'Arblay* 3: 365–66).

Burney's diary also offers young Virginia an angle absent in Scott's diaries. Burney attends to women and their treatment throughout her diary and thus models a way of seeing Woolf will follow throughout her life. Burney's diary was an especially happy early find, for diary historian Blodgett notes that Burney's diary "violate[s the] female acculturation to self-abnegation, modesty, and silence" present in most English women's diaries (*Centuries* 37). Young Fanny despairs of dress and social rites quite as fully as fifteen-year-old Virginia. Burney's views, in fact, may have shaped and fortified Virginia's own. "Miss Crawford" was Burney's "Ida Milman": "Miss Crawford called here lately—she is very earnest for us to visit her—but *we* are not very earnest about the matter:—however, the code of custom makes our spending one evening with her necessary. O! how I hate this vile custom which obliges us to make slaves of ourselves!—to sell the most precious property we boast, our time;—and to sacrifice it to every prattling impertinent who chooses to demand it!"(*Early Diary* 1: 54). A month later, seventeen-year-old Burney queries: "why are we not permitted to *decline* as well as *accept* visits and acquaintances?" (*Early Diary* 1: 62).

That Burney, at a later age than Virginia's fifteen, feels anguish at social pressures can be seen in this diary entry at age nineteen: "About three o'clock, the rest of our company came. And from that time, was *my* comfort over, for my uncle is so [word omitted] yet, I should not have regarded *him*, if mama had been at home, but, upon my word, appearing as *Mistress of the* house [for the first time] distressed me beyond imagination. . . . I would not go through such another day for the world" (*Early Diary* 1: 168). Ward notes the irony of Burney's post as Second Keeper of the Robes, for "Dress had always been one of the last subjects about which she troubled herself" (*Diary and Letters of Madame D'Arblay* 1: 290).

Burney observes in her diary small nuances of gender. Of Mrs. Wall of Gloucester she notes, "she makes it a rule never to look at a woman when she can see a man" (*Early Diary* 2: 183). Burney asks, not only her diary but also "Mr. Turbulent" at court, "what choice has a poor female with whom she may converse? Must she not, in company as in dancing, take up with those who choose to take up with her?" (*Diary and Letters of Madame D'Arblay* 2: 26). And when "taken up," Burney repeatedly scorns men who believe they can talk only nonsense to women (*Early Diary* 1: 242, 301). She poses questions to challenge cultural codes—a practice Woolf later will use. At the end of her first diary entry, sixteen-year-old Burney shrewdly inquires: "but why, permit me to ask, must a *female* be made Nobody? Ah! my dear, what were this world good for, were Nobody a female?" (*Early Diary* 1: 6).

Across more than fifty years of diaries, Burney records women's restriction. At age sixteen she decries her own narrow education, for she tells her diary: "you must consider how very, very, very bad a judge I am, as I read with nobody, and consequently have nobody to correct or guide my opinion."[16] In her preface to Burney's *Early Diary*, Ellis observes that "There were many more educated ladies in the eighteenth century than it is customary to think there were, but it would be difficult to overstate the poorness of teaching in the schools for girls"—information young Virginia may have stored (1: lxxvi). Burney records in her diary her father's words to a visitor after *Evelina's* success: "why she has had very little education but what she has given herself,—less than any of the others!" (*Diary and Letters of Madame D'Arblay* 1: 74).

That women of Burney's era often limited each other is an ongoing diary theme. When Burney is sixteen Miss Dolly Young "very seriously and earnestly" advises her to give up her diary (*Early Diary* 1: 19). Fanny defends herself: "I told her, that as *my* Journal was *solely* for my own perusal, nobody could in justice, or even in sense, be angry or displeased at my writing any thing" (*Early Diary* 1: 20). However, only by showing her diary to Miss Young does she earn the older woman's approval. Burney burned her early prose and verse, Ellis tells us, because of hints from her new stepmother that "girls who wrote lost their time, and risked their good repute" (1: lxv). Because of this, as Woolf notes in "Dr. Burney's Evening Party," Burney reorders her life in a manner harmful to her gifts. "I make a kind of rule, never to indulge myself in my two *most* favourite pursuits, reading and writing, in the morning," Burney explains; "no, like a very good girl I give that up wholly . . . to needle work, by which means my reading and writing in the afternoon is a pleasure I cannot be blamed for by my mother, as it does not take up the time I ought to spend otherwise" (*Early Diary* 1: 15; *CR* 2: 97). Ten years later, sister Susanna writes to Fanny of a Mrs. Hales "who would think it destruction for a girl to read a novel" (*Early Diary* 2: 224), and in the 1780s Queen Charlotte and Mrs. Mary Delaney, both revered by Burney, discourage her writing for the stage as "too public and hazardous a style of writing for her quiet and fearful turn of mind" (*Diary and Letters of Madame D'Arblay* 1: 294). As a result, Burney composes her tragedies in secret.

Burney notes male disdain for women as well as female discouragements, and she defends women, again striking a path Woolf will follow. Burney's intellectual poise came early. At age sixteen, she writes of Homer's *Iliad*: "Thus has Homer proved his opinion of our poor sex—that the love of beauty is our most prevailing passion. It really grieves me to think that there certainly must be some reason for this insignificant opinion the greatest men have of women—at least I fear there must. But I don't in fact believe it" (*Early Diary* 1: 30). When Burney meets misogynists, she takes note in her diary. She boldly retorts to writer Richard Owen Cambridge: "if agreeable women are rare, much more so, I think, are agreeable men; at least, among my acquaintance they are very few" (*Diary and Letters of Madame D'Arblay* 1: 274). In 1792, she reports the Duke de Liancourt's speaking "with great asperity against all the *femmes de lettres* now known; he said they were commonly the most disgusting of their sex, in France, by their arrogance, boldness, and *mauvais mœurs*" (*Diary and Letters of Madame D'Arblay* 3: 27). Dr. John Shebbeare, a novelist who "absolutely ruined" Burney's evening, offers an early model for Woolf's "Professor von X" in *A Room of One's Own*. (Woolf was re-reading Burney's diary during that volume's composition.) "[W]hat most excited his spleen," Burney notes, "was *Woman*, to whom he professes a fixed aversion" (*Early Diary* 1: 285).

Most unsettling to young Virginia, however, may have been the discovery that Burney's own father derails her first comic play. Dr. Burney insists on the play's withdrawal, and at a time when the d'Arblays badly need the funds—a time, in fact, when his daughter is forty-seven and a celebrated novelist. Fanny's letter to her father is poignant as well as pointed:

This release gives me present repose, which, indeed, I much wanted; for to combat your, to me, unaccountable but most afflicting displeasure, in the midst of my own panics and disturbance, would have been ample punishment to me had I been guilty of a crime, in doing what I have all my life been urged to, and all my life intended,—writing a comedy. . . . My imagination is not at my own control, or I would always have continued in the walk you approved. (*Diary and Letters of Madame D'Arblay* 3: 193–94)

Burney then begs her father to allow her the same creative space he claims for himself. She urges Dr. Burney to say to himself: "Why then, after all, should I lock her up in one paddock, well as she has fed there, if she says she finds nothing more to nibble [in fiction]; while *I* find all the earth unequal to my ambition, and mount the skies to content it? Come on, then, poor Fan! the world has acknowledged you my offspring, and I will *disencourage* you no more. Leap the pales of your paddock" (*Diary and Letters of Madame D'Arblay* 3: 194). Across her diary Woolf repeatedly uses a horse figure for her own writing and spurs herself to leap her fences. Each time she affirms her tie to Burney.[17]

Beyond its words on gender, Burney's diary also offers young Virginia an early anti-military view. When only seventeen, Burney questions the social response to a three-year-old boy who tortures insects: "The poor boy belongs to a sex sufficiently prone to cruelty: is it for *women* thus early to encourage it?" (*Early Diary* 1: 100). At age fifty, viewing Napoleon's troops in Paris in 1802, she writes: "while all the pomp and circumstance of war animated others, it only saddened me; and all of past reflection, all of future dread, made the whole grandeur of the martial scene, and all the delusive seduction of martial music, fill my eyes frequently with tears, but not regale my poor muscles with one single smile" (*Diary and Letters of Madame D'Arblay* 3: 232–33).

Woolf's defiant "As a woman I have no country..." in *Three Guineas* may have had its earliest root in this 1803 Burney diary statement: "war [between England and France] therefore seems inevitable; and my grief, I, who feel myself now of two countries, is far greater than I can wish to express" (*Diary and Letters of Madame D'Arblay* 3: 240). Burney cannot escape the horrors of war. In Brussels in 1815 during the Battle of Waterloo, she indelibly captures the slaughter: "For more than a week from this time I never approached my window but to witness sights of wretchedness. Maimed, wounded, bleeding, mutilated, tortured victims of this exterminating contest passed by every minute: the fainting, the sick, the dying, and the dead, on brancards [litters], in carts, in waggons, succeeded one another without intermission" (*Diary and Letters of Madame D'Arblay* 3: 361).

Two mysteries surround Woolf's later use of what appears to be an extraordinarily potent early source. The first is the meager space accorded Burney in the 1929 *A Room of One's Own*, the text where Woolf utters her immortal "we think back through our mothers if we are women" (79). Burney was clearly on Woolf's mind during the volume's composition, for Woolf begins her essay by wondering if the invitation to speak about "women and fiction" might mean "simply a few remarks about Fanny Burney" (3). However, in the volume's famous chapter 4 historical march through English women authors, Woolf leaps from Aphra Behn (1640–1689) to Jane Austen with only a one-sentence note that Austen "should have laid a wreath upon the grave of Fanny Burney"—a spiritual act of necessity since Austen died twenty-three years before the long-lived Burney (69).

Woolf might easily have offered a paragraph or two on the author of *Evelina*; *Cecilia*; *Camilla*; and *The Wanderer; or Female Difficulties*. In a 1918 review of R. Brimley Johnson's *The Women Novelists* Woolf had written that Burney "showed that it was 'possible for a woman to write novels and be respectable,' but the burden of proof still rested anew upon each authoress" (*E* 2: 315). In point of fact, Burney balks at the word "novel" long before Woolf does. Of her third volume, *Camilla*, Burney writes to her father: "I own I do not like calling it a novel; it gives so simply the notion of a mere love-story, that I recoil a little from it" (*Diary and Letters of Madame D'Arblay* 3: 96). In chapter 4 of *A Room of One's Own*, Woolf writes "'the novel' (I give it inverted commas to mark my sense of the words' inadequacy)"—a view often repeated in her diaries (80).

That Woolf did not pay greater tribute to Burney in *A Room of One's Own* might be explained in several ways. I believe it was not primarily as a novelist that Burney figured in Woolf's mind; rather it was Fanny Burney *diarist* who inspired. Woolf's topic in *A Room of One's Own* is women and fiction, and Burney's place is, accordingly, pared. A further, and more practical, explanation for the few sentences on Burney is that during the writing of *A Room of One's Own* and after, Woolf *was* celebrating Fanny Burney—Frances Burney the diarist, that is. "Dr. Burney's Evening Party" appears in July 1929 and "Fanny Burney's Half-Sister" in August 1930. Both essays pay tribute to Burney. In each Woolf enters imaginatively into Burney's diary world—in truth, expands this world—as if *she*, not Maria Allen, were Burney's half-sister. "Fanny Burney's Half-Sister" re-imagines scenes cut from Burney's diary. "Dr. Burney's Evening Party," in turn, might be read as Woolf's creative response to this Macaulay line on Mr. Crisp: "he pressed Fannikin to send him full accounts of her father's evening parties" (*Diary and Letters of Madame D'Arblay* 1: xxiii). After meeting seventy-four-year-old Burney on November 18, 1826, Walter Scott also reprised in *his* diary the evening party where Dr. Johnson first praised *Evelina* (Lockhart 9: 44–45).

Woolf saw the creative boost Burney's diary gave, for in revising her 1926 essay "How Should One Read a Book?" for the 1932 second *Common Reader*, she compresses to one phrase her feat in "Fanny Burney's Half-Sister" and inserts it into the essay as her final illustration of reading "to refresh and exercise our own creative powers":

> It may be a few sentences—but what vistas they suggest! Sometimes a whole story will come together with such beautiful humour and pathos and completeness that it seems as if a great novelist had been at work, yet . . . it is only Maria Allen letting fall her sewing in the empty drawing room and sighing how she wishes she had taken Dr. Burney's good advice and had never eloped with her Rishy. None of this has any value; it is negligible in the extreme; yet how absorbing it is now and again to go through the rubbish-heaps and find rings and scissors and broken noses buried in the huge past and try to piece them together while the

colt gallops round the field, the woman fills her pail at the well, and the donkey brays.[18]

Fanny Burney and her diary, I believe, hover (literally) in the background of *A Room of One's Own*. Judith Shakespeare may have "set fire" to her early "scribblings," Woolf speculates there (49). Woman before the eighteenth century "never writes her own life and scarcely keeps a diary" (47). *Diarist* Burney, in fact, may be so important that Woolf cannot directly own the legacy. Instead she demonstrates the influence separately and creatively through the engaging Burney essays, works allowing the colt (Burney) to gallop around the field, and the woman (Woolf) to fill her pail at the well—and any donkey who wishes to bray.

On May 5, 1930, Woolf writes to Vita Sackville-West from Taunton in Somerset: "Every street like Pope or Dryden: and everywhere Burke stayed or Sir Walter Scott, Wordsworth and Fanny Burney" (*L* #2173, 4: 162–63). That Burney remains in Woolf's imagination as late as 1932 can be seen not only in her revision of "How Should One Read A Book?" but also from her June 22, 1932, letter to Lady Ottoline Morrell confessing that she "wasted an hour very happily this afternoon looking for a Burney for you in an old bookshop" (*L* #2600, 5: 71). On September 16, 1932, she again writes to Lady Morrell, "what I wanted to ask is Have you got Fanny Burney's diary? I find there are two editions . . . and want to send you one (if you'd like it) but dont know which you'd prefer" (*L* #2638, 5: 106–7).

We know from the 1939 allusion in "A Sketch of the Past" that Burney's diary was again in the background as Woolf begins her memoirs. The most disturbing mystery is why this mother figure was unable to sustain Woolf in her final days. Woolf's regard for Burney and her diary was not unalloyed. In "Dr. Burney's Evening Party" she observes: "There was something a little prudish in [Burney's] nature. Just as she avoided the name of Tomkins, so she avoided the roughnesses, the asperities, the plainnesses of daily life. The chief fault that mars the extreme vivacity and vividness of the early diary is that the profusion of words tends to soften the edges of the sentences, and the sweetness of the sentiment to smooth out the outlines of the thought" (*CR* 2: 98). Burney's diary also differs from Woolf's. It was not only heavily expurgated—with erasures, mutilations, and defacements—but it also used fictitious names at times for its more public audience and was extensively rewritten.[19]

However, this expurgated diary—with its missing days and months—may have shown young Virginia that diaries need not be daily (like Scott's) to recall a world.[20] Burney's motives for diary-writing are nearly as complex as Woolf's. Like Scott, Burney keeps a diary to preserve what would otherwise be forgotten. She laments, for instance, in 1812, "There are few events of my life that I more regret not having committed to paper while they were fresher in my memory, than my police adventure at Dunkirk" (*Diary and Letters of Madame D'Arblay* 3: 249). Like Scott, Burney values her diary for its family use. At twenty-one, she exclaims, tongue fast in cheek: "But for my pen, all the adventures of this noble family might sink to oblivion!" (*Early Diary* 1: 282–83).

Like Scott, Burney turns to her diary to confide. At sixteen, in her opening apostrophe "Addressed to a Certain Miss Nobody," Burney expresses her wish to write "A Journal in which I must confess my *every* thought, must open my whole heart! . . . I must imagion [*sic*] myself to be talking—talking to the most intimate of friends—to one in whom I should take delight in confiding" (*Early Diary* 1: 5). And like Woolf, Burney finds in diary confiding, in diary stroking, a psychological release. In an interesting entry at age eighteen lamenting her neglect of her diary, Burney asks: "how many subjects of joy, how very many of sorrow have I met with of late, without the least wish of applying to my old friend for participation, or rather relief?" (*Early Diary* 1: 120). More than forty-eight years later, a year-and-a-half after her beloved husband's death, Burney unfolds in her diary General d'Arblay's final illness. "Ever present as it is to me," she writes, "it will be a relief to set it down" (*Diary and Letters of Madame D'Arblay* 3: 423).

Beyond reinforcing these motives for diary-keeping, Burney also provides teenage Virginia with the image of "Old Virginia"—the Burney-like older self returning to relish her diary and further it as art. When she is twenty-one, Burney tells Mr. Crisp her wish for her diaries: "to *me*, who know all the people, and things mentioned, they may possibly give some pleasure, by rubbing up my memory, when I am a very tabby, before when I shall not think of looking into them" (*Early Diary* 1: 228). In introducing the early diaries, editor Ellis observes that "These journals gave Frances in old age, the delight which she had looked forward to receiving from them in her youth. . . . A singular proof of unity of character is given in her finding at seventy the pleasure which she had anticipated in reading her old diaries when she began to write in them at sixteen" (1: viii, lxxviii). Burney's first diary sentence is this: "To have some account of my thoughts, manners, acquaintance and actions, when the hour arrives in which time is more nimble than memory, is the reason which induces me to keep a Journal" (*Early Diary* 1: 5).

Burney's much edited and revised diary offers a vision of what Woolf's diary might have looked like had she lived to be eighty-seven (like Burney) and followed Burney's path of not only mining her diary for published memoirs but also revising it for publication. In 1939 Woolf begins her memoirs as she had long planned, mentioning Burney's diary in the process. She also carries forward the name of Dr. Burney's friend, Mr. La Trobe, bestowing it on her female artist in her final novel, *Between the Acts* (*Early Diary* 1: xiv). Burney herself, however, supplied a model of an actual long-lived female artist (and diarist). Burney outlived Mr. Crisp and Dr. Johnson, her beloved sister and father, her husband, and even her son.

In 1976, Barbara G. Schrank and David J. Supino suggested that "Although her fame was as a novelist during her own lifetime, it is her diary, published posthumously, that assures Fanny Burney an enduring place in literature" (1). That Woolf wrote "Why not write about Scott's diaries?" in the final years of her life, and not "Why not write about Burney's diaries?"—that she did not return to the colt in the field and find a way yet again "to refresh and exercise" her imagination—is a matter of infinite woe.[21]

Samuel Pepys's Diary

Although penned in the 1660s, Samuel Pepys's famous diary did not reach the public until 1825.[22] Sir Walter Scott's admiration for Pepys's diary—and for the poet Byron's diary also published that year—likely spurred him to try his own hand at the form. Scott's many delighted nods to Pepys in his diary may have piqued fifteen-year-old Virginia Stephen's interest, for after finishing John Lockhart's *Memoirs of the Life of Sir Walter Scott* February 24, 1897, she begins to borrow Pepys's *Diary* from her father's library on March 29.[23] Remarkably, she finishes the nine-and-a-half-year, 1.25 million-word diary in only twelve days—the very days leading to Stella's April 10 wedding (Latham and Matthews lxi). "After all books are the greatest help and comfort," she confides to her diary during Stella's May illness (*PA* 79). On April 4 she calls "My dear Pepys . . . the only calm thing in the house" (*PA* 66).

Pepys's diary offered young Virginia a vastly different atmosphere, not only from the fevered wedding march invading the lower regions of her house but also from Scott's highland writer's diary. Like Woolf's diary mother, Fanny Burney, Pepys is a fellow Londoner, another nobody who becomes immortal through his pen. As he scurries back and forth across 1660s London—from home to office to coffee house to play to home and so to bed—Pepys offers the girl a vision of a busy London life, a life (if we substitute "shops" for "office") that she is already living and recording. Pepys also writes of his excursion to Holland, showing her (as had Scott and Burney) that a life diary can be a travel diary too. As Pepys biographer Claire Tomalin notes, Pepys's diary "lets us know that each of us inhabits a perpetually fluctuating environment"—a fact that likely resonated with Woolf (xxxi). His habit of yearly summing up his life and times (on occasion, he does this monthly) is one she will often follow too.

Pepys's swift prose may have reinforced hers, for he moves briskly through his diary reports, switching seamlessly from outer to inner worlds, from personal to political. "It snowed hard all this morning, and was very cold, and my nose was much swelled with cold. Strange the difference of men's talk! Some say that Lambert must of necessity yield up," runs a typical Pepys passage (Wheatley 1: 8). His diary shows a mind absorbing its world: "Her husband walked through to Redriffe [Rotherhithe] with me, telling me things that I asked of in the yard; and so by water home, it being likely to rain again to-night, which God forbid" (Wheatley 3: 198–99).

Again one cannot say for certain what, or how much, young Virginia took from this, her first brush with Pepys's diary. Pepys dines with a Mrs. Ramsay, for instance, and mentions two Pargiters, one a "cheating rogue," but one hesitates to make too much of this (Wheatley 2: 66, 67, 116). We do know Woolf refers to Pepys regularly throughout her life and nods to him often in her own diary with his signature "and so to bed." In 1911, in a review of *The First Duke and Duchess of Newcastle-upon-tyne*, Woolf offers a vivid picture of Pepys "puffing behind" the Duchess's coach, remarking its strange color.[24] Walter Scott mentions this moment in *his* tribute to Pepys's diary. Woolf here remakes her diary father as she does later when she remakes Scott's diary note of "Dr Burney's Evening Party."

In 1918, Woolf follows Scott again in penning her own tribute to Pepys. In her review of *Occasional Papers Read by Members at Meetings of the Samuel Pepys Club*, she insists that Pepys was not "poetic"; nevertheless his prose, though "slipshod . . . never fails to be graphic" (E 2: 234, 235). The following brief sentence shows Pepys's swift, graphic, englobing prose: "My wife and I to church this morning, and so home to dinner to a boiled leg of mutton all alone" (Wheatley 1: 296). One thinks of Woolf's own famous sausage and haddock diary phrase. In 1918 *she* turns poetic to praise Pepys's concrete prose. His language, she writes, "catches unfailingly the butterflies and gnats and falling petals of the moment" (E 2: 235).

Pepys balances the record of his personal life with reports of the larger events of his time—the restoration of Charles II, the Black Plague, the London fire—a practice Woolf attempts as well when she seeks to capture in her diary the 1926

General Strike, King Edward's 1936 abdication, and the preparations for war.[25] Diaries offer hospitable space for disparate matter, for democratic mingling of the high and the low, of great events and small. Pepys's diary, even more than Scott's, shows this leveling grace. In 1918, Woolf recognized Pepys's virtue in this regard: "And thus it comes about that the diary runs naturally from affairs of State and the characters of ministers to affairs of the heart and the characters of servant girls; it includes the buying of clothes, the losing of tempers, and all the infinite curiosities, amusements, and pettinesses of average human life" (E 2: 234).

Pepys was fond of having his portrait painted. He used portraits of himself as bookplates. How early did Woolf recognize Pepys's gifted self-portraiture as well as his sharply etched portraits of others? By 1925, with numerous superb portraits lodged in her own diaries, Woolf noted Pepys's skill in an essay on "Montaigne." She asks: "After all, in the whole of literature, how many people have succeeded in drawing themselves with a pen? Only Montaigne and Pepys and Rousseau perhaps" (CR 1: 58). As scholar Colin Burrow has noted, "What makes Pepys matter as a writer is the fact that he is a man totting up his sins before God, and a man out to take sexual favours and greedily sums them up, and a man who works honestly, and a man who manoeuvres for bribes, and a man who can feel for a pigeon, and a man who knows that all of this does not quite add up to the total of what he is" (12). In 1918, Woolf calls Pepys modern in his "quick and varied sensibility" (E 2: 235). Was he an early exemplar for her that "nothing was simply one thing" (To the Lighthouse 186). And if so, how soon did she see this?

Did Virginia see in 1897 what her later self so clearly valued? Pepys writes: "as I am in all things curious" (Wheatley 2:105). In 1918 Woolf observed that "Insatiable curiosity, and unflagging vitality were the essence of a gift to which, when the possessor is able to impart it, we can give no lesser name than genius" (E 2: 234). In 1897, curiosity has not yet entered her diary. That questions will become her diary's hallmark will become apparent as this book unfolds. Pepys's genius in this regard, as in others, will become her own.

In 1918 and later, Woolf saw in Pepys's diary the human impulse to confide. Scott's and Burney's diaries stressed this motive as well. Scott starts *his* diary with this old song as his epigraph: "As I walked by myself / I talked to my self / And thus my self said to me." He repeats these lines to launch his essay on Pepys. Woolf writes in 1918 that Pepys wished "to hold intercourse with the secret companion who lives in everybody" (E 2: 237). Eleven years later, in the more private space of her diary, she alludes to Pepys again as she ponders her own diary-keeping. "And why do I write this down?" she asks of her just-expressed pique at Vita's lovers. "I have not even told Leonard; & whom do I tell when I tell a blank page? The truth is, I get nearer feelings in writing than in walking—I think: graze the bone; enjoy the expression; have them out of me; make them a little creditable to myself; I daresay suppress something, so that after all I'm doing what amounts to confiding. Why did Pepys write his diary after all?" (D 3: 239). When she is fifteen, Pepys's diary shows her a confiding mind both skeptical and eclectic. His diary, like Burney's, gives her a model of London vitality and success—and of diary success across the ages.

"Miss Jan"

Like Fanny Burney before her and Anne Frank after, teenage Virginia Stephen created a persona, a projection of herself, in the first months of her 1897 diary: "Miss Jan." Diary editor Mitchell Leaska suggests this family nickname may have been a shortening of "Miss January," the month of Virginia's birth (PA 5n3). Virginia uses this name in a dozen contexts in the 1897 diary's first five months, and commentators have made much of the alter ego. Louise DeSalvo suggests that Virginia "used the cover of Miss Jan to express emotions that, in the Stephen household, . . . might have been difficult or dangerous for her to express overtly" (Impact 243). Elizabeth Podnieks endorses and expands De-Salvo's analysis. Podnieks sees "Miss Jan" as evidence of Woolf's early aesthetic of impersonality and as a sign that from the first Woolf "donned masks" and "used her diary as a place in which she could play multiple roles, refusing . . . to be fixed to any one identity" (150). Noting that while we can see "Miss Jan" as a convincing sign of trauma "repressed and expressed," Podnieks believes we should also view her as an invention of an aspiring journalist and novelist (146).

I do not wish to make too much of the twelve references to "Miss Jan" in the first five months of Woolf's diary. Certainly the construction is important, as DeSalvo and Podnieks imply. However, "Miss Jan" also seems much more casually and variously employed than Anne Frank's desperately needed "friend," Kitty, or Fanny Burney's droll and durable "Miss Nobody."[26] Unlike Burney and Frank, Virginia used her alter ego outside her diary as well as in it. "It is so windy to day, that Miss Jan is quite afraid of venturing out," she writes to Thoby March 6, 1896 (L #2, 1: 2). On February 24, 1897, her letter to him reports that "Poor Janet was almost crushed by the agitated ladies" vying to see the Queen (L #5, 1: 6). "Miss Jan," then, is not a private diary construct; it is a public family nickname Virginia adopts in several contexts. As with "poor creature," I believe young Virginia is not so much dissociating herself from her emotions and projecting them onto "Miss Jan," as DeSalvo claims, as she is setting off this important identity for attention, sympathy, and study. A playful dramatic heightening sounds in these constructions; in the 1897 diary Vanessa on occasion is "Miss Maria" and "poor Marmot" (*PA* 13, 80).

In four of the twelve uses, "Miss Jan" does indeed serve as a vehicle for expressing feelings. Discomfort is noted and its source named in Virginia's very first diary entry: "Miss Jan rode her new bicycle, whose seat unfortunately, is rather uncomfortable" (*PA* 5). On February 1, "Poor Miss Jan is bewildered" at being pressed into the role of Stella's chaperone—a sentence that allows the diarist not only to identify her emotion and its cause but also to administer sympathy to herself (*PA* 27). Nineteen days later "Poor Miss Jan utterly lost her wits" at the Stillmans. In this more extended use Virginia again offers sympathy to her distressed self ("Poor Miss Jan"); however, she also owns her behavior through vivid description and appears, through analysis, to accept her social limits: "So we left, I with the conviction that what ever talents Miss Jan may have, she does not possess the one qualifying her to shine in good society" (*PA* 39). One can read these "Miss Janisms" as Virginia examining, comforting, and coming to understand herself. On May 2, "Miss Jan's" last appearance in the diary is to express joy at Stella's recovery from illness: "Jan most jubilant—& went comfortably to bed for the first time" (*PA* 80).

If four of the twelve references to "Miss Jan" disclose feelings (of discomfort, bewilderment, distress, or joy), in four others "Miss Jan" makes judgments and assesses intellectual levels: "The Pantomime was Aladdin and very good Miss Jan thought, more suited to her comprehension than a grown up play" (*PA* 6). On May 2 she again seems keen to gauge her own intellectual rung compared to others. Her father's Town Hall lecture on Pascal, she writes, "was very deep rather too deep for the audience; very logical & difficult for the ignorant (i.e. Miss Jan) to follow" (*PA* 79). On January 5, Virginia writes that "Miss Jan thought" Adrian's purchase of a bicycle luggage carrier "a piece of great extravagance," while on February 4 dances are judged of no interest to "Miss Jan" (*PA* 7, 29). Here Virginia personifies that part of herself that assesses and asserts values.

Perhaps the four most important references to "Miss Jan," however, associate her with a writer's identity. Virginia was composing in tandem with her 1897 diary a work called the "Eternal Miss Jan," the title revealing the girl's wish for enduring life. On February 5, she tells her diary: "After tea wrote the Eternal Miss Jan" (*PA* 30). The nearness of "Miss Jan," the heroine of this fiction, to "Miss Jan" of the diary, and to fifteen-year-old Virginia herself can be seen in

Virginia's April 28 diary entry expressing alarm at Stella's chill: "Oh dear—how is one to live in such a world, which is a Miss Janism, but very much my mind at present" (*PA* 77).

Eight days earlier it is "Miss Jan" as writer-persona who probes the type of writer Virginia seeks to be. After capturing a bit of the exhilaration of a downhill bicycle ride, Virginia is thinking very much as a writer when she observes: "If I was a poet (which Miss Jan does not claim to be) I should write something upon this way of traveling. This diary is too small to allow of very much prose" (*PA* 73). In an earlier, February 11, entry, it is "Miss Jan" the writer-persona who again determines what will enter the diary. Outside of Bognor, during their chaperone ordeal, Vanessa and Virginia meet a "school of little boys" marching toward them. "Their remarks shall not be entered here, Miss Jan says" (*PA* 33).

As noted earlier, "Miss Jan" makes her final diary appearance to express joy at Stella's recovery: "Jan most jubilant" (*PA* 80). After this May 2 reference, "Miss Jan" disappears from the diary. Readers have expressed frustration that the 1897 diary makes no direct mention of Virginia's sexual abuse. However, in May she repeatedly documents George Duckworth's intellectual trespass. Her May 6 entry ends with the complaint that "Georgie insisted upon my putting out my light early or I should have finished the 3rd vol. of Macaulay" (*PA* 82). On May 20 she notes that she "read in bed as usual, The Scarlet Letter, & was stopped by Georgie & Nessa at 11 o'clock" (*PA* 88), and she ends her May 24 entry with the rather ominous, though triumphant, "I determined to finish the 1st vol. of the F[rench]. R[evolution]. . . . [I]n the middle of my nightly forbidden reading, I shut up, thinking G[eorge]. was coming. However it was a false alarm, & the 1st vol. was finished" (*PA* 90). In this month she gives George a diary for his birthday. Does she hope a diary might allow him to see himself, that it might reflect his intrusive behavior back to him or invite, at the least, introspection?

"Miss Jan" the writerly persona fades from the diary in early May, and the diary—itself so often personified—begins to wither after Stella's shocking July 19 death. Virginia struggles on half-heartedly through the end of July and all of August and September, but by October long gaps begin, and they continue to the end of the year. On January 10, Virginia had mused, "It is a week today since I began this diary. How many more weeks has it to live," revealing that she thought of her diary from the first as a person, a "life" (*PA* 10). By August 9 she is writing, "This poor diary is in a very bad way," and by September 14 the diary is projected as a kind of corpse (like Stella) eaten by worms: "This poor diary is lingering on indeed, but death would be shorter & less painful—Never mind, we will follow the year to its end, & then fling diaries & diarising into the corner—to dust & mice & moths & all creeping crawling eating destroying creatures" (*PA* 121, 128).

William Johnson Cory's *Journals*

Before her diary begins to sputter in October 1897, fifteen-year-old Virginia Stephen spends time in early September reading William Johnson Cory's diary. A poet, adored master of Eton, and fellow at King's College, Cambridge, Cory left behind a diary at his 1892 death. Virginia was thinking of college for herself at this time, and the just-published *Extracts from the Letters and Journals of William Cory* gave her an intimate look at both the British male public school and the Cambridge life her brother, Thoby, soon would taste.

In 1847, Cory wrote that he and Sir Henry Sumner Maine "went through several hard subjects in the old Cambridge way, in that method of minute comparison of opinions without argument which I believe to be peculiar to the small intellectual aristocracy of Cambridge" (46). Cory was a Cambridge Apostle, and his *Extracts* describe Apostle talks and meetings, including a visit by the poet Alfred Tennyson (422). "The Society will do you no good if you pick up in it only or chiefly the banter or irony," Cory writes to Frederick Pollock in 1865. "It will do you good if it makes you hammer out your own thoughts till they are intelligible and till they fit into other men's thoughts" (159). Cory mentions another Apostle, Leslie Stephen's older brother, Fitzjames Stephen, and this may explain the book's presence in the Stephen home and its further appeal to young Virginia.

Her father had been a day student at Eton, which may have quickened her interest in Cory's Eton scenes. Cory tutored girls and young women when his Eton days were done. Virginia might have found him an amiable tutor for herself through his diary *Extracts*. After all, he calls Walter Scott "*the supreme man of letters*" after William Shakespeare (454). At age forty, Cory confides to his diary that when he was twenty-three:

The love of literature had then been overlaid by a half-hearted love of science, and though I went to see Scott's trees and books, I did not care for Scott in '46 as I did in '32, when he died, and I subscribed five shillings to the fund for saving his library from creditors. And now [1863], my ambition being trodden under foot, my hopes of improving the world withered away, social liberty attained, tongue loosed, shyness diminished, theories given up, I find I love Walter Scott as well as I did in boyhood, and take Tweedside for the home of my fancy. (95)

Cory confesses to his diary that at a London portrait exhibition in 1868 he saw Scott's portrait "through a mist of weeping. He is my lost childhood, he is my first great friend. I long for him and hate the death that parts us" (223).

Like Scott, Cory uses initials in his diary and writes a diary of emotional reserve. Offering to share his diary with his brother, the Reverend C. W. Furse, Cory explains: "I often write at considerable length, leaving out all sordid and vexatious things" (238). Unlike Scott, he shuns speed in his diary to achieve a more conservative, pondered style; however, he confesses to his brother that "To write rapidly is a great pleasure, like skating; it is a pity I don't do it more" (238).

Cory calls his diary "a genuine, original book," and, like Burney and Scott, he values his journal for preserving life that would otherwise be lost (204). Sounding regrets similar to Burney's over her lost Dunkirk police adventure, Cory tells his brother: "I wish I had written more at school; as it is there are records of a whole fortnight and of a month (last May) which may some day be valued as data for an account of Eton life. In another way I sometimes think my journals will be valuable, they will contain some careful studies of people whose biographies will be written, if not published" (238). One wonders if fifteen-year-old Virginia took note of *this* Cory statement: "I wish King David had remembered his fifteenth year. Luckily St. Augustine did; so did Isaac Williams" (215).

William Cory "purred over books" (153); in fact, like Virginia, he speaks of devouring books and calls the London Library an "inestimable resource" (8, 27). His diary portrays British male public school education, Cambridge university life, and the atmosphere they fostered. She saw what she was missing. However, Cory also shared his reservations, which may have also influenced the fifteen-year-old who was soon, in November, to begin at King's College (Kensington) herself. "The faults found with Eton, dress and gluttony, are after all the faults of the English 1 ½ million or upperclasses," Cory declares in 1879 (444). Dress and gluttony, however, are never Woolf's sins. "As a general rule I have . . . very little faith in schools or schooling," this master of Eton surprisingly writes (206). "I lately read my old Journal kept at Cambridge when I was an undergraduate," he writes to A. D. Coleridge. "It is full of melancholy scrupulosity and morbid combination of piety with opinion-breeding. In those days we had a great difficulty in sorting the contents of our minds: I got so sick of it that when I was about twenty-five I used to tell people that I declined having any 'opinions' at all—'went in for facts.' Luckily, I never quite gave up poetry" (375). When he resigns his fellowship at King's College and retires from Eton, Cory confesses, "I begin to see that neither Eton nor Cambridge was good for my poor body, which has greatly improved these six months. . . . I am healthier and happier, and more needed by others, in this quiet parish near my ancestral town of Torrington, than I used to be in King's" (293, 290).

Beyond a candid look at English education, Cory's *Extracts* offered Virginia images and scenes of perhaps even greater use. He may have planted in her mind the importance of "a room of one's own." In an 1872 letter to a young Eton student, Cory offers this assurance: "You will soon have a room of your own and get away from the more childish boys" (281). He may have hastened her interest in the lives of the obscure. That Cory thought, at times, of women's views can be seen in this intriguing 1867 journal entry on Bolton Abbey: "I wish there were . . . some few lines about the loves and the sorrows of the very people who saw these most poetical of buildings when fresh in their first marvellousness. The bereaved mother could not say—for there were no words then to say it in—'My grief shall arise and stand fast in the pillars of the house of prayer, and the memory of my child shall endure in beauty of carven stone.' Did she see the stones put together in these fair forms? Did the masons care for her loss? Did the widows widowed by the Sword of William Fitz Duncan come to pray in the new church?" (190).

In an 1874 letter, Cory unfolds this delightful scene of a country entertainment:

Ten days ago they played for the first time in public; it was in our barn, on the estrade where the piano was. The audience was the Dolton choir, and my Brother's tenants, old servants, &c.; of course all my people too. . . . Willink was there—he had worked briskly at lighting up the barn with wooden chandeliers wreathed. Mrs. and Mr. Furse worked at the hanging wreaths—we put up my old sconces and red Indian shields. We made tables for the supper. . . . Many of the old people had never had such an evening. . . .

I liked, above most things, seeing Philip here, and next to him old Milles the farmer, who is very musical and a meek, well-bred man, delightfully free from anxiety. Our party amounted to sixty, including the twenty in the house. . . . [I]magine the sweet little thrill it gives a Dolton girl, of the humblest birth . . . and the tearful gratitude of Mary L., the literary woman who lives at the corner by Budd's mill, and of Mary the slowly dying wife of Philip. (369–70)

Could this country day have lodged in young Virginia's mind, become part of the compost heap, the seedbed for the extraordinary country theatrical of Woolf's final novel *Between the Acts*?

Virginia Woolf's 1897 Diary Concluded

In November 1897, fifteen-year-old Virginia begins to study Greek, Latin, and history at King's College in Kensington, a challenge that might explain her neglect of her struggling diary. More has been written on this, her first extant, diary than on any of her other diary books—and the range of readings dazzles. Clinical psychologist Katherine Dalsimer notes "occasional . . . undisguised venomousness, even sadism" in the diary, invariably directed against an older woman (49). This I do not find. Dalsimer writes: "In the diaries and letters of her adult years, this aspect of Woolf's character is modulated to a sort of zestful maliciousness that makes these volumes delicious reading"; however, in the 1897 diary Dalsimer finds "no pleasure either for the writer or for the reader" (49).

Roger Poole calls the 1897 diary "cautious" and "censored" (302), and Joanne Campbell Tidwell, focusing on Woolf's development of self, stresses the fading self in the diary's second half. "The young Virginia cannot maintain the female sense of self imposed upon her from the outside, and she is unable to create a satisfying lingual self in her diary," Tidwell suggests. "Virginia's retreat from written language marks an inability to express her self" (15). Elizabeth Podnieks, in turn, sees the 1897 diary as Virginia's "means of suppressing or controlling the chaos of her life" (140). Certainly diary-writing, in its regularity, can provide an island of stability in a whirlpool of activity, a refuge for reflection, yet also a bridge of continuity from the past to the future. In the 1897 diary we see Virginia record everyone's activities and chart her place within this busy flow.

Louise DeSalvo, who has written of the 1897 diary in articles and books across a decade, comes finally to consider this diary both a covert record of abuse and repression and a triumph over them. DeSalvo suggests that in reading so many histories and biographies across the year, Virginia "carved out an identity for herself, as a historian in the making" ("1897" 87). In contrast to Tidwell's stress on the teenager's fading "self," Woolf biographer Hermione Lee calls the 1897 diary style "rapid, energetic, [and] self-engrossed" (166), while Andrew McNeillie, the assistant editor of Woolf's 1920 to 1941 diaries, considers the 1897 journal "a triumph" (*CM* 2: 43).

I believe the achievement of the 1897 diary far outweighs its constrictions.

Amid the breathless dashes and the telegraphic record of family comings and goings, small signs of literary promise appear as the teenager records her world. We see an observing eye. When her cousin, the architect Edmund (Jo) Fisher, invites the Stephens to his office in January, she writes: "Jo plunged us down a little back street and so to his office, which is one small room, with a hideous green paper, with yellow peacocks and lions, and with a window looking on to the river" (PA 8). We see thumbnail portraits and discover how early Virginia deflates pomposity by noting people's animal traits. In June, Aunt Dorothea arrives "as fat as a grampus, & blowing like that animal—terrible in her heat, & perspiration; & general cowlike stout appearance" (PA 105). We see first tries at balanced portraits when Virginia writes in June of cousin Adelaide's fiancé, the composer Ralph Vaughan Williams: "Poor Ralph is a *calf*—according to [Stella]—& also, I am afraid, to us—However they are very much in love, & there is a chance that he has genius" (PA 101).

Like Fanny Burney, Virginia strives to record talk as well as looks and character. On March 5, she delivers the following small scene, with its humorous parallel "verys": "Lady Stephen and Katherine came to lunch. Lady Stephen very proper and talkative. Katherine, very massive and intellectual—Tried to talk to father but she was snubbed—She eat, however, an enormous luncheon, almost demolishing a pineapple. Lady Stephen was very full of Miss Walpoles broken off engagement, which Georgie heard of yesterday. 'They have ceased to understand each other' she said" (PA 48).

Three days later, Virginia borrows Burney's italics and manages a more sophisticated substitutionary narration in her portrait of Mrs. Howard Smith, whom they interviewed regarding a prospective cook: "She was a horrid little skinny lady—would not answer for the cook's honesty—would not say she was dishonest, that would not be right, the old hag said, but we agreed that under such a mistress our tempers and our honesty would be very much tried—so Mary Smith will most likely—with her *dreadful* temper and her suspicious honesty become cook at No. 24" (PA 50). On March 31, the young diarist tries her hand with Henry James: "We met Mr James in Oxford Street. 'Most extraordinary coincidence, my dear Stella Duckworth! I was just this moment, this very moment, thinking of you—in fact I had stopped 10 doors back to get you something—now I meet you!' This was carried on at great length with great difficulty in the midst of the crowd" (PA 63).

Beyond modest, yet lively, portraits, young Virginia also reveals her awareness of nature and nature-writing. On March 10 she mimics a form of natural history prose met often in the daily press: "A reverend gentleman has written to the Times to record the first hawthorn flower—the earliest that has appeared in the Parish since 1884 when, as will be remembered, there was an uncommonly mild winter, and favourable spring—still I think your readers will agree with me, when I say that it is not an unprecedented phenomenon, this early visitor, etc etc. *Hear hear!*" (*PA* 52). The young diarist cheers her own parody.

A week later she continues to delight in this refined country-parson naturizing: "At about one [Stella], Adeline and I went in to the gardens and looked at the flowers—the almond trees out, the crocusses going over, squills at their best, the other trees just beginning to seed—I shall turn into a country clergyman, and make notes of phenomena in Kensington Gardens, which shall be sent as a challenge to other country clergymen" (*PA* 55–56). Within the send-up (and too vague description of flora) we notice the observant eye and the ability to imagine herself as another. Five months later, she sounds a different note—and one of her first probing diary questions—when she finds herself in the country for real: "we strolled about, with the bluest of skies above us, & the fir trees—scenting the air strongly. Down in the valley there are gypsies, & blue straight pillars of smoke—One ought to be a poet if one lives in the country—& one is? what—" (*PA* 119).

The year also brings fodder for later works. On April 8, Stella loses the opal ring her fiancé has given her, and Virginia and Vanessa join the search party, a scene reprised in *To the Lighthouse*, Stella transformed into Minta Doyle and her opal ring into Minta's grandmother's brooch (*PA* 67). (An actual brooch is lost in 1897 as well.) On August 5, Thoby's school friend, C.E.W. Bean, seems a model for Charles Tansley, Mr. Ramsay's annoying disciple in *To the Lighthouse*. "A red headed conceited youth," Virginia tells her diary; "very Cliftonian & talkative" (*PA* 120). Virginia also personifies books in her diary in a manner foreshadowing her 1925 essay "Lives of the Obscure." She must decide what to do with a birthday gift, a "gorgeous" copy of Dr. Mandell Creighton's 1896 *Queen Elizabeth* (*PA* 21). On February 7 Virginia ponders, "what shall become of her—She is far too beautiful to lie about the nursery at the mercy of the ink pot or of Pauline, and far too big to live in any of our bookshelves" (*PA* 31). The first paragraph of "Lives of the Obscure" offers this library scene: "The obscure sleep on the walls, slouching against each other as if they were too drowsy to stand upright.... Why disturb their sleep?" (*CR* 1: 106). Even at fifteen, biographies and diaries are "lives" for Virginia, lives famous or obscure.

The seeds of Woolf's many later allusions to Shakespeare's "Fear no more the heat o' the sun" can also be traced to this year. Young Virginia immerses herself in Thomas Carlyle across 1897. On January 29, two days after she reads Carlyle's *Reminiscences* for the second time, her father takes her to Carlyle's Chelsea home. "Went over the house, with an intelligent old woman who knew father and everything about him," Virginia tells her diary. "We saw the drawing room, and dining room, and Cs sound proof room, with double walls—His writing table, and his pens, and scraps of his manuscripts—" (*PA* 24). On display in Carlyle's home today, and perhaps in 1897 as well, are four stanzas from Shakespeare's *Cymbeline*, copied in Carlyle's hand, beginning "Fear no more the heat o' the sun."

Virginia Stephen's 1897 diary offers clear signs of literary aspirations, and of literary gifts as well; however, it sounds another note too—one of spatial restriction. "No room for more!" resounds nine times in the diary from April onward, a practical note on her diary's small size (*PA* 98). The 1897 diary may have been handsome with its brown leather cover, gilt edges, "beautiful boards," and key, but it was also only three-and-a-half inches wide and five-and-a-half inches long and allotted only a page for each day's entry. "This diary is too small to allow of very much prose," Virginia recognizes April 20 when she is tempted to write, as a poet, about her thrilling bicycle ride (*PA* 73). Had she a larger diary, she might have tried further to capture this flight, and she could have expanded her character studies as well. On June 8, she writes of Frances Noel and a Miss Baldwin, the latter "an emaciated female who plays the piano loudly & badly," "No room to say more of this wonderful pair" (*PA* 97). On July 30 she describes a letter from Helen Holland: "Helen splendid—but I have no room to reproduce her choicest bits" (*PA* 118). We receive only "a very bare record" of Virginia's trip to Windsor in June—"no room for more"—and nothing of her "many adventures" on the way to Brighton in April or of the "great water party" in May: "My space is gradually dissappearing [*sic*], & I cannot say in the shortest way all that we did" (*PA* 107, 72, 89). How sad the young writer was not given a larger diary page.

The small canvas may figure in her growing neglect of her diary—or perhaps her college work interferes. Whatever the cause, she closes her 1897 diary with a final entry on January 1, 1898:

I write this morning what would more fitly have been written last night. But my diary has ever been scornful of stated rules! Here then comes the "Finis" What a volume might not be written round that word—& it is even hard to resist the few sentences that naturally cling to it. But I will be stern. Here is a volume of fairly acute life (the first really *lived* year of my life) ended locked & put away. And another & another & another yet to come. Oh dear they are very long, & I seem cowardly throughout when I look at them. Still, courage & plod on—They must bring something worth the having—& [illegible] they *shall*. Nessa preaches that our destinies lie in ourselves, & the sermon ought to be taken home by us. Here is life given us each alike, & we must do our best with it: your hand in the sword hilt—& an unuttered fervent vow! (*PA* 134)

Podnieks finds in this final entry "the weariness of spirit and psyche which was overwhelming [Virginia] and which she was projecting onto her future state of mind" (140). DeSalvo focuses on the sword image to find the fifteen-year-old both besieged and forearmed: "her vision of herself was in part an embattled one" (*Impact* 232). I would stress as well the exclamatory pride in her diary: a diary "ever scornful of stated rules!"—the phrase foreshadowing the convention-expanding writer to come. Was there pride, too, in a diary written at speed, with dashes connecting rather than periods concluding? We note, too, the literary diarist who finds, even as she closes, that the word "Finis" invites her pen.

2

The Experimenter

Virginia Woolf's 1899 Warboys Diary

"This book has now got to be a kind of testing ground..."

(PA 416)

ifteen-year-old Virginia appears to have followed her inclination to "fling diaries & diarising into the corner." At least no diary for 1898 survives. Her imagination stirs again, however, in late summer 1899. Now seventeen, she embarks with her family in August on a seven-week holiday in the fen country of Huntingdonshire (now Cambridgeshire). Warboys Rectory, where they stayed, was a five-mile bicycle ride from a different St. Ives, but a reminder of their happy Cornwall summers before her mother's death. Another's diary may have renewed Virginia's diary pulse. On August 7, the fourth day of the sojourn, she describes herself adrift "in the punt, which has been padded with rugs & cushions & read[ing] a sleepy preaching [?][1] book; the diary of some ancient Bishop written in flowing ancient English that harmonized with this melancholy melodious monotony (what an awful sentence!) of bank & stream" (PA 138).

The ancient Bishop and his diary in ancient English remain, alas, unidentified. Virginia's sentence describing them, however, conveys the character of the 1899 diary, which differs greatly from her 1897 diary. The 1897 diary is a *life diary*; the 1899 diary a *travel diary*. While the 1897 diary offers 309 entries—the most entries of any of Woolf's diary books—the 1899 diary contains only 19 entries across 47 Warboys days. To compensate, however, its sentences are less breathless and more elaborate than those of 1897—as are the entries themselves. The journal begins as a daily diary on August 4, 1899; however, after five consecutive entries—or perhaps eleven, if one includes two undated entries—a gap then occurs and, beginning August 18, the diary becomes a periodic diary. In fact, it becomes a different diary altogether, for four of the final eight entries are *titled*, as if they are diary *essays* or simply set pieces unto themselves.

With the 1899 diary, the seventeen-year-old becomes self-consciously literary; in fact, she uses her Warboys diary for writerly exercises of all kinds. On the most practical level, the diary serves as a "testing ground" for new pens and inks. Quentin Bell calls the 1899 diary "an exasperating document"—exasperating to read, that is, for its pages contain diary entries but also pen practice, Virginia writing the same phrases over and over in different nibs and inks (*VW* 1: 65). As Mitchell Leaska, who edited the early journals, notes, this gives the journal "its appearance of immense chaos."[2] However, what may first appear to be fussy adolescent pen and penmanship play also marks the young writer's growing sense of audience and concern for writing standards. "I have made the most heroic resolution to change my ideas of calligraphy in conformance with those of my family, which are more generally accepted by the world as the correct ones," she grandly explains (*PA* 416). No more, then, is the diary quite "scornful of stated rules!" (*PA* 134). On August 13, she pauses in her description of tree sugaring to reveal again her sensitivity to readers' needs: "(I suppose a reader sometimes for the sake of variety when I write; it makes me put on my dress clothes such as they are)" (*PA* 144). This parenthetical confession suggests that she considers a public writing style something adopted, put on to impress readers, like formal clothes. She tries on this formal style often in this diary.

Her "such as they are," however, forms part of the motif of deficiency, hesitancy, yet qualified assertion that pervades the 1899 diary. The seventeen-year-old follows conventional diary practice by launching her diary with an explanation for her act; however, the end of her sentence shows her tentative state. "This being our first night, & such a night not occurring again, I must make some mark on paper to represent so auspicious an occasion," she begins strongly, with Fanny Burney–like mock seriousness (*PA* 135). However, she then adds, "tho' my mark must be frail & somewhat disjointed," as though she distrusts the new "very fine pen" she uses, or distrusts this strong stance and wishes to qualify it, to declare her voice different (Bell *VW* 1: 65). Across her stay she struggles with "details," their necessity and ratio to other material in her entries. She tries to become a nature writer but repeatedly stresses her trials. Her August 6 entry begins with a reference to "My Garden Acquaintance," an essay by her godfather, the American poet James Russell Lowell, and it seems itself more an essay than a diary entry. After considering whether she might simplify into a country naturalist like Gilbert White if she stayed longer in the country, and after mimicking (again) the country clergyman style, she explains her plight: "Alas, tho,' as a Cockney I have no sound country education to go upon. I must blurt out crude ecstasies upon sky & field; which may perchance retain for my eyes a little of their majesty in my awkward words."[3] She admits here her fumblings, yet hopes her attempt may serve some use, if only a private one. On August 12, she uses the "I wish" mantra to paint a picture of the fens. Again she notes her failure, but ends: "Nevertheless I own it is a joy to me to be set down with such a vast never ending picture to reproduce—reproduction is out of the question—but to gaze at, nibble at & scratch at" (*PA* 143). Here is the first sign of Woolf's mimetic view of art. She wishes she could capture the fens; she notes the impossibility, and, having acknowledged this fact, she can then make her small inadequate picture.

On September 3, when she assays "A Chapter on Sunsets," she must three times note her difficulty before she finally succeeds. In her final diary entry, after a fine description of the change from summer to fall, again her sense of inadequacy sounds. "I cannot attempt to explain in words the charm & melancholy, the colour & the interest, of the picture," she writes, yet saying she "cannot" paves the way for her to try.[4]

The aspiring writer experiments with more than pens, inks, calligraphy, diary formats, and nature writing in her 1899 diary; she tries her hand at other literary styles as well. Her essay-entry titled "Extract from the Huntingdonshire Gazette. TERRIBLE TRAGEDY IN A DUCKPOND," skillfully parodies journalistic conventions—and gothic narratives as well. At seventeen, she can mimic newspaper accident reports as wittily as letters from country parsons. In her "Extract from the Huntingdonshire Gazette" she places her audience in the role of newspaper reader, her capital letters capturing the blare of tabloid headlines. "A terrible tragedy which had its scene in a duck pond has been reported from Warboys," the piece begins. "Our special correspondent who was despatched to that village has had unrivaled opportunities of investigating the details" (*PA* 150). The account then assumes a mock tragic tone, the gothic clichés trotted forward: "ill fated," "meet their doom," "harrowing tale," "terrible shrieks & agonized struggles for air," "the green shroud" (*PA* 151).

In her 1989 volume *Virginia Woolf: The Impact Of Childhood Sexual Abuse On Her Life and Work*, Louise DeSalvo considers "TERRIBLE TRAGEDY IN A DUCKPOND" Virginia's covert communication of her sexual abuse, first to her private diary, and then revised and sent twice to Emma Vaughan, eight years her senior, who had been one of the participants in the (more happily resolved) punt adventure. In DeSalvo's overdetermined reading, "DUCKPOND" symbolizes Duckworth (that is, Virginia's half-brothers George and Gerald Duckworth); the "carpet of duckweed—the green shroud" covering the duck pond and perhaps gagging the victims, represents the same. The gagging, suffocating death is linked to sexual force, even oral sex (259). Read in this way, the "Extract" is much more than an attempt to parody newspaper and gothic conventions; it is, according to DeSalvo: "a dress rehearsal for what Woolf would do to herself in 1941," it is "an enactment of her identification with her mother" (who "sank" in 1895), and it is a prediction of "what will happen to her if no one comes to her rescue and allows her to continue to be subjected to abuse" (257).

Many motives might join in this mock dramatic piece. I believe the entry shows the young writer parodying prose styles, yet also *expanding* them, for amid the gothic excesses appear phrases of simple (yet vivid and moving) poetic prose: "the green caverns of the depths opened—& closed—The cold moonlight silvered the path to death—& perhaps tinged the last thoughts of the unfortunate sufferers with something of its own majestic serenity" (PA 151). Whatever its motive, this is the first diary entry we know Virginia shared with others.

Other set pieces also distinguish the Warboys diary. On August 13, an entry for which Virginia also "suppose[s] a reader," she captures their "Sugar campaign" in an extended comic scene worthy of Fanny Burney. She introduces her moth-hunting siblings one-by-one in high-spirited mock-heroic fashion, as if it were a travel or battle narrative. The entry bursts with droll thrusts. "[S]o have we perverted the morals of moth land," she observes of their rum-sugar-and-beer concoction smeared on the trees (PA 145). However, as with "Extracts from the Huntingdonshire Gazette" that will soon follow, the send-up of expedition narratives mixes close observation with simple prose to achieve more than a comic end:

By the faint glow we could see the huge moth—his wings open, as though in ecstasy, so that the splendid crimson of the underwing could be seen—his eyes burning red, his proboscis plunged into a flowing stream of treacle. We gazed one moment on his splendour, & then uncorked the bottle. I think the whole procession felt some unprofessional regret when, with a last gleam of scarlet eye & scarlet wing, the grand old moth vanished. (PA 145)

The August 18 "Warboys Distractions" essay-entry recounts another comic expedition, this time an excursion to Godmanchester for a water outing with their "terrible oppressive" relatives, the Stephens (PA 146). For the first half Virginia tries her hand at traditional travel narrative: a journey, filled with mishaps, by pony cart, train, and trap. With the second half, however, she offers her first diary portrait of a "type"—here the Stephens, who are "immensely broad, long & muscular; they move awkwardly, & as though they resented the conventionalities of modern life at every step. They all bring with them the atmosphere of the lecture room; they are severe, caustic & absolutely independent & immoveable. An ordinary character would be ground to a pulp after a weeks intercourse with them" (*PA* 149).

The young writer then picks up her narrative, compresses the hour's rowing and landing into two sentences, and this separates the two shades of her portrait, the immoveable independence from its social effect:

> One remarkable sign of character in this race is that they are able to sit speechless without feeling the slightest discomfort while the whole success of the party they have invited depends on them. They acknowledge that it is drizzling & grey, that their guests are depressed & think the whole party a bore; they can bear the knowledge of these facts & support the discovery without turning a hair. I admire this as I should admire a man who could stand on the line immoveable while an express train rushed towards him. This kind of heroism however, is not calculated to smooth a tea party. (*PA* 149)

We see here the seventeen-year-old's grasp of the dry skewering last line. She has used it in the paragraph before in her portrait of a single Stephen—Rosamond—that concludes: "As we went down to the river she lectured us on the various objects of interest. I fear I did not profit" (*PA* 149).

Woolf tries single portraits and family types in this diary and further tests literary types when she compares curates in books to an actual curate, Blake Milward. "I had a dim idea of mythical curates, dwelling in the pages of novels, & receiving satire at the hands of all wielders of Pens," she writes, "—but the fact that a Black Coated gentleman could be a Human Being & not a Hypocrite . . . was quite strange to me" (*PA* 141). She tests literary formulae against personal observation again and again in the 1899 diary. The tension between the two creates this diary's unusual quality: stilted formality mixed with the natural and new.[5] "Methinks," "methought," and "perchance," the seventeen-year-old writes across the diary, aping the Elizabethans (*PA* 136, 138, 155, 159, 160, 424). "[L]et us hope," she declares grandly in her first diary entry, and "Let me remark" (*PA* 135, 136). "Behold Nessa," she declaims in the Godmanchester entry (*PA* 146).

The awkward flourishes reside particularly in her tropes, for with the 1899 diary, the seventeen-year-old becomes metaphorical. Virginia *personifies* the natural world across the diary's nineteen entries, perhaps following the classical Greek models she has studied. The sun most frequently is personified: as a hunter, soldier, or god. "[T]he sun shot a shaft of light down," she writes in her first entry, depicting the sun as an ancient bowman (*PA* 136). Clouds "catch" the sun's glory on September 3; more elaborately, "a low lying bank of gray cloud . . . fixed to receive into its arms the impetuous descent of the sun god" (*PA* 155). The duck pond is personified in fury; its "angry waters . . . rose in their wrath," we are told, "to swallow their prey" (*PA* 151). In the diary's final entry, flames "leapt out & lashed their tongues" (*PA* 162). Trees are shown "casting their arms against the sky" in the "Chapter on Sunsets" (*PA* 155). Earlier, the pollard trees are personified "sobbing in the wind" (*PA* 146).

How Homeric all this seems in lovely Huntingdonshire, a try-out of classical tropes, ancient vehicles for the tenor at hand. Virginia's nature personifications may have been spurred by Tennyson as well as by Homer. Tennyson's poem "Tithonus" is on her mind as the summer wanes and autumn starts, for she practices its line "The vapours weep their burden to the ground" four times in her pen and penmanship exercises and incorporates the personification into her final diary entry which celebrates the air of "autumn in its youth, before decayed woods & weeping vapours have come to end its substance" (*PA* 420, 421, 161).

Katherine Dalsimer stresses the "insistent subtext" of these often-overlooked Tennyson lines. "Tithonus," she reminds us, is about "the *yearning* for death": "The theme of the poem whose opening lines Woolf wrote and rewrote . . . is that long life is cruelty. Death is release" (66, 64). For Dalsimer, the "chaos" of the Warboys journal "is part of the story she was telling" (67). However, that Virginia also is studying poetic tropes is evident in this passage also copied into the diary: "When he describes a fine day, he gives it the epithet 'firm' which at once conveys to the mind an idea of solidity & almost flesh" (*PA* 422).

If the diary's classical personifications seem archaic and unnatural, its similes are more original and suggestive. After referring to the Bishop's diary on her fourth Warboys day, Virginia pauses for this reflection: "Activity of mind, I think, is the only thing that keeps one's life going, unless one has a larger emotional activity of some other kind. Ones mind thats like a restless steamer paddle urging the ship along, tho' the wind is fallen & the sea is as still as glass" (*PA* 138). What a vivid picture this offers of the seventeen-year-old's diary— and life—her restless mind propelling her on. And *this* simile leads to a more elaborate one:

that I am a Norseman bound on some long voyage. The ship now is frozen in the drift ice; slowly we are drifting towards home. I have taken with me after anxious thought all the provisions for my mind that are necessary during the voyage. The seals & walruses that I shoot during my excursions on the ice . . . are the books that I discover here & read. . . . What a force a human being is! There are worse solitudes than drift ice, & yet this eternal throbbing heat & energy of ones mind thaws a pathway thro'; & open sea & land shall come in time. (*PA* 138)

DeSalvo sees much in this extended simile. At seventeen, DeSalvo claims, Virginia sees that she has been "immobilized in the frozen waste of a Victorian female adolescence, immobilized and isolated and threatened by her sexual abuse" (*Impact* 253). Yet DeSalvo also is forced to acknowledge that Virginia here seems to feel "fully capable of rescuing herself if only she could have patience enough to wait out the situation in which she was living" (*Impact* 253). The metaphor certainly offers a more hopeful end than that of "TERRIBLE TRAGEDY IN A DUCKPOND." That the two outcomes co-exist in the 1899 diary should bear weight. More simply, however, the paddlewheel and Norseman conceits may convey Virginia's sense of the Warboys interim: she entertains herself with books and propels her mind as they are "slowly . . . drifting towards home."

Similes figure in the most important passage in the 1899 diary: the moment when, after repeated declarations of inadequacy and impossibility, the apprentice writer finally delivers her sunset—although she resorts to a drawing to aid her verbal picture: "This is one observation that I have made from my observation of many sunsets—that no shape of cloud has one line in it in the least sharp or hard—nowhere can you draw a straight line with your pencil & say 'This line goes so.' Everything is done by different shades & degrees of light—melting & mixing infinitely—Well may an Artist despair!" (*PA* 155–56). Surely this represents Woolf's first expression of her literary aesthetic—at seventeen (not twenty-five, as Leaska has suggested): "Everything . . . done by different shades & degrees of light—melting & mixing infinitely."

Woolf's first extant diary, the palm-size, brown leather 1897 diary with its lock and key, was, Elizabeth Podnieks reminds us, the only conventional diary she ever kept (102). That she considers her 1899 diary experiments worth preserving can be seen in the fact that she buys a calf-bound book to protect them and enhance their aesthetic appeal. "[T]he aspect of this book distresses me," she writes as early as her fourth entry (*PA* 139). Two days before her September 20 departure, she reveals her move to enhance her text: "This work has undergone so many changes since I last wrote. . . . The work heretofore was contained in one modest paper book, that fronted the world in a state of nature—naked but not ashamed. Boards it recked not of, now it boasts boards that amount to the dignity of a binding, being ancient tooled calf—the tooling resplendent today as a hundred years ago" (*PA* 158–59).

She describes the "sudden idea" that struck her "that it would be original useful & full of memories if I embedded the foregoing pages in the leaves of some worthy & ancient work, the like of which might I knew be bought at St Ives old Curiosity Shop for the sum of 3d" (*PA* 159). She describes the hunt with Adrian that produces the book she appropriates for her diary, *LOGICK: OR, THE Right Use of REASON WITH A Variety of RULES to Guard Against ER-ROR in the AFFAIRS of RELIGION and HUMAN LIFE as well as in the Sciences* by Isaac Watts D.D. She pastes her 1899 diary pages on top of his.

Commentators have made much of this textual transformation. DeSalvo believes Virginia sought to hide the original manuscript of "TERRIBLE TRAG-EDY IN A DUCKPOND" from the "prying eyes of her family" (*Impact* 260, 249). Podnieks believes the seventeen-year-old sought to elevate her diary to the status of published work: "if her entries were contained within 'some worthy & ancient work,' then they would themselves take on the respected qualities of such a work. In this way she could approach the 'patriarchal' literary status of Watts, and her diary—a traditionally devalued & feminine genre—would be elevated to literary status" (103). In choosing *LOGICK: OR, THE Right Use of REASON*, Podnieks suggests, Virginia may have sought subconsciously "to prove to herself (and to her future readers) that her recorded thoughts were those of a logical, reasonable, and hence sane person" (103). Other readers have viewed the action as the diarist's subversive challenge to masculine logic and reason and literal replacement of male words with female.

I find Podnieks persuasive in her reminder that the seventeen-year-old's "attention to the aesthetic construction of her journal coincided with its becoming more of a writer's notebook" (103). I am also inclined to take Woolf's words at face value. Watt's volume, she writes, "attracted my attention firstly because of its size, which fitted my paper—& 2ndly because its back had a certain air of distinction among its brethren. I fear the additional information given on the title page that this is the Logic of the 'Late Reverend & Learned Isaac Watts D.D.' was not a third reason why I bought it" (*PA* 160). Certainly a wry jibe at religion might be seen in these last words, and Virginia further suggests she thought Watts' *LOGICK* suitable for "desecration," for "no one methought could bewail the loss of these pages" (*PA* 160). Whatever the motive for the physical diary upgrade, the result was that a sturdy, handsome, calf-bound, self-designed and handmade 1899 diary joins the smaller leather-covered 1897 tome.

Within its handsome bindings, the 1899 diary offers a tentative, awkward, amusing, yet boldly experimental writer's diary. Virginia Stephen at seventeen lacks the diaristic poise and sophistication of Fanny Burney at sixteen. However, her range, even in these tentative testings, appears wider than Burney's. In the 1899 diary, the young writer tries her hand at travel writing, narrates comic scenes, creates single and group portraits, and parodies newspaper, gothic, and expedition narratives. Her attempts at place-writing include guidebook descriptions of both Ramsey and St. Ives, and she pens her first offering of what today is called "public history": her August 8 description of the women and children of the Huntingdonshire harvest. Most important, the aspiring writer seeks to capture with her pen—"frail & somewhat disjointed" as it is—the natural world around her (*PA* 135). She articulates a Platonic, mimetic theory of art and articulates for the first time a modernist aesthetic vision: "shades & degrees of light—melting & mixing infinitely" (*PA* 156). By acknowledging the difficulty—even the impossibility—of her writing goals, she frees herself to try.

Across her *first* diary, fifteen-year-old Virginia expressed panic and despair whenever forced to leave her London home. "Oh for London," she exclaimed regularly in her 1897 diary (*PA* 119, 32, 70, 99, 132). The 1899 diary marks her growing sense of the country's writerly worth. "Tomorrow at this hour I shall be in my room in London!" she still exclaims in the Warboys final entry. Then, however, she adds: "The roar of the city will be booming in my ear, which 7 weeks of Warboys will have made as sensitive as any country cousins. I write this down to see if it looks any more credible in pen & ink; but I cannot bring my mind to bear upon the change" (*PA* 162).

3

Choosing the Outsider Role

Virginia Woolf's third diary, her 1903 diary, may be the most important of all her thirty-eight diary books. In the crucible of family crisis—her father's slow death—a saving move occurs. The twenty-one-year-old compares London with the country across her 1903 diary: London represents for her culture, the male literary tradition, even (social) death; the country stands for nature, the female, and the unconscious mind.

Wiltshire, the site of their eight-week summer holiday, only accentuates (in Woolf's diary) the male/female, culture/nature rub, for the Stephen family lodges in the shadow of "the great man of the place": near Wilton, Wilton Hall, and the Pembrokes (*PA* 189). Virginia visits Salisbury Cathedral and, finding it surrounded by its restrictive close, contrasts it with nearby Stonehenge lying open on the Salisbury plain. The 1903 diary offers the first sign of the crucial role the downs and solitary country strolls will play in Woolf's creative life.

As she rejects London social success and chooses the outsider role, Woolf reads (and lauds) James Boswell's *Journal of a Tour to the Hebrides with Samuel Johnson* during her Wiltshire stay. Boswell's Hebrides *Journal* was a three-month "sketchbook," like her own diary-in-progress, and across its pages Boswell and Johnson contrast the country with "great cities," the very theme of her 1903 diary. Boswell, she finds, has visited Wilton Hall as a guest of Lord Pembroke; he is himself an ambiguous "outsider," redefining in his *Journal* the "Great Man" tradition. Boswell's *Journal* introduces Woolf to Samuel Johnson. She offers in her 1903 diary the first glimpse of the uncommon literary critic she will become in her *Common Reader* essays.

An *outsider* is one excluded from a party, an association, or a set—one detached from the activities or concerns of her community. The dictionary even defines an "outsider" as "a contestant given little chance of winning." To be "Outside the Walls," as Woolf titles one of her 1903 diary's essay-entries, is to be in a space beyond boundary or limit. By choosing the outsider role at this pivotal moment, Woolf chooses to be detached, apart, and divergent. She moves at age twenty-one to the frontier—to unmarked territory she will make her own.

Virginia Woolf's 1903 Diary

> *"Outside the Walls"*
>
> (*PA* 188)

Nearly four years pass between the 1899 and 1903 journals. Were diaries written but—sadly—lost or destroyed? Or did the diary pulse retreat on return to the city? Whatever transpired, Virginia rediscovers her 1899 diary in 1902, for she writes in its pages "Time disentombs a certain number of things, & among them this sheet of paper" (*PA* 416). She rereads her Warboys diary and sees its historical worth. "This book in days to come will contain one of the very rare records of Warboys before the fire," she notes.[1] Perhaps this thought fuels the 1903 diary. The new diary resembles the 1899 diary, only amplified and smoothed. While the 1899 diary contains nineteen entries across forty-seven Warboys days, four of them titled pieces, the 1903 journal offers thirty titled essay-entries across a three-month span. Like the 1899 journal, the 1903 diary begins with four (or five) daily entries before finding its periodic rhythm.

However, the 1903 diary differs importantly in both place and structure from the 1899 holiday diary. The 1903 diary begins in late June, and its first ten entries survey London before the family's July 31 departure for an eight-week holiday in Wiltshire. Virginia uses the word "chapter" across this diary, suggesting that she sees the volume as a shaped work, its opening third a London study, followed by eighteen entries that offer a contrasting Wiltshire "country" chapter, and concluding with a return to the city for a short (two-entry) epilogue at September's end.

A portrait that praises a woman, Lady Katherine Thynne, starts the 1903 diary; in fact, this free and self-assured woman provides a blessing on the twenty-one-year-old diarist's work. "An Afternoon With The Pagans," the title Virginia gives this late June entry, offers her first portrait of the English aristocracy. It foreshadows the admiration she will feel for Vita Sackville-West decades later and defines the qualities she will always find attractive in the English upper class. Lady Katherine Thynne, the Countess of Cromer, and her sister, Lady Beatrice Thynne, were the daughters of the fourth Marquis and Marchioness of Bath. Virginia and Vanessa visit them at St. Albans with Lady Robert Cecil, daughter of the second Earl of Durham, who will soon become Virginia's friend. Woolf depicts all three aristocrats as pagans, and Lady Katherine more particularly as Venus, as a "divine Giantess," and as "a great benevolent goddess" (PA 184, 185). Even before this diary entry, Woolf's equation of Lady Katherine with a pagan goddess can be followed in her letters to Violet Dickinson in the first months of 1903. Her most suggestive reference occurs April 10, 1903, where she links the country to pagan renewal (and to women). "Spring in the country is like a clean bath," Virginia writes to Dickinson. "I get born anew into the bosom of my God once a year—a God half Katie and some rakish old Pagan, like you" (L #76, 1: 73).

In "An Afternoon With The Pagans" Virginia makes clear what she admires in the Countess: "She doesn't think how she looks. . . . Indeed the whole atmosphere of the place was one of careless ease. . . . She held forth as of old; declaiming her impossible theories in the same half laughing half serious way; pouring scorn upon us all" (PA 184, 185). Lady Katherine's "impossible theories" authorize Virginia's own in the entries that follow. "I would be a pagan—if I could," the twenty-one-year-old declares (PA 184). "'Good bye' [the Countess] said, in a voice which sounded like a blessing—a half humourous blessing," Virginia writes at entry's end (PA 185). The Countess was in her sixth month of pregnancy during this visit; therefore her blessing may have been felt as a mother's blessing as well.

The other portrait in this opening London "chapter" celebrates another theorizing woman: Virginia's Greek teacher "Miss Case." This undated essay is included among the first ten diary entries and reveals that Virginia now thinks of her diary as a "sketchbook." "Two days ago I had my Greek lesson from Miss Case," the entry begins. "I reflect that it may be my last, after a year & a half's learning from her—so wish, entirely presumptuously I know, to make a rough sketch, which is at any rate done from life" (PA 181–82). Like Lady Katherine Thynne, Janet Case was a woman of "ardent theories & she could expound them fluently. She used three adjectives where I could only lay hands on one," Virginia writes (PA 182). Case took her pupil "quite seriously," and, as a result, Virginia notes, "I was forced to think more than I had done hitherto" (PA 182, 183). In a few years, the Bloomsbury circle will offer similar push. However, the importance at this moment of Janet Case and Lady Katherine Thynne as self-confident woman theorizers should not be overlooked.

After receiving the blessing of "pagan goddess" Lady Katherine Thynne, Virginia pens three essay-entries June 29, June 30, and July 1 on the London social scene—each from an "outsider's" perspective and each critical of society life. In her June 29 entry, "A Dance In Queens Gate," she describes a dance as seen and heard from her bedroom window. (This is the most literary of the 1903 entries, and Virginia places it first when later she shapes and binds the diary.) The 1903 diary compares city and country life. Here Virginia contrasts the eternal natural world with the ephemeral, artificial, even destructive social world of the London dance. She takes note of a great glass skylight "under which I suppose the dancers are drinking champagne & devouring quails" and then presents an image of her own role as outsider: "I dont know why it is but this incongruity—the artificial lights, the music—the talk—& then the quiet tree standing out there, is fantastic & attracts me considerably" (PA 165–66).

The first half of "A Dance In Queens Gate" captures the lure of the social whirl: "oh dear—the swing & the lilt of that waltz makes me almost feel as though I could jump from my bed & dance it too. . . . [Y]ou . . . yield to that strange passion which sends you madly whirling round the room—oblivious of everything save that you must keep swaying with the music . . . . If you stop you are lost" (PA 165). However, as an outsider, she can shift her eyes at will. She looks at the skylight and the tree; she sees the fiddlers as well as the dancers and notes that "these fiddlers dont believe a word of it," that is, of dreams of "love & freedom & life moving in rhythm & waltz music" (PA 166). However the social dance calls, and "A Dance In Queens Gate" mounts, like Poe's "Masque of the Red Death," to a vision of mad and ghastly destruction: "they dance as pale phantoms because so long as the music sounds they *must* dance—no help for them. . . . They are sucked in by the music. And how weary they look—pale men—fainting women—crumpled silks & trampled flowers. They are no longer masters of the dance—it has taken possession of them" (PA 166–67). In the end the natural world, the dawn, triumphs. "No lamplight can burn in the radiance of that whiteness—no music can sound in the pause of that awful silence. The Dance is over," the entry prophetically ends (PA 167).

"A Garden Dance," the next day's essay-entry, describes another musical evening, this one actually attended. In a December 1902 letter to Violet Dickinson, Virginia expressed a more positive view of dance: "Adrian and I waltzed (to a Polka!), and Adrian says he can't conceive how anyone can be idiotic enough to find amusement in dancing, and I see how they do it but feel all the pretty young Ladies far removed into another sphere—which is so pathetic—and I would give all my profound Greek to dance really well, and so would Adrian give anything he had" (L #62, 1: 63). Six months later, her view changes. In her previous 1899 diary, she imagined a reader for her journal, stating, "it makes me put on my dress clothes such as they are" (*PA* 144). In 1903, dress clothes are scorned in favor of the writer's nightgown. "Honestly, I enjoyed my window dance the most," she writes, contrasting the previous night's experience with the current evening's dance at Sir Walter Phillimore's:

> To begin with, for this dance one had to be properly dressed—& that is a penance—while last night I could lie with my nightgown open & my hair tumbled over my forehead as it is at this moment. . . . Though I hate putting on my fine clothes, I know that when they are on I shall have invested myself at the same time with a certain social demeanour—I shall be ready to talk about the floor & the weather & other frivolities, which I consider platitudes in my nightgown. A fine dress makes you artificial—ready for lights & music—ready to accept that artificial view of life which is presented to one in a ballroom—life seen by electric light & washed down by champagne. (*PA* 169–70)

The twenty-one-year-old rejects this ballroom life, her outsider role once more offering other views. She feels "pleasantly detached" at the dinner dance "& able to criticise the antics of my fellows from a cool distance" (*PA* 170). She is "thoroughly content to lie in an arm chair & watch the Ladies in their light dresses pass and repass. . . . It was like some French painting" (*PA* 171). She aestheticizes the moment, the dance serving as material for art. As in "A Dance In Queens Gate," she observes nature as well as society and contrasts the two. "Again I noticed that strange blending of the two lights—the pale light of the sky & the yellow light of lamps & candles both together illuminating green leaves & grass," and the entry ends with her delighted escape to her home where she can "open my book of astronomy, [and] dream of the stars a little."[2] The next day's entry, "An Artistic Party," focuses again on dress. Once more she thinks "dress clothes (a rude test of merit!)," and confesses she "could have been well content to take [her] evening's pleasure in observation merely" (*PA* 176).

These three entries, all critical of London society life, lead to the July 15 essay-entry "Thoughts Upon Social Success." Significantly, when she binds her diary, she places this entry out of chronological order to follow "A Dance In Queens Gate." The essay's spur is that evening's "very typical entertainment," during which she rarely speaks but savors the "outsider" role yet again (*PA* 167). "We always seem to be outsiders," she acknowledges. "All the same I can sit by & watch with pure delight those who are adepts at the game" (*PA* 167, 168). She ponders the "social gift" (*PA* 167). It is not out of reach, she acknowledges; however, once more she resists its cultivation. She imagines most young women her age as social flowers coming alive only at night. They are flowers, however, not human beings, and she finds "this very beautiful & attractive but always a little puzzling" (PA 168). She protests, perhaps excessively, that she "most honestly admire[s] such scraps of society . . . even though I myself take no part in it"; however, she sees in the social ideal just that—an ideal fundamentally false, for it ignores much of the world:

> You must consciously try to carry out in your conduct what is implied by your clothes; they are silken—of the very best make—only to be worn with the greatest care, on occasions such as these. They are meant to please the eyes of others—to make you something more brilliant than you are by day. This seems to me a good ideal. You come to a party meaning to give pleasure; therefore you leave your sorrows & worries at home—for the moment, remember, we are all dressed in silk—without sorrow or bother that is—more than that, you must be prepared to be actively happy: if you talk it must be at least to express pleasure at something; better still if you can, say something amusing: seriousness is just as much out of place here as an old serge skirt. . . . The talk is very swift & skimming: it is not part of the game to go deep: that might be dangerous. All this a moralist might say, is very artificial. . . . [I]t is easy to conclude that society is hollow— that the men & women who make it are heartless. (PA 168, 169)

Here the social critic seeks "another side to the picture" and locates "the courage of a hero" in the masquerade (PA 169). However, the best the twenty-one-year-old can do is find something of Walter Scott's laconic nobility in society life. To be socially successful, she concludes, "one must be a Stoic with a heart" (PA 169).

In the 1903 diary's opening London "chapter," four of the ten essay-entries reject the narrowness and artificiality of society life, finding it ultimately destructive, while two celebrate theorizing women. The London chapter closes with two further striking entries, the first, "The Country In London," the pivotal entry in the 1903 diary.[3] This entry develops in fits and starts, the diarist allowing her mind to associate freely and capture subterranean impressions. "[W]e are getting ready for Salisbury," Virginia writes, and explains that "getting ready" for her means "I collect books on all conceivable subjects & sew together paper books like this I write in—thick enough to hold all the maxims in the world" (PA 177). Revealingly, she confesses that she actually begins her "country" planning in October—that is, almost immediately on her return each year from the country. And then come seven startling sentences:

It is quite true that I read more during these 8 weeks in the country than in six London months perhaps. Learning seems natural to the country. I think I could go on browsing & munching steadily through all kinds of books as long as I lived at Salisbury say. The London atmosphere is too hot—too fretful. I read—then I lay down the book & say—what right have I, a woman to read all these things that men have done? They would laugh if they saw me. But I am going to forget all that in the country. (*PA* 178)

These words signal the twenty-one-year-old's conscious turn from the masculine literary tradition associated with the "too fretful" London "atmosphere" toward a more natural, almost bovine or ovine, existence in the country (*PA* 178). The country seems not only more natural to her than the city but also linked to the unconscious: "I am going to forget all that in the country" (*PA* 178). Perhaps the country is natural *because* one can be more unconscious there. "I write— with greater ease, at times, than ever in London," she continues, and this leads to an epiphany: the first articulation of her vision of the "common mind": "I think I see for a moment how our minds are all threaded together—how any live mind today is of the very same stuff as Plato's & Euripides.... It is this common mind that binds the whole world together; & all the world is mind.... I feel as though I had grasped the central meaning of the world" (*PA* 178–79).

Here stands the writer's worldview (and further literary aesthetic), offered at age twenty-one. She notes that when this vision fades, movement in the "free air" of the country "soothes" her and makes her "sensitive at once" (*PA* 179). The free air of her diary does the same. London, in contrast, erects obstacles to her vision: "In London undoubtedly there are too many people—all different—... & they must all be reconciled to the scheme of the universe before you can let yourself think what that scheme is" (*PA* 179).

Nevertheless, she remains ambivalent regarding the city. She recognizes its challenges. "Of course, people too, if one read them rightly, might illuminate as much as if not more than books. It is probably best therefore in the long run to live in the midst of men & women—to get the light strong in your eyes as it were—not reflected through cool green leaves as it is in books" (*PA* 179). However, she ends the entry by again taking the outsider stance and prizing the country's essential role in her creative life: "Nine months surely is enough to spend with ones kind!" (*PA* 179). "The Country In London" captures a vital moment in Woolf's emergence as a writer. She is not prepared to give up London (and the male literary tradition it represents). She will face its strong light.

She titles her entry "The Country In London," signaling her drive to find her own free, unconscious space from which to write.[4]

Of the thousands of entries in Virginia Woolf's diaries, few can match the importance of "The Country In London." "Retrospect," the July 30 entry that follows, continues its theme. "We close here our London Chapter with regret," she writes, but then adds, "For 8 weeks, I shall not miss you, great City; in October we may meet on more friendly terms" (*PA* 186). She then offers an assessment of her diary's first ten entries that underscores her present view of herself as a visual artist and her diary as an artist's pad:

> But the only use of this book is that it shall serve for a sketchbook; as an artist fills his pages with scraps & fragments, studies of drapery—legs, arms & noses—useful to him no doubt, but of no meaning to anyone else—so I take up my pen & trace here whatever shapes I happen to have in my head.
>
> It is an exercise—training for eye & hand . . . . I have gone on this plan for something over a month now, & propose, Ladies & Gentlemen, to continue it in the country. . . .
>
> Tomorrow I shall open at a new chapter. (*PA* 186–87)

The new chapter, however, continues the outsider theme. Fanny Burney visited Wilton and Stonehenge in 1791 when she finally escaped King George III's court (*Diary and Letters of Madame D'Arblay* 2: 417–18). Virginia's eighteen "country" entries personify Wilton, Stonehenge, and the other Wiltshire sites she visits to far surpass Burney's diary sketch. Appropriately, the family lodges in Netherhampton House, an artist's retreat. The sculptor J.H.M. Furse owned the house and leant it to the Stephens. In the "chapter's" opening essay-entry, titled "Netherhampton House," Furse's home is personified as "humble" and "unpretentious," "with a certain quaint dignity of its own," although its coat of arms reveals aristocratic ties (*PA* 187, 188). Virginia notes that the house was built in the Elizabethan age as a dower house for the Pembroke family, a dower house that was part of a deceased man's real estate given to his widow. Consequently "various old countesses . . . have had their lodging here, after the splendours of Wilton," she writes (*PA* 187–88). Netherhampton House thus exudes a female history as well as a contemporary artist's aura. It is also outside the "splendours" of the great house.[5]

From this congenial site, the diarist sets forth "to find out our position in the world" (*PA* 188). The title of her entry supplies the answer: "Wilton—From Outside The Walls." The entry underscores the young writer's continued sense of herself as an outsider and her continued rejection of male traditions. The statue of the thirteenth Earl of Pembroke (1850–1895) is "at least 3 feet taller than the most gigantic of ordinary mortals. As a work of art therefore," she jibes, "the statue is not convincing" (*PA* 189). In contrast to her humble but dignified widows' and artists' lodge, the village of Wilton is "more smug & well pleased with itself than the majority of English villages" (*PA* 189). In fact, it "has the look of a very faithful old family retainer" to the Pembrokes in their manor (*PA* 189). Neither the superiority nor the servility of Wilton village pleases: "We— that is Adrian & I—commented upon all this—in no very friendly spirit. We professed to find the whole country side 'demoralised' & clinging to the great man of the place. This I suppose is an exaggeration; at any rate if we had been inside those high brick walls our point of view might have changed—but it is safe to say that the feudal spirit in England is not yet dead" (*PA* 189–90).

"Wilton From Inside," however, also disappoints. Wishing to change her position and to view firsthand her first English "stately home," the twenty-one-year-old presents herself on the "one day . . . in every week when from the hour of 2 till 5—the public can enter the great gates of Wilton as freely as any Herbert in the land" (*PA* 195). If she has personified Wilton village as a smug and "very faithful old family retainer," she finds at Wilton Hall its literal counterparts: "A massive lodge keeper in livery" at the gate; a dignified but condescending housekeeper within (*PA* 195). "Honestly, I was disappointed in my first view of a great house," Virginia declares, and she is delighted to find herself "soon out of range" (*PA* 196, 197).

Boundaries and gatekeepers are noted regularly in the country "chapter" entries, making the 1903 diary a dress rehearsal for *A Room Of One's Own*. The diarist casts herself as a "restless devil" in her essay-entry titled "Salisbury Cathedral" (*PA* 192). She "invaded the sanctuaries of the [Cathedral's] Close . . . where motor cars may not penetrate, or butchers carts, unless bearing clerical provisions" (*PA* 193). When she returns with Adrian for "An Evening Service" and drives slowly round the Close, she notes its artificiality: "It is as though you shut thick ivy grown walls between yourself & the world" (*PA* 194). She declares she "would no more live here than lie myself down tomorrow in a venerable grave in the cloisters" (*PA* 194). The cathedral's 404-foot spire, the tallest in England, that dominates the landscape, she likens to "an extinguisher," and she once more notes that this institution of moribund privilege is "circled by a rich layer of turf—& beyond that, like a zealous bodyguard, stand round all the houses of the close. . . . [L]ike the beefeaters, or some other ancient guard, they are eminently picturesque without rivalling the splendour of their monarch" (*PA* 194). As with Wilton Village, she finds such patriarchal eminence demoralizing and even destructive of its surroundings. She closes her "Salisbury Cathedral" entry with a striking simile drawn from nature: "So much ancient stone however fairly piled, & however rich with the bodies of Saints & famous men, seems to suck the vitality of its humble neighbours. It is like a great forest oak; nothing can grow healthily beneath its shade. All this is a form of heresy I know. . . . A bare hilltop would have pleased me better than all the Closes & Cathedrals of England."[6]

Stonehenge, lying open on the Salisbury plain twelve miles away, provides the pleasure she seeks. This "recognisable temple" is surprisingly humble: "a tiny compact little place" (*PA* 199). "I had imagined something on a much larger scale," she observes (*PA* 199). Even more pleasing is the site's lack of male tradition: "[N]o one in the world can tell you anything about it" (*PA* 199). The stone circle is the work of the obscure. "[S]ome forgotten people built here a Temple where they worshipped the sun," she writes (*PA* 199). More importantly: "Man has done nothing to change Salisbury plain since these stones were set here" (*PA* 200). Pagans created Stonehenge:

> I like to think of it; imagine those toiling pagans doing honour to the very sun now in the sky above me, & for some perverse reason I find this a more deeply impressive temple of Religion—block laid to block, & half of them tumbled in ruin so long that the earth almost hides them, than that perfect spire whence prayer & praise is at this very moment ascending.
>
> It is matter for thought surely, if not for irony, that as one stands on the ruins of Stonehenge one can see the spire of Salisbury Cathedral. (*PA* 200)

In "Stonehenge Again," her September 5 entry recounting her second visit to the pagan shrine, Virginia substitutes the word "pilgrimage" as more fitting than her first entry's term "expedition" (*PA* 204). "The solitary policeman whose strange lot in life it is to mount guard over Stonehenge," has taken shelter behind one of the stones, leaving the scene to the sheep and the women.

Interspersed among the five "country" entries critical of patriarchal structures—and therefore functioning with the two Stonehenge entries as counterpoint—are three entries ("The Downs," "The Talk Of Sheep," and "Life In The Fields") in which the "outsider" to society and male traditions seeks to become one with nature.[7] These entries are important, for they serve as early sign of the crucial role the downs and solitary country strolls will play in Woolf's creative life.[8] "Since we came here, for various reasons, I have spent many of my after-noons in solitary walks," she explains at the opening of "The Talk Of Sheep" (*PA* 197). "I walk generally straight out of the house & on to the downs. . . . A curious content, which I cannot put into words, comes over me when I reach the top of the down, & lay myself flat on the grass" (*PA* 197, 198).

In another early piece of women's public history, "The Wilton Carpet Fac-tory," she declares: "I like to feel that I am in harmony with nature" (*PA* 200). In "The Talk Of Sheep," her "high ambition" is to converse with the ewes and the rams (*PA* 197). In "The Downs," she deplores Adrian's dismissal of this country as dull and likens the downs to "the long curved waves of the sea."[9] As at Stone-henge, "Man . . . has done nothing to change the shape of these breakers. . . . The villages have all sunk into the hollows between the waves; & the result is a peculiar smoothness & bareness of outline. This is the bare bone of the earth" (*PA* 192). By "Life In The Fields," the diarist has become "absorbed by the spirit of Nature, let us say—a vast quantity of it is distilled by these fields & downs" (*PA* 203). Like "The Downs," "Life In The Fields" closes with a poetic evocation of the earth as a figure for female wholeness: "If you lie on the earth somewhere you hear a sound like a vast breath, as though it were the very inspiration of earth herself, & all the living things on her" (*PA* 203).

"The Water Meadows," which follows "Wilton—From Outside The Walls," dramatizes the conflict between the male and the female, between the social and natural domains, that unfurls across this diary. The entry can be read as a cautionary tale with a triumphant close. Virginia and Vanessa set off across the water meadows to visit "a certain romantic looking church" in the distance (*PA* 190). For Virginia, the church is a literary landmark, for she thinks it the church where Renaissance poet George Herbert served as rector. Vanessa, in turn, "was anxious to find the mythical railway, which is to supply the express train in her great Landscape" (*PA* 190). This "pilgrimage," therefore, holds meaning for both female artists. However, access to the church proves more difficult than the women foresee, the journey fraught with obstacles. They scramble through hedges, flatten themselves under barbed wire barriers, encounter fences "with but one sound rung left" (*PA* 190).

Finally, they hear male voices and are laughed at—just as Virginia foresaw in "The Country In London" when she writes "what right have I, a woman to read all these things that men have done? They would laugh if they saw me" (*PA* 178). Woolf's words are suggestive: "We were brought to a stop by hearing male rustic voices, alarming to pedestrians of the womanly sex—Men were making hay in the adjoining field & not only were they talking but they were talking of us—possibly to us" (*PA* 190). Again a male functions as gatekeeper: "one of them advanced to the gate; we had to move up to hear what he said. . . . 'You dont mean to say you've lost the road in broad daylight?' That was an excellent joke too—'You wont find no road here—better go back the way you come'" (*PA* 190). *Better go back*, the patronizing gatekeeper declares, discouraging the women artists from achieving their goals. This emblematic tale ends happily, however, but only when the male destination is abandoned and nature embraced. Vanessa agrees to Virginia's suggestion that "for the rest of this walk we should be independant [*sic*] of bridges or lack of bridges—that we should bare our feet, & use them for the purpose—after all—for which they were created" (*PA* 191). The aspiring artists remove their shoes, emblems of civilization, and begin to savor nature: "It was thus strangely charming to walk barefoot across two or three fields & streams. We found our road—& put on our shoes—only too soon" (*PA* 191).

The Wiltshire interlude was a time of an acute sense of boundaries, gatekeepers, and the "great man of the place" aura, of feeling an outsider "Outside The Walls." However, it was also a time of solitary walks on the downs and in the fields seeking a more inclusive and sustaining nurture. In "The Country In London" essay-entry penned in London, Virginia imagines herself a contented cow (or ewe) "munching steadily through all kinds of books" (*PA* 178). In "Country Reading," toward the close of her Wiltshire holiday, she confesses her "boast of reading in the country has not been altogether fulfilled" (*PA* 205). However, she describes three books that please her, and her descriptions reveal once more that she is thinking at this time as a visual artist. Henry James's novel *Roderick Hudson* reminds her of "an infinitely fine pencil drawing; it lacks colour, it lacks outline, but it is full of exquisite drawing, as an artist would say—& the slightest stroke, you see, has its meaning" (*PA* 205). Nevertheless, she finds James's technique not "an altogether satisfactory style of art" (*PA* 205). It lacks "that spontaneous & unreflecting pleasure" one gets from the great books, she suggests, revealing her preference for spontaneity and accessibility. With James, she declares, one needs to be "a little of an epicure to see how very fine & rare" he is (*PA* 205).

Thomas Hardy and his *Tess of the D'Urbervilles* please her more, although she harbors some reservations. She finds his criticism of social conventions so overt that "he tends to spoil his novel as a novel": Tess, Clare, and D'Urberville represent types and, therefore, "rather lose their individual features" (*PA* 206). However, she finds other facets of the work "purely admirable": "Joan Durbeyfield for instance—the Dairy maids at the Farm, & Hardy is one of the few writers who can bring the fresh air into their books. His country is solid" (*PA* 206). In the context of this diary's country/city probe, this praise bears added weight. However, the diarist saves her greatest praise—as soon we will see—for a diary.

Woolf's final Wiltshire essay-entry, "Out Of The Windows," mirrors the London entry "A Dance In Queens Gate," for here, on the eve of her departure, she considers the *country* life outside her window. She repeats the words of her final night in London: "The journey is not to be measured by its miles" (*PA* 209). Once more she associates London with "months of lessons & restraint" and thinks to abandon the country until Easter a "sad thought" (209). Her final page is missing from this entry. Did she explore further her country/London theme?

"London," the first of the two essay-entries that bring the 1903 diary full circle and to its close, finds the city "in deshabille" in mid-September: "she is not at her best" (*PA* 210). The final 1903 entry, titled "The Serpentine," also links back to "A Dance In Queens Gate." There, in late June, London society life is described as a current of water, exhilarating but finally destructive. The dancers "must keep swaying with the music—in & out, round & round—in the eddies & swirls of the violins. It is as though some swift current of water swept you along with it" (*PA* 165). Ultimately, the social current overpowers the exhausted dancers: "the music that seemed to ebb before, has gathered strength . . . no one can stop dancing now. They are sucked in by the music. . . . And all joy & life has left it, & it is diabolical, a twisting livid serpent, writhing in cold sweat & agony, & crushing the frail dancers in its contortions."[10] She offers here an image of death by drowning, by (social) suffocation. The diabolical "twisting livid serpent" returns in "The Serpentine." London once more destroys—but here a woman, a woman with "No father, no mother, no work," a woman rejected by the city who finally, "slipping off the weight that had been too much for her, . . . sank in the waters" of the Serpentine pond in Kensington Gardens, a pond Virginia knew well (*PA* 213).

The 1903 diary as bound by Virginia Stephen begins and ends with visions of death—of death from a heartless London society that sucks one in and under, yet swirls heedlessly on. However, within this frame of evil and death, we find a young woman repeatedly and courageously rejecting the social current, rejecting the "great man" tradition in its myriad forms, a twenty-one-year-old seeking survival in nature rather than culture, seeking a freer, more unconscious space from which to create.

The 1903 diary's thirty essay-entries emerge during the drama of Leslie Stephen's losing fight with cancer. The family, in fact, gives up the country and returns to London a week earlier than planned due to this consuming illness. In such a context, the 1903 diary entries become even more courageous. We see how closely death and life touch for the diarist: how thin the boundary between. Does her father's pending death propel her drive to separate from the "great man" tradition? Does his illness spur her toward female nurture—to the pagans and to nature personified as a woman?

Whatever the spur, we know that in this time of family crisis, Virginia Stephen uses her diary to mark a space for herself—an outsider's space—from which she can survive and create. The importance to her of this "Country In London" diary can be gauged from the care she took with its creation. As she noted, she stitched the volume herself and made the gray-paper-covered diary "thick enough to hold all the maxims in the world."[11] She thought enough of some of her entries to send them to Violet Dickinson for critique, and when she came to bind the thirty entries, she made changes in chronological sequence to fit aesthetic and thematic goals, placing an "Index" at the front, as if this were a book of essays rather than a diary.[12] Elizabeth Podnieks writes that the 1903 diary reveals the twenty-one-year-old's continuing development of a "writerly sensibility" and notes that her occasional diary-style dating of titled essays reveals "how early on she was blurring genre boundaries" (103, 104).

The 1903 diary marks a huge stride from the 1899 Warboys diary. Virginia's personifications are much more natural in 1903 than in 1899, and her language less stilted and archaic. In fact, she exudes at times a Boswellian confidence. "But this is not what I meant to write," she declares in "The Country In London," before she refocuses to launch her "common mind" epiphany (PA 178). "But it is of carpet manufactories that I am going to write," she declares in "The Wilton Carpet Factory" (PA 201). We see an artist's concern for truth and an emerging artist's wariness of the sentimental or picturesque. More than anything, her conscious turn from male traditions and decision to write "from outside the walls" position her to become the writer we know.

James Boswell's *Journal of a Tour to the Hebrides with Samuel Johnson, LL.D.*

In 1903, Virginia Stephen closes her diary entry titled "Country Reading" with praise of a fellow diarist: James Boswell and his *Journal of a Tour to the Hebrides with Samuel Johnson, LL.D.* Having read by age fifteen the diaries of Walter Scott, Fanny Burney, and Samuel Pepys, the young writer now meets in Boswell another great British diarist. A word must be said about the text she read.

Boswell kept a journal intermittently for thirty-seven of his fifty-five years. (A similar sentence can be written of Woolf: she kept a diary intermittently for thirty-four of her fifty-nine years.) However, in 1903 the world believed that all of Boswell's papers (including his journals) were destroyed at his 1795 death. It was not until 1925 that his papers surfaced in Ireland at the estate of his great-great grandson Lord Talbot de Malahide—a staggering find. In 1936 a new edition of the *Hebrides* travel diary appeared, drawn from the newly found original manuscript. This longer and livelier original *Journal* differs materially from the earlier published editions.

The paler *Journal of a Tour to the Hebrides* available in 1903 proved sufficiently colorful nevertheless to fire twenty-one-year-old Virginia's imagination.[13] The Hebrides *Journal* was a three-month diary—like her own 1903 diary-in-progress—and across the text Boswell and Johnson contrast the country with great cities. They examine, in short, the very theme of her 1903 diary. "I have a notion that [Dr. Johnson] at no time has had much taste for rural beauties. I have myself very little," Boswell notes early in the tour (Carruthers 78). Three times we hear of Johnson's thirst for London, his desire "to be again in the great theatre of life" (Carruthers 317). Boswell writes of his own stay at Wilton and talk with Lord Pembroke. In truth, Boswell was an ambiguous "outsider" himself, addressing, in fact, *redefining* in his *Journal*, the "great man" tradition.

Most importantly, Boswell's Hebrides journal was a sketchbook offered in those very terms and therefore likely to be of great interest to a young woman attempting her own. With supreme confidence Boswell introduces his journal's star: "Dr. Samuel Johnson's character, religious, moral, political and literary, nay his figure and manner, are, I believe, more generally known than those of almost any man; yet it may not be superfluous here to attempt a sketch of him" (Carruthers 4). After a few pages of respectful diffidence, Boswell cannot help but think his own portrait will be desired as well. "I have given a sketch of Dr. Johnson," he declares; "my readers may wish to know a little of his fellow-traveler" (Carruthers 32).

As in Pepys's diary, Woolf found a diarist aware that flaws add charm and interest to a portrait. Boswell does more than merely report in his *Journal* his own occasional drunkenness, "excessive levity," and social malice; he draws attention to them. In fact, he provides Johnson's authoritative view of this tack: "Macleod asked, if it was not wrong in Orrery to expose the defects of a man with whom he lived in intimacy.—*Johnson*. 'Why no, sir, after the man is dead; for then it is done historically'" (Carruthers 188–89). If seventeen-year-old Virginia worried about "details" in her 1899 Warboys diary, she saw in 1903 that

Boswell prized them. "Let me not be censured for mentioning such minute particulars," he begs following a sentence describing Johnson's large oak walking stick and "very wide brown cloth great coat, with pockets which might have almost held the two volumes of his folio dictionary." To Boswell, "Everything relative to so great a man is worth observing" (Carruthers 5–6).

The 1903 diary marks Woolf's introduction to Samuel Johnson. "Boswells Hebrides," she tells her diary, "has fired me to read all I can find of Johnson" (*PA* 206). Her discriminating paragraphs on Henry James, Thomas Hardy, and Boswell in "Country Reading" resemble Johnson's incisive assessments of Alexander Pope, Edmund Burke, and other writers as reported in Boswell's *Journal*. In short, we see in Woolf's 1903 diary the first signs of the critic of the *Common Reader* essays to come.

Her interest in (and affinity with) Johnson likely came from several shared traits. Boswell speaks twice in his *Journal* of Johnson's "constitutional melancholy" and associates it with his genius (Carruthers 5). "'I inherited,' said [Dr. Johnson], 'a vile melancholy from my father, which has made me mad all my life'. . . . Lady Macleod wondered he should tell this.—'Madam,' said I, 'he knows that with that madness he is superior to other men'" (Carruthers 169). Virginia, who has just penned her own "Thoughts Upon Social Success," may have marked Johnson's repeated refusal to descend to social platitudes. His mind instead is "so full of imagery," Boswell reports, "that he might have been perpetually a poet" (Carruthers 4). In a revealing simile in her 1899 Warboys diary, seventeen-year-old Virginia likened her mind to "a restless steamer paddle urging the ship along" (*PA* 138). She may have quickened, therefore, in 1903 to Boswell's equation of Johnson's mind with a mill "in which a subject is thrown to be ground. It requires, indeed, fertile minds to furnish materials for this mill. . . . I know not if this mill be a good figure; though Pope makes his mind a mill for turning verses" (Carruthers 211).

Boswell's *Journal* favored speedy prose—as had Sir Walter Scott's. Dr. Johnson endorses the practice: "I . . . would advise every young man beginning to compose, to do it as fast as he can, to get a habit of having his mind to start promptly; it is so much more difficult to improve in speed than in accuracy. . . . But, if a man is accustomed to compose slowly, and with difficulty, upon all occasions, there is danger that he may not compose at all, as we do not like to do that which is not done easily; and, at any rate, more time is consumed in a small matter than ought to be" (Carruthers 44). When Boswell confides to Johnson that he fears "writing in a slovenly manner" in his journal—a concern Woolf too will raise periodically across her diary, using that precise word "slovenly"—the good doctor is most assuring: "'Sir,' said he, 'it is not written in a slovenly manner. It might be printed, were the subject fit for printing'" (Carruthers 179).

Boswell's *Journal* may have inspired Woolf to start a reading notebook to complement her diary. On September 30, 1773, Boswell ends his day's entry by noting the books he has read: "This is a very slight circumstance, with which I should not trouble my reader, but for the sake of observing, that every man should keep minutes of whatever he reads. Every circumstance of his studies should be recorded; what books he has consulted; how much of them he has read; at what times; how often the same authors; and what opinions he formed of them, at different periods of his life.—Such an account would much illustrate the history of his mind" (Carruthers 216–17). Woolf's first extant reading notebooks are dated 1905 (Silver).

Boswell's *Journal* also repeatedly endorses diary-writing. Boswell justifies his *Journal* as a preservative act. "[T]his specimen of the colloquial talents and extemporaneous effusions of my illustrious fellow-traveler," he explains, "will become still more valuable, when, by the lapse of time, he shall have become an *ancient*; when all those who can now bear testimony to the transcendent powers of his mind, shall have passed away; and no other memorial of this great and good man shall remain, but the following Journal" (Carruthers xxviii). He notes that Johnson agrees with him that "there should be a chronicle kept in every considerable family, to preserve the characters and transactions of successive generations" (Carruthers 173). At the close of their tour, Boswell rests his pen, a lapse he bitterly regrets. He mentions a sermon Johnson gives them on the origin of evil and adds, "Much do I upbraid myself for having neglected to preserve it" (Carruthers 291). On November 1, 1773, he repeats:

> Often must I have occasion to upbraid myself, that, soon after our return to the main-land, I allowed indolence to prevail over me so much, as to shrink from the labour of continuing my Journal with the same minuteness as before; sheltering myself in the thought that we had done with the *Hebrides*, and not considering that Dr. Johnson's *Memorabilia* were likely to be more valuable when we were restored to a more polished society. Much has thus been irrecoverably lost. (Carruthers 299)

In point of fact, on August 18, 1773, Dr. Johnson leaves "one volume of a pretty full and curious diary of his life" in a drawer in Boswell's home near Edinburgh, a diary Boswell laments has been destroyed (Carruthers 33). The Scotsman includes at the close of his *Journal* this praise from Sir William Forbes: "I am not sure that an ordinary observer would become so well acquainted either with Dr. Johnson or with the manners of the Hebrides, by a personal intercourse, as by a perusal of your journal" (Carruthers 325–26). Dr. Johnson himself frequently praises Boswell's diary. "This will be a great treasure to us some years hence," the great man declares (Carruthers 219). Would twenty-one-year-old Virginia have been impressed by Johnson's declaration that "The more I read of this, I think the more highly of you" (Carruthers 209)?

As with Scott, Burney, and Pepys, Woolf returns to Boswell again and again across her life. She must have written on him soon after reading the *Hebrides* journal, for in a letter to Violet Dickinson likely written in early 1905, she reports being "crosser than ever" that Reginald Smith, the editor of *Cornhill Magazine* (which her father edited from 1871 to 1882), rejected without comment a short article she sent him on Boswell's letters: "[A]ltogether I feel, as you read in the Bible, despised and rejected of men. I was a fool not to find something suitable for the Cornhill, instead of sending an old and fragmentary bit" (*L* #206, 1: 171–72).

Four years later she succeeds with this, or perhaps another, piece. The *Times Literary Supplement* publishes her review of the *Letters of James Boswell to the Rev. W. J. Temple* titled, interestingly, "The Genius of Boswell." In this 1909 review, Woolf locates Boswell's genius in his curiosity, powers of observation, vitality, and inspired presentation of self, others, and the world. She pictures a perpetual "twinkle of curiosity in his eye" and praises his "elegant and half-quizzical attitude" (*E* 1: 252, 250). He notices everything, she notices admiringly; in fact, he searches for more than surface show. Boswell possessed the sense "that something of value lay hidden in other people also beneath the babble of talk," she explains (*E* 1: 251).

She notes that Boswell appears astonished himself by his own range and vitality, and she quotes this line from him in her 1909 homage: "It is hardly credible what ground I go over, and what a variety of men and manners I contemplate every day, and all the time I am myself *pars magna*, for my exuberant spirits will not let me listen enough."[14] Such heroic consciousness reflects more than mere vanity, Woolf asserts in 1909; it reveals the hypersensitivity of an artist. "He was always imagining himself," she writes (*E* 1: 250). "He was not anxious merely to display all his emotions, but he was anxious to make them tell. He left out much that other people put in, and directly that he had a pen in his hand he became a natural artist" (*E* 1: 251). (The last can be said of Woolf.)

As with Pepys, she admires the multifaceted character Boswell unabashedly displays. "[S]hould he be a Don Juan, or the friend of Johnson and Paoli, or the 'great man at Adamtown'?" (*E* 1: 250). Most importantly, he brings himself and his world to life. In 1909, Virginia asserts that Boswell "had something of the clown in Shakespeare in him. It was granted to this scatter-brained and noisy man with a head full of vanity and grossness to exclaim with the poets and the sages, 'What a motley scene is life!'" (*E* 1: 252).

On January 4, 1909, twenty-six-year-old Virginia boasts to Violet Dickinson that she thinks her "Genius of Boswell" article "rather good" (*L* #465, 1: 379). Seven months later she reflects in another *Times Literary Supplement* article—this one on Dr. Johnson's friend Giuseppe Baretti: "It is strange to reflect what numbers of men and women live in our minds merely because Boswell took a note of their talk" (*E* 1: 272). In 1921, she reveals in a review of "Henley's Criticism" that her thoughts on Boswell were hard-won. "[H]ow persistently we must do battle with Carlyle's Boswell . . . before [he] will let us come by an opinion of our own!" she exclaims (*E* 3: 286). We know from her *Reading Notebooks* that she likely read Chauncey Brewster Tinker's *Young Boswell* in 1922, for she made notes on the women he loved (238), and on September 12 she writes in her diary: "I told Lytton I should try to write down his talk—which sprang from a conversation about Boswell" (*D* 2: 201). In her July 17, 1923, entry, in a pause between two tries to capture talk, she reports that Augustine Birrell has given her Boswell's *Journal of a Tour to Corsica*.

Woolf's 1929 diary reveals (yet again) that she thinks of diaries as living entities, for she exults when Boswell's journals emerge from a croquet box in Ireland: "Think! There are 18 volumes of Boswell's diaries now to be published. With any luck I shall live to read them. I feel as if some dead person were said to be living after all" (*D* 3: 237–38). Two months later, when she learns of Geoffrey Scott's tragic early death, she exclaims in her diary of the man chosen to edit the new Boswell: "He is dead in New York, and all those papers about Boswell—what will become of them; and the life . . . will never be written" (*D* 3: 245). In late March 1930, *she* is tapped to write Boswell's life—and offered a sizeable sum to do so. Her refusal signals continued rejection of the "great man atmosphere" in favor of her own outsider views still associated (in 1930) with the country and nature: "Yesterday I was offered £2,000 to write a life of Boswell by Doran Heinemann. L[eonard]. is writing my polite refusal this moment. I have bought my freedom. A queer thought that I have actually paid for the power to go to Rodmell & only think of The Waves by refusing this offer" (*D* 3: 295).

Although she refuses to write his life, Woolf finds that Boswell's journals, like Burney's diaries, refresh and revive her across her days. In an important October 15, 1934, diary entry, Woolf reveals herself so depressed following Roger Fry's death and Wyndham Lewis's attack that she asks Leonard what she should do now "of a morning—creation flagging" (*D* 4: 252). "Read," her husband advises, and Virginia reports that "I am as slack as a piece of maccaroni: & in this state cant shake off a blackness, a blankness. Now (10 to 1) after writing & beginning to read an old life of Boswell I feel the wheels grinding" (*D* 4: 252).

In a February 1937 entry, she thinks of "dear old Desmond [MacCarthy]" as "a kind of Goldsmith or Boswell; a congenial spirit" (*D* 5: 62), and in late June 1938 she even tries her hand at a Boswellian journal of the Hebrides during their Scottish tour. That she destroys part of this travel diary gives pause and is to be lamented. "[S]ick of copying," she writes, revealing more perhaps than she knows, "I tore the rest of it up—a lesson, next journey, not to make endless pencil notes that need copying. Some too I regret: some Boswell experiments in Inns" (*D* 5: 154). As late as May 14, 1939, she again confesses, "I wish I could repeat more words. Boswell did it. Could I turn B. at my age?" (*D* 5: 218). She tries her hand at talk from C. Day Lewis, and then tries again: "Boswell at Sissinghurst" (*D* 5: 218).

In the final pages of her memoir "A Sketch of the Past," written November 15, 1940, or later, she returns again to the Boswell of circa 1903 as she contrasts the "pure convention" of George Duckworth downstairs (awash in his dances and dinner parties) with the "upstairs pure intellect" of her father:

> Thus I would go from the drawing room, where George was telling one of his little triumphs—"Mrs Willie Grenfell asked me to come for a weekend. And I said on the whole I thought I wouldn't . . . She was taken by surprise . . ."—up to father's study to fetch a book. I would find him swinging in his rocking chair, pipe in mouth. Slowly he would unwrinkle his forehead and come to ground and realize with a very sweet smile that I stood there. Rising he would go to the shelves, put the book back, and ask me gently, kindly; "What did you make of it?" Perhaps I was reading Boswell . . . (*MOB* 157)

On February 7, 1941, in the last article she wrote in her life, Woolf reports writing "with some glow" of Boswell's rival, the diarist Hester Thrale (*D* 5: 355).

Almost thirty-eight years before, in her 1903 diary, twenty-one-year-old Virginia Stephen probed the source of Boswell's diary success. "What is the receipt I wonder for making such a book as this?" she asks, and finds her answer in Boswell's ability to capture life: "Boswell apparently sat up at night—fuddled with wine as likely as not—& wrote down word for word the sayings that had dropped from Johnson's lips during the day. Many people could do this & have done it—but without success. . . . Boswell somehow manages to cut out a whole chunk of the earth & air & stick it all alive under a glass case for us to come & see" (*PA* 206).

4

Professional Writer

Virginia Woolf's 1904–1905 Diary

"my work gets established"

(February 8, 1905; PA 234)

ed-letter dates color the 1904–5 diary. That is, Virginia Stephen stamps or writes the *dates* in red ink, then shifts to black ink for the entry proper. Like her last (1903) journal, this 1904–5 diary is self-bound with a gray paper cover. However, it is much smaller than the 1903 diary: only four-and-a-half inches wide and five-and-three-quarter inches long (rather than six-and-one-quarter inches wide and eight-and-seven-eighth inches long).

Leslie Stephen succumbed to abdominal cancer on February 22, 1904. On May 10, twenty-two-year-old Virginia—bereft now of father, mother, and work—suffers a nervous breakdown and attempts suicide. While convalescing in Cambridge with her aunt Caroline Stephen, she finds in October a "hoard" of her aunt's diaries and those of her paternal grandmother, Jane Catherine Venn (*L* #185, 1: 146). Her grandmother's diaries were "most amusing and interesting," she writes to Violet Dickinson. "She kept records of all her children said and did from the time they were born till 1873. Some of the child sayings are quite delightful, and extraordinarily characteristic of him [her father] as a man, and of the Quaker [Caroline Stephen], who always makes haste to agree and to offer Lellie [Leslie] her best toy when he has broken his!" (*L* #185, 1: 146). As with her 1899 Warboys journal, reading others' diaries may have ignited the diary flame. A further note-worthy event occurs in December 1904 as well: the publication of her first professional work in *The Guardian*, an Anglo-Catholic clerical journal with a women's supplement, edited by Violet Dickinson's friend Margaret Lyttelton.

Like her first diary at age fourteen, the diary Woolf maintains from "Christmas 1904" to May 31, 1905, is an almost daily diary accented with dashes and showing the diarist's deep private interest in history as she records the public comings and goings of the Stephen children now "four square" against the world (*PA* 244). This diary ranks third in *number* of entries in Woolf's diaries, its 135 entries trailing only the 309 entries in her first diary and the 143 entries in her 1917–18 Asheham House natural history diary. The diary documents, almost to the exclusion of all else, her emergence as a professional writer.[1]

While this diary harkens back in noteworthy ways to Virginia's first extant diary, its first four entries reprise themes of her 1899 and 1903 diaries. Like the 1899 Warboys diary, the 1904–5 diary comes to life in the country—at New Forest during the Christmas 1904 holidays. Virginia's opening entry also calls to mind her 1903 Stonehenge entries. "The trees stand round in a circle," she writes; "far away voices of men shouting, all sound as in some distant romantic dream; as though falling through an ocean of waters" (*PA* 215). Male voices distant, the writer's voice can sound. Her first two entries show her still drawn to changing light and recall her 1899 Warboys "Chapter on Sunsets." "The sunset makes all the air as though of melted amethyst; yellow flakes dissolve from the solid body of amethyst which is the west," she writes on Christmas 1904 (*PA* 215). "The afternoon was a beautiful specimen of winter light," she states again in her next entry, January 1, 1905; "the air as clear as though sheets of glass had been dissolved into atmosphere & all the colours were lively & delicate" (*PA* 216).

But she must leave the country on January 4. Her January 5 entry compares the country to London to the latter's disadvantage: "A London day. That is to say only narrow strip of sky to be looked at, no bird noises, no sighings & moanings of trees & green growing things—no splash of water—only the interminable roar & rattle & confusion of wheels & voices" (*PA* 217). However, the new professional writer makes the best of it. "But ones mind 'grows mouldy in the country,'" she writes, quoting I know not who (*PA* 217). However, on March 19 Virginia takes Vanessa on a bus ride "to the top of the Steep Hampstead Rd. & then on to the edge of the Heath, from which we looked miles into a land of green fields, blue distance, & cloudy trees. This did refresh our eyes; & birds sang here as in the country, & it was pitiable to have to turn our backs on such beauty; & descend again into the black pit of London—but we had to" (*PA* 254). On May 7 she takes another trip to Hampstead, which, she writes, "still manages to delight me—There is something fantastic—I mean phantom like—about this little vision of country in the heart of London" (*PA* 271). Here is "The Country In London" she seeks.

In a letter to Violet Dickinson written perhaps four days before her May 10, 1904, nervous breakdown, Virginia made this desperate plea: "Oh my Violet if you could only find me a great solid bit of work to do when I get back that will make me forget my own stupidity I should be so grateful. I *must* work" (*L* #178, 1: 140). That Dickinson finds her "a great solid bit of work" at *The Guardian*, work that can hardly be thought of as less than a lifeline, must be praised. That the twenty-two-year-old was willing and able to seize her opportunities matters as well. The 1904–5 diary records the young writer's preparations for professional work and the red-letter days that herald her immediate and rapid success: January 16, 1905 (invitation to write for the *National Review*); February 8 (invitation to write for *The Outlook* and *The London Times*); February 17 (invitation to write for *Literature and the Academy*). By February 17, she is writing articles and book reviews for five newspapers and journals.

On January 11 and 13 she reports framing letters left by her father, letters written by George Eliot and the poet James Thomson, as well as verses from her godfather, James Russell Lowell. She stands these on her mantelpiece, perhaps for inspiration. On January 13 she begins to read "a book about the relations of poetry & music" (*PA* 221). The 1905 diary contains more references to the arts than any other of Woolf's diaries. The arts conjoin in this year of professional success. On February 25, Virginia writes: "as my ear craved music I went . . . & listened to a stiff, but on the whole interesting, programme" (Richard Strauss's *Symphonia Domestica*) at the Queens Hall (*PA* 242). On March 26 she notes her weekly attendance at concerts (*PA* 257). In lobbying for an early escape from Cambridge in an October 30, 1904, letter to Dickinson, Virginia explained that for her London meant a unity of art: "London means my own home, and books, and pictures, and music, from all of which I have been parted since February now,—and I have never spent such a wretched 8 months in my life" (*L* #186, 1: 147).

Having studied the relation of poetry to music in January 1905, on February 21 Virginia begins Aristotle's *Poetics* "which will fit me for a reviewer!" (*PA* 240). February 21 to March 2 belong to *The Poetics*, which offers, she asserts, "the first & the last words" on literary criticism (*PA* 241). On March 13 she buys books by Robert Louis Stevenson and Walter Pater: "I want to study them—not to copy, I hope, but to see how the trick's done. Stevenson is a trick—but Pater something different & beyond" (*PA* 251). On March 25, preparing to write travel pieces on her upcoming trip to Portugal and Spain, she buys an attaché case "which will just hold my books & writing paper, & can lie on my knee in the carriage" (*PA* 256). She acquires thus the texts and tools of her trade. The next day she constructs her Spanish diary, "by means of which I hope to pay some at least of my travelling expenses. It is a Grub St. point of view—but all the same, rather a nice little bit of writing might be made out of the sea & land" (*PA* 256–57).

Elizabeth Podnieks writes that "The 1905 diary presents a young woman constructing herself as a dedicated, hard-working professional. She hid the part of herself that had suffered breakdowns and abuses behind the persona of this confident writer, whose identity was fully bound to a work ethic" (147). I would argue with the second claim, for Virginia speaks more directly of her illness in this diary than in any of her previous journals. On January 10, 1905, for instance, she writes, "Discussed the [teaching working women at] Morley College scheme, & settled to get [Dr.] Savages advice first, as to my capabilities of work at present. Otherwise, to wait till October to begin" (*PA* 220). She reports his approval on January 14: "Savage . . . was well satisfied, thinks me 'normal' & able to return to all my usual ways, going out, work, &c—so that horrible long illness which began in the 2nd week of April last year, is now fairly put away, & I need think no more of it—for which the Lord be praised!" (*PA* 222). This certainly whistles in the dark, for two weeks later she still thinks on her illness, for she confesses her subversive joy in penning her "Street Music" article, "since I have been ordered not to write for my brains health" (*PA* 230). Three days later, when she starts to translate Thucydides on February 2, she observes to her diary that "This is the first Greek I have done since my illness—since February, that is—almost a year ago. I remember the last morning's work at Thucydides, & how my brain felt sucked up. I am glad to find that I dont forget Greek & read Thucydides which is tough, as easily as I ever did" (*PA* 231).

This does not seem a person hiding her illness; rather, she is recalling it, dating and examining it, and comparing her current state of mind to her past, as she does two weeks later when she recalls reading Latin with Thoby in September 1904: "Even that little bit of Virgil with T. in the summer, when I was hardly able to use my brains, brought a sense of harmony into them, such as for many months they had not known; & therefore I dont forget it" (*PA* 238).

She does some censoring, some hiding, in the 1904–5 diary. On March 2 she writes, "Violet & the clergyman's wife to tea—who was not—this is too indiscreet"—and says no more of the clergyman's wife (*PA* 245). But her discretion relates to others more than to herself. When it comes to her own person, she will report her three-hour talk with Vanessa on the ethics of suicide and record her close observations of her mind (*PA* 269). Her verbs suggest she sees herself as actively, even forcibly, pressing her brain. "I must cudgel my brains for a lecture," she writes in the January 14 entry reporting Savage's okay (*PA* 222). In February she "pegged away" at her review and "had to beat [her] brains a little" (*PA* 240). In March, given all the space she likes for a review, she "cant screw out words at any price" (*PA* 252). Creation for this writer—be it lecture, translation, or review—requires active mental force and sustained pressure.

So focused is the 1904–5 journal on the diarist's professional start—she lists at the end the reviews and articles she has written and payments per column—that for all its entries this diary is (ironically) the least literary of her first four diaries. Vanessa painted her first professional portraits during the diary's timeframe; in contrast, Virginia's *diary* portraits are minimalist (like her first 1897 portraits). Nowhere can be found the deliberate and elaborate sketchbook portraits of the 1899 and 1903 notebooks. A few portraits are amusing although brief. Lady Alice Shaw Stewart is "really a delightful person, like a tame & combed out Beatrice [Thynne, the pagan], but very full of character, & even beauty" (*PA* 250). People still resemble animals. When he drops in for tea on April 29, 1905, Clive Bell is seen rather ominously as "a nice garrulous old man, with his odd information oozing out—rather pouring buckets full, so that we sit & are pumped into" (*PA* 269). The 1904–5 diary rarely poses questions. Woolf's curiosity has not yet dawned. References to the wider world are likewise spare. On January 23, 1905, she records "Russian massacres, & the poor timorous Czar in hiding," but less than a month later she writes: "Politics in the rough dont much interest me, & seem mostly a waste of time & good English words" (*PA* 227, 239–40).

Like her first diary, Virginia's almost daily 1905 diary weakens and finally dies. A daily diary never succeeds for this periodic diarist who, like Ralph Waldo Emerson, will take a long time to find her diary stride. The 1905 diary appears to founder on the shoals of travel writing—both her private travel diary and the public travel articles she meant her diary to detail. Her twenty-six entries for her travels to France, Portugal, and Spain lack, surprisingly, both description and incident. She struggles in late April "to fix some kind of sketch of our journey for Mrs. L[yttelton of *The Guardian*]: but as usual the thing wont come. . . . I can only hope for better luck next time" (*PA* 268).

Metaphors of scarcity succeed those of plenty in the 1904–5 diary. When material is ripe and plenteous, Virginia relishes her role as writer. Preparing a lecture on sculptor Benvenuto Cellini for her working women in mid-February, she reports that "there are a great many plums which it is no trouble to pick" (*PA* 237). Translating Sophocles three weeks later, she finds him "really not hard, & I have unearthed some gems" (*PA* 248). It is when she finds a concert "threadbare" April 30; her Spanish travel pieces "dry bones to preserve" May 2 and "three dry little sketches" May 3; and the Royal Academy exhibition a "painted desert" that the diary begins to die of enervation—too feeble to survive. (It could also have foundered on jealousy, for Virginia reports on April 29 that Vanessa has received her first commission—from a "Mrs. Seton" (*PA* 269)).

"As it must be confessed that I write this [entry for May 12] on 27th May, it is useless to pretend that I can record what happened on the 12th," she confesses (*PA* 273). Her May 13 entry reveals that she continues to view her diary as a life, but one now sinking "into a premature grave" (*PA* 273). At the start of her life as a professional writer, public writing displaces the first 1905 diary. "It is a hopeless attempt:" she confesses, "writing an extra [diary] page every day, when I write so many of necessity[; diary-writing] bores me, & the story is dull" (*PA* 273). This will not be true with later diaries which will refresh her for her professional prose (and will prove far from dull). Her final entry echoes Walter Scott's repeated praise of spontaneity and resistance to Dame Duty. "Such an exercise can only be fulfilled when it is voluntary, & words come spontaneously," she writes May 31. "Directly writing is a task—why, one asks, should one inflict oneself thus? The good is nullified" (*PA* 273).

The 1904–5 diary is an important volume biographically. Its single-minded focus reveals the intensity of the emerging writer's drive for success. "I want to work like a steam engine," Virginia writes Violet Dickinson in early January 1905, and she does (*L* #206, 1: 172). The diary records her accumulating lessons as a professional writer: the risks of exceeding one's word-limit and being insensitively edited ("I shant waste words again!" *PA* 251); the difficulties of reviewing when one knows little of the subject; and her encounters with the Angel in the House phantom that must be vanquished ("How I wish I could be brave & frank in my reviews, instead of having to spin them out elaborately" *PA* 270). We see a writer learning to protect her time ("Really I must find some way of doing these lecture jobs at other times—mornings are too precious" *PA* 237); and one wishing, even as she starts, to write free of editors' demands ("Wrote this morning—*not* for any editor to see, which becomes a relief" *PA* 252). The 1904–5 diary ends with dismissal of concern for its death in favor of praise for its success: "All but six months find some sort of mirror of themselves here; the sight is one that profits or pleases" (*PA* 273).

5

Embracing the Unconscious

t age twenty-one Virginia Woolf chooses the outsider role; at twenty-three she turns inward. "All greatness is unconscious, or it is little and nought," Thomas Carlyle wrote in "Sir Walter Scott"—an essay Woolf likely knew (37). Her 1905 ghostly, haunted Cornwall diary and the 1906 to 1908 Great Britain travel diary that follows it display her growing trust in her own unconscious as both reservoir and compositor.

In her 1905 Cornwall diary, Woolf abandons date and subject markers as she pursues "a vast trackless country, without mark or boundary" (*PA* 297). Her Cornwall "Walk by Night," repeated five times in the 1907 Playden diary in Sussex, reveals her growing embrace of the night-conscious—the unconscious—and with it, in 1906, the first diary signs of unwilled, spontaneous invention and, in 1907, of her "scene-making" gift.

Untouched land and uncharted waters draw Woolf repeatedly across these years, her own creative space found only after insistent turns from male voices. She reads and reviews three works in 1907 and 1908 that showcase for her further the protean diary form. The *Diary* of William Allingham, a Victorian poet who knew her family, plants the seed for *Freshwater* and more. *Leaves from the Note-books of Lady Dorothy Nevill* displays the merits of scrapbook-keeping and lays the path toward "Miss Ormerod" in "Lives of the Obscure" and to Cassandra Otway and Mrs. Hilbery in *Night and Day*. Lady Charlotte Bury's *Diary of a Lady-in-Waiting* gives Woolf a first look at an officious, letter-writing political toady named Whitbread—the name Woolf will give to her own destructive letter-writing politico in *Mrs. Dalloway*. It shows her, too, the trials of women writers in the early nineteenth century.

Virginia's Woolf's Ghostly 1905 Cornwall Diary

"some persistent phantom had at last taken shape"

(PA 289)

"The Ghost Diary" should be the title of Virginia Stephen's fifth journal, for phantoms and a ghostly aura haunt the Cornwall diary. If her first 1905 diary withers in May, becomes a dull private work to a twenty-three-year-old more absorbed by her public prose, the diary pulse revives in the country (as it has before). The Cornwall diary resembles physically her last two diaries in its self-binding and soft paper cover—although now a blue-gray shade for Cornwall instead of the previous deep gray. However, it departs completely in *form* from these earlier journals, for Virginia now tries something new.[1] Fifteen entries capture the fifty-six-day Cornwall holiday August 10 to October 4, 1905; however, only the first two entries are *dated*. After that, the tenth entry is *titled* ("The Lands End"), but the other twelve entries sport neither date nor title. Only white space separates them, as if they are vestiges of some larger whole. Each of the fifteen entries addresses a separate topic, and they appear to have been written at different times; however, Woolf's abandonment of date and subject markers shows her both suspending—and expanding—conventional diary terrain.

The diary's first sentence introduces this altered dimension: "It was with some feeling of enchantment that we took our places yesterday in the Great Western train" (*PA* 281). Her next sentence personifies the train as a "wizard who was to transport us into another world, almost into another age" (*PA* 281). Mist and magic envelop the diary as traditional boundaries fade. "We would fain have believed that this little corner of England had slept under some enchanters spell since we last set eyes on it ten [eleven] years ago," she writes, "& that no breath of change had stirred its leaves, or troubled its waters" (*PA* 281). When they creep up the driveway to Talland House the first night, the site of more than a decade of happy summers in their youth, and gaze through a chink in the escallonia hedge at the "two lighted windows," she reports that they "hung there like ghosts" (*PA* 282).

The unmarked third entry hints that the Cornwall "persistent phantom" lost but recovered in this diary is a woman: the diarist's dead mother, Julia Stephen. When Virginia and Adrian take shelter from the rain in a fifteenth-century parish church, they are stopped by the church's elderly caretaker, a woman dressed in black who has been seeking news of them. The woman weeps and "poured forth her memories, her constant remembrance & gratitude" for Julia Stephen's beauty and charity. "And as I heard those humble words of the love that one woman felt for another," Virginia ends this entry, "I thought that no acclamation of praise throughout the whole world could sound so sweet, or could mean so much" (*PA* 285).

When they visit Mr. Pascoe, the old man who kept the bathing tents, Virginia notes in entry five that, "'I cant believe that I see you there before me in the flesh' was a phrase that recurred, as though some persistent phantom had at last taken shape" (*PA* 289). In the next entry, she describes the waves at ebb tide, equating the waves—this crucial Woolf symbol—with the mother: "The slope of the beach gleams as though laid with a film of mother o' pearl where the sea has been, & a row of sea gulls sits on the skirts of the repeating wave" (*PA* 290). In "A Sketch of the Past," written thirty-four years later, Woolf recounts her first memory: herself sitting on her mother's lap in a train heading, perhaps, toward Cornwall (*MOB* 64). In this 1905 Cornwall diary entry, the "row of sea gulls" might be the Stephen children sitting on the skirts of the wave.[2] Birds will symbolize the young writer as the Cornwall diary unfolds. "The pallor of the sandhills makes the scene yet more ghostly," the diarist continues, evoking now the sandhill cranes, "but the beautiful sights are often melancholy & very lonely" (*PA* 290).

"These are rough notes to serve as land marks," she begins her ninth entry (*PA* 291). This entry precedes the sole titled entry in the Cornwall diary, "The Lands End," a title hinting that traditional "land marks" now will cease. In "The Lands End," Woolf confesses that she has private landmarks not easily accessible to others that are more important to her than traditional tourist sites. "The Lands End" marker sets the stage for the most important entry in the Cornwall diary: the unmarked thirteenth entry recounting a ghostly walk home from the inland sea. This dateless, titleless entry serves as both climax to and emblem of the entire haunted Cornwall diary with *its* turn inward to Woolf's inland sea. Like the striking "Country In London" entry in the 1903 diary, it reveals her drive to claim her own creative space.

The Cornwall diary, like the 1903 diary, affirms the importance of solitary walks to the writer. Virginia's seventh entry dwells on just such rambles. She delights in the "scarcity of good roads in Cornwall" that "keeps the land fluid, as it were, so that feet may trace new paths in it at their will" (*PA* 290). Acknowledging that "the stranger must often prefer the cut & dry system of regular high roads," she suggests, however, that a walker "should sketch his path with a free hand, & trust that he will find some little trodden line to guide him" (*PA* 290).

In fact, she concludes, "for the walker who prefers the variety & incident of the open fields to the orthodox precision of the high road, there is no such ground for walking as this" (*PA* 291).

The thirteenth entry limns such terrain. "It is a mistake to keep rigidly to the coast; strike inland," Woolf begins, suggesting that the interior voyage is her goal (*PA* 297). The trek home begins at dusk, that amorphous blend of light and dark, of the conscious and the unconscious, and is delayed by their inclination "to take a long look at the Gurnard's Head [promontory] & the misty shapes beyond, through which suddenly there flashed the fitful glare of the St Just lighthouse" (*PA* 297). Because their long gaze makes them late, they resolve "to keep safe upon the road," but when they find the road it is only "a vague white mist." (*PA* 297). Adrian "stalking ahead was blurred & without outline," Virginia writes, "& at a hundred yards distance we had to send our voices out after him to make sure that we had not lost him. In this mystification we left the road, & stepped into a vast trackless country, without mark or boundary" (*PA* 297). They are unbound. "Before us dozens of lights were scattered, floating in soft depths of darkness without anchorage on the firm ground" (*PA* 297). A farmer's voice bidding them goodnight "recalled us for a moment to the cheerful land of substance, but our path lay on into the darkness again" (*PA* 297–98). They stumble across fields "which swam in dusky vapours," meet another road, and then dark spectres of death: "lighted windows, scarcely able to irradiate a yard of the blackness that pressed on them"; "long black figures leaning against the walls quiescent" (*PA* 298). Are these the "lighted windows" of her first entry—at Talland House—that stand for her parents? At last they find the road and finally home, but it is home with a difference. It is home with a profound sense of the potent land crossed. "But how narrow were those walls [of home]," begins the entry's last line, "& how intense that light after the vague immensity of the air; we were like creatures lately winged that have been caught & caged" (*PA* 298).

In her bold "Country In London" entry in 1903, before becoming a professional writer, twenty-one-year-old Virginia acknowledged her need "to live in the midst of men & women—to get the light strong in your eyes as it were" (*PA* 179). Two years later, she rejects the "intense light" of civilization for her own "vague immensity" of air. In entry seven, a row of seagulls "sits on the skirts of the repeating wave" (*PA* 290). In entry twelve, Virginia equates passing ships with birds: "all day long these silent voyagers are coming & going, alighting like some traveling birds for a moment & then shaking out their sails again & passing on to new waters. Where do they come from, & whither are they bound?" (*PA* 296). In entry thirteen, the Stephen children are like these bird/ships: "creatures lately winged" (*PA* 298). They have tried "the vague immensity" of air and feel the constriction of "familiar lamps" (*PA* 298). Surely this entry—in fact, the entire Cornwall diary—reveals the young writer's intent to chart unmarked waters and find richness in her own misty dappled terrain.

The Cornwall diary's fifteenth and final entry recalls entries in the 1899 and 1903 diaries and should be understood as one of Woolf's habitual diary gestures. The young writer confesses: "[S]o . . . it comes to pass that I write these words upon the eve of our return. The lights of London will be round me at this time of evening tomorrow, as the lighthouse gleams now. That is a thought which comes with real melancholy, for, besides the actual beauty of this country, to part with it is to part with something which we knew long ago. . . . There is in truth, as I thought once in fancy something of our own preserved here from which it is painful to part. . . . On the whole I prefer to think that there is good reason to regret this departure more than others" (*PA* 299).

The country will prove vital to Woolf across her diaries, and the inner landscape of Cornwall memories makes it doubly evocative. As she writes in entry four, "The delight of the country is that all moods of the air & the earth are natural, & therefore fit and beautiful."[3] The open fields invite her to "sketch [her] path with a free hand" (*PA* 290). If in the 1903 "Country In London" entry she sought to forge her own natural space within the city, by 1905 she embraces both an inland sea and "a vast trackless country, without mark or boundary" (*PA* 297).

Gone in the 1905 Cornwall diary are the notes of hesitancy and inadequacy of the 1899 diary. In their place is the surer hand of a professional writer who begins strongly with metaphors of wizards and enchantment and then cloaks her personal and writer's quests in symbolic nature scenes. That she now thinks as a writer can be seen in her response in her fifth diary entry to a report of a farmer's daughter who left her new husband after only nine days: "There is a curious little plot, or rather psychological study for a novelist" (*PA* 287). Her eighth entry tries to re-create the St Ives Regatta as a French impressionist painting, and her portraits are as confidently sketched as her boat scenes. She etches fine extended portraits of the Pascoes, capturing both their look and their talk. Her similes and metaphors are also fresh and appealing. Two-and-a-half weeks into the holiday, she writes to Violet Dickinson, "I am writing 2 large works; one upon the letters of the Paston family; the other upon the nature and characteristics of the country of Cornwall; I want to learn how to write descriptions without adjectives" (*L* #248, 1: 206). The diary's lively scenes of pilchard fishing (entry nine), card playing (entry fourteen), and the haunting walk home from the inland sea (entry thirteen) reveal that she is learning not only to write descriptions but also that the most ordinary acts can be imbued with vivid life.

In years to come Woolf will transplant the Pascoe name to her first modernist novel *Jacob's Room* and re-present in *To the Lighthouse* many facets of the 1905 Cornwall stay. Entry two of the Cornwell diary, for instance, describes the sea becoming calm as they sail across the bay—an important moment in the 1927 novel. Entry nine in 1905 begins in disappointment, "we sat over our breakfast despondently, the mist deciding us to give up our expedition to Mullion"; however, the entry ends in triumph with a brilliant vision of pilchard catching in the bay (*PA* 291–92).

Even more significantly, the diarist turns her important entry thirteen into a public essay, "A Walk By Night," published in *The Guardian* on December 28, 1905. In so doing, she expands her diary entry and equates the night more directly with water—that is, with the unconscious and with death. Adrian is depersonalized in the transformation; he becomes even more ghostly than before: "A figure withdrawing itself some yards wavered for a moment and was then engulfed as though the dark waters of the night had closed over it, and the voice sounded like one reaching across great depths" (*E* 1: 80). The "vast trackless country" of the diary entry becomes "the trackless ocean of the night" in *The Guardian*, and there the farmer "recalled us as though a firm hand had grasped ours, to the shores of the world, but in two strides the immense flood of darkness and silence was over us again" (*PA* 297, *E* 1: 81). In *The Guardian* revision, darkness again overcomes the light. "How puny were the rays of the lamp against the immeasurable waves of darkness surging round them!" Woolf exclaims, and the Stephen children are universalized into "a little village" at the mercy of darkness and death (*E* 1: 82). "A ship at sea is a lonely thing," Virginia writes, "but far lonelier it seemed was this little village anchored to the desolate earth and exposed every night, alone, to the unfathomed waters of darkness" (*E* 1: 82).

And yet the writer finds nourishment in the dark. She elaborates her diary closing ("But how narrow were those walls, & how intense that light after the vague immensity of the air; we were like creatures lately winged that have been caught & caged") into an entire paragraph suggesting that the dark gives her access to "the phantoms and spirits of substantial things": "And yet, once accustomed to the strange element, there was great peace and beauty in it. It seemed as though only the phantoms and spirits of substantial things were now abroad. . . . The eye might bathe and refresh itself in the depths of the night, without grating upon any harsh outline of reality; the earth with its infinity of detail was dissolved into ambiguous space. The walls of the house were too narrow, the glare of the lamps too fierce for those thus refreshed and made sensitive; we were as birds lately winged that have been caught and caged" (*E* 1: 82). Away from the "harsh outline" of the earth and its "infinity of detail," one can pause and refresh oneself at night. Form dissolved will leave space to forge new forms of one's own.

Virginia Woolf's 1906–1908 Great Britain Travel Diary

"a blank sheet of hill & valley"

(August 8, 1907; *PA* 367)

London fades in Virginia's sixth and seventh diaries—a telling fact in itself. The years 1906 to 1908 become the years of her travel diaries. The first book preserves holidays at seven sites in England and Wales from 1906 to 1908; the second, her travels outside the British Isles to Greece and Turkey in 1906 and to Italy in 1908 and 1909. Why Woolf chose to *be* a travel diarist rather than a life diarist remains an intriguing question. She likely wished to preserve the memories of her holidays and travels. Furthermore, the drive to capture *place* figures strongly in these diaries. Travel diaries offer useful practice ground for one honing her skills in scenic description as she broadens (literally) her geographical and cultural horizons. Finally, as we have seen, the "country" away from London offers vital artistic terrain, space that refreshes and sensitizes her eye perhaps *because* it supplies less structured paths than the city's. The same can be said of her loosely structured diary: it refreshes and sensitizes her eye. Therefore while London at this time might be linked with her public prose, the travel diaries mark the private work that feeds it.

The Great Britain travel diary, with its hand-binding and sturdy brown board cover, preserves Virginia's 1906 Easter holiday alone in Giggleswick on the Yorkshire moors; the family's summer sojourn at Blo' Norton Hall, a moated Norfolk Elizabethan manor house; her rejection of the New Forest in Hampshire at Christmas 1906; her renewed search for "the country in London" at Hampstead in July 1907; and a new diary style during their summer 1907 holiday in Playden, Sussex. The diary ends full circle in August 1908 with solitary sojourns in Wells, Somerset, and Manorbier, South Wales.

꓾

Virginia did not choose to be alone for the Easter 1906 holiday. Emma and Marny Vaughan, her cousins, proposed to go "somewhere" with her; however, the plans collapsed, and with Vanessa in Sussex professionally engaged in painting Lady Robert Cecil's portrait, Virginia asked Madge Vaughan in Giggleswick to help her find a Yorkshire inn (*L* #265, 1: 220). She may have recalled with fondness her stay with Madge and her family at Giggleswick School at the close of her convalescence in November 1904. "I promise not to bother you: you shant see me at all, except passing in the road," the twenty-four-year-old writes to Madge in April 1906. "I am bringing a great box of books, and I shall shut myself in my room and read" (*L* #265, 1: 220).

She mentions Madge's diary in this letter, and she clearly has read all or parts of it, for she sees it as a work of promise. "It strikes me that you might make a really good book out of that Diary," Virginia states. "Suppose you went on day by day, writing out soberly and exactly, what you think, feel, see, hear and talk about, as you have done that one day [in 1889, when Madge was twenty], all things growing naturally out of each other as they do—wouldn't the result be something very true and remarkable? Because, without counting your mind, your life is remarkable, and lived in a remarkable place. It is a book I should very much like to see, and I believe you could do it" (*L* #265, 1: 220–21). Once more another's diary may have sparked Virginia's own. She may have felt that she, too, might supply "something very true and remarkable" by recording her days.[4]

Nine entries capture the fifteen-day Easter holiday April 12 to 26, 1906, the diarist inclining still to undated entries as in her last ghostly Cornwall diary. This practice has the effect of universalizing the Giggleswick entries which unfold untethered to specific days. Woolf's wry mockery of Easter destabilizes time even more. She paganizes Easter in her second, Good Friday, entry, turning a Yorkshire road and its Christian procession into the Greeks' Sacred Way and her own taking of bread into "sacrifice to the gods" (*PA* 302, 301). Her fourth, Easter Sunday, entry closes in similar pagan allusion: "Tomorrow, all the furies will be let loose once more, & then, perhaps, peace" (*PA* 304).

Her nine diary entries, separated only by white space, may have been written on consecutive days, the diary shut with Vanessa's arrival April 21. In her opening entry, Virginia exalts in her solitary state, noting the absence of distractions and her freedom to order meals when she likes. This may be partly bravado though, for she appears to seek succor as well. She may have reread her Cornwall diary before starting anew, for echoes of Cornwall and that diary resound across the nine Yorkshire entries, as if she still seeks parental ghosts.[5] In her second entry, describing her walk on the moors, she observes that "In many ways this land is like Cornwall," and in her first she notes that "the moors rise in waves all round" (*PA* 302, 301). In an April 16 letter to Violet Dickinson, she boasts of walking "with gigantic strides over the wild moorside, shouting odes of Pindar, as I leap from crag to crag, & exulting in the air which buffets me, and caresses me, like a stern but affectionate parent!" (*L* #266, 1: 221).

Woolf animates the moors in the Giggleswick diary, likening them repeatedly to the sea. In entry two "The moors rise & roll away, for miles on either side, tossing themselves into great promontories . . . & then surging on their way again," and in entry four she reveals this country's pull: "You get into a desolate sea of moors. . . . No road or house seems to adventure out there; & the likeness to a barren sea scape is unavoidable" (*PA* 302, 304). The moors provide the unmarked space she prefers.

In 1903 the aspiring writer sought "The Country In London." In the 1906 Giggleswick diary she repeats the move: "I amused myself with planning the countryside into Bloomsbury & Piccadilly" (*PA* 303). However, she then reverses the move: "& setting St James Streets & Marble Arches on all the hills and valleys" (*PA* 303). She invites her country and London worlds to merge: to fertilize each other. However, the feeling of inadequacy re-enters the diary. She ends her first entry—the one crowing of her independence—with "& really, as one may gather, nothing profitable is to be looked for in the scratching of a pen tonight" (*PA* 301). Entry six ends with her failure to find suitable words for the moors: "But words! words! You will find nothing to match the picture" (*PA* 305). Her effort in entry eight to describe her happy afternoon walk, "a gift set down in the course of an ordinary day," also falters. "I delay in truth," she confesses, "because I shall get no nearer the words by making a direct search for them than by thus dallying upon the outskirts" (*PA* 306). Her final Giggleswick entry resists traditional diary (and narrative) forms. "I will not attempt here the most dreary catalogue that exists: that of a day's expedition," she writes defiantly. "I shall say only that we found ourselves at the Manchester Zoo at 11:30: or thereabouts: & if that fact does not write its own history in more pertinent figures than I can come by, imagination is a broken winded jade" (*PA* 307).

Unlike her solitary sojourn on the Yorkshire moors in April 1906, guests filter through the family's summer holiday four months later at Blo' Norton Hall in Norfolk.[6] This change does not sound in the diary, however, which focuses almost exclusively on the manor hall, the Norfolk country, and the narratives they inspire. Eight undated and untitled entries preserve this twenty-nine-day holiday August 3 to August 31, 1906. Virginia continues the untethered form of her Giggleswick and Cornwall diaries.

In her first entry she captures first impressions, analyzes them and their resilience, but then swiftly leaves them behind. She first recoils from moated Blo' Norton manor and its environs. However, she moves quickly to a more favorable second view. She ends this first entry by observing that her first rash "notes are the things one thinks before one begins to reason or to know. And like the images of childhood, they stay bright" (*PA* 310). However, her drive in this entry to look beneath the manor "surface," beyond childhood images, and to "reason or to know" reveals her growing resolve, as she will write in her Italian diary two years later, "to write not only with the eye, but with the mind" (*PA* 384).

By entry four she has completely revised her first view. Her growing delight with this country relates directly to her discovery of the open heath less than a mile from her door. She confesses in entry five that the heath attracts her most—far more than the muddy fens—"because there are no fields" (*PA* 312). Once more it is the *absence* of human design that draws her. Like the moors and the downs and her beloved Cornwall landscape, the uncultivated heath invites her imagination. In entry six, she celebrates the paradox of civilization and its absence: "I am half inclined to state that Norfolk is one of the most beautiful of counties. . . . And truly, it would need a careful & skilful brush to give a picture of this strange, grey green, undulating, dreaming, philosophising & remembering land; where one may walk 10 miles & meet no one; where soft grass paths strike gently over the land; where the roads are many & lonely, & the churches are innumerable, & deserted" (*PA* 312). The roads and churches do not draw her; rather their lonely vacancy.

On the second day of her Blo' Norton sojourn, Virginia writes to Violet Dickinson that "Nessa paints windmills in the afternoon, and I tramp the country for miles with a map, leap ditches, scale walls and desecrate churches, making out beautiful brilliant stories every step of the way" (*L* #282, 1: 234). The heath seems to abet this story-making, for immediately after disclosing her discovery of "the real heath" in diary entry four, she writes: "It is a strange lonely kind of country; a carriage comes bowling over the hill, & you watch it pass & disappear & wonder where it comes from & whither it goes, & who is the lady inside" (*PA* 312). Intriguingly, a page is torn out at the end of her sixth entry just as she personifies the *land* as a woman: "[Norfolk] is so soft, so melancholy, so wild, & yet so willing to be gentle: like some noble untamed woman conscious that she has no beauty to vaunt, that nobody very much wants her" (*PA* 313).

Could this be the genesis of Mistress Joan Martyn, the fictional, early Renaissance diarist of Virginia's untitled work begun at this time? (The work titled "The Journal of Mistress Joan Martyn" when published posthumously in 1979.) Did Virginia tear out her diary page for use in her story? Joan Martyn's tale is set in Norfolk just a few miles from Blo' Norton Hall. Louise DeSalvo believes Virginia re-creates Blo' Norton manor in the fictional Martyn Hall ("Shakespeare's *Other* Sister" 63). That the young writer was conjuring stories is clear from her fourth diary entry, in which she speculates on the life of the unknown lady in the carriage, her sixth entry which projects Norfolk itself as a melancholy and unclaimed woman, and her seventh (and next-to-last) entry, in which she describes her visit to Kenninghall and its cemeteries and imagines lives of departed women from their epitaphs. In "The Journal of Mistress Joan Martyn," Joan dies at age thirty. The "Journal" ends, in fact, with Joan gazing down at her ancestors' gravestones in the church cemetery.

By her eighth and closing entry, Norfolk has become rich in life for Woolf. She paints a telling portrait of Thetford village. "For when you come upon stalwart men leaning their elbows on a parapet & dreaming of the stream beneath, while the sun is still high in the air," she writes—a scene that anticipates her portrait of the artist fishing in the subconscious in her 1931 "Professions for Women"—"you reconsider what you mean by life. Often in London shall I think of Thetford" (*PA* 315). Once more she images a nourishing country-*in*-London: "coming home in the evening through great open spaces of field it was born [*sic*] in upon the mind that something was alive enough" (*PA* 316).

Two further passages at the close of this vibrant Blo' Norton diary suggest the writer begins now both to recognize and to trust her unconscious as a *reservoir* in the fullest sense of that word: as both a *source* and a subtle *compositor* of her art. Her seventh entry offers the first diary sign of her emerging gift for spontaneous creation. "It is one of the wilful habits of the brain . . . that it will only work at its own terms," she complains. "You bring it directly opposite an object, & bid it discourse; it merely shuts its eye, & turns away. But in one month, or three or seven, suddenly without any bidding, it pours out the whole picture, gratuitously" (*PA* 313). In her next (and final) entry, she anticipates her later figure of her diary as a compost heap, for she ventures: "A very hot August day, a bare road across a moor, fields of corn & stubble—a haze as of wood fire smoke—innumerable pheasants & partridges—white stones—thatched cottages—sign posts—tiny villages—great waggons heaped with corn—sagacious dogs, farmers carts. Compose these all somehow into a picture; I am too lazy to do it" (*PA* 315).

She may have been too lazy to compose this picture further in her *diary* because she has been composing it fully in "The Journal of Mistress Joan Martyn." Three weeks into her four-week Norfolk holiday, she writes to Dickinson that she has written forty pages of manuscript since she arrived (*L* #283, 1: 235). Here she is, a twenty-four-year-old woman keeping a diary in an Elizabethan manor house, thinking all the while of Norfolk women of the past. Perhaps this suggested a story of a twenty-five-year-old pre-Elizabethan Norfolk woman (and aspiring writer) who also keeps a diary. Joan Martyn's fictional diary, which comprises the second half of "The Journal of Mistress Joan Martyn," resembles in form Woolf's eight-entry Blo' Norton diary. Joan's diary consists of seven entries and ambiguous "Last Pages." Furthermore, only three of Joan's entries are titled (marking the passage of the year: "May," "Midsummer," "Autumn"); the rest, like Virginia's, are unmarked.

That a diary contains a "life" Virginia understood from her very first tiny diary. A diary revives the past. Joan Martyn's fictional diary supplied a form for evoking the Norfolk land and its inhabitants. Miss Rosamond Merridew, the fictive forty-five-year-old historian who discovers Joan's diary at the story's start, might be read as Virginia's projection in 1906 of herself in middle age. Miss Merridew boasts that she has "exchanged a husband and a family and a house in which I may grow old for certain fragments of yellow parchment" (*SF* 33). The historian thinks of these fragments as her children, "as cripples with fretful faces, but all the same, with the fire of genius in their eyes" (*SF* 33). We learn that she has "given and taken many shrewd blows" regarding her work over the years; however, she also has "won considerable fame" (*SF* 34, 33). Medieval England, Miss Merridew's historical specialty, holds for her the charm of Virginia's empty landscapes. It is "more bare than any other of private records," Miss Merridew explains; "unless you choose to draw all your inspiration from the *Paston Letters* you must be content to imagine merely, like any other story teller" (*SF* 35).

Rosamond Merridew borrows Joan's diary from John Martyn, Joan's descendant, the current owner of Martyn Hall. An engaging but ambiguous figure, he considers Joan a "[q]ueer old lady" and believes Willoughby's stud book and Jasper Martyn's household book of far greater interest than Joan's diary (*SF* 41). "Horses or Grandfathers!" he offers Rosamond Merridew, holding out those two male texts.[7] Nevertheless, he has read Joan's diary from start to end and allows he "learnt a deal about the land from her, one way and another" (*SF* 41).

If Rosamond Merridew offers a portrait of Virginia Stephen's projected *fu-*

ture self, Joan Martyn should be read as the fifteenth-century counterpart of her *current* self. Joan's father, we learn, taught her to read and to write, and he sends her manuscripts to read from London. Joan's diary ends with this father, but it begins with a tribute to her mother who manages the Martyn lands ably while her husband is gone to London or to the wars. "[Y]ou see what a noble woman she is," Joan affirms in her first diary entry. "It is a great thing to be the daughter of such a woman, and to hope that one day the same power may be mine. She rules us all" (*SF* 46). This beloved mother can write, but she cannot read, and she "draws the Gates close, clamps them with the lock, and the whole world is barred away from us," Joan explains (*SF* 45). Joan differs from this mother. The twenty-five-year-old confesses to being "very bold and impatient sometimes," and she longs to travel to London (*SF* 45). "It is a fearful ride," she admits in entry two, "but, truly, I think I should like to go that way once, and pass over the land, like a ship at sea" (*SF* 49).

Joan's first diary entry ends with a rush of wind and Joan's sense "that horses and men in armour are charging down upon me" (*SF* 47). In entry three they materialize in the form of a written request for her hand from Sir Amyas Bigod, the Lord of Kirflings, an estate touching the Martyn land. Sir Amyas Bigod, "a man of ancient name," has gray hair, Joan reports, so he likely is much her senior (*SF* 50). Joan understands from her mother that marriage is "a great honour and a great burden," but she does not wish to leave her mother (*SF* 50).[8] Entry four celebrates Norfolk as a woman—as does Virginia's Blo' Norton diary. Norfolk, Joan writes, "is to me what my own grandmother is; a tender parent, dear and familiar, and silent to whom I shall return in time. O how blessed it would be never to marry, or grow old; but to spend one's life innocently and indifferently among the trees and rivers which alone can keep one cool and childlike in the midst of the troubles of the world!" (*SF* 52).

First the mother is celebrated in the diary, then the land as ancestral mother. With entry five comes "May" and a celebration, not of marriage, but of story and song. Richard Sir, the songster from Cornwall, arrives with the spring, though he acknowledges "The times are not favourable to songs" (*SF* 54). Joan's mother bids her son open the Gates, and all the people crowd in to listen and to dance. Art, here, opens the gates and unites. Joan admires the Cornwall singer beyond measure. "[W]ords seemed dear to him, whether he spoke them in jest or earnest," she writes (*SF* 55). "[H]e had a kind of gaiety and courtesy about him, as though the fine music of his own songs clung to him and set him above ordinary thoughts" (*SF* 54). Joan likens him to a bird—that suggestive symbol of the artist in the Cornwall diary. When he finishes his song, he is "like a man who lets something slip from his clasp; and beats thin air" (*SF* 56). They try to retain him, but he soon departs: "we felt as though some strange bird had rested on our roof for a moment, and flown on" (*SF* 57).

This important entry ends with a celebration of *written* texts as well as spoken. Richard places his great book in Joan's hands—surely a passing on of the Cornwall legacy—and as she looks at the words and pictures, she explains, "They were like little mirrors, held up to those visions which I had seen passing in the air [when he sang] but here they were caught and stayed for ever" (*SF* 56–57). Richard's book "was as yellow and gnarled outside as the missal of any pious priest; but inside the brilliant knights and ladies moved, undimmed, to the unceasing melody of beautiful words" (*SF* 57).

"May" is followed by "Midsummer," entry six, and the return of Joan's father and older brothers. During this interlude of tranquility, they embark on their midsummer pilgrimage to Our Lady of Walsingham. Sober thoughts accompany the journey, for Joan learns her marriage to Sir Amyas has been set for December 10, and she thinks ahead to "the serious things of life—such as age, and poverty and sickness and death" and recognizes she must meet them (*SF* 58). But again her thoughts turn to her art: "it seemed to me that one might enter within such feelings and study them, as, indeed, I had walked in a wide space within the covers of Master Richard's manuscript," she declares (*SF* 58). "Midsummer" ends with an ecstatic experience—and a kiss of female devotion. "For one moment I submitted myself to her [Our Lady of Walsingham] as I have never submitted to man or woman, and bruised my lips on the rough stone of her garment," Joan reveals. "White light and heat steamed on my bare head; and when the ecstasy passed the country beneath flew out like a sudden banner unfurled."[9]

This moment of midsummer ecstasy contrasts sharply with "Autumn," the seventh diary entry that follows. To prepare Joan for her December marriage, Joan's mother allows her to help run the manor. Sir Amyas, Joan acknowledges, is a "good gentleman, who treats me with great courtesy and hopes to make me happy" (*SF* 59); however, her mother insists her life will not be that of the princesses in fairy tales. The princesses "did not live in Norfolk, at the time of the Civil Wars" (*SF* 59). Joan describes in this entry her mother's view of England to come, a vision British readers of this story would likely embrace, and in fact, would say had arrived: "a small island set in the midst of turbulent waters; how one must plant it and cultivate it; and drive roads through it, and fence it securely from the tides" (*SF* 59). In 1480, Joan's mother dreams of civilization, commerce, and safety. Her daughter, revealingly, yearns for more.

"The Journal of Mistress Joan Martyn" closes with a paean to diaries and to Joan Martyn as a writer of promise. In these "Last Pages" Joan's father finds her at the desk, writing in her diary. She is ashamed, but he cries:

Ah, if my father had only kept a diary! . . . There's John and Pierce and Stephen all lying in the church yonder, and no word left to say whether they were good men or bad. . . .

And so my grandson will say of me. And if I could I should like to write a line myself: to say "I am Giles Martyn; I am a middle sized man, dark skinned, hazel eyed, with hair on my lip; I can read and write, but none too easy. I ride to London on as good a bay mare as is to be found in the Country."

Well what more should I say? And would they care to hear it? And who will *they* be? (*SF* 60–61)

Giles Martyn can write, "but none too easy." His daughter does better, and he knows it, for he asks for her diary so he will have "some token of you when you are away; and our descendants shall have cause to respect one of us at least" (*SF* 61).

The closure of Joan's life and diary, like that of all diaries, is left of necessity in the reader's hands.[10] Woolf does not tell us what happens to Joan Martyn beyond the fact that she dies at age thirty. Perhaps she married Sir Amyas Bigod and died in childbirth. Perhaps she fell to the plague or the wars. Perhaps she set out boldly for London and was killed. Another scenario, hinted at in entry three of Joan's diary, is that events stopped her December wedding. The war? Sir Amyas's death? Or perhaps a failure in final terms. "[D]uring the last two or three years there have been several contracts almost made I know," Joan writes, "that came to nothing in the end" (*SF* 51). How ever readers wish to imagine Joan's last years and too early death, she leaves her father her diary which is carefully preserved.

"The Journal of Mistress Joan Martyn" ends with Joan's pride in "the many sheets that lie written in my oaken desk" and her plans to write "stories" beyond those of "Norfolk and myself" (*SF* 61, 62). DeSalvo calls "The Journal of Mistress Joan Martyn" "a meditation upon Rosamond Merridew's quest for a female past" and an early revelation of "Virginia Woolf's own epic quest for a mythic mother as muse" ("Shakespeare's *Other* Sister" 79). Joan Martyn is Shakespeare's *other* sister, DeSalvo reminds us, not Judith Shakespeare who left us nothing, but "the one who kept her journal for more than a year and who has been the historian of her own times" ("Shakespeare's *Other* Sister" 79).

Staggering events unsettle Virginia Stephen between her richly imaginative Blo'
Norton diary in August 1906 and her single late-December 1906 diary entry
titled "The New Forest   Christmas." The family's eagerly anticipated tour of
Greece and Constantinople in September and October (preserved in her Continental travel diary) concludes in tragedy with young Thoby Stephen's shocking death from typhoid on November 20, a loss compounded two days later
when Vanessa accepts Clive Bell's marriage proposal. On December 21, Vanessa
travels to the Bells' Wiltshire country estate to meet Clive's parents, abandoning
Virginia and Adrian to Aunt Minna (Sarah Duckworth) and the New Forest for
the Christmas holidays.[11]

A psychological reading of her sole New Forest diary record seems inescap-
able. Virginia's daily 1904–5 diary had come to life two years before at the New
Forest. In 1904 she found the New Forest trees appealing, standing "round
in a circle" like the pagan Stonehenge pillars (PA 215). In 1904 she heard "the
distant music of hounds running. The note of the huntsmans horn, & far away
voices of men shouting . . . as in some distant romantic dream" (PA 215). Male
voices "far away," her own diary voice sounds in 1904, capturing the dissolving
sunset.

Clive Bell was an avid huntsman, and in 1906 Virginia can no longer feel the
male hunter a distant dream. One feels in her 1906 critique of the New Forest
veiled thrusts at her sister's fiancé. "For why," she asks, "does the forest always
disappoint me? & why does Christmas disappoint me too?" (PA 363). By comparing Christmas with the New Forest and noting her dissatisfaction with both,
Virginia telegraphs her apprehensions regarding Clive Bell as well: "Is it not
that they both promise something glittering & ruddy & cheerful, & when you
have it you find it not quite as good as you expected? The forest is too benign &
complaisant; it gives you all that you can ask; but it hints at no more. . . . To be
candid the forest is a little sleek & a little tame; it is Saxon without any Celtic
mysticism; it is flaxen & florid, stately & ornamental" (PA 363–64).

She declares no need for the New Forest, now associated with the male
hunting tradition rather than with the female pagan. "We have no use for forests
now, & yet this one is preserved reverently, when the old spirit has died out of
it," she writes, suggestively. "So it comes about that there is always something
artificial about the place, & its lovers. You will not find the real country man or
woman here. . . . [T]here is the old colonel of course who never misses a meet &
knows his way through the forest better than any of the tufters; such old gentle-

men are not unusual, but in other countries surely they have fewer grooves in which to run so smoothly" (*PA* 364).

Woolf rejects the New Forest and its male traditions in this 1906 diary entry, finding it artificial and too much revered. "But O for the dusky roll of some Northern moor, or the melancholy cliffs of Cornwall," she concludes the entry, once more showing her preference for her own less-charted terrain. "There," she exults, "you hear the wind & the sea" (*PA* 364).

Half a year later, she turns again from male traditions in her solitary "Golders Green & Hampstead July" 1907 diary entry. Vanessa marries Clive Bell on February 7, 1907, and in early July the Bells and Adrian decide to spend the Bank holiday in Cambridge. Virginia refuses to join them at this male enclave. She writes to Violet Dickinson that she means "to read, or write, or somehow enjoy myself" alone (*L* #369, 1: 298). Across her early diaries she has associated the "country" with nature and with authentic—as opposed to artificial, man-made—"Life." Regret at leaving the country is one of her persistent diary gestures, as is her effort to access "The Country *In* London." In 1905, her Sunday, March 19 diary entry captures just such a moment: "I took Nessa on a yellow bus, branded with a red H, all the way to the top of the Steep Hampstead Rd. & and then on to the edge of the Heath, from which we looked miles into a land of green fields, blue distance, & cloudy trees. This did refresh our eyes; & birds sang here as in the country, & it was pitiable to have to turn our backs on such beauty; & descend again into the black pit of London—but we had to" (*PA* 254).

More than two years later, a similar need for country refreshment, for the bird to sing, recurs. That weekend, Virginia takes out all of her books, "French and Latin and English and Greek," she writes to Dickinson on Sunday, July 7: "I read on and on, and never was so happy in my life—a little beast in a green forest, with all its fruit and nuts. But this morning I knew I must see Life; so I went in the Tube to Golders Green, and walked through some dusty fields to Hampstead" (*L* #369, 1: 298).

Her single "Golders Green and Hampstead" diary entry records her struggle to find genuine "country in London" in 1907. Like her 1903 diary's "Water Meadows" essay-entry, this 1907 entry foregrounds barriers and gatekeepers and functions as a cautionary tale. Virginia abandons the houses and pavements of London and arrives at Golders Green seeking the "soft green fields" (*PA* 365). "But no real country road . . . is raked so persistently by huge barrelled motor cars," she laments, "nor do strings & knots & couples of brightly dressed people fill all the way, so that you must steer to get past them" (*PA* 365–66). She spots fields on either side of this populous road, "though one had to violate some instinct which held them forbidden before one crept under the paling. It seems so natural that all open spaces should be hedged off, or only available on payment; & half the people I think kept to the road in obedience to this traditional belief" (*PA* 366).

This "Golders Green and Hampstead" entry marks Woolf's recognition of the power of "traditional beliefs," but also her rejection of them. "My way was across a field of long grass towards a slight mound," she declares. "—O if I could but use the real country names!" (*PA* 366). She defies hedge and fences and in the field finds "occasional tracks, like those a ship leaves on the sea, to show that bold travellers had gone before" (*PA* 366). Such a bold traveler she wishes to be. However, the social beat is clamorous. "But while I heard the throb of brass I could not count myself free," she confesses. "A line of moving heads at a little distance showed me that there was, as I expected, a regular channel up to Hampstead, along which one might legitimately walk" (*PA* 366). However, she refuses the "legitimate" path and positions herself instead "where the bushes shut out all sights except the fields, & there eat my luncheon" (*PA* 366). Afterward, she finds herself "gravitating, half sulkily, towards that cut in the land where I should find a real road, & people" (*PA* 366).

Significantly, she does not seek to understand her actions. "What motive it was, I will not determine," she observes (*PA* 366). The "real road" had been "but a short time before, a foot path; & the glamour of the afternoon to me was caused by the fact that it led us past a real country farm, with a yard & a dog; I looked in at the window & saw the family at dinner, & there was a stuffed jay in a case" (*PA* 366). She finds her country-in-London once more.

Although she does not stop to analyze her need for the country in this entry, the fact that she thinks this afternoon worth recording—not just in a letter but in her travel diary as well—suggests its subconscious import. "Last Sunday . . . I made an expedition which seems to me to deserve commemoration," she begins this suggestive entry.[12]

The "real country" in London, hard-won in July 1907, serves as prologue to the important Sussex diary that follows in August and September. On August 8, 1907, Virginia and Adrian rent a cottage for their summer holiday in Playden, a village a mile north of Rye in Sussex. Eleven entries preserve this fifty-day country sojourn: the opening entry titled "Playden," three entries marked by dates ("22 August," "3 September," and "19 September"), and the remaining seven undated and untitled as in the Blo' Norton, Giggleswick, and Cornwall diaries.

Mitchell Leaska believes "[s]omething new" appears in Woolf's diary style with her fall 1906 travel to Greece and Turkey (*PA* xxiii). I hope I have shown that *each* of her early diaries attempts something new: the 1899 diary that tests pens, inks, calligraphy, poetic tropes, and narrative forms; the 1903 diary comprised of thirty titled essay-entries; the daily diary of a fledgling professional writer in 1904–5, followed by the ghostly, inward-turning Cornwall diary of autumn 1905; and now the two travel diaries from 1906 to 1909. Leaska suggests Woolf's diary becomes more suggestive and resonant in the fall of 1906, that she "began to pause longer over what she saw, catching the smallest details of people, places, manners and morals" (*PA* xxiii).

It seems to me that something new evolves from the ghostly Cornwall diary of late summer 1905 that gathers force across 1906 and unfurls in the 1907 Playden diary. A growing sense of the *unconscious,* and trust in it, shows. Greater intellectual depth seems to be sought as well. The opening Playden entry reprises the opening of the Blo' Norton summer holiday diary the year before in which Woolf moves from first impressions to those that emerge when "one begins to reason or to know" (*PA* 310). In 1907, she probes the steps of this process even further. "It would need a great deal of time to begin with—then knowledge—then insight—then language to write here of Rye in such a way as to do it justice," she begins the Playden diary, acknowledging the difficulties before her (*PA* 367). Right language ranks for her highest. "[B]etter than all insight & knowledge, final & supreme fruit of it," she declares, "is one single sentence, six words long maybe; & that if you have not this forming at the top of your pen you had better write sedately of other things; accumulating touches" (*PA* 367). She seems to accept here an indirect, accumulative approach to truth (and life)—a good description of a diary. She has come to the country, she continues, "to see the land that has kept its own counsel, obeyed its own will, since the day it carved itself thus, before any gave it name or likeness" (*PA* 368). This is her own artistic goal: to carve her own path and to obey her own will.

Curiosity begins to form in the 1906 and 1907 diaries, and it perhaps propels the dips into the unconscious and the intellectual probes. Woolf raises an occasional provocative question in her diaries before age twenty-four; however, starting with her Christmas 1906 diary entry, questions press her mind and lead to diary expansion.[13] Merely writing the words "The New Forest   Christmas" as the heading for her 1906 entry spurs multiple questions and a speculative train of thought. "Just now as I wrote these words & saw them dry in juxtaposition it struck me that perhaps their alliance was natural & not accidental," she observes. "For why does the forest always disappoint me? & why does Christmas disappoint me too? Is it not that they both promise something glittering & ruddy & cheerful, & when you have it you find it not quite as good as you expected?" (*PA* 363).

Eight months later, in her unmarked fourth Playden entry, multiple questions recur as her scene-making gift blooms. We see her enter imaginatively into another's life: that of a small boy carrying beer to the harvesters.[14] In the passage below, she springboards from their talk to imagine his whole future life. She addresses him, enters his mind, and speaks in his voice:

> He could not measure distances, nor did his mind seem able to get beyond the shadow of the hall. This year he will not pick hops, which is sleepy work; he will, so soon as the harvest is in, undertake a job in Bexhill; since he has left school.
>
> The nut trees promise to bear well; as do the blackberries. "Look at them filberts." He was agile in mind & body; swift to see all things in hedges, reading signs all the way, invisible to us; brown quick little animal; & you shall become an airdrugged old labourer, with a crick in your back, living to be 80, & picking up in that time only a few habits of birds in this part of Sussex, some knowledge of the signs of the weather, & an animal kinship with the people in your village; perhaps at moments you will have a queer sense that this isn't all, & that you have had scarcely your rights here. But there will always be beer, & the knowledge that your fathers lived this life for centuries, & found it good enough. After all, one might fare worse; Uncle Bill, for example, went to sea, & never came back again. Ah they do say that there's fine things overseas; but I guess a man may bide here. "Tidy bit" was his word;
>
> Then there were great horses, stamping up the hill with a waggon of brushwood; where did they cut it—what will be its use—? O the wish to know & to understand how this toil is organized, how the whole land yields it fruits punctually in the right places. A great imaginative feat it would be to understand the point of view of a Sussex labourer. (*PA* 370–71)

She has, of course, just attempted this feat. And what intense curiosity about the world and its ways! And how rapidly she passes from outer to inner worlds and from herself to another. Note, too, the same rhythm of her questions: "where did they cut it—what will be its use—?"

The diarist projects herself imaginatively into places as well as into people. Her second Playden entry, dated "22 August 1907," reveals not only that she thinks her diary an ongoing text but also that she rereads this accruing work. We find here the first expression of another diary motif. "Perhaps some day it may be amusing to read here the name Peasmarsh," she muses regarding a "little snails shell" of a cottage three miles north of Rye she thinks to buy (*PA* 368). She imagines living there, and her description suggests it represents for her yet another "country-in-London": "Still it would be pleasant—how pleasant I can still imagine—to think of it in certain London days, when all the world seems made of brick; to know that it lies moored there, ready for us to embark upon" (*PA* 368). The Peasmarsh cottage becomes a ship, an artist's ship—and an escape. The scene then materializes, and it is an erotic one:

I think especially of walking up at night, from Rye, all the vague scents & coolnesses of a country evening washing over one's body, though things can scarcely be seen in that light: how it will slowly go out; and only lamps will be seen: at last "our lamp"; & I shall tramp up the flagged path; and see my chair ready, the table spread, some garrulous old woman, carpenters wife or such like, will attend & tell me the news of the village—how there has been a sale, & someone has had a baby; & the postman is dead. She will apologize for her cooking, but hope I have everything I want; & leave me, lighting her lantern "O I can find my way Miss, & the Moon's getting up."[15]

Surely it is significant that five of the eleven 1907 Playden entries—the second, third, fifth, sixth, and ninth—describe such "walks by night," the title of her polished and published 1905 Cornwall diary entry that embraces the nighttime consciousness, the unconscious. Two Playden entries especially recall that key Cornwall entry and its published expansion. Her entry three record of a walk at night *into* Rye and home again depicts "our frail little house" (*PA* 369). This recalls the "lighted windows, scarcely able to irradiate a yard of the blackness that pressed on them" in Cornwall (*PA* 298). Two entries later, an evening walk to Winchelsea, the companion town to Rye, concludes: "The road is but a blurred grey vapour. . . . The light of a carriage lamp cast on the hedge has the effect of some spectral shrouded figure, just about to taper into a point & disappear. Happy ecstasies float the mind out into the vague; spur it & seek not to recall it" (*PA* 372).

What causes "the scene making" gift (as Woolf will call it) to burst forth in the Playden diary? Curiosity and questions accompany and, perhaps, evoke the scenes, as can be seen in the untitled ninth entry re-creation of a sunset at Rye. Woolf first describes the moment, then poses questions: "a breeze drives the old creatures who are drinking their last dose of sunlight, to shelter. Will they have a lamp, & read some pious gross old book? or the letter from some daughter in service?" (PA 374). Questions shape her imaginative entry into others' lives. One or all of the following may explain the flowering at Playden of these expansive diary traits: the evocative Sussex landscape; her many encounters with Henry James at Rye across the fifty days (never, interestingly, acknowledged in the diary)[16]; her growing interest in Clive Bell, who will become a valued literary confidant in the coming months; or simply the natural growth of a writer constantly practicing her art. That the Playden holiday proves productive can be gauged from Virginia's Sunday, September 22 letter to Violet Dickinson. "We go back on Thursday," she writes, "and I want to write for six months unceasingly—about the pace I go now—ink pots drying beneath me—paper withering, as beneath the blast of some Tropic wind" (L #383, 1: 311).

William Allingham's *Diary*

Did Virginia Stephen continue this firestorm of prose? That could explain the lack of diary of any kind across the next ten months, until her solitary August 1908 holiday in Wells, Somerset, and Manorbier, Wales. Although she keeps no diary herself during this time, she reads diaries of others and writes reviews of them. She celebrates *William Allingham: A Diary* in the December 19, 1907, *Times Literary Supplement*—and why wouldn't she praise it? Like William Cory's diary, which she read at age fifteen, Allingham's *Diary* conveys the life of a Victorian poet who knew her family.

Twenty-five-year-old Virginia might have found much to identify with in Allingham's *Diary*. The poet lost his mother even earlier than she—when he was only nine—and his words of tribute might have struck a chord. "I dimly recollect my mother as thin, pale, delicate, gentle in voice and movement," he wrote. "She was kind, sweet, and friendly, and a great favourite with all who knew her; but her ill-health and early death left us, alas! to learn these her merits by hearsay and to love her shadowy memory when the mild presence had vanished for ever" (8). An aspiring writer, Allingham was sickly in his youth and kept from university study. Virginia might have admired his dogged drive to teach himself Greek, Latin, and history at ages twenty-six to twenty-nine. Was she not doing the same? She may also have admired his enterprise at age thirty in moving from his native Ireland to London to embark on a literary life and "to make what use I can of the means afforded me by London to compensate for the defectiveness of my education" (70).

Although he lives in London at regular intervals across the years, Allingham also savors nature and his country walks. He publishes a series of *Rambles* under the pen name Patricius Walker. However, like Virginia, he relishes society too. "Has anybody walked habitually alone as much as I?" he asks in an 1865 entry when he is forty-one (and unmarried). "Many, doubtless,—but none that I know. And who fonder of genial company?" (124). Water draws the poet as well, and he writes of it in ways that may have stayed with Woolf: "In some moods it sounded like ever-flowing Time itself made audible" (18). In her review of Allingham's *Diary*, Woolf highlights the exchange Allingham preserves between himself and Alfred Lord Tennyson: "They came to a 'large tangled fig tree' . . . 'It's like a breaking wave,' says I. 'Not in the least,' says he. Then, as his thought swept round, 'Man is so small! But a fly on the wheel'" (*E* 1: 155).

While parallels in life and thought may have touched Woolf, a further pull lay in the glimpses Allingham offers her of Tennyson, William Thackeray, Julia Cameron, Ellen Terry, G. F. Watts, and the Isle of Wight in the 1860s. Diarist William Cory may have seen Tennyson across the room at an Apostles' dinner, but Allingham *participated* in and preserved in his *Diary* (often in play form) the lively Freshwater scene. In 1907, his diary confirmed Stephen family lore and made abundantly plain that Freshwater harbored rich material for art.

During his slow rise across the nineteenth century from bank clerk to customs agent to sub-editor and then editor of *Fraser's Magazine*, Allingham took a position in customs in Lymington, Hampshire, in 1863. This allowed him to make regular visits to Farringford, Tennyson's home on the Isle of Wight, which led to encounters with the Thackerays and Julia Cameron, Tennyson's neighbors. On July 29, 1865, while dining at the Sun Inn, Allingham spies a portrait of Ellen Terry on the wall. He identifies the actress to the landlady's daughter, who replies, "Yes, it's Mrs. Watts—she's staying here"—which surprises Allingham greatly. "It seems she used to put up here in old times, when playing at the Ryde Theatre," he notes, "and now, being married—and separated—she goes about by herself from place to place, and has come for a while to her friendly old quarters. She gave them this likeness on some former visit" (120).

His diary portrait of another great nineteenth-century woman artist, Woolf's great aunt, the pioneer photographer Julia Margaret Cameron, is even more elaborate. It glows with humor and incident, Allingham noting her household's total disregard of time, her passion for photographing Mrs. Tennyson's maid as "Desdemona," and her donkey-chaise waiting in the moonlight (182, 186, 127). Yet Woolf likely also gleaned from Allingham's *Diary* a sense of the obstacles her predecessor battled. "[T]rain comes in with Mrs. Cameron, queenly in a carriage by herself surrounded by photographs," Allingham writes June 1, 1867: "We go to Lymington together, she talking all the time. 'I want to do a large photograph of Tennyson, and he objects! Says I make bags under his eyes—and Carlyle refuses to give me a sitting, he says it's a kind of *Inferno*! The *greatest* men of the age (with strong emphasis), Sir John Herschel, Henry Taylor, Watts, say I have *immortalised* them—and these other men object!! What is one to do—Hm?' This is a kind of interrogative interjection she often uses, but seldom waits for a reply. I saw her off in the Steamer, talking to the last" (152–53). Carlyle later relents. However, perhaps he lamented the effects of Cameron's art as did Tennyson, who exclaimed: "They charge me double! and I can't be anonymous (turning to Mrs. Cameron) by reason of your confounded photographs" (185).

Three months later, Allingham receives "several pressing notes from Mrs. Cameron to come and bring D[ante]. G[abriel]. R[ossetti] to her—'photograph you both.' I ask him will he come to-day. Decidedly, 'No!'" (161). The next day Allingham coaxes Rossetti only as far as the Lymington pier (161). Beyond sitter reluctance, technical challenges further thwart Cameron's art. In 1865, Allingham arrives at Tennyson's retreat to find "people in the hay-field and Mrs. Cameron photographing everybody like mad. . . . Mrs. Cameron focuses me, but it proves a failure and I decline further operations. She thinks it a great honour to be done by her" (117).

If his diary snapshots of her great aunt proved lively, imagine Woolf's response in 1907 when her father enters the frame courting Thackeray's younger daughter "Minnie." "Enter Mr. Leslie Stephen, tall and pale," pronounces Allingham in an entry a year after they wed (171). He notes, too, Carlyle's sneer at Leslie Stephen's work. In November 1873, Allingham tells Carlyle that Stephen is writing on Jonathan Edwards: "C[arlyle]: What is the use of it?—sticking like a wood-louse to the old bed-post and boring one more hole in it" (228). The *Diary* also supplied Woolf with this heartbreaking glimpse of her father on December 1, 1875: "Carlyle and I walk in the snow and dusk in Cromwell Road. We meet Leslie Stephen, whose wife died on Sunday; he turns and shakes hands, but does not speak. Carlyle says 'I am very sorry for you, sir. My own loss did not come in so grievous a way.' S. departs without a word" (241). When readers complain of reticence in Woolf's diary, perhaps they need look no further than her father's silence in crisis and to Walter Scott's stoicism as well.

As the above passages hint, Allingham's diary held riches beyond mere family portraits. Even more than Cory's journal, his is a writer's diary. Allingham wrote a poem every evening for many years, and he had the poise as a young man to write to other poets. He corresponds with Ralph Waldo Emerson, who sends him gifts (152); in fact, Emerson recites Allingham's poem "Touchstone" in his funeral oration for John Brown (199).[17] Tennyson, of course, is Allingham's lodestar, but the likeable young Irishman also knows Charles Swinburne, Leigh Hunt, and the Shelley and Rossetti families and meets and mingles with almost every other literary figure of note. He meets and corresponds with Nathaniel Hawthorne, knows Henry James and Woolf's godfather, James Russell Lowell, and preserves in his 1851 diary the night Tennyson listens "attentively" as he recites Edgar Allan Poe's "Raven" (62).[18] The diarist meets the Russian writer Ivan Turgenev at Carlyle's home and entertains George du Maurier in his own. He first meets Jane Carlyle and Charles Dickens at an 1850 Thackeray lecture. Dickens, he finds, lives only two streets from him in London. Later, Allingham attends a performance in which Dickens plays Mrs. Gump in a brown bonnet and corkscrew curls. The diarist encounters Anthony Trollope with Julia Cameron on the Yarmouth steamer, and when he meets Arthur Sullivan, he beguiles the composer with the origins of the Sullivan name. All of this deftly recorded in the *Diary*.

When Allingham visits Charles Darwin in 1868, he pens a provocative diary note on illness that Virginia may have absorbed, for she repeats the idea in her 1926 essay "On Being Ill." "Upstairs Mrs. Darwin, Miss D. and Mr. Charles Darwin himself,—tall, yellow, sickly, very quiet," Allingham records. "He has his meals at his own times, sees people or not as he chooses, has invalid's privileges in full, a great help to a studious man" (184). Similarly, Allingham's scenes with George Eliot, and particularly her remarks on death, may have lingered: "George Eliot said, 'I used to try to imagine myself dying—how I should feel when dying, but of course I could not'" (313). Woolf makes this imaginative feat in her 1940 diary.

In her 1907 review of *William Allingham: A Diary*, Woolf calls his diary "true in the best sense of the word" (*E* 1: 156). Surely she relished his portrait of Thomas Carlyle as much as that of Julia Cameron. Allingham reports that Carlyle's niece, Mary Carlyle, tells her uncle, "People say Mr. Allingham is to be your Boswell," and he replied, "Well, let him try it. He's very accurate" (202). Allingham seems to spend more time with Carlyle than even with his beloved

Tennyson, dodging carriages on walks with the Scotsman, who carries his stick "so as to poke it into a horse's nose at need" (208). The diarist accompanies Carlyle to haircuts and keeps a lock of his hair. On February 5, 1881, Mary Carlyle writes Allingham that the great writer's end is near. Allingham sits awhile with the corpse, and his wife, the watercolor painter Helen Paterson, makes two pencil sketches, but then the street bell rings bringing a messenger from Queen Victoria—probably John Brown, Allingham thinks—inquiring after the great man's health.[19]

As noted earlier, Carlyle may have first directed Woolf to the lines from Shakespeare's *Cymbeline* she would recall across her days and deploy in *Mrs. Dalloway*. She may have read the line "Fear no more the heat o' the sun" in Carlyle's own hand during her visit at fifteen to his Chelsea home. If she did not see that document then, we can date the influence of these words to 1907 and Allingham's *Diary*. On September 22, 1872, Allingham records this resonant scene: "go to Cheyne Row at 3, and find C[arlyle].—friendly. We walk to Kensington Gardens—sunshiny but cold. . . . C. quotes Shakespeare's—

Fear no more the heat o' the sun,
Nor the furious winter's rages;
Thou thy worldly task hast done,
Home art gone, and ta'en thy wages;

'One of the prettiest things ever written—that [says Carlyle]. It is like the distant tinkle of evening bells. Much comes of the rhymes—rhymes are valuable sometimes, answering somehow to the melody within a man's thought and soul'" (210).

William Allingham: A Diary was a life diary rather than a travel diary. In truth, it is an instance of that diary hybrid, a *memoir-diary*, for Allingham meant to use his diary as the foundation for his memoirs, but died (like Woolf) before the memoir was done. In 1907 Woolf read an expurgated version of Allingham's diary edited by his wife, Helen, and Dollie Radford. Their cuts make it even more of a periodic diary than it actually was; however, it offered Woolf another illustration (along with Fanny Burney's diary) that a periodic diary could well convey a life and world.[20] Allingham possessed a Boswellian and Burneyan eye for detail and the gift for preserving talk. He also uses initials in his diary, as does Virginia and several other diarists she has read.

When Allingham becomes ill, he writes at the end of his life, "I have no wish to keep the diary of an invalid" (383). When he starts to neglect his diary in the final six years of his life, he writes interestingly: "Have neglected my diary again for many weeks. See no particular good in keeping it up, yet feel uneasy when I don't" (369). Among his memoranda, he leaves this tribute to his diary: "I care for my old diaries for the sake of the Past, the sad, sacred, happy Past, whose pains, fears, sorrows, have put on the calm of eternity,—mysterious Past, for ever gone, for ever real, whose footsteps I see on every page, invisible to other eyes!" (387).

In 1904 William Butler Yeats wrote to Allingham's wife: "I am sometimes inclined to believe that [Allingham] was my own master in Irish verse, starting me in the way I have gone whether for good or evil" (Warner 9). In 1975, biographer Alan Warner called Allingham's diary his "most important prose work": "Had he never written a line of poetry, the diary would still entitle him to a modest place in the annals of literature" (66, 74). Twenty-five-year-old Virginia Stephen clearly valued Allingham's diary in her 1907 review. "Are we on the whole to regret the fortune that left William Allingham's autobiography unfinished, and gave us the chance of reading his diaries and notebooks unprepared as he wrote them?" she asks. "How often, in the future, biographers will come here," she later exclaims, "who want to know exactly what Carlyle said of Browning, or how it was that he disposed of his old pipes!" (E 1: 154, 156).

Lady Dorothy Nevill's *Note-books*

A rarer diary hybrid next crosses Virginia Stephen's view: the *scrapbook-memoir. Leaves from the Note-books of Lady Dorothy Nevill* appeared in 1907 on the heels of Lady Nevill's successful first volume of memoirs, *The Reminiscences of Lady Dorothy Nevill.* Woolf reviewed both works in the April 1908 *Cornhill Magazine.* The daughter of the third Earl of Orford and a descendant of the Walpoles, Lady Nevill lived from 1826 to 1913 and kept notebooks and scrapbooks across the decades. *Leaves from the Note-books* offers several charming glimpses of painter G. F. Watts—further *Freshwater* fodder. They also report soon-to-be-read diarist Lady Elizabeth Holland's marital scandal (embellished by Byron's verse) and retail a fine mot involving Dr. Burney and Lord Nelson's nightcap: "Dr. Burney, whilst staying with Nelson at Merton, discovered that he had omitted to bring any nightcaps with him, and so borrowed one from the great admiral. . . . [T]he cap somehow caught fire in a candle, the end portion of it being consumed, upon which Dr. Burney wrote out the following lines, which he sent with the remains of the cap to his host . . . 'Take your nightcap again, my good lord, I desire, / I would not detain it a minute; / What belongs to a Nelson, where'er there's a fire, / Is sure to be instantly in it'" (269–70).

Lady Nevill grew up in Norfolk, the heath and fen country of Virginia's evocative 1906 Blo' Norton diary, and this may have quickened her interest in the *Note-books*. Wolterton Hall, the Walpole country seat, was Lady Dorothy's Norfolk home. She mentions Thetford in her *Leaves* and gives Woolf a portrait of an actual nineteenth-century Norfolk woman.[21]

Leaves from the Note-books makes no attempt to reproduce Lady Nevill's actual notebooks; rather, items in her scrapbooks and notebooks launch her memories of her life and times. "It has always been a passion with me to collect odds and ends of every sort and put them into scrap-books and note-books," she begins her volume, revealing she is not a life diarist in the usual sense. "Consequently I now have many volumes filled with odd squibs, cuttings, photographs, scraps of verse, menus of banquets, and other trifles which, together with notes scribbled at the side, recall many pleasant and amusing days now long vanished into the past." Later she observes that "Anything which recalls the past becomes of interest as time goes on, and some of the mementoes of other days which I have carefully preserved bring vividly back to one's mind scenes now almost historical, as well as the people who figured in them" (9).

Leaves may have shown Woolf the merit of scrapbooks. She begins scrapbooks of her own in 1929 or early 1930 with clippings that date from 1927 (Pawlowski 304). Like Lady Nevill's "notes scribbled at the side," Woolf types reading notes on cards or ruled paper which she pastes or attaches with gummed labels alongside her scrapbook items.[22] As Lady Nevill foresaw, *Leaves from the Note-books* grows in value as the decades pass, for she recalls deer hunts in Hyde Park and the era of running footmen. She notes when certain customs ended—wigs, nightcaps, dueling, hanging criminals in chains, the May fair at Mayfair—and describes the advent of trains in Norfolk and a London of old lampposts, barrel organs, and Punch and Judy shows.

Beyond showcasing rather impressively the worth of scrapbook-keeping, Lady Nevill's *Note-books* also supply an early model for "Miss Ormerod," the dedicated entomologist of Woolf's 1924 *Dial* article incorporated into "Lives of the Obscure" in the 1925 *Common Reader*. With her marriage, Lady Nevill moves to an estate near Tennyson in Sussex and begins an extensive garden. "In my greenhouses I had at one time a large collection of insectivorous plants, specimens of which I used occasionally to send to Mr. Darwin, who carried on a correspondence with me about these curious things, in which he was very much interested," she confides in *Leaves*. "[H]e told me a great deal about the digestive powers of the secretion of the *drosera* or sun-dew, which, as he had actually proved by experiment, acted upon albuminous compounds in exactly the same manner as does the gastric juice of mammals" (239). How like this all sounds to Miss Ormerod's Hessian Fly and Paris Green!

Lady Nevill also breeds silkworms. Her amusing tale of her efforts (and her failures) may have been the inspiration for Cassandra Otway's similar eccentric practice in Woolf's 1919 novel *Night and Day*.[23] Even more noticeably, Lady Nevill anticipates *Night and Day*'s Mrs. Hilbery as a grand dame of the Victorian Age lamenting the Edwardians' decline. "People of original character and brilliant intellect were undoubtedly more frequently to be met with some thirty or forty years ago than is now the case, when almost every one seems to be cast in a mould of a more or less mediocre kind," Lady Nevill declares in *Leaves* (14). Woolf quotes these further lines in her 1908 review: "Society in old days cannot in any way be compared with the motley crowd which calls itself society to-day. . . . The general level of conversation in the so-called society of modern days must, of necessity, be low, for society, or what passes for it, is now very large, whilst wealth is more welcome than intellect. Good conversation, therefore, is practically non-existent" (22, 26; *E* 1: 179–80). Biographer Hermione Lee calls writer Anny Thackeray Woolf's model for Mrs. Hilbery (76–78); however, Lady Nevill surely contributed too.

Lady Charlotte Bury's *Diary of a Lady-in-Waiting*

"I have got 2 huge volumes of Ly Bury's Diaries to read and write about," Virginia Stephen crows to Violet Dickinson in July 1908—three months after her review of Lady Nevill's *Note-books* appears (*L* #422, 1: 337). This work further showcased the protean diary form. The volumes' full title was *The Diary of a Lady-in-Waiting: Being the Diary Illustrative of the Times of George the Fourth interspersed with Original Letters from the Late Queen Caroline and from other Distinguished Persons.* Here, then, was not a memoir-diary combination (like William Allingham's) or a notebook/scrapbook-memoir (like Lady Dorothy Nevill's) but a diary interlaced with letters.

Furthermore, like James Boswell's *Journal of a Tour to the Hebrides with Samuel Johnson*, Lady Bury's was a designedly public diary (as published) and a diary focused not so much on the *diarist's* life (the practice of most diarists) as on a famous person, here the ill-treated Princess Caroline of Wales who became (briefly) Queen Caroline. Lady Bury's *Diary* created *un succès de scandale* and enjoyed a huge sale when published (anonymously) in 1838—Queen Caroline and King George IV both conveniently dead. Woolf reviewed a new edition of this clever text edited in 1908 by A. Francis Steuart. Steuart fills in some of the names tantalizingly offered as initials in 1838—but not enough for most twentieth or twenty-first century readers.

Nevertheless, much in the *Diary of a Lady-in-Waiting* might have engaged Woolf. Handsome Lady Charlotte, the scribbling daughter of the fifth Duke of Argyll, lost her mother when only fifteen, and, like Woolf, dealt with bouts of depression across her days. In May 1812, for instance, Lady Charlotte writes, "To-day, I experienced the most gloomy melancholy I ever felt, without at *the time* having a cause for so doing."[24] In February 1815 she confesses to being "weary of myself and of all the world," and in late March, she further alarms when she reports that "This last week, one of my overcoming periods of returning sadness stopped my pen" (1: 310, 341).

Lady Charlotte knows Woolf's diary father, Sir Walter Scott. Woolf notes in her review that at age twenty-one, following her 1796 marriage to her kinsman, "handsome Jack Campbell," Lady Charlotte was "queen of the [Edinburgh] literary society . . . scribbling her own verses, and receiving the compliments of Walter Scott" (*E* 1: 195). The *Diary of a Lady-in-Waiting* refers often to Scott and his works, as well as to Madame de Staël, whom Lady Charlotte also admires.

Lady Charlotte meets other famous writers as well. In June 1814, she dines with the Princess of Wales and "the two Doctors Burney"; the *Diary*, in fact, includes a letter from Princess Caroline impugning Fanny Burney's English— the German princess was hardly one to talk—and authorship of *Evelina*.[25] The Princess entertains Lord Byron and the golden-haired Lady Oxford. Lady Charlotte befriends Caroline Lamb and paints diary portraits of her and of Adam Smith. In her 1908 review, Woolf quotes Lady Charlotte's astute first impression of "'another eccentric little artist, by name Blake,' who talked to her about his painting, and seemed to her full of imagination and genius" (*E* 1: 198). The *Diary* refers, too, to three women whose diaries (or lives) Virginia soon will read: Lady Elizabeth Holland, Lady Hester Stanhope, and Miss Mary Berry. Thus *this* diary primes Woolf for others.

"Handsome Jack Campbell" dies in 1809, leaving Lady Charlotte at age thirty-four a widow with nine children. She married for love rather than for wealth. Her uneasy financial state leads her to accept Princess Caroline's 1810 invitation to serve as one of her ladies in waiting, "[t]he natural profession, for a women with her connexions," Woolf explains in her review (*E* 1: 195). Lady Charlotte also sympathized with, and showed social courage in associating with, the much-maligned Princess who was, at that time, separated from the Prince of Wales and estranged from the Royal Family.

Lady Charlotte's views of marriage might particularly have interested Virginia Stephen in July 1908. "[N]ot all [Lady——'s] eloquence could convince me that I was wrong in preferring a state of single blessedness," the Scotswoman confides to her 1816 diary when she is forty-one: "A happy marriage I should think the height of human felicity; but I fear there are few which are truly such. On the other hand, an unhappy marriage must be the extremity of misery, and even a poor old maid must be happy in comparison, and a rich old maid in the third heaven of delight. But riches I think are more necessary for that state of solitude than any other" (2: 101). Yet a mere eleven months later, Lady Charlotte—perhaps beleaguered—also declares: "Every woman should make it her business, as a duty she owes herself, to find a husband; for no other interest in life is ever stable, abiding, or sufficient to the happiness of a woman" (2: 144).

Lady Charlotte writes her first novel, *Self-Indulgence*, in 1812—probably also to pay the bills. She will pen thirteen more starting in 1822, but this comes after Queen Caroline's sudden death in 1821 and the end of the *Diary*. Lady Charlotte says nothing in the *Diary* of her first novel, perhaps because her focus is on the Princess of Wales.[26] Nevertheless, she clearly delights in literature and includes in her volume letters from her friend Susan Ferrier, the Scottish writer, and from other unidentified women writers expressing their uncertainties regarding women's literary pursuit. In 1817, for instance, Ferrier writes to Lady Charlotte: "With regard to my own performances, I must confess I have heard so much of the ways of booksellers and publishers lately, that I find a *nameless* author has no chance of making anything of the business, and am quite dispirited from continuing to finish my story, and very much doubt if it will see the light of day" (2: 177). The following 1820 letter from an unidentified woman reports the counsel of a Mr. Millar regarding publication:

When I spoke of Lady [——]'s name as being worth thousands in itself, he shook his head, and replied that it would indeed excite a *strong sensation*, and cause a temporary run upon the book; but that was not enough; unless it was likely to become a standard one it was impossible to give a large sum for it. With regard to Miss Edgeworth, Madame D'Arblay [Fanny Burney], and those heroines of romance, he said their publishers could venture to give them almost carte blanche, for their names were now so celebrated, and their fame so firmly established and so widely diffused, that before their books were printed there were thousands and thousands of copies bespoke, besides large orders for America and the

Continent.... In short, I got such a complete history of the uncertainty of authorship, that I have resolved never to make a trade of it. Walter Scott is flourishing like a palm tree. (2: 262)

Readers may wonder where Woolf came by her conviction that women (and women writers) were despised. One answer: from primary sources, including diaries. Among the ten letters from writer Monk Lewis in *The Diary of a Lady-in-Waiting* is this one exuding such excessive ire at women writers that one thinks of the threatened Professor von X in *A Room of One's Own*:

I wish [Susan Ferrier] would let such idle nonsense alone, for, . . . as a rule, I have an aversion, a pity and contempt, for all female scribblers. The needle, not the pen, is the instrument they should handle and the only one they ever use dexterously. I must except, however, their love-letters, which are sometimes full of pleasing conceits; but this is the only subject they should ever attempt to write about. Madame de Staël even I will not except from this general rule; she has done a plaguy deal of mischief, and no good, by meddling in literary matters, and I wish to heaven she would renounce pen, ink, and paper for evermore.... In a word, ... I hate a blue; give me a rose any day in preference, that is to say, a pretty woman to a learned one. What has made you inflict this long harangue upon me? you will exclaim, and I must beg your pardon for so doing; but the fact is, I am full of the subject, being at the present moment much enraged at Lady [————], for having come out in the shape of a novel; and now, hearing that Miss F is about to follow her bad example, I write in great perturbation of mind, and cannot think or speak of anything else. (2: 327–28)

The Diary of a Lady-in-Waiting was an engrossing, but also an unreliable, masking text when it appeared anonymously in 1838, and it continues maddeningly untrustworthy in the 1908 version Woolf reviewed. It exudes all the allures and snares of Anaïs Nin's twentieth-century diaries and a bit of their fictive nature as well. Beyond faulting the diary's tedious length and "insipid" travel observations, twenty-six-year-old Virginia Stephen paid no attention to matters of authorship, authenticity, and motive in her 1908 review. She works instead to re-create "the watery Georgian atmosphere" the *Diary* conveys (*E* 1: 195). Still a new professional writer, she seems content to retail the *Diary's* most colorful revelations: the Princess of Wales sticking pins, voodoo style, into tiny wax figures of the Prince of Wales, then roasting them in the fire; the Princess's horrid after-dinner singing ("squall—squall—squall," writes Lady Charlotte);

the Princess in her carriage which was "shaped like a sea-shell, lined with blue velvet and drawn by piebald ponies" (*E* 1: 197). The young reviewer skillfully captures the meat of the lengthy *Diary* text.

She also mentions in her review a name she will employ herself in her 1925 novel *Mrs. Dalloway*. "Brougham and Whitbread were always coming with documents for her to sign, and good advice for her to follow," Virginia writes (sardonically) of the court politicos who sought to smooth Princess Caroline's way in a court that scorned her—or at least, so they said (*E* 1: 196). Hugh Whitbread will be Woolf's political frog in *Mrs. Dalloway*. She meets Samuel Whitbread, the brewer and officious politician, in July 1908 in Lady Charlotte's *Diary*, and she will meet him again within six months in *The Journal of Elizabeth Lady Holland (1791–1811)*, again in 1912 as a "mischievous politician" in *The Diary of Frances Lady Shelley, 1818–1873* (1: 85), in 1916 in Mary Berry's diary, and in 1918 in Henry Crabb Robinson's ebullient diaries.

Soft-hearted Lady Charlotte wishes to think Whitbread "a most upright, kind-hearted man" (1: 234); however, Princess Caroline often thinks differently. In his sixteen appearances across Lady Charlotte's *Diary*, Whitbread acts most often to curtail Princess Caroline—both physically and financially. On May 31, 1813, for instance, Lady Charlotte writes that Whitbread has sent Princess Caroline a letter "begging that she would be very careful about *her dress,*—in short explaining that she ought to cover *her neck*" (1: 152). A year later to the day, when Queen Charlotte writes to Princess Caroline, "by desire of the Regent," to forbid her attendance at court, the Princess "then related what had been her answer, namely *a determination* to go; but Whitbread, without even reading her letter, insisted upon it, she was not to go; and, in the most peremptory manner, almost ordered the Princess to copy a letter *he* had written to the Queen, which was a submissive acquiescence *respecting the two drawing-rooms* immediately in question" (1: 200). Seventeen days later, when Whitbread advises the Princess not to force herself on the public or to seem to defy her husband, he says, "I trust, madam, you will believe me sincere, when I declare that no party interest whatever sways me in this or any other advice I have ever given your Royal Highness, nor ever shall, to the detriment of your interest." The Princess, Lady Charlotte reports, "bowed coldly in reply to this speech, and did *not* seem to believe Mr. Whitbread's sincerity" (1: 218).

On July 1, 1814, after the Prince Regent has persuaded Parliament to pay Princess Caroline's debts and increase her income to £50,000 a year, Whitbread urges the Princess to ask the House to reconsider and give her only £35,000 (1: 236). On *this* matter, Lady Charlotte sees more deeply: "The fact is, (and perhaps he hardly knows the fact himself, for we are all deceived by our passions,) that Mr. Whitbread does not like the Princess should make all the play herself; he likes the idea, that it is to him, and to the weight of his politics, she should owe whatever advantages she may reap from the present contest. . . . [H]e has the notion which all Englishmen, nay, perhaps men of all countries, entertain, namely, that *men* only can act on the public stage of life. He has imbibed this prejudice with the air he breathes; and one cannot blame him. If I were the Princess, however, I would show him the contrary" (1: 234).

In 1908, Virginia Stephen does not much admire Lady Charlotte as a writer or as a woman. "She was little more . . . than a correct and kindly woman, with a diffuse taste for sentiment of all kinds, whether in people, or art, or letters," Virginia writes in her review (*E* 1: 197). The *Diary* offers signs that Lady Charlotte knew her own failings. She admits to a "natural suavity [in] my manner and temper . . .—a suavity that I sometimes blame myself for, when it induces me to gloss over sentiments to which a more bold frame of mind would express its dislike or abhorrence" (1: 53). Nevertheless, her *Diary of a Lady-in-Waiting* continues the mural of Georgian court life begun in Fanny Burney's diary and reveals the trials of lady scribblers in the first decades of the nineteenth century. It gives Woolf a glimpse of a destructive letter-writing politician named Whitbread, and, battling him and the whole court, a courageous and defiant woman.[27] As Lady Charlotte writes at the beginning of her *Diary*, "The Princess of Wales . . . has a bold and independent mind, which is a principal ingredient in the formation of a great queen, or an illustrious woman" (1: 20).

Virginia Woolf's Great Britain Travel Diary Concluded

Virginia's Great Britain travel diary of 1906 to 1908 ends full circle with a holiday alone, but now in Wells, Somerset, and Manorbier, Wales. Male dismissal served as psychological backdrop for the single "New Forest   Christmas" 1906 and "Golders Green and Hampstead   July" 1907 diary entries, and similar turns from the male undergird the 1908 Wells and Manorbier pages. Four of the seven Great Britain travel diary locales preserve this determined move. In August 1908, Virginia's brother, Adrian, embarks with Saxon Sydney-Turner for the Wagner Festival in Bayreuth, Germany. Virginia likely could have joined them—she does so a year later; however, in 1908 she turns again from male voices and refuses to sit at a male composer's feet, preferring again her own solitary path and work.

Through the good offices of Violet Dickinson, whose grandfather had been

Bishop of Bath and Wells, she secures lodging at The Vicars' Close in Wells for herself and her dogs, Hans and Gurth. Built in the mid-fourteenth century for the College of Vicars Choral, the Close in 1908 housed theological students during the academic year (*PA* 376n2). Four diary entries preserve Virginia's two-week working holiday, the first labeled "Wells 1 to 14 August" and the remaining three undated and untitled.

Woolf's first entry reveals again that she rereads her previous diaries—and does so with a critical eye. "When I read this book, which I do sometimes on a hot Sunday evening in London," the Wells diary begins, "I am struck by the wildness of its statements—the carelessness of its descriptions—the repetition of its adjectives—& in short I pronounce it a very hasty work, but excuse myself by remembering in what circumstances it was written" (*PA* 375). Mitchell Leaska chose this entry as the epigraph for *A Passionate Apprentice*, his edition of Virginia's 1897 to 1909 diaries. Certainly it opens a window on her diary practice. "After a days outing, or when half an hour is vacant, or as a relief from some Greek tragedy—at different times, & in different moods it is written," she continues, "& I am certain that if I imposed any other conditions upon myself it would never be written at all. Did I not take it to Cornwall at Easter, & determine to note something serviceable—& did I even write my address? So once more I return to the old method; & protesting merely, that I am conscious of its faults—the protest of vanity" (*PA* 375–76).

This critique suggests she now brings her professional eye and the sensibility of a novelist to her diary. Placed beside the opening of her last (Playden) diary a year before—"It would need a great deal of time to begin with—then knowledge—then insight—then language to write here of Rye in such a way as to do it justice" (*PA* 367)—the Wells opening seems yet another version of an essential diary gesture, a kind of warm-up. By acknowledging her literary failings and the difficulty of her task, the writer lowers the psychological bar sufficiently to proceed.

As we saw in her Easter 1906 Giggleswick diary, confronted with Christianity, Woolf will usually transmute or retort. In her untitled and undated second Wells entry, she criticizes Christianity even more forthrightly than in 1906. Woolf describes her surroundings and suggests their resistance to change. "[W]hat breath can ever blow down these crooked alleys, all crusted with medieval stone," she complains; "a print of Wells in the 17th Century is precisely the same as a photograph of Wells in the 19th" (*PA* 376). That she feels embattled in the Vicars' Close in a town where "The Cathedral of course dominates the whole place" seems clear. "But if Christianity is ever tolerable," she allows, "it is tolerable in these old sanctuaries; partly because age has robbed it of its power, & you can fondle a senile old creature, when you must strike with all your force at [a] young & lusty parson" (*PA* 376).

This entry, as it continues, recalls as well the important Playden entry a year before in which Virginia's dismissal of conventional expedition narratives releases her scene-making gift. In 1908 in Wells, Woolf turns from Christianity to what truly grips her. "When I came here first, in the evening, I was delighted by the little wave like hills which seemed to form all round me," she writes (*PA* 376). These vacant hills lead to an extended portrait of a Somerset workingwoman, Mrs. Wall, to place beside the 1907 vision of the Sussex boy laborer. Woolf follows her first impression of Mrs. Wall with deeper vision. As with the Sussex boy, she moves from the woman's appearance and conversation to enter imaginatively into her past and her future:

> When I first saw her, wavering about in the passage with clasped hands & bent shoulders, ready to welcome me, but keeping her distance, I said This is exactly what I had imagined of Mrs. Wall. She does not change, but it is a subtler study than I expected. She has had this house for 30 years, & the number of students she has had in her charge must be some hundreds. She speaks of them as "my gentlemen" or, when she warms, "my boys." "It hurts me when they go, as though I lost a child." She has been intimate with many, not a landlady, but a comfortable old gossip & confidante. It begins with care for their teas & dinners, & she keeps an eye on their punctuality, & would perhaps say something if they missed a lecture, or stayed too late in bed. She knows more than they do—who stay a year & pass on—of rules & characters, & must often put them up to useful information. They in their turn, ask after her rheumatics, & spoil her cat. So far as I know her, she is a woman of patient, deft & indefatigable industry. . . .
>
> Indeed, a woman of 75, who has had ten children, placed them & lost them, a widow, who for 30 years has paid her rent, & kept her house going, must have come by a certain insight & tact besides what we call commonly "knowledge of the world." I can imagine shrewd wisdom issuing from her lips, in no weak shape; & a distinct course taken deliberately, through difficult matters. (*PA* 377–78)

Fanny Burney's diary had offered a portrait of a Mrs. Wall, a woman "who makes it a rule never to look at a woman when she can see a man" (*Early Diary* 2: 183). Woolf here depicts a more admirable Mrs. Wall; in fact, those who criticize Woolf's class snobbery should note this early tribute to a working woman.

The diarist is forced from the Vicars' Close after a week, eviction she does not much regret. "The Close has filled itself with theological students, & I am not sorry to leave," begins her third (and next-to-last) Wells entry. "[T]he cheery male voice is as the drone of bluebottles in my ear" (*PA* 378). She finds shelter for herself and her dogs for the remaining week at 5 Cathedral Green in a lodge run by Mrs. Dorothy Oram, the verger's wife. That the twenty-six-year-old continues to be leery of the droning "male voice" and acutely conscious of gender barriers is evident, for she offers the dry observation that "The Cathedral Green is rather spent by the time it reaches this far corner [number 5], & the grass, upon which you may not walk, elsewhere, seems here to lose its sacred character & to become a playground of the children of the neighboring houses" (*PA* 378–79).

The remainder of this entry focuses on the Oram family's two children and leads to questions about herself as a child and about "the nature of children" (*PA* 379). Vanessa is pregnant now with her first child, and this may have spurred Virginia's interest in children. Once more, description leads to questions—and to diary expansion: "They [the Oram children] play all day in front of me. Did I ever play all day when I was a child? I cant remember it. . . . Now, if they could think on waking, that today was to be like other days, & they would do no more than kick a ball, would they enjoy it? I believe not. The truth is, that each kick is an adventure, that may be entirely unlike anything else"(*PA* 379). Here again she writes with her mind as well as her eye.

Her second lodging, sadly, seems as unsuited for work as her first. "[I]t is very difficult to sit down after breakfast in a lodging parlour, opposite a portrait of Prince Albert," she writes Violet Dickinson August 9, "without a desk, or a table that stands, and conceive scenes in a novel" (*L* #430, 1: 346). The final Wells entry opens to reject the place: "This country has to my mind one fatal fault—no sea" (*PA* 379). She then offers again her aesthetic: "Yesterday however, did its best to shroud this fact; all the air was hung with tattered clouds—or watery drifts of air, not rounded into a form; the most beautiful sky there is, perhaps; it is always moving, always letting through different lights & shades . . ." (*PA* 379). *Formless* movement once more strikes her, revealing the shifting shades and lights.

Virginia declined male company to come alone to Wells, and, once there, she turns again from "the cheery male voice" and the dominating Christian scene. In fleeing to the sea at Manorbier, Wales for her final fifteen days of summer holiday, she rejects another male, Hilton Young, choosing again her own work.[28] As early as the third day of her two-week Wells holiday, Virginia was writing to Clive Bell, "I am tempted to rush up to Manorbier for 10 days after this in order to look at some waves and cliffs; I am almost drowned in earth and antiquity here" (*L* #426, 1: 340). In the next day's letter to Vanessa, we learn she persists for Manorbier despite an invitation that morning to another locale from Hilton Young, the twenty-nine-year-old assistant editor of *The Economist*, an invitation both sisters read as prelude to a marriage proposal. "This morning I had a letter from Hilton Young, sending me an address at a farm house, and asking when I should be in Marlborough, so that he might come and have tea with me," Virginia writes to Vanessa August 4. "I am rather pleased with the idea of Manorbier; so I shall tell H. Y. that I shant be at Marlborough. I shall write with friendliness—but I have no discretion—no kind of instinct in me, such as most women have, in affairs of sex" (*L* #427, 1: 341). She chooses Manorbier and her writing over another invitation as well: this one from Mary Sheepshanks, principal of Morley College, who asks her to a village in Devon to meet the Bertrand Russells, the Gilbert Murrays, Jane Harrison, and Francis Cornford. "Too much elderly brilliance for my taste," Virginia writes her sister on August 12. "However, I have no doubt I am missing lifelong friendships, and all for the sake of lonely walks along the sea shore, with an occasional leap over a fissure" (*L* #434, 1: 351).

That she grabs at the meager Manorbier digs available—ones lacking hot water for baths—suggests the pull of the place. Manorbier held sticky associations. The Stephen children and George Duckworth stayed in Manorbier for about a month in March 1904 after Leslie Stephen's death. In this sense, her return to Manorbier is a return to the father—or to mark a father's loss. Perhaps even more importantly, Virginia had suggested Manorbier to Clive Bell and Vanessa as the site for their honeymoon seventeen months before. In coming to Manorbier was she (subconsciously) seeking to retrace her sister's footsteps, to see what Clive and Vanessa saw, to appropriate Manorbier, in short, for herself? "Marlborough is impossible," she writes to Vanessa from Wells August 10, again referring to Hilton Young, "and I am taken with a passionate desire for Manorbier" (*L* #432, 1: 348).

"There is no doubt but that I was well advised in telling you to come here for your honeymoon," she begins a letter to Clive Bell on August 19, the third of fifteen Manorbier days: "I am surprised to find how beautiful it all is—more than I remembered—how lovely, and how primitive. . . . Ah, it is the sea that does it! perpetual movement, and a border of mystery, solving the limits of fields, and silencing their prose. . . . There was a day when I never talked of my writing to you. I have passed your house, and imagined numbers of things. There is a certain road, with shadows across it, leading to the sea where Nessa and I walked, and she declared that Romance was not a thing of the past, as she had thought, but was going on all round us. . . . Next year we might come here" (L #438, 1: 355–57).

Virginia pens only one diary entry across her fifteen days in Wales, an entry evoking the country in language like that above. She finds Manorbier "as different a place from Wells as [she] could have chosen. It is a lean country, scarcely inhabited, & the one church which does duty for many miles, is a threadbare place" (PA 380). Her lodgings also please her: "a perfectly genuine cottage, inhabited by a stone mason & his wife. . . . Ah, the loneliness of these little distant places!" (PA 380). Once more lonely vacancy delights.

The spare 1908 Manorbier diary might serve as warning to Woolf diary readers of an error easily made. Faced with a single diary entry for fifteen days, readers might easily assume illness or depression and conjure visions of the twenty-six-year-old repining and distraught on the cliffs of South Wales. Nothing could be farther from the truth. As it happened she found an ideal place to write: a private room a short distance from her lodging "with a great bow window facing the sea," its gentlemanly owner opening his library to her just as her father had done (L #438, 1: 356). All evidence suggests that she neglects her diary at Manorbier because she is pouring herself into three other literary forms: her journalism; letters; and her novel-in-progress, "Melymbrosia [The Voyage Out]." "I think a great deal of my future," she writes to Clive Bell August 19, "and settle what book I am to write—how I shall re-form the novel and capture multitudes of things at present fugitive, enclose the whole, and shape infinite strange shapes" (L #438, 1: 356). She also tells Bell in this letter that she is "observing intensely" (356). On August 28, she offers a critique of Clive's letters that sheds light on her diary practice. Clive asks her if she likes his letters, and she responds seriously. "[T]he only view I will put forward is that you might put your style at the gallop rather more than you do," she suggests. "After all, the only way of expanding it is to try to grasp things that you dont quite grasp: and a slight tone of monotony, which I detect sometimes, seems to me to come from the fact that you are content to do things that you can do very well" (L #442, 1: 362).

The Great Britain travel diary of 1906 to 1908 registers huge strides in the writer's art. The dreaming fishermen at Thetford in 1906 and the many Sussex "walks by night" in 1907 show Woolf's further embrace of the unconscious begun in Cornwall in 1905—and with it, the first signs of spontaneous creation. With the plunge into the unconscious (as both reservoir and compositor) comes a parallel drive "to reason or to know." Curiosity enters the diary—multiple questions now with tentative answers—and propels the scene-making gift. That this crucial growth takes place in her *diary*, diary-writing integral to the work, is hinted in the 1906 "Journal of Mistress Joan Martyn," the story of a daughter, an aspiring bard, who surpasses her father and pens a diary that lasts across time. Each advance, furthermore, involves the land—and the land as woman—and the lonely vacancy of land and sea. If Virginia Stephen turned from London and male laughter in her pivotal 1903 diary, she repeats the move again and again across her Great Britain travel diary. The whole diary elides London—surely a step required.

6

The Problem of Description

The many paths to apt description occupy Virginia Woolf's mind across her seventh and eighth diary books. Her first task in her 1906 to 1909 Continental travel diary is to skirt the trap of guidebook prose during her trip to Greece and Turkey. In Constantinople she works hard to rid herself of Western notions of the East. Her problems intensify, however, with her 1908 and 1909 Italian travels. "I begin to distrust description," she writes in 1908 as she seeks to expand her diary (and other) art (PA 384). She wants to write now "not only with the eye, but with the mind; & discover real things beneath the show" (PA 384). In 1909 Florence she begins to seek less definition and more subtlety in her descriptions. She first fears "empty & ladylike writing" and then rejects it, choosing to be a blazing furnace instead (PA 395). In her newly found 1909 life diary, she tries out a new kind of description, one in which place and portrait join: décor disclosing character. We leave her in this 1909 diary pressing for finer and finer discriminations.

The diaries she reads from 1908 to 1910 become part of her steady march toward a view, voice, and form of her own. Of Lady Elizabeth Holland, whose *Journal* she reviews in 1908, Woolf exclaims admiringly: "But what numbers of likenesses she struck off, and with what assurance!" (E 1: 237). Lady Holland and Lady Hester Stanhope, whose exploits Woolf follows gleefully across six diary volumes, are women who boldly break conventions. In 1910 Woolf reads diary extracts of a more recent foremother, those in *Gathered Leaves from the Prose of Mary E. Coleridge*, Samuel Taylor Coleridge's great-great niece. Mary Coleridge forged the path Woolf is following in 1910. Coleridge writes in multiple forms, savors fantasy, relishes change, and deplores women's depiction in literature.

In contrast, in a 1910 review, Woolf defines herself *against* Ralph Waldo Emerson and *his* early journals. She rejects as "platitudes" the American's simple thoughts (each a match to a single idea in his mind), just as she rejected the simple static beauty of Perugino's fresco in Italy in 1908. She wants instead complexity, multiplicity, suggestive discords, and movement: the flight of the mind.

Virginia Woolf's 1906–1909 Continental Travel Diary

"And is it not to study sides of all things that we travel?"

(October 1906; PA 338)

The productive summer sojourn at Norfolk's Blo' Norton manor had barely ended in 1906 when Virginia departed in September with Vanessa and Violet Dickinson for nearly two months' travel in Greece and Turkey. Rather than record her Continental travels in her travel diary in progress, Virginia chose to begin a new diary book, one slightly longer and thinner than the Great Britain travel diary with cream unruled paper instead of white. Perhaps she wished a new book for her lengthy travel—or did she see her Continental forays as something apart? The latter gains weight from the fact that when she journeys to the New Forest at Christmas 1906, after her return from Greece and Turkey in November, she takes her brown-covered Great Britain travel diary from her shelf; she does not simply continue in her last diary, the Continental diary. Her seventh diary book, the Continental travel diary of 1906 to 1909, preserves her explorations of Greece and Constantinople in 1906 and her travels in Italy in 1908 and 1909.

⸙

The Greek tour begins auspiciously enough on Thoby Stephen's twenty-sixth birthday, September 8, 1906. Virginia has been studying Greek and the Greeks for almost a decade. Her eagerness for Greece can be gauged from the fact that she passes completely over her first six days of travel in France and Italy to begin the diary with their reunion with Thoby and Adrian in Olympia, Greece. In fact, her first diary *heading* exclaims "Olympia. September 14th!" Twenty-four entries convey her thirty-seven-day Greek holiday. The first seventeen entries are *titled*: fifteen with the names of *places* she visits (including four on the Acropolis) and two with *subject* headings ("Germans and Modern Athens" and "Modern Greeks"). The diary's final seven entries bear no dates or titles at all, a return to the unmarked form of the previous Blo' Norton, Giggleswick, and Cornwall diaries.

Woolf's drive to avoid guidebook prose becomes the recurring theme of the diary. In her second entry, titled "Olympia," she acknowledges that "[O]f Olympia it is difficult to write. Baedecker [*sic*] will count the statues; a dozen archaeologists will arrange them in a dozen different ways; but the final work must be done by each fresh mind that sees them" (*PA* 318–19). Writing, she implies here, consists of sight shaped by mind. "The pediments of the temple line the two sides of the museum; but we wont write guide book," she continues (*PA* 319). Olympic Stadium offers a similar snare. "The theatre is—once more we might quote the Guidebook," she acknowledges; "for our purposes it is simply a flat circle of grass, scattered with innumerable fragments of stone" (*PA* 319). In Athens, in entry thirteen, she resists both guidebook color and a man in Albanian dress to seek the *women* of Greece instead. She first describes the colorful Albanian male, but then writes: "But this you may see written in a dozen guide books. I have seen no native women who could be distinguished from an Italian woman; & indeed, you see very few women. The streets are crowded with men drinking & smoking in the open air, even, in the country, sleeping beneath the wall; but the women keep within" (*PA* 328). At "Mycenae," in her last titled entry, she describes her challenge most clearly: "I tremble to write of the classics, because that might savour of the perfunctory impulse of the guidebook; but the taste of Homer was in my mouth" (*PA* 331). She captures the thyme in the valley "kindled by the sun," and lets that suffice: "These lines hint, at least, that Mycenae leaves a great body of confused meaning in the mind; nor will it be possible to spin a coherent tale till I have made sure of the earth & the sky. And then guide books will do the rest" (*PA* 332, 333). The natural, rather than the man-made, remains her goal: nature ("the earth & the sky") before culture.

The twenty-four-year-old counters the guidebook lure with vigilance and patience. "There is so much to grasp in Athens that there is no need to attempt any single description," she tells herself in entry four. "By proceeding quietly looking here & there at leisure, a solid picture slowly composes itself" (*PA* 321). Her method mirrors the diary's cumulative tack. By entry sixteen she is declaring that Athens resembles St. Ives and the Greek countryside, Cornwall—a sign they suit her imagination (*PA* 330). When she travels to the coast, she finds it "very steep, & gray; like Cornish cliffs" and "all the more beautiful because it was so unknown" (338). In fact, she prefers this less celebrated landscape to Athens or Olympia. "Here flourished the unknown artists of the soil, working for the delight of their own peasants," she writes in her unmarked entry twenty (*PA* 338).

Illness enters the Greek diary only, ironically, to enrich it. Vanessa's appendicitis attack temporarily halts Virginia's sightseeing, allows her to pause and look about her lodgings and even to read. This brings welcome variety to the travel diary. In entry thirteen she had looked for "native women" (*PA* 328). She locates them in her unmarked twenty-first entry in a Greek mother and daughter staying at their hotel. She imagines the two might be in Athens "to buy clothes for the coming season; . . . may be little officials in Sparta or Nauplia" (*PA* 339). Marriage, she hints, may be their covert goal, for she describes the mother talking to a "young man from Patras" who makes the daughter smile (*PA* 339).

Marriage likely hovered in Virginia's mind this 1906 autumn, despite the sights Greece supplied. Vanessa had refused Clive Bell's first marriage proposal in August 1905, and in a letter to Violet Dickinson dated provisionally June 1906, Virginia pondered whether marriage might aid her own art. "Madge [Vaughan] tells me I have no heart—at least in my writing," she confesses to Dickinson: "really I begin to get alarmed. If marriage is necessary to one's style, I shall have to think about it. . . . 'The air is full of it [marriage],' says Madge: but I breathe something else" (*L* #273, 1: 228). Between this June letter and the autumn diary scenes in Athens, Virginia creates a foremother, the fictional diarist Joan Martyn, who prefers writing to marriage. Surely it is noteworthy that in the fall of 1906, the twenty-four-year-old finds few attractions in the Greek daughter; in fact, treats her with pity and scorn. The daughter plays the piano dreadfully after meals, and Woolf muses (with a whiff of superiority), "Perhaps she can't read literary Greek" (*PA* 339). In fact, she observes, "there is no reason to suppose that she can read, write or talk. And although much can be done without those accomplishments, still, if you meet her, sitting by herself in the drawing room, dull, vacant, pallid, & infinitely bored, you can even pity her" (*PA* 339). She pities the conventional daughter she chooses not to be.

A more accomplished woman supplants this Greek daughter who sadly lacks literary Greek. Tellingly, she is the "unknown woman" of Prosper Mérimée's *Lettres à une inconnue*. Virginia celebrates *this* woman and her unconventional relationship with a man in her next-to-last diary entry. She begins this twenty-third entry by confessing she prefers nonfiction to fiction in times of distress. The novels about her seem "too far & visionary" for the sickroom, "but Merimée [*sic*] was dealing with a real world in which people were ill & angry, where the rain was wet & the sun was hot, & it was rather agreeable to be told that such things went on outside the bedroom door just as usual" (*PA* 341).

Woolf did not know when she penned this entry that Mérimée's mysterious correspondent was Jeanne-Francoise Dacquin (1811–1895), the well-educated French woman who published verse and prose under a pen name across the thirty years of Mérimée's letters. However, Virginia sensed enough from the one-sided correspondence to suggest the woman possessed "a rare mind, & perhaps, a rare nature" (*PA* 342). In fact, she declares, "there is no question of a step down between [hers and Mérimée's] minds" (*PA* 342). Woolf spins out twenty-four paragraphs speculating on the correspondents' relationship. That the woman was "unknown," I believe, particularly invited her fancy.[1] Her speculative portrait of an unknown woman, a woman with "a rare mind, & perhaps, a rare nature," a woman who "could read Greek," is the longest entry in the entire Greek diary (*PA* 342, 343).

"[T]he Letters of Merimée [*sic*] to an unknown woman," she writes, is one of those books that "send an occasional thrill of oblivion down your spine, & let you dream that you are free to follow them whither they call" (*PA* 341). Six years before her marriage to Leonard Woolf—four years, in fact, before he even reenters her life—she imagines in this entry an unconventional love. "They were scarcely affectionate, very often," she writes of Mérimée and his "unknown lady": "the great bond lay perhaps—outside those many intellectual sympathies—in their common boredom & in their common candour. . . . [I]t must have been such an odd kind of concord; if you could hear these two voices speaking together it would not be a dulcet sound, or a loving sound, or a passionate sound that they would make in unison; but it would be something sharp & curious, something that would ring a new note in the ear, not to be forgotten" (*PA* 344, 342).

⌁

Constantinople and the Cathedral of St. Sophia become mysterious women in the ten entries that make up the Turkish diary that follows. Undated and untitled, these ten entries may have been penned on consecutive days, October 20 to 29, 1906—the time frame of the Turkish travel. Guidebook prose persists as a trap to be skirted. In her fourth entry Virginia declares, "As for those observations upon manners or politics with which all travelers should ballast their impressions, I confess I find myself somewhat out of pocket today. The truth is that travelers deal far too much in such commodities, & my efforts to rid myself of certain preconceptions have taken my attention from the actual facts" (*PA* 351).

The Turkish diary shows Woolf's drive to resist all preconceptions of the East, to view it fresh and whole. In this fourth entry she places her *own* experience against conventional western views of eastern women: "Were we not told for instance, that the female sex was held of such small account in Constantinople—or rather it was so strictly guarded—that a European lady walking unveiled might have her boldness rudely chastised? But the streets are full of single European ladies, who pass unmarked; & that veil which we heard so much of—because it was typical of a different stage of civilization & so on—is a very frail symbol. Many native women walk bare faced; & the veil when worn is worn casually, & cast aside if the wearer happens to be curious" (PA 351–52).

"And is it not to study sides of all things that we travel?" she had asked her Greek diary a few days before (PA 338). On her arrival in Constantinople, she refuses to view the country through a European lens. "[Y]ou felt yourself in a metropolis; a place where life was being lived successfully. And that did seem strange, &—if I have time to say so—a little uncomfortable," she acknowledges in her second entry. "For you also realized that life was not lived after the European pattern, . . . [Y]ou knew yourself to be the spectator of a vigorous drama, acting itself out with no thought or need of certain great countries yonder to the west" (PA 348). Woolf ends her fourth entry by insisting that "when we come to consider the question of the West & the East—then indeed—we lay down the pen, & write no more," and in her ninth and next-to-last entry, she declares: "Indeed the only remark I can make with any confidence is that no Christian, or even European, can hope to understand the Turkish point of view" (PA 352, 355).

When she tries to summarize and say goodbye in her tenth and final entry, she treats Turkey and Constantinople as another unknown woman. "[T]here is the puzzle of S. Sophia," she begins: "why is she the most cryptic church in Europe? Why does she grow more beautiful & more mysterious the better you know her—or the shell of her?" (PA 357). To answer her questions she addresses the Turk as a man but quickly transforms him to a woman (or an androgynous soul): "You must begin at the beginning & confess that the Turk himself is the riddle; a tough, labyrinthine riddle, by which wise heads—the Times newspaper even—are still constantly confounded. . . . Constantinople is a place of live nerves, & taut muscles; so we read directly we saw the town laid at our feet; but continuing the metaphor we also said that the eyes of this great giantess were veiled" (PA 357).

In light of her oft-expressed preference for bare and unmarked places, we should not be surprised that she discovers in Constantinople a mosque that appeals to her even more than St. Sophia. The "most beautiful mosque in Constantinople," she writes in entry five, "is none other than a vast empty drawing room; you might dance in silk here, or drink afternoon tea, or merely live a gentle life. . . . And the devotion seemed none the less sincere that it could stand the light of the day & the brilliance of silk & mosaic; nor did it seem in any way strange that men should say their prayer to rare carpets & painted tiles, without the figure of a saint or the symbol of a cross to inspire them" (*PA* 352–53).

Hermione Lee calls the Greek and Turkish diaries "carefully written . . . with essays in mind" (787n69). Joanne Campbell Tidwell, tracking Woolf's development of self, asserts that her "self is more and more confident. She has fully entered the Symbolic Order and become as comfortable in it as she ever will be" (22). I find her consciously seeking in her diary her own view, voice, and form.

Two years later, Virginia returns from another productive summer holiday— the fifteen days solitude in Manorbier, South Wales—to embark for Northern Italy with Vanessa and Clive Bell. Ten entries preserve the September 1908 visits to Milan, Siena, Perugia, and Assisi—all undated and untitled save entry nine (headed "Perugia"). She thus continues the unmarked form of her last Continental (1906 Turkish) diary and the final seven entries of the 1906 Greek diary.

The first entry discloses again that she rereads her diaries. Even more important is her wish now to expand her diary art. "There are many ways of writing such diaries as these," she begins: "I begin to distrust description, & even such humorous arrangement as makes a days adventure into a narrative; I should like to write not only with the eye, but with the mind; & discover real things beneath the show" (*PA* 384). She acknowledges, however, the challenge of this task—specifically, the limited time and energy she has for diary prose. Once more she lowers the bar so she can start. If she fails to write with the mind as well as eye, she tells herself, "& I shall neither have time nor perseverance for much thought, I know, I shall try to be an honest servant, gathering such matter as may serve a more skilled hand later—or suggest finished pictures to the eye" (*PA* 384). Here again the diary serves as reservoir and subconscious compositor. "The fact is, that in these private books, I use a kind of shorthand, & make little confessions," she continues, "as though I wished to propitiate my own eye, reading later. Besides I feel (at the moment) great distrust of my own words. Is it worth while to write? As I have had some amusement from reading about Greece, I may as well do what I can with Italy" (*PA* 384–85).

The 1908 Italian diary resembles the 1906 Greek diary in offering a mother-daughter hotel scene and continued contempt for conventional marriage. After dinner at Perugia's Brufani Palace Hotel, twenty-six-year-old Virginia observes a scene "as like that wh[ich]. takes place in an English drawing room as possible"—a scene she deplores (PA 390). A mother sits with a plain daughter and a pretty one:

> the pretty one, with great curves of red & white flesh on her bones, leans back to look up into the parsons face, & laugh friendly when he speaks. Her mood is invariable; she is as simple in her heart as on her lips; The deepest of her plots is to be mistress of a good mans home, & bear him children.
>
> She would blush that you should guess it, but everyone can see that the cheerfulness & sweet temper, which compose her charms & wiles, proceed directly from such ambition; no one could blame them, & there is something so perpetual about them, that it seems as tho' generation[s] of mothers had found them effective & bequeathed them as sufficient armour to their daughters. Viewed in this light, there is cause for alarm, & even for disgust. Old mother nature is not a skinflint; human beings might soar very high so long as such tools are adequate. (PA 390)

Clearly, this daughter's flight strikes Woolf as low. In marriage, as in writing, she places faith in nature's riches. After all, has she not just been reading in her Greek diary of a woman with "a rare mind, & perhaps, a rare nature" (PA 342)? Has she not herself just completed one hundred pages of "Melymbrosia [The Voyage Out]" in Manorbier and sent them to Clive Bell to read? Has she not envisioned in that work a very different heroine?

No further mention of marriage—or even of Clive Bell—occurs in the 1908 Italian diary. Instead, Virginia seeks to become one with (or rival) her sister by treating the Italian scene as a painter. In this respect the 1908 Italian diary resembles her 1903 diary "sketch book." She treats the books she reads as visual art as well (as she did in her 1903 diary). Thomas Hardy's drawing room women in Two on a Tower (and his distrust of them) remind her of Charles Keene's drawings of 1870s women in Punch. Hardy "forces his warm human beings against a wire frame work of plot, as though they could not stand up by themselves," she declares (PA 387). Five entries later, she finds George Meredith's Harry Richmond even more disappointing. "Instead of supporting his fabric, as Hardy does, with an intricate wire netting, Meredith contents himself . . . with flimsy vapour, shot with all the colours of the sunset, but without substance where there should be substance," she writes, treating Meredith, like Hardy, as a painter or sculptor. "I doubt though that the patient reader takes away one complete character, consistently developed. . . . In his novels, then, we get the shadow of something magnificent, & without likeness; red silhouettes of men, extravagant grotesques, an earth & sky all on fire as in perpetual sunset" (*PA* 391–92).

A connoisseur of sunsets herself, she knows they do not last. Her reflections on Meredith's art lead directly to the climax of the 1908 Italian diary, an entry of equal importance to the opening entry in which she resolves to write with the mind as well as with the eye and to discover real things beneath the show. Mitchell Leaska calls this eighth entry her artistic credo (*PA* xxvi). It represents the fullest statement to 1908 of views she has expressed in her diary as early as 1899. On a hot day in Perugia, Woolf writes with the mind as well as the eye. "[L]et me try to grasp some ideas about painting," she begins, and then seeks to distinguish her writer's art from Perugino's (*PA* 392). She finds Perugino's fresco beautiful but frozen: "not a hint of past or future. . . . infinitely silent." She wishes to express beauty too—but beauty of life and the world in motion: "Isn't there a different kind of beauty? No conflict. I attain a different kind of beauty, achieve a symmetry by means of infinite discords, showing all the traces of the minds passage through the world; & achieve in the end, some kind of whole made of shivering fragments; to me this seems the natural process; the flight of the mind. Do they really reach the same thing?" (*PA* 393).

Curiosity and questions have now fully entered the diary—expanding her thought and art. "Is it worth while to write?" she asks herself in entry one (*PA* 385). "Is Thomas Hardy among the Classics?" (*PA* 386). Has George Meredith "really made so sure of his subjects that he can exhibit them in crisis?" she asks in entry seven, which leads to the question series that propels her statement of her own aesthetic: "beauty (symmetry?) of life & the world, in action. Conflict?—is that it? . . . a different kind of beauty?" (*PA* 391–93). The 1908 Italian diary marks a turning point and a crisis on the diarist's path to becoming Virginia Woolf. She distrusts and questions as she moves to expand her art.

The Journal of Elizabeth Lady Holland

Between her first Italian diary in September 1908 and her second in April 1909, Virginia Stephen reviews *The Journal of Elizabeth Lady Holland (1791–1811)* for the December 1908 *Cornhill Magazine*. She had written of Elizabeth Vassall, Lady Holland, in 1905 as one of eight Georgian beauties whose "genius" she then called elusive, for it "seemed inseparable from the living voice" (*E* 1: 62). Now the voice sounded in a two-volume edition of Lady Elizabeth's diary. The *Journal* begins as a Continental travel diary, a fact that may have drawn twenty-six-year-old Virginia to the work. Lady Elizabeth spends much of ages twenty to twenty-five touring Italy and recording its art and architecture in her diary—as Virginia has just (more briefly) done.

Lady Holland writes that she "devoured books" as a young girl, the very verb Virginia used for her own reading in her first (1897) diary.[2] "[A] desire for information became my ruling passion," Lady Elizabeth declares (1: 159). When she is twenty and twenty-one, she attends lectures on chemistry, natural history, and philosophy in Italy. Lady Elizabeth "picked up her learning where she might," Woolf notes in her review (E 1: 230). "The young lady was indefatigable"—full of passions and theories (E 1: 232).

Unlike Virginia, however, Elizabeth Vassall was sacrificed on the marriage altar when she was only fifteen. A mariage de convenance was forged with Sir Godfrey Webster, a baronet twenty-three years her senior and a member of Parliament from Battle Abbey in Sussex. The young woman's determined escape from this moody tyrant, first with him to the Continent and then from the marriage entire—though it caused a scandal and "she was nowhere received in society"—was a bold act Virginia could understand and admire (1: xviii). The young wife's Italian diary records Sir Godfrey's anger, and we see he impedes her growth. "In all the collections much escapes me," Lady Elizabeth writes when she is twenty-two, "as I am always accompanied by one whose impetuosity compels me to hasten from objects I would willingly contemplate, and whose violence of temper throws me into agitations that prevent me distinguishing the objects when they are before me" (1: 38). In Frankfort, Germany, later that year, Sir Godfrey "in a paroxysm" tears the book she is reading from her hands and throws it at her head (1: 83). She considers suicide on the seventh anniversary of her wedding and comes to call her husband "my tormentor" (1: 129).

Woolf observes in her review that we cannot trace "accurately" in the diary the developing "friendship" between Lady Elizabeth and Henry Richard Fox, the third Lord Holland, two years her junior (E 1: 233). Perhaps Lady Elizabeth's diary discretion served as a model for Woolf's own in matters of courtship and love. "[I]t was not the purpose of her diary to follow her feelings closely, or indeed to record them at all," Woolf observes, "except to sum them up now and then in a businesslike way, as though she made a note in shorthand for future use" (E 1: 233). This was exactly how Virginia characterized her *own* diary practice at the opening of her 1908 Italian diary three months before: "I use a kind of shorthand, & make little confessions, as though I wished to propitiate my own eye, reading later" (PA 384–85). The latter motive she also gives to Lady

Holland: "to propitiate her own eye when she reads [her diary] later in Sussex" (*E* 1: 231). To "propitiate my eye" will become another of Woolf's repeated diary drives.

Lady Elizabeth's return to London in 1797, divorce of Sir Godfrey, and marriage to Lord Holland gives her diary a new turn. "Having a very bad memory, and many odd irregular half-hours," she writes in 1797, "it has occurred to me to assist the one and occupy the others by writing down any events, conversations, anecdotes, etc., that may interest me at the moment; and though my nature is too lazy to allow me to hope that I can act up to anything like a systematic pursuit, yet whilst the fit is upon me to be so employed, I will yield" (1: 148). Unlike Virginia, Lady Holland harbors no love for Sussex—or even for nature.[3] Politics is her landscape, and her diary quickens in its transformation from a travel diary to a life diary, particularly when Lord Holland's uncle, Charles Fox, becomes England's foreign minister to France and negotiates with Napoleon, and when the Whigs come to power in 1806.

Lady Holland's London diary offers keen analysis of unfolding events from an insider who is also an outsider. She discusses the Divorce Bill (of special interest to the Hollands), the charges of immorality against Princess Caroline of Wales, the abolition of the slave trade in 1807, and King George III's "madness" in 1801 and 1810. "Lady Holland is far from eccentric in her journal, and adopts more and more as time goes by the attitude of a shrewd man of business who is well used to the world and well content with it," Woolf astutely comments in her 1908 review (*E* 1: 237).

As noted earlier, Lady Charlotte Bury's *Diary* portrait of the meddling letter-writing politician Samuel Whitbread may have prepared the way for Hugh Whitbread in Woolf's 1925 novel *Mrs. Dalloway*. Samuel Whitbread reappears even more despised in Lady Holland's *Journal*. In fact, he seems an annoying hanger-on, the very role Hugh Whitbread enacts in *Mrs. Dalloway*. Whitbread's name rarely appears in Lady Holland's *Journal* without her scorn. In 1806 he oversteps himself regarding Prussia's offer to go to war with France, causing Lady Holland to call him "absurdly extravagant in his views and demands" (2: 183). In 1811 she derides "the unpopular and odious manners of Whitbread, whom unfortunately all parties concur in hating, however they may respect him as a public character" (2: 285). In creating the odious Hugh Whitbread, Woolf could have been recalling the odious Samuel Whitbread of Lady Holland's *Journal* and the harmful letter-writing Samuel Whitbread of Lady Charlotte Bury's *Diary*.

In 1908, Woolf finds much to praise in *The Journal of Elizabeth Lady Holland*.

"From her earliest youth Lady Webster seems to have had a quality which saved her diary from the violent fate of diaries, and spared the writer her blushes," Woolf notes in her review; "she could be as impersonal as a boy of ten and as intelligent as a politician" (*E* 1: 231–32). That Lady Holland could exert mastery over so many people was proof in itself of a "remarkable mind," Virginia stresses, and the younger woman admires her predecessor's confidence and courage.[4] "But what numbers of likenesses she struck off, and with what assurance!" Virginia exclaims (*E* 1: 237). "[H]er past life had given her a decision and a fearlessness which made her go further in one interview than other women in a hundred" (*E* 1: 235). Lady Elizabeth Vassall Webster Holland not only went further but also defied traditions: "a spoilt great lady who confounds all the conventions as it pleases her" (*E* 1: 236). Was that not what Virginia Stephen also sought to do?

Virginia Woolf's Continental Travel Diary Concluded

A second Italian diary, the Florence diary of April 1909, concludes Virginia Stephen's Continental travel diary book. This diary sheds light on—in fact, invites us to reconsider—a time Woolf's biographers almost universally call unhappy. Quentin Bell, Hermione Lee, Mitchell Leaska, and others focus on the marriage malaise. They note Lytton Strachey's impetuous and withdrawn marriage proposal in late February 1909, his inability to join Virginia and the Bells in Florence in April, and Virginia's flirtation with Clive Bell and its painful results as possible reasons Virginia mysteriously cuts short her Florence stay (and diary) after only a fortnight and returns to England alone. The Florence diary reveals the twenty-seven-year-old's *literary* preoccupations rather than her familial and matrimonial maneuvers and suggests blessings as well as blight.

In point of fact, she begins a new diary—and one not a travel diary—within a week of Strachey's aborted proposal. New diary-keeping hardly seems the act of an immobilized soul. Like Strachey's retracted proposal, the April 7 death of Woolf's aunt, the diarist Caroline Stephen, also meant loss preceding gain. Caroline Stephen bequeathed £100 each to Vanessa and Adrian, but £2,500 to Virginia. Did this spur resentment and trouble the Florence holiday? Virginia writes Clive Bell that she plans to share her gift with Adrian (*L* #481, 1: 391). Whatever the family vibrations, Woolf's receipt of what today would be at least $277,000 freed her from economic worries—hardly an unhappy fate.

If one Aunt Stephen's April legacy aided artistic freedom, another Aunt Stephen's criticism chills the Florence diary. "It is with great timidity that I write,"

Woolf begins this diary, "remembering strictures upon empty & ladylike writing" (PA 395). Vanessa's April 28 letter to Lytton Strachey reveals that Dorothea Stephen pronounced this judgment on Virginia's prose—that it was "ladylike & empty" (*Selected Letters of Vanessa Bell* 83). Timidity, subtlety, and *force* become the themes of the Florence diary. We see Woolf counter Aunt Dorothea's chill with quiet self-assertion. Robert Browning, who lived in Florence, may have "attended" to criticism. "As for me—I write," Virginia declares. "The instinct wells like sap in a tree" (PA 395).

The instinct, however, appears to be undergoing change, and this change of literary style may have been more challenging and absorbing to Virginia Stephen than any marriage prospect. The change centers on her view of description, a concern that links the 1908 and 1909 Italian diaries. "I begin to distrust description, & even such humorous arrangement as makes a days adventure into a narrative," she writes at the start of her September 1908 Italian diary (PA 384). Seven months later her distrust persists. "The fault of most of my descriptive writing is that it tends to be too definite," she ends her first brief Florence entry, perhaps wondering if her description is "empty & ladylike" (PA 395). She picks up the theme in her second entry. "Descriptive writing is dangerous & tempting," she declares. "It is easy, with little expense of brain power, to make something. One seizes some broad aspect, as of water or colour, & makes a note of it. This single quality gives the tone of the piece. As a matter of fact, the subject is probably infinitely subtle, no more amenable to impressionist treatment than the human character. What one records is really the state of ones own mind" (PA 396).

She tries to describe Florence but reverts to the difficulty: "to tell of this would need immense concentration. To make a good passage requires an heroic grinding of the mind—& here am I, half asleep" (PA 396). She seems to recognize in the Florence diary that the subtle description she seeks requires a different approach and great mental press. This causes her to abandon the descriptive prose of her previous travel diaries—and perhaps to abandon Florence as well. She turns to human portraits instead. She writes retrospectively toward the close of her diary—perhaps even from London—that "Laziness, or some feeling, akin to laziness perhaps, that the task was hard enough to require more thought than I could give it, prevented me from writing any thing more about Florence. Also, I became familiar with the marked aspects; & was on the search for something subtler" (PA 399).

The turn from place-writing gives the Florence diary its unusual form. At first glance it appears that only two entries convey the fourteen-day Florence stay: the first, dated "25 April," comprised of a mere five sentences and fifty-three words; the extensive second, titled "Florence," offering some twenty-one hundred words. A closer look, however, reveals that the long "Florence" entry unites accounts of at least four separate days and events and that the diary's final two paragraphs were likely penned in England.

When Woolf drops *scenic* description as requiring more subtlety than she now can muster, she turns her diary into a portrait gallery instead. "It would be possible, though," she considers, "to note something about the people we met" (*PA* 399). She passes over a portrait of famed art critic Bernard Berenson to offer likenesses of five women (and one man, a woman's spouse). However, only one of the women pleases: Mrs. Campbell, "over seventy," who was "tender & affectionate" and "had done the life of Father Damien" in rhyme—a detail the beginning novelist will place in both *The Voyage Out* and *Jacob's Room* (*PA* 400, 401n10). Principessa Lucrezia (Rezia) Rasponi and Mrs. Janet Anne Ross, in contrast, are "distinguished old ladies" who lack appeal (*PA* 398). Woolf resists the narrow role she must play with them. "Only one position is possible if you are a young woman," she laments: "you must let them adopt queenly airs, with a touch of the maternal. She [Mrs. Ross] summons you to sit beside her, lays her hand for a moment on yours—dismisses you the next—to make room for some weakly young man" (*PA* 398).

Woolf's portrait of morbid "Miss Murray"—probably Margaret Alice Murray, the Egyptologist and prolific writer on the occult, Leaska suggests—offers yet another instance of her balanced portraits (*PA* 399n9). After finding Miss Murray lacking in spirit and atmosphere, "infinitely arid, & out of tune," Woolf concludes: "And yet I think she was honest, unselfish, & clever above the average. I am never comfortable with these acute analytical minds. They seem to me to miss the point, & yet light on something which one cant deny" (*PA* 399–400).

Her portrait of poet and essayist Alice Meynell resonates most with the spirit of the Florence diary. The young writer who begins her diary in "great timidity," finds in Meynell precisely the skittishness she deplores. Woolf rejects Alice Meynell with her face like "a transfixed hare," the woman "who somehow, made one dislike the notion of women who write" (*PA* 398). "Did Mrs Browning look like that too?" Woolf wonders, and then offers her theory: "a writer should be the furnace from which his words come—& tepid people, timid & decorous, never coin true words."[5]

Woolf wishes to coin true (and subtle) words—and it appears she must leave Florence to do so. "The discomfort of writing here is intense—constrains my style to be tense, in the form of lapidary inscriptions," she writes, and then describes the following vision that came to her during an evening walk on San Miniato—another "walk by night." "[I]t occurred to me that the thing [her writing?] was running into classic prose before my eyes. I positively saw the long smooth sentence running like a ribbon along the road—casting graceful loops round the beggar woman & the dusky child—& curving freely over the bare slopes of the hills. London!" (*PA* 396–97). Here country ("bare slopes of the hills") and London again combine.

 ↷

The Continental travel diary of 1906 to 1909 reveals Virginia Stephen's determined march toward a style of her own. In 1906, she refuses to write "guidebook" in Greece and Turkey and firmly resists Western notions of the East. She turns as well from conventional marriage—played out in Greek and Italian hotels—toward an "unknown woman," a woman with "a rare mind, & perhaps, a rare nature" and the unconventional love she maintains. In Italy in 1908, the diarist poses her own aesthetic against Perugino's silent beauty: her art one of infinite discords, shimmering fragments that capture life in motion, the very flight of the mind. Her wish for greater subtlety in her scenic description—to write with the mind as well as with the eye—leads her to abandon places in April 1909 to turn from places to portraits. She rejects timidity and chooses instead to flame.

Virginia Woolf's 1909 Life Diary

"determination to find out the truth for herself"

(*CH* 7)

Virginia Stephen returns to London diary-writing in the period between her two Italian travel diaries, and she resumes this London diary *after* Italy as well. The 2002 discovery of a previously unknown 1909 diary is extraordinarily important, for it reveals Virginia's return to a life diary (of sorts) after nearly four years of travel diaries. The two Italian travel diaries and the newly found 1909 life diary—the three covering the period from September 1908 through November 1909—should be studied as a unit, for they focus on the problem of description, and on marriage as a problem as well.

The 1908 Italian travel diary and the 1909 life diary that follows it mirror

Virginia's pivotal 1903 diary. In Italy in 1908, the twenty-six-year-old seeks to write with a painter's eye as she did at age twenty-one. In both diaries she describes not only the landscape she sees but also the books she reads as works of visual art. While the 1908 Italian diary returns to the painterly *diction* of the 1903 diary, the 1909 life diary adopts its *form*. The 1903 diary consists of thirty titled essay-entries treated as a book with a table of contents; the 1909 life diary offers six titled (and dated) essay-entries with a similar "contents" page. Virginia seems to return in 1909 to an earlier moment of artistic growth as she ponders new paths.

The 1909 life diary begins February 24, within a week of Lytton Strachey's withdrawn marriage proposal, and five of its six entries come in February and March. In late April and May, Virginia switches to her Continental travel diary for her fortnight in Florence with Vanessa and Clive Bell, but she then returns to the life diary November 3 for an essay-entry she titles "Jews and Divorce Courts." London supplies the setting for five of the six life diary entries: "Carlyle's House," "Miss Reeves," "Hampstead," "A Modern Salon," and "Jews and Divorce Courts." The sixth, "Cambridge," contrasts negatively with "Hampstead" (the country-in-London).

⁓ᕤ

David Bradshaw, the editor of this newly found diary (published in 2003 under the masking title *Carlyle's House and Other Sketches*), suggests that in making at least her third visit to Thomas Carlyle's home in late February 1909, twenty-seven-year-old Virginia was seeking "to reach back to her father—and mother—at a time of emotional upset" (*CH* 26–27). The 1909 diary's *form* returns to that used during her father's 1903 illness. Virginia literally retraces her steps recorded in her first diary at age fifteen. Bradshaw sees her visit, too, as her effort to imagine via the gifted Carlyles how a marriage with Strachey might have unfurled (*CH* 28–29). That she launches a new diary at this moment of personal crossroads strikes me as an act of self-assertion and self-definition. A complex rather than simple regression occurs. At this time of marital uncertainty, Virginia returns to early sources of nourishment: her father and Carlyle, via "Carlyle's House"—and to a diary as well. She touches base with what is most essential to her identity, including a diary.

Bradshaw also notes helpfully that professional—even more than psychological—need may have spurred the visit (*CH* 26). Virginia was preparing to review *The Love Letters of Thomas Carlyle and Jane Welsh* for the *Times Literary Supplement*. She tries to imagine herself into the Carlyles' world across her

February 24 diary entry. "This was how it looked 50 years ago, I suppose," she writes of the brown sails on the Thames at the entry's start: "This was how it looked to the Carlyles; but their Row has stucco pillars now, and the fields are stamped out by great municipal buildings of grey brick. I imagine that Carlyle tramped off into muddy lanes, and really got a salt breath from the river, almost at his door" (*CH* 3). Her scene-making gift is working nicely here. "But Cheyne Row is spoilt," she then declares, and we discover her dissatisfaction with the Carlyles' house in 1909 derives from its unnaturally formal presence (*CH* 3). "Carlyle's house already has the look of something forcibly preserved," she complains; "it is incongruous now"—a suggestive remark with respect to her father as well as to Carlyle.[6]

Questions pepper this first entry. "Why does one do these things?" Virginia asks herself of her visit, suggesting (as with her 1907 "Golders Green and Hampstead" entry) that she feels some unconscious need (*CH* 3). In 1909, her diary focuses more on Jane Carlyle than on Thomas, and she treats her predecessor as a fellow questioner. Jane Carlyle's portraits "seemed to look out quizzically upon the strangers as though she asked what they really found to look at: did they think that her house and her had been like that? Would she have tolerated them for a second?" (*CH* 3).

We see the diarist thinking as a professional writer as she nears this entry's end: "The house is light and spacious; but a silent place, which it needs much imagination to set alive again—one must show it with all her bright little 'contrivances'; and see, somehow, his long gaunt figure, leaning or lying back, pipe in hand; and hear bursts of talk, all in the Scotch accent; and the deep guffaw. Mrs Carlyle, I suppose, sat upright, but very fragile, amused, but critical too— telling her day's narrative" (*CH* 4). The 1903 diary began with "An Afternoon With The Pagans," time spent with the motherly love goddess (Lady Katherine Thynne) who authorizes Woolf's own "theorizing." Jane Carlyle serves as muse for the 1909 diary, a muse "very fragile, amused, but critical too—telling her day's narrative."

⌁

Amber Reeves, the "Neo-Pagan," comes to life two days later in the diary's second entry. "I met her at dinner last night," begins this February 26 entry (*CH* 5). "Miss Reeves," as Virginia titles the portrait, is five years younger than she, a graduate of Newnham College, Cambridge, a Fabian, and the mistress of H. G. Wells. Woolf begins the portrait, as she often does, with close physical description and an animal link: "She has dark hair, an oval face, with a singularly small mouth: a line is pencilled on her upper lip. She reminds me of the girl whose mother was a snake. There is something of the snake in her" (*CH* 5).

Despite this serpent aspect (and a few more reservations), Woolf's portrait of the young activist strikes me as mostly favorable. "She always leans forward, as though to take flight; her whole figure and pose indicating an ardent inter-ested spirit," Woolf writes: "When she is silent, she thinks—her eyes intent on one spot. But she talks almost incessantly, launching herself with the greatest ease—but says nothing commonplace. Her talk at once flies to social questions; is not dry exposition, but very lucid and vigorous explanation. 'We think . . . ,' 'we find' and so on; as though she spoke for the thinking part of the nation. Her vigour struck me most—and the fact that she was not pedantic" (*CH* 5).

Woolf then pauses to reflect critically on Amber Reeves, perhaps like Jane Carlyle. "I imagine that her taste and insight are not fine" she muses; "when she described people she ran into stock phrases, and took rather a cheap view" (*CH* 5). However, she then notes that Reeves "seemed determined to be human also; to like people, even though they were stupid" (*CH* 5). This pause for fastidious judgment done, she then continues her admiration.

Bradshaw believes twenty-seven-year-old Virginia views the younger woman, the college woman, with envy in this entry, particularly for her "social ease and intellectual lucidity" (*CH* 31). Near the close of the portrait, when Woolf de-clares that Reeves "lacks mystery; and the charm people have who withdraw, and don't care to coin their views," Bradshaw believes Virginia "obviously has herself in mind" (*CH* 5, 31). However, he wonders, "is her tone self-possessed, haughty, or inflected with pathos?" (*CH* 31). We know from her previous diaries that mystery and vacancy—in landscape and architecture as well as in peo-ple—attract Woolf more than definition. In this light, the entry's criticism likely says more about the diarist's own aesthetic than it does about Amber Reeves.

Virginia seeks to capture another woman, an older woman, a month later in "A Modern Salon." Bradshaw calls this early portrait of Lady Ottoline Morrell "spiteful" and evidence of the general "tendency to fault-find" of the 1909 diary (*CH* xv). Doris Lessing also believes Woolf does not "come out very well" in this "collision with money and aristocracy" (*CH* xi).[7] However, as with "Miss Reeves," the entry strikes me as, on the whole, an admiring portrait. The text is titled "A Modern Salon" after all. It opens with the suggestion that Lady Ot-toline's salon approaches in design the "great French salons" of Madames de Staël and de Sévigné (*CH* 12). The diarist then explores the endeavor, and, as with "Miss Reeves," finds much to praise. "Lady Ottoline has a definite end in view," Woolf asserts; "she is a great lady who has become discontented with her own class, and has found what she wanted in the class of artists, writers, and professional people" (*CH* 12).

The strange, yet luminous, atmosphere that rises from this mix becomes the subject of the entry. The artists: "are always conscious that she comes from a distance, with strange colours upon her; and she, that these humbler creatures have yet a vision of the divine. Her parties have always a certain romance and distinction from the presence of this incongruity" (*CH* 12). Woolf denies to Lady Morrell the "purer" gift of art *production*; however, she lauds her for knowing art's divinity, for coming a great distance, and for producing a lustrous and evocative atmosphere.

Woolf pauses after this description, wondering if more needs to be said. She credits Lady Morrell with devoting all her energies to her "salon" and for a consistency of attitude and approach. She then turns to the hostess's appearance and finds her "remarkable if not beautiful in her person" (*CH* 13). Her critique of Lady Morrell's facial beauty is rendered as art criticism, and rather droll and satirical criticism at that: "She takes the utmost pains to set off her beauty, as though it were a rare object. . . . It always seems possible that the rich American connoisseurs, who finger her Persian wrapper, and pronounce it 'very good,' should go on to criticize her face; 'a fine work—late renaissance, presumably; what modeling in the eyes and brow!—but the chin unfortunately is in the weaker style.'" (*CH* 13). Woolf here displaces the critique from herself to others, and skewers the American connoisseurs as much as Lady Morrell.

The entry closes with an image of Lady Morrell's head and manner: "the way she draws her head back and looks at you blankly gives her the appearance of a cast from some marble Medusa" (*CH* 13). Bradshaw, as I have noted, calls this entry "spot on and spiteful," but is it really spiteful? Lady Morrell is celebrated for coming a long way to create a luminous and distinctive salon. She is called "remarkable if not beautiful in her person" and treated as a strange but colorful spirit. Surely the Medusa reference continues the theme of "strangeness" the entry seeks to convey—along with, perhaps, mythological color. The notion of a strange and exotic "monster" might not also be amiss.

The centerpiece of the 1909 life diary, both literally and in terms of importance, is the difference limned between "Cambridge" and "Hampstead." On March 1, Virginia travels to Cambridge and offers a survey of three Cambridge "types":

the Darwins, parents and daughters, and the exclusive society of Cambridge male undergraduates.[8] "I begin to distrust description," she had confessed at the start of her September 1908 Italian diary, declaring her wish to write "not only with the eye, but with the mind" (*PA* 384). She attempts a new kind of description in the 1909 life diary, one in which décor discloses *character*, eye thus joined to mind. Bradshaw dubs "Cambridge" a "pompous" entry, but again I find the varied portraits much more positive than he (*CH* xv).

Virginia begins with the Darwins' home and describes a generational conflict in décor. The "comfortable" but "homely" eighteenth-century house reflects Sir George Darwin's character: "The ornaments, of course, are of the kind that one associates with Dons, and university culture. In the drawing room, the parents' room, there are prints from Holbein drawings, bad portraits of children, indiscriminate rugs, chairs, Venetian glass, Japanese embroideries: the effect is of subdued colour, and incoherence; there is no regular scheme. In short the room is dull" (*CH* 6). Sir George Darwin appears to her equally bland. However, she also acknowledges his gifts. "Sir George is now a very kindly ordinary man, with whom his children are entirely at their ease. . . . The liveliest thing about him is his affection for his children. . . . He notices small things; and that, at his age, gives him a certain charm" (*CH* 6, 7). Like "Miss Reeves," however, Sir George lacks mystery, a major weakness to Woolf. "His sensible and humorous remarks, his little anecdotes, and his shrewd judgments, are natural to him; no mask, as one had hoped," she declares, disappointed. "It is also clear that he has no feeling for beauty, no romance, or mystery in his mind; in short, he is a solid object, filling his place in the world, and all one may ever hope to find in him is a sane judgment, a cheerful temper" (*CH* 6, 7). Clearly, she wants more.

The Darwin *daughters* show more promise. In fact, Virginia might be describing her own Hyde Park Gate/Bloomsbury (and Victorian and Modern) poles in the contrasting Darwin rooms and goals. "'The children's room revolts against the parents,'" she writes immediately after dubbing the parents' quarters "dull" (*CH* 6). The daughters prefer "white walls, modern posters, photographs from the old masters. If they could do away with the tradition, I imagine that they would have bare walls, and a stout table" (*CH* 6). Interestingly, she critiques *both* poles in this essay-entry. She finds the Darwin daughters "naturally more interesting" than their parents (*CH* 7). She suggests they are "anxious to get rid of Darwin traditional culture and have a notion that there is a free Bohemian world in London, where exciting people live. This is all to their credit; and indeed they have a certain spirit which one admires" (*CH* 7).

Thinking critically once more, however, she also finds them (like "Miss Reeves") lacking the finest discrimination and settling for easy answers. We find here, as in the other entries, a mix of praise and critique, an observer who seeks to be discriminating yet also fair. The Darwin daughters:

aim at beauty, and that requires the surest touch. Gwen tends (this is constructive criticism) to admire vigorous, able, sincere works, which are not beautiful; she attacks the problems of life in the same spirit; and will end in 10 years time by being a strong and sensible woman, plainly clothed; with the works of deserving minor artists in her house. Margaret has not the charm which makes Gwen better than my account of her; a charm arising from the sweetness and competency of her character. . . . Margaret is much less formed; but has the same determination to find out the truth for herself, and the same lack of any fine power of discrimination. . . . I think I find them content with what seems to me rather obvious; I distrust such violent discontent, and the easy remedies. But I admire much also: only find the Darwin temperament altogether too definite, burly, and industrious. They exhibit the English family life at its best; its humour, tolerance, heartiness, and sound affection. (CH 7–8)

Is this smug and "cutting," as Bradshaw declares, or is it rather "constructive criticism" by a writer who favors indefiniteness to definition? Is it not the constructive criticism of one who shares "the same determination to find out the truth for herself"?

Of the three "Cambridge" types, Woolf's portrait of James Strachey and his college rooms and roommates stands out as most memorable. Virginia has tea with the male undergraduates and finds she has "to consider a very different state of things" (CH 8). The men's rooms appeal to her much more than those of either the Darwin parents or daughters. Strachey's rooms are "dim and discreet; French pastels hung on the walls and there were cases of old books" (CH 8). The décor delights, but the conversation fails. "The three young men— [H. T. J.] Norton, [Rupert] Brooke and James S.—sat in deep chairs; and gazed with soft intent eyes into the fire," Virginia writes. "Mr Norton knew that he must talk, and he and I spoke laboriously. It was a very difficult duet; the other instruments keeping silent" (CH 8). She tries to account for their silence, and her assessment is as startling as it is precise: "their views seem to me honest, and simple. They lack all padding; so that one has convictions to disagree with, if one disagrees. Yet, we had nothing to say to each other; and I was conscious that not only my remarks but my presence was criticized. They wished for the truth, and doubted whether a woman could speak it or be it. I thought this courageous of them; but unsympathetic. I had to remember that one is not full grown at 21" (*CH* 8).

Doris Lessing describes the last sentence as "the wasp's swift sting" (*CH* xi). Bradshaw calls it putting the men "firmly in their place" (*CH* xx). However, we might also read "I had to remember that one is not full grown at 21" as compassionate—even hopeful the college men will outgrow these narrow views.

⁊

Surely it is no accident that Virginia turns from the male disdain of "Cambridge" to the more nourishing and inclusive (female) setting at "Hampstead." As I hope by now is clear, Hampstead is linked in Woolf's early diaries with the country, with nature as woman, and with the fertile unconscious mind. Woolf's move from culture to country and her drive to merge the two are among her most significant diary acts. In the pivotal 1903 diary entry titled "The Country In London," the twenty-one-year-old reflects that men would laugh at her and her bookish aspirations, but she then dismisses the patriarchal tradition with "But I am going to forget all that in the country" (*PA* 178). In March 1905 she takes Vanessa to Hampstead for "country in London" refreshment, and in the summer of 1907 she refuses Cambridge in favor of her own work which is refreshed again at "Golders Green and Hampstead" (*PA* 254, 365–66). Should we be surprised, then, that on March 19, 1909 she turns from unsympathetic "Cambridge" to affectionate "Hampstead" and contrasts the two worlds? "Hampstead is always refreshing," begins the "Hampstead" entry (*CH* 10).

She continues her new descriptive tack in her "Hampstead" portrait: room décor signals character. "The ladies themselves are of a piece with the house," she writes of the Case sisters, Euphemia (Emphie) and Janet, who reside in Hampstead: "one of them [Emphie], that is, is pale and fresh, and rather shabby, like the furniture, and the other [Janet] seems to represent the fine and rather austere intellect, tempered by suburban residence, which has filled the rooms with solid works and her Greek archaeology, and hung the walls with photographs from old masters. The look of them is very valiant, humane, and perhaps a little too amiable to be consistent with the very keenest edge of intellect" (*CH* 10).

Woolf has already celebrated her Greek teacher, "Miss Case," in her 1903 diary. The Case sisters' visitor, Margaret Llewelyn Davies, becomes the focus of the 1909 entry.[9] The "harmonious" conversation of these three college women contrasts with her awkward "duet" with the three male undergraduates in "Cambridge." The three women, she writes, "together made an harmonious picture" (*CH* 10). Davies, in fact, becomes another admirable "pagan." Virginia thinks her the most rigorous of the three women: "Miss Davies comes of a sterner stock. Her features are sharper, her eyes burn brighter; once she must have had something of the beauty of a delicate Greek head. . . . Miss Davies, it is clear, has far less tolerance than her friends; and has done what she has done through the force of conviction. She has organized a great co-operative movement in the North. . . . [She] has a mind like one of those flint coloured gems upon which the heads of Roman emperors are cut, indelibly" (*CH* 10, 11).

The three women attended college together, we are told, and they "drop easily into what I suppose is their shop" (*CH* 11). But how their talk differs from that of "Cambridge"! "[T]hey describe the last problem play; they discuss the last development in the fight for the franchise," Woolf records. "It is all admirably sane, altruistic, and competent; save for a certain sharpness of edge, it might be the talk of capable members of parliament. I was struck by the conviction with which they spoke; a conviction that justice ought to be done, not to them or their children, but to the whole of womankind" (*CH* 11). How different the two settings and conversations seem—the attractive but exclusionary rooms of Cambridge and the shabby, austere, but inclusive Hampstead. Surely this contrastive portrait represents an early tryout for *A Room of One's Own.*

Portraits dominate the 1909 life diary. Three of the six entries—"Miss Reeves," "A Modern Salon," and "Hampstead"—offer portraits of women, while "Carlyle's House" centers on Jane Carlyle, and more than a third of "Cambridge" is devoted to Mrs. Darwin and her daughters. Virginia appears to be studying female "types" at this moment, seeking her own niche. The first portion of the final diary entry, "Jews and Divorce Courts," offers another woman's portrait: that of Mrs. Annie Loeb. Bradshaw describes Mrs. Loeb's son, Sydney, as "one of the most consummate Wagnerians of his generation" and suggests Virginia likely met him in August 1909 at the Wagner Festival in Bayreuth (*CH* 41). This may have led to the November invitation to Mrs. Loeb's home in Lancaster Gate.

Curiosity launches this November 3 entry. "One wonders how Mrs Loeb became a rich woman," Woolf begins (*CH* 14). After a paragraph of description, she pauses again to ask, "What was the truth of the matter, I wonder?" (*CH* 14).

She follows this question with an admiring view: "I imagine her to be a shrewd woman of business, in the daytime, moving in a circle of city people" (*CH* 14). However, despite these questions and laudatory speculation, Woolf offers in the remainder of the sketch the harshest of all the female portraits in this diary. Two aspects in particular expose her to charges of anti-Semitism. In the first place, she dislikes Mrs. Loeb's cuisine: "Her food, of course, swam in oil and was nasty" (*CH* 14). Certainly this shows cultural narrowness and insensitivity. Woolf recoils from the pressure to partake: "at dinner she pressed everyone to eat, and feared, when she saw an empty plate, that the guest was criticizing her. Her food, of course, swam in oil and was nasty."[10]

More troubling than this food jibe, however, is Woolf's title, "Jews," for the opening half of the November 3 entry, as if Mrs. Loeb's (predominantly negative) portrait stands for all Jews. After all, Woolf does not title "Miss Reeves'" portrait "New Zealanders"—or even "Neo-Pagans." Why not, then, title Mrs. Loeb's portrait simply "Mrs Loeb" on the model of "Miss Reeves"? We note, furthermore, that the final entry is not even called "*A Jew* and Divorce Courts," but "Jews and Divorce Courts," Mrs. Loeb apparently standing for "Jews."

In trying to understand for myself the title "Jews and Divorce Courts," I recognize that Virginia's ire at Mrs. Loeb rises from a long-standing (and not anti-Jewish) grievance. Virginia has offered two previous diary portraits of mothers and marriageable daughters, and now, in Mrs. Loeb's music salon, she finds herself similarly framed. In her 1906 Greek diary, Woolf expressed pity for the Greek daughter who lacked classical Greek but possessed a mother chatting up a young man from Patras. More recently, in her 1908 Italian diary, she castigates at greater length an *English* mother with her plain and pretty daughters, declaring their behavior unworthy of nature's riches. The conclusion of Mrs. Loeb's portrait provides the motive for this angry sketch. Woolf feels herself in the plight of the plain daughter. Mrs. Loeb acts the role of marriage broker for Woolf and the harpist Miriam Jane Timothy, and, as is clear, Woolf finds it a very low game:

> She adjusted her flattery, to suit me, whom she took to be severe and intellectual, and Miss Timothy whom she thought lively and flirtatious. To me she talked of . . . the "companionship of books for a lonely woman" (and yet she only dines alone once in the week)[,] of her white bedroom, with its bare walls and open windows. She rallied Miss T. . . . upon the attentions of the hundred men of the orchestra; upon her fat arms; upon

the attentions of Syd, her son. What was the truth of the matter, I wonder? . . . [S]he wishes to be popular, and is, perhaps, kind, in her vulgar way, ostentatiously kind to poor relations. The one end she aims at for them, is the society of men and marriage. It seemed very elementary, very little disguised, and very unpleasant. (CH 14–15)

The one end she aims at for them, is the society of men and marriage. This "aim" is resisted strongly in this November 3, 1909 entry. Furthermore, does it mitigate at all our sense of anti-Semitism to acknowledge that Mrs. Loeb is not the only woman described as "coarse" in the 1909 life diary? She joins Mrs. Darwin in "Cambridge" and Miss Lewis in "Divorce Courts" soon to come—neither of them Jewish (CH 7, 17). Furthermore, Amber Reeves' "taste and insight are not fine" and the Darwin daughters "lack . . . any fine powers of discrimination" (CH 5, 8). It may mitigate our sense of Woolf's anti-Semitism if we note that it is Mrs. Loeb's "very elementary, very little disguised, and very unpleasant" marriage brokering that is chastised here (15).

The link between the two November 3 essay-entries, separated only by space, lies precisely in their focus on marriage, Woolf examining the marriage machinations of a Jewish mother in the first half of the entry and the tyrannies of a male Anglican rector in the second. Bradshaw appears baffled by the second half of the November 3 entry. He writes that one would expect Woolf to show greater sympathy for the rector's wife seeking "judicial annulment" of her marriage on the grounds of cruelty, or more admiration for her supporter, the lesbian nurse Miss Lewis. However, he declares, "if they lie anywhere, her sympathies seem to lie with the Old Etonian, the solidly Victorian cleric" (CH 49). I do not read the entry as sympathetic to the Victorian rector. However, his tyrannies have brought Woolf to the divorce courts and he remains the major focus of the entry.

Curiosity sparks the second half of the November 3 entry, just as it does the first, and in her opening line Woolf reveals her motive: "Curiosity took me to the divorce courts, because I had read of a clergyman who seemed to have a bigoted faith, so that he brought religion into contact with his most private life" (CH 16). The "contact" she alludes to here was literal—part of the sensationalism of the case. The rector had "raised a crucifix" to his wife (CH 18). A writer's tone can be hard to gauge; however, Woolf's treatment of the Reverend Herbert Oakes Fearnley-Whittingstall strikes me as arch, even broadly contemptuous of his patriarchal display:

He vindicated the position of the ideal husband, who must teach, forbear, and help the weaker party.

He spoke the literal truth and enforced it with oaths. He had taken care never to sin: at the same time, he had not any pliancy. . . . [His wife] had fallen into the hands of Miss Lewis, who had revealed to her that she was misunderstood. . . . No one could doubt the man who remembered every date; was scrupulous enough to own his hot temper—and yet he had tried to control it by prayer and silence; who said outright that he "adored" his wife; but his character as a clergyman of the Church of England was more to him; who had clearly suffered, and done right, so far as he could see it. (*CH* 16, 17)

[H]is character as a clergyman of the Church of England was more to him. Surely this is the heart of Woolf's critique. Her next line reveals her true assessment: "One believed him; but he explained the other side as he spoke. He was a man without pity or imagination; a formalist and, perhaps, a selfish man. Moreover, his religion absorbed him. Religion had had much to do with it, I thought" (*CH* 17).

Although she gives less space to Alice Mary Fearnley-Whittingstall, the much put-upon wife, in her focus on religious tyranny, one senses profound sympathy for the wife as victim of both church and court. "Mrs W. felt desperate that no one could see what cruelty his right doing implied," Woolf writes, and we sense that *she* can see it. "It was a nightmare to her. Miss Lewis, and one or two women friends and a hospital nurse, were the only people who saw: the whole male world was against her" (*CH* 17).

⌐҅

The 1909 life diary captures an important turn in Woolf's diary history. It marks her return to a life diary (of sorts) and a London diary after nearly four years of travel diary. *Places*, in fact, become *portraits* in the 1909 life diary: "Carlyle's House," "Cambridge," "Hampstead," and "A Modern Salon" sketches of *persons* more than locales. Portraiture reenters the diary, and in this respect the 1909 life diary sets the stage for both the 1909 Florence diary, with *its* many female portraits, and the life diary that will follow in 1915. The discovery of this 1909 diary particularly pleases, for it reveals that Virginia Stephen summons her resources to counter the marriage rub. She returns to her earlier sources of nurture (Thomas Carlyle, Jane Carlyle, Hampstead, Janet Case, and diary-keeping) and focuses insistently on the finer discriminations that lift her life and art.

Dr. Charles Meryon's Diaries Celebrating Lady Hester Stanhope

Virginia Stephen's 1909 life diary ends with her November 3 entry "Jews and Divorce Courts." For the next five years no diary survives. However, she read and reviewed *others'* diaries. Across thirty years she recalled her Christmas 1909 holiday, made merry by six volumes of diaries that told the extraordinary life of Lady Hester Stanhope who escaped England and, dressed as a Turkish sultan, held sway from a mountaintop in Lebanon in the first half of the nineteenth century. In late 1909, the *Times Literary Supplement* editors asked Woolf to review Julia Anne Roundell's lively new memoir *Lady Hester Stanhope*. The book offered much to engage Virginia, for Lady Hester, William Pitt's niece, preceded her as a traveler to the Levant. In 1810, Lady Hester journeyed to Greece and Constantinople, just as Virginia did in 1906. However, Lady Hester saw Byron dive into the Hellespont, and she boldly entered Constantinople riding side-saddle on a horse.[11] Roundell depicts Lady Hester taking Byron "briskly to task for [his] deprecating opinion . . . of all female intellect" (25).

Proof of Woolf's interest in Lady Hester (and of her devotion to her journalism) can be seen in the fact that she moved swiftly from Roundell's memoir to its primary source: the six volumes of diaries Lady Hester's physician, Dr. Charles Meryon, published in 1845 and 1846, following her death in 1839. The doctor's first three diary volumes, covering the years 1818 to 1839, were so popular in 1845 that in 1846 he published a second three-volume set titled *Travels of Lady Hester Stanhope: Forming the Completion of Her Memoirs Narrated by Her Physician*. These volumes detail her early life and her travels from 1810 to 1817. Woolf's December 27, 1909 letter to Violet Dickinson from Cornwall suggests she considers Lady Hester another inspiring pagan: "I . . . spend my time, reading, not a silly new book by a woman called Roundell, but the old diaries written by her doctor, which keep me entirely happy. She seems to have been an insolent noble aristocrat, not unlike Beatrice [Thynne], only crazed about the Messiah, and the stars; with a passion for conversation" (*L* #514, 1: 418). Virginia's letter to Clive Bell the day before reveals that she found in Dr. Meryon's diaries just the rich ore she sought: "It makes me rock with delight—thinking what a number of wonderful things I shall dig out of it in my article" (*L* #513, 1: 416). As this letter continues, Woolf imagines herself Lady Hester in Cornwall.

Like Lady Charlotte Bury's *Diary Illustrative of the Times of George the Fourth* which Woolf had reviewed eighteen months before, Dr. Meryon's diaries were private diaries turned public to defend a maligned woman.[12] His diaries also resembled James Boswell's journals; that is, they preserve the talk of a brilliant raconteur. The Boswell link might explain Virginia's preference for the diaries.[13] Dr. Meryon titled his first three published diaries *Memoirs of the Lady Hester Stanhope, As Related By Herself In Conversations With Her Physician*. In his "Preface" he declares, "My object being to portray a character which is not duly appreciated by people in general, I could devise no better means than that of giving a diary of her conversations, wherein her observations on men and things fall naturally from her own mouth" (*Memoirs* 1: iv). Lady Hester would sleep until midafternoon, then rise to engage the doctor in talk across the evening— often for eight to twelve hours at a stretch. Many nights she would dismiss him, only to call him back for another hour of chat.

Dr. Meryon speaks in his "Preface" of "the profound impression which her conversation always left on the minds of her hearers," and, as Woolf writes in her January 20, 1910 review, "When he got back at dawn from those long audiences, by the end of which the lady was hidden in smoke, he tried to put down the stories and to express the kind of stupefaction with which she overwhelmed him" (*Memoirs* 1: x; *E* 1: 326). In introducing his diary, Dr. Meryon insists that:

> Everybody who has visited Lady Hester Stanhope in her retirement [to Mount Lebanon] will bear witness to her unexampled colloquial powers; to her profound knowledge of character; to her inexhaustible fund of anecdotes; to her talents for mimicry; to her modes of narration, as various as the subjects she talked about; to the lofty inspirations and sublimity of her language, when the subject required it; and to her pathos and feeling, whenever she wished to excite the emotions of her hearers. . . .
>
> It was this comprehensive and searching faculty, this intuitive penetration, which made her so formidable. . . . Everybody who heard her for an hour or two retired humbled from her presence. (*Memoirs* 1: 135, 136)

Woolf likely saw she shared some of Lady Hester's gifts: the "searching faculty," the range, the intuitive penetration. Lady Hester knew even as a child her talk was as brilliant as her complexion and her teeth. "[M]y language—ah! there it was—something striking and original, that caught every body's attention," she declares (*Memoirs* 2: 19). When the Prussian Prince Pückler-Muskau prolongs his stay with her in April 1838, leaving the Emir Beshýr to cool his heels, he, too, sought to preserve "the extraordinary powers and animation of Lady Hester Stanhope's conversation" in the diary he dictated to one of his courtiers (*Memoirs* 3: 93). Two months later, it is Lady Hester's refusal to see Maximilian, Duke of Bavaria—"I have neither breath nor strength enough to undergo the exertion of conversation," she confides—that convinces the doctor she soon will die (*Memoirs* 3: 249).

In late 1909, Lady Hester offered Woolf another illustration that, like imperious Lady Holland and subversive Lady Charlotte Bury, a woman must be convention-breaking and courageous to make her mark. Lady Hester lost her mother at age four. Her brilliant father was "a tyrant in his own family" who refused to send his *sons* to college, much less his gifted daughter (Roundell 4). Nearly six feet tall and "majestic in her movements," Lady Hester lived to command but had to leave England to do so (Roundell 7). In 1812, "[t]o the terror of those with her," Roundell writes, Lady Hester rode into Damascus unveiled in broad daylight (57). In 1813, she dared the dangerous desert crossing to Palmyra to see the place Zenobia governed. "She sought the remains of Zenobia's greatness, as well as the remains of Palmyra," Dr. Meryon explains (*Travels* 2: 176). In the "Preface" to his diaries, Dr. Meryon begs appreciation for "a heroine who marches at the head of Arab tribes through the Syrian desert; who calls governors of cities to her aid, whilst she excavates the earth in search of hidden treasures" (*Travels* 1: vi).

Lady Hester disdained marriage as "slavery" and threw an aura of mystery around herself "in the commonest circumstances"—both inclinations likely to interest Virginia Stephen in 1909 and 1910 (*Memoirs* 3: 262, 4; *Memoirs* 2: 350). One of Lady Hester's favorite stories, recounted by both Roundell and Dr. Meryon, is of a man who observed to William Pitt: "'I suppose [Lady Hester] waits [to marry] till she can get a man as clever as herself.' 'Then,' answered Mr. Pitt, 'she will never marry at all'" (*Memoirs* 2: 31–32).

Following the 1811 shipwreck that sinks all her clothes, Lady Hester dresses as a Turkish gentleman for the rest of her days. That her dress change was unplanned, practical, and astute rather than whimsical can be seen in her 1812 letter to her London solicitor following the shipwreck: "To collect clothes in this part of the world so as to dress like an Englishwoman would be next to impossible; to dress as a Turkish woman would not do, because then I must not be seen to speak to a man" (Roundell 41). Her saga, of course, puts one in mind of *Orlando*, and, in truth, both Roundell and Dr. Meryon present Lady Hester as an androgynous soul. Lady Hester reports that King George III once declared that: "There is not a man in my kingdom who is a better politician than Lady Hester; and . . . I have great pleasure in saying, too, there is not a woman who adorns her sex more than she does. And, let me say, Mr. Pitt, you have not reason to be proud that you are a minister, for there have been many before you, and will be many after you; but you have reason to be proud of her, who unites everything that is great in man and woman" (*Memoirs* 2: 230–31). Lady Hester tells Prince Pückler-Muskau that "The Arabs have never looked upon me in the light either of a man or of a woman, but as 'un être à part'" (Roundell 186).

Lady Hester's life, as conveyed in Dr. Meryon's diaries, offered seeds for more than *Orlando*. In fleeing England and shaving her head (for greater comfort under her cashmere turban) Lady Hester supplied the plot for *Flush*.[14] This description in Dr. Meryon's "Preface" may have caught Woolf's fancy and lodged in her mind: "Every year brought her nearer to the simplicity of nature, and taught her to throw down those barriers with which pride, reserve, and etiquette have hedged in persons of rank in this country" (*Memoirs* 1: iv). Lady Hester's repeated remarks on this subject likely fortified a writer who, from her 1903 diary forward, consciously chooses nature over culture.

Lady Hester keeps no watch or clock. "I cannot bear anything that is unnatural," she declares. "I like nothing but nature" (*Memoirs* 1: 125, 126). "Nature, doctor, makes us one way, and man is always trying to fashion us another," she complains (*Memoirs* 2: 14). Seeking the doctor's return in an 1823 letter, she writes, "I have been thought mad—ridiculed and abused; but it is out of the power of man to change my way of thinking upon any subject. . . . my reasoning is profound according to the laws of Nature" (*Memoirs* 1: 9). In 1827, she urges him to "never act contrary to the dictates of conscience, of honour, of nature, or of humanity," and in the last years of her life she boasts that "There is perhaps no one in the world who has ever done justice to everything in the creation, man or brute—even down to an ant—like me" (*Memoirs* 1: 57; *Memoirs* 3: 120).

Disgusted with England, Lady Hester escapes to Lebanon and cultivates her own Voltairian garden, a garden Dr. Meryon describes as "entirely of her own creation, . . . richly diversified with covered alleys, serpentine walks, summerhouses, pavilions, arbours, and other embellishments, in which she displayed such admirable taste, that it would not be easy, even in England, to find a more beautiful garden within similar limits."[15] When she dies alone June 22, 1839 with no European to attend her, Lady Hester is buried in her garden and surrounded by roses, as she ordained. The American missionary who arrives the next day and reads the Church of England service over her, writes, "I have rarely seen a more beautiful place; neither time, labour, nor expense had been spared to convert this barren hill into a wilderness of shady avenues, and a paradise of sweet flowers" (Roundell 228).

From this natural harbor, Lady Hester launches sharp critiques of British (and European) imperialism. In 1816 she writes to the Marquis (afterward Duke) of Buckingham: "The grand-daughter of Lord Chatham, the niece of the illustrious Pitt, feels herself blush . . . that she was born in England—that England, who has made her accursed gold the counterpoise to justice; that England who puts weeping humanity in irons, who has employed the valour of her troops, destined for the defence of her national honour, as the instrument to enslave a free-born people" (*Travels* 3: 304–5). In the final years of her life, when a petty British government withholds her pension due to minor claims of debts, she writes to Queen Victoria: "I shall not allow the pension given by your royal grandfather to be stopped by force; but I shall resign it for the payment of my debts, and with it the name of English subject, and the slavery that is at present annexed to it" (*Memoirs* 2: 267). In this regard, too, Lady Hester foreshadows Woolf's immortal words in *Three Guineas*: "as a woman, I have no country. As a woman I want no country. As a woman my country is the whole world" (109).

In her 1910 review, Woolf challenges the dismissive label "eccentric" the *Dictionary of National Biography* hangs on Lady Hester (and others).[16] Instead, she praises Dr. Meryon and his diary. "The charm of Dr Meryon's work lies in its comprehensiveness," she explains. "He lived with her off and on for twenty-eight years, and the people we live with are the last we seek to define in one word. Dr Meryon never attempted it" (*E* 1: 325). We see here further sign of Woolf's press for range and subtlety, her belief that we are not just "one thing."

And like Scott, Burney, Pepys, and Boswell, Lady Hester Stanhope remains in Woolf's mind across her days—largely through Dr. Meryon's lively diaries. When Woolf resumes her own diary in 1915, defense of Lady Hester and "eccentrics" rises almost at once. "I think one day I shall write a book of 'Eccentrics,'" Woolf tells her diary on January 19, 1915. "Mrs Grote shall be one. Lady Hester Stanhope. Margaret Fuller. Duchess of Newcastle. Aunt Julia [Margaret Cameron, the photographer]" (*D* 1: 23). She fulfills this vow, not with a book but with an article called "The Eccentrics" in the April 1919 *Athenaeum*. In this essay she insists that "perhaps after all there is something to be said for the eccentrics" (*E* 3: 38). Reminding readers that eccentrics usually go unrecorded, she notes that "Sometimes, though it happens far too seldom, lives have been written of these singular men and women, or, after they are dead, someone half-shamefacedly has put together their papers. Dr Meryon, for example, wrote the memoirs of Lady Hester Stanhope, thus earning our eternal gratitude" (*E* 3: 39).

Eight days before this defense of "Eccentrics" sounds in the April 25, 1919 *Athenaeum*, Woolf expresses disappointment at Lytton Strachey's two-part article "Lady Hester Stanhope," which appeared in the first two issues of the *Athenaeum* April 4 and 11. His piece, she tells her diary, was "not one of his best"

(D 1: 264). One wonders, in fact, if she writes "The Eccentrics" as a riposte to Strachey's portrait, for in it he twice calls Lady Hester "eccentric" and describes her as "peculiarly imbalanced," "overstrained," and "preposterous" (Part I: 131, 132, 133; Part II: 166, 167). He derides Dr. Meryon as well. He calls the doctor "a poor-spirited and muddle-headed man" and questions how he could have left Lady Hester at the end, when any reader of the six volumes of diaries would understand fully why the doctor leaves and likely would rate Dr. Meryon both generous and astute.[17]

Nine months later, reviewing *The Life of Thomas Coutts, Banker* for the March 12, 1920 *Athenaeum*, Woolf includes Lady Hester among the noble and beautiful people who besiege "the richest man in England" for funds (E 3: 187). "Lady Hester Stanhope thundered and growled melodiously enough from the top of Mount Lebanon," Woolf engagingly reports (E 3: 188). In 1923, in her important essay "How It Strikes A Contemporary," the essay she chooses to close her first *Common Reader*, Woolf offers Lady Hester as a model for critics. Let the book critic, she writes, "slam the door upon the cosy company where butter is plentiful and sugar cheap, and emulate rather that gaunt aristocrat, Lady Hester Stanhope, who kept a milk-white horse in her stable in readiness for the Messiah, and was forever scanning the mountain tops, impatiently, but with confidence, for the first signs of His approach" (E 3: 359).

In her March 20, 1940 diary entry, a year before her death, Woolf rebounds from two "attacks" of illness and from Leonard's criticism of *Roger Fry* through thoughts of Lady Hester and of writing of her once more. Woolf wants "to be winging off on small articles & stories. . . . Harpers wants an essay on Ly Hester Stanhope: the book I read that Christmas at Lelant [in Cornwall], & finished too soon, & put Lytton on the scent of. Yes; so I'm set up" (D 5: 272). Regrettably, she dies before beginning this assignment, before returning to Lady Hester Stanhope and to Dr. Meryon's diaries, for they might have refreshed and fortified her. Nevertheless, in 1909 Dr. Meryon's six diary volumes gave her rich matter for later work and showed her at age twenty-eight the wide reach of the diary form. A diary could preserve, and also *defend*, a life—and could also immortalize a diarist.

Ralph Waldo Emerson's Early *Journals*

"Emerson's *Journals* have little in common with other journals," Virginia Stephen begins her March 3, 1910 review of his early diaries (E 1: 335). She knows whereof she speaks for by 1910 she has read at least ten published diaries, including those of Pepys, Boswell, Burney, and Scott; has written reviews or essays on six of the ten; and has devoured several private family diaries, including those of her grandmother Stephen, her aunt Caroline Stephen, her cousin Madge Vaughan, in addition to, of course, repeatedly, her own.

Emerson's complete journals span more than fifty years. The two volumes twenty-eight-year-old Virginia reads in 1910 offer his first extant journals, kept from 1820 to 1832. These show Emerson from ages sixteen to twenty-nine, almost exactly the timeframe of Woolf's own diary-keeping to this point. Edward Waldo Emerson and Waldo Emerson Forbes, Emerson's son and grandson who edited the 1909 edition she read, also knew their forebear wrote a journal quite apart. In his "Introduction," Edward Emerson warns readers they will find everything in Emerson's journals "but what might be expected in a boy's diary; for of incidents, of classmates, of students' doings, there is hardly an entry. Throughout, and increasingly in later years, these are journals, not of incidents and persons, but of thoughts" (1: ix).

At Harvard, Emerson joins the Pythologian Society dedicated to writing and speaking. However, as Woolf observes in her review, while the journals "show that Emerson occasionally read and listened to papers comparing love and ambition, marriage and celibacy, town life and country life, they give no impression of intimacy" (E 1: 336). Emerson knew his coldness. "What is called a warm heart, I have not," he tells his journal at age twenty (1: 366). In a revealing entry two years before, he writes that the weather and his social calls have been so pleasant "that the mind has not possessed sufficiently the cold, frigid tone which is indispensable to become . . . *oracular*" (1: 117). Emerson seems to court emotional distance for his literary art. At twenty-four he confesses that "whilst places are alike to me, I make great distinction between states of mind. My days are made up of the irregular succession of a very few different tones of feeling" (2: 219).

At age twenty-eight Woolf finds Emerson's early journals narrow. Her critique particularly arrests, for it emerges in the face of all she shares with him. Both begin diaries in their early teens. Both adopt diary names but quickly drop them: Miss Jan, Virginia's diary persona; Junio, Emerson's bow to *The Spectator* and *Rambler*. Both are experimenting periodic diarists, Woolf sharing Emerson's "immoderate fondness for writing," which, he writes at age twenty, "has swelled these pages to a voluminous extent" (1: 361).

Both diarists read greedily many books at once. Emerson rebukes himself more than Woolf does for this "cardinal vice," this "sinful strolling from book to book" (2: 55); however, he cannot help himself. He keeps lists in his journals of the books and authors he reads each year and may have underscored for Woolf the merit of maintaining separate reading notebooks in this advice at age twenty-nine to his young cousin: "The best of all ways to make one's reading valuable is to *write* about it, and so I hope my cousin Elizabeth has a blank-book where she keeps some record of her thoughts" (2: 462).

Emerson studies Greek in the mornings and saves his beloved Walter Scott for day's end (2: 21). At age seventeen, he directs himself to "Take Scott's Novels and read carefully the mottoes of the chapters; or, if you prefer reading a novel itself, take the 'Bride of Lammermoor'" (1: 72). The latter was his favorite Scott novel across his days. At Harvard, Emerson organizes a book club that buys new poems and fiction, especially Scott's novels, and he often reads them aloud at meetings (1: 33n1). At twenty-five, in a journal entry titled "Novels," he writes: "The passion for novels is natural. Every child asks his Grandpapa to tell him a story. . . . Walter Scott is the grandpa of the grown up children" (2: 263).

Emerson's frail health across the dozen years of these *Journals* and his comments on it may also have interested his fellow diarist. At age eighteen Emerson uses his journal as a testing ground. "Amid my diseases and aches and qualms I will write to see if my brains are gone," he tells his journal, words that echo Virginia's in her 1905 diary (1: 137). The American calls himself "the melancholy Jacques," and his editors speak of "the general vital depression" that from 1822 to 1827 "nearly cost [Emerson] his life" (2: 245; 1: 142n1). The editors omit the first part of Emerson's twelfth journal because it reflects that depression (1: 267).

Did it edify (and fortify) Woolf to learn that in his thirties Emerson "stood condemned by many of the elder professors, clergy, and leading citizens, as visionary, dangerous, or insane" (1: xi)? Emerson embraces rather than shuns his ills—as Woolf also will do. "He has seen but half the Universe who never has been shown the house of Pain," he writes his aunt at age twenty-three, and when his wife of sixteen months dies in 1831, he asks his journal at age twenty-eight (Virginia's age when she reads him): "May I not value my griefs, and store them up?" (2: 180, 433). Emerson's editors report that walks—the diarist's "rambling tendencies"—helped restore his health (1: vii). Woolf may have quickened to his journal declarations of his "strong propensity for strolling" and belief that "The Poet, of course, is wandering, while Nature's thousand melodies are warbling to him" (2: 244; 1: 20).

Emerson's early journals, in short, offered much that might have spoken to twenty-eight-year-old Virginia Stephen. The American treats his journal as a consoling confidant. Even more importantly, he believed, as Woolf will come to believe, that journal-writing improves his prose. At age seventeen he calls his diary-keeping "an improving employment decidedly. It has not encroached upon other occupations. . . . It has prevented the *ennui* of many an idle moment and has perhaps enriched my stock of language for future exertions. . . . [I]ts office was to be a hasty, sketchy composition" (1: 31). Emerson uses his journal to spur himself on. At sixteen, he writes, "Mount on thy own path to Fame, nor swerve for man," the Pegasus horse trope used by Fanny Burney: in fact, the very lesson Virginia has gleaned from Lady Hester Stanhope, Lady Elizabeth Holland, and Princess Caroline of Wales (1: 14). At eighteen, in a journal entry titled "Greatness," Emerson suggests that this summit cannot be so rare as widely thought: "This very *hope* [of greatness] . . . is, in some sort, an earnest of the possibility of success" (1: 122).

In spite of these commonalities, Woolf views Emerson's journal sentiments as "platitudes" in her 1910 review and dubs his many journal essays "frigid exercises" (*E* 1: 338, 336). She reads James Eliot Cabot's two-volume *Memoir of Ralph Waldo Emerson* in tandem with the *Journals*.[18] The *Journals'* editors twice recommend it, the first time pointing readers to Cabot's inclusion of "a pleasant letter" from Emerson on the joy of dwelling in the country.[19] Perhaps she also sought atmosphere in Cabot's *Memoir* to surround the *Journals'* "thoughts."

To prepare for her review, she likely also reread her father's essay on Emerson, for her criticism of the American diarist reprises and extends his critique. Leslie Stephen's essay turns on Emerson's *simplicity*. Calling the American a "pure, simple-minded, high-feeling man, made of the finest clay of human nature," Leslie Stephen declared that Emerson's "special function" was to "find effective utterance for . . . 'simplest truths,'" truths "altogether above the sphere in which controversy is possible" (*Studies of a Biographer* 4: 155, 126, 128). His simple truths are delivered in "a 'mosaic' of separate sentences," explains Stephen, who complains that "His characteristic want of continuity made him as incapable of evolving a central idea as of expounding an argument. . . . [H]e often coins exquisite phrases, but he is abrupt and fragmentary and apt to break down both in grammar and rhythm" (4: 127, 151).

Virginia's 1910 review elaborates this critique. "[T]he wonder is," she writes, "that, treating as he does of platitudes and expounding them for our good, he yet contrives to make them glow so frequently, as if, next minute, they would illumine the world" (*E* 1: 338). Such a gift is not negligible, she acknowledges, though it is not one she much esteems: "He had the poet's gift of turning far, abstract thoughts, if not into flesh and blood, at least into something firm and glittering. In the pages of his diary one can see how his style slowly emerged from its wrappings, and became more definite and so strong that we can still read it even when the thought is too remote to hold us" (*E* 1: 338). She, of course, wants "flesh and blood." Taking up her father's word "fragmentary," she, too, focuses on Emerson's syntax, faulting him for single (simple) thoughts rather than commingling (complex) ones. "Emerson did not see that one can write with phrases as well as with words," she explains. "His sentences are made up of hard fragments each of which has been matched separately with the vision in his head. It is far rarer to find sentences which, lacking emphasis because the joins are perfect and the words common, yet grow together so that you cannot dismember them, and are steeped in meaning and suggestion" (*E* 1: 338). This criticism echoes her 1908 diary rebuke of Perugino's painting. The elements in Perugino's fresco "compose one idea in his mind," just as Emerson's fragments are "matched separately with the vision in his head," but that "one idea" fails to capture the world in its rich suggestive flux (*PA* 392).

Woolf finds Emerson's tack "priggish" and impoverished (*E* 1: 338). Born in a new world with few traditions of its own—the barely trammeled space she prefers—Emerson disappoints her by failing to capture the moving shades. He becomes a priggish schoolmaster instead, she observes, and remains an immature artist:

> born among half-taught people, in a new land, [Emerson] kept always the immature habit of conceiving that man is made up of separate qualities, which can be separately developed and praised. It is a belief necessary to schoolmasters; and to some extent Emerson is always a schoolmaster, making the world very simple for his scholars, a place of discipline and reward. But this simplicity, which is in his diaries as well as in his finished works . . . is the result not only of ignoring so much, but of such concentration upon a few things. By means of it he can produce an extraordinary effect of exaltation, as though the disembodied mind were staring at the truth. . . . But these exaltations are not practicable; they will not stand interruption. (*E* 1: 339)

Her critique of Emerson's early journals reflects her own steadily evolving artistic vision. Has she not just resisted the single word "eccentric" for Lady Hester Stanhope? Her review says at least as much about her own literary preferences as about Emerson's self-acknowledged "very few different tones of feeling" (2: 219). Scholar Lawrence Rosenwald calls Emerson "the greatest American diarist of the [nineteenth] century" (53). Woolf resembles Emerson in her long period of diary experiment and late arrival to mature diary form. However, her review precisely captures their differences in method and in view.

In his excellent *Emerson and the Art of the Diary*, Rosenwald describes Emerson's efforts to resist the simplifications of the Lockean commonplace book:

> Clearly, [John] Locke's commonplacer lives in a world of sharply and evidently differentiated topics. . . .
> But the real genius of Locke's method is its elimination of the circumstantial. . . . [H]is method cleverly and efficiently removes the detritus of historical or personal context clinging to the passages we dredge up and leaves them bright, clean, and isolated, isolated not only from us who found them, from the context in which they emerged as interesting, but also from one another. . . . [W]hat better way to prevent that association of ideas that Locke identified as the great source of error? (31–32)

In 1910, Virginia Stephen recoils from these bright but isolated fragments; in fact, the *historical, personal,* and *communal* are just what she desires. Rosenwald argues that Emerson himself rebelled against Lockean narrowness, and that it was in his gradual rejection of Lockean dominance in 1833, *after* the *Journal* volumes Woolf read, that he moves from an immature to a mature diarist. We lack, however, Woolf's view of these later journals, and suspect she would not accept the transcendentalist view that "every thought is a world," that, as Emerson also told his journal: "the World reproduce[s] itself in miniature in every event that transpires, so that all the laws of nature may be read in the smallest fact. So that the truth speaker may dismiss all solicitude as to the proportion (of) & congruency of the aggregate of his thoughts so long as he is a faithful reporter of particular impressions" (*Journals and Miscellaneous Notebooks* 4: 53; 7: 302–3).

Woolf retained her view of Emerson's simplicity across at least fourteen years. In her January 30, 1920 review of *A Treasury of English Prose*, she questions the inclusion of eleven pages of Emerson at the expense of other writers and once more faults his inorganic form:

> Passages seem to break off in one's hands like ripe fruit without damage to the tree. The first passage reads beautifully; the second almost as well. But then—what is it? Something bald and bare and glittering—something light and brittle—something which suggests that if this precious fruit were dropped it would shiver into particles of silvery dust like one of those balls that were plucked from the boughs of ancient Christmas trees, and slipped and fell—is Emerson's fruit *that* kind of fruit? Of course the luster is admirable—the dust, the dust of the stars. (*E* 3: 173)

Woolf wants, of course, the fruit *and* the tree, something *this* worldly—not broken off and glittery like the distant, separate stars. Nearly three years later, in her fascinating August 17, 1923 diary entry that pictures *The Common Reader*, she lists Emerson among the authors to treat. However, she never writes at length on him again. In her lively July 3, 1924 bashing of *The Week-End Book* in the *Times Literary Supplement*, she again singles out Emerson as a dubious inclusion in this book of poems, songs, games, and cocktail recipes—all of which she rejects for the greater outdoors.

Mary Coleridge's Diary

"Dont you think that Miss Sichel, that talented Jewess, has trampled Mary Coleridge a little flat?" Virginia Stephen asks her friend, Lady Eleanor Cecil, in 1910 (*L* #525, 1: 426). She refers to *Gathered Leaves from the Prose of Mary E. Coleridge*, a new collection of writings from Samuel Taylor Coleridge's great-great niece. The book includes extracts from Mary's diary introduced by a forty-four-page memoir from historian and poet Edith Sichel. Woolf never knew Mary Coleridge whereas Lady Cecil likely did.[20] Nevertheless, Woolf treats Coleridge as a kindred spirit. Her wish for a richer portrait of this recently deceased foremother hints at her regard. In fact, Coleridge stays in Woolf's mind across many years.

Mary Coleridge was born in 1861 into a literary family even more distinguished than the Stephens. "As a child she was delicate and shrinking, the prey of an almost painful sensitiveness," Sichel discloses in her memoir, a second trait Mary shared with Virginia (and with Virginia's diary mother, Fanny Burney) (3). Like Burney and Woolf, Coleridge possesses a beloved sister. Like them, too, she escapes from the world through books. Mary adores Walter Scott. She was "one of the leading spirits among a circle of eager children, who met together every Saturday to act the Waverly novels," Sichel notes (4). The shy girl assumes the role of Ivanhoe! At age thirteen, she meets William Cory, the poet and master of Eton whose own diary Virginia read at age fifteen. Once more figures in Woolf's diary world meet and mingle.

Mary's education surpassed Virginia's in rigor, a fact the younger writer no doubt saw. According to Sichel, at age nineteen Coleridge was well versed in Hebrew, German, French, and Italian, and a little later, with Cory's help, she becomes a keen reader of Greek. She takes classes in English literature at King's College for Women and travels to Perugia and Florence—sites Virginia has just preserved in her own 1908 and 1909 diaries. Mary steeps herself in history, poetry, and art. She often visits Tennyson at Farringford on the Isle of Wight, although she is "too timid to reveal herself" to him (25). She places a wreath on G. F. Watts' grave at Compton (260). Thus, like diarist William Allingham, she witnesses the Freshwater scene. When Robert Browning calls upon her parents, Mary again shies from speech, but he exerts a strong influence on her life, and it grieves her that Cory "cared not at all about Browning" (14, 331). She, in turn, dislikes Thomas Carlyle (219). Mary Coleridge and Virginia Stephen shared a side vocation as well, although again Virginia would have seen that Coleridge taught night classes at the Working Women's College for a dozen years (from 1895 to 1907)—service much longer than her own.

Mary Coleridge, in short, forged a path Virginia Stephen is following in 1910, for Mary, that sensitive, shy reader and admirer of Walter Scott, becomes a reviewer, essayist, and novelist (and a poet too). And she kept a diary as well. "The tail of the comet S.T.C.," as she was called, wrote reviews, first for the *Guardian* and *Monthly Review* and then, starting in 1902, for the *Times Literary Supplement*—three years before Virginia starts her own *Times* reviews. Some readers said of Coleridge's essays what they would later say of Woolf's: that they were "the prose work of hers they love the best" (26). And the never-married writer enjoyed her success. "She no longer came into a room apologetically—her presence gained a certain repose," Sichel writes (29). Although "she hardly knew what she had on. . . . she began to like accepting invitations" (41, 29). All this will prove true of Virginia Stephen Woolf. In fact, Coleridge's 1905 novel *The Shadow on the Wall*, derived from one of her earlier short stories, likely inspired Woolf's own short story "The Mark on the Wall."[21]

Mary Coleridge's life and work offered much to inspire twenty-eight-year-old, unmarried Virginia Stephen in 1910. Sichel praises Coleridge's "airy treatment of the real" (28). "Fantastic she was to excess," Sichel declares, "and there were hours when she let her fancies, light as thistle-down, take her anywhere so long as she need not tread on solid earth" (1–2). Coleridge's moods shifted rapidly. "She was as changeful as the sea she so adored," Sichel reports. "No one was more affected by Nature" (16). Coleridge herself writes in a diary entry (or letter): "How I do love the tossing and kissing and crushing of the waves" (237).

Coleridge embraces change and range. "Talk of myriad-minded Shakespeare," she writes in either her diary or a letter (extracted in *Gathered Leaves*). "Why, the commonest man breathing has many, many more than a myriad minds. I am a different person every twelve hours. I go to bed as feminine as

Ophelia, fiery, enthusiastic, ready to go to the stake for some righteous cause. I get up the very next morning, almost as masculine as Falstaff, grumbling at Family Prayers" (221). Here is another possible seed for *Orlando*.

According to Coleridge, whim should be prized, not decried. "Besides the terrific knowledge," she writes of William Cory, "he had that vein of caprice which seems to me sometimes to mark out all the really great critics—men who were poets before they turned to criticism—men like Sir Philip Sidney, Charles Lamb, Mat Arnold, FitzGerald, and so on" (241). "[L]*ife* lives in her books," Sichel declares, a phrase likely to attract Woolf, and Coleridge sees talk as a key ingredient (28). She preserves not just Cory's own "Table Talk" but, within it, his praise of Plato's *Apology*: "Such easy, trickling talk! In Plato it is all talk and not artificial speech. This is his art" (293).

When obstacles rise, Coleridge reaffirms her wish to write. "I shall always go on writing, because it amuses me so" is "the conclusion of her moral questionings, when debating her right to make books at all," Sichel reports (21)—a sentiment akin to Virginia's 1909 Florence diary declaration: "As for me—I write. The instinct wells like sap in a tree" (*PA* 395). And Coleridge "corrected and re-corrected and re-wrote, with a scrupulous perseverance" (34).

After Sichel's opening memoir, *Gathered Leaves from the Prose of Mary E. Coleridge* offers 9 of Mary's short stories, 8 essays, 6 unpublished poems (despite the volume's titular promise of "prose"), and 149 passages from her diaries and letters from age twenty-one to forty-six—along with a 49-page appendix printing her "Notes from the Table Talk of William Cory" and a concluding poem, "Mary Coleridge." Regrettably, Sichel chose to omit the dates of many of the diary and letter excerpts. Worse still, she does not reveal whether a given extract comes from the diary or from a letter. We do learn that Coleridge created a diary persona, like Fanny Burney's "Miss Nobody" and Woolf's early "Miss Jan." The following passage, which describes her diary method and intentions, suggests that Coleridge saw herself as an artist shaping her life:

[The diary] shall be just my daily life, the life behind the scenes, and the audience shall sit at the back, and for the Dramatis Personae I will myself represent them, for of what other do I know anything? and lest this *I* should grow troublesome and importunate, I will christen myself over again, making George Macdonald my godfather, and name myself after my favourite hero, Anodos in *Phantastes*. . . . If Anodos dies or gets married, the work will be discontinued; no one writes diaries in Paradise. If not, *vogue la galère*. (23–24)

Diary (or letter) extracts reveal Coleridge's interest in women and their plight. Like Woolf, Coleridge imagines herself back to earlier times as this droll 1897 diary (or letter) excerpt reveals:

I take personal interest in the Anglo-Saxon nuns of the ninth century, because if I had happened to be born then instead of in the nineteenth, I should have had to enter a convent from the impossibility of getting books anywhere else. They were obliged by their abbesses to read two hours a day, and they wore fringes (for which the bishops had them up), and corresponded with St. Boniface, or any other saint they could find, in bad Latin, and went to Rome on pilgrimage whenever they were tired of one another, and were dreadfully afraid of meeting Saracens there. Five hundred of them once danced for joy on the grave of a novice-mistress whom they hated, till the earth sank in half a foot, and the Abbess condemned them to fast three days on account of the hardness of their hearts. My opinion is that unmarried ladies had a high old time of it in those days. (236)

This more serious 1890 reflection may have intrigued—and fortified—Woolf: "Ibsen's delicate way of unfolding character seems to me wonderful, and a man that thoroughly understands a woman was a very great man indeed. There are two or three people who can tell stories about her, and one or two who can put her into a book without killing her during the process, but how few can get her alive on to the stage not laughing only, not crying only, but doing both, and that not hundreds of years ago in blank verse, but dressed in the latest fashion, and talking prose" (227).

In an 1897 diary (or letter) passage, Coleridge decries the treatment of "Woman," both en mass and in literature. "Woman with a big W bores me supremely," she writes. "How γυνὴ would have puzzled the beautiful concrete Greeks. It is a mere abstraction born of monks and the mists of the North. A woman I know, but what on earth is Woman? She has done her best to spoil history, poetry, novels, essays, and Sir Thomas Browne and Thoreau are the only things safe from her; that's why I love them" (234). Such sentiments anticipate Woolf's similar complaint of women's role in fiction in *A Room of One's Own.*

Coleridge's diary (or letter) views of literary structure may also have struck Woolf. "I have rapidly come to believe that construction is not nearly so important as people think," Coleridge declares. "It is to a book what morality is to a person. But there are delicious books without any construction at all, and delicious people with no morality" (264). Coleridge chooses madness over rigid design. "The Blake pictures in Ryder Street are amazing," she tells her diary (or an unidentified correspondent). "I am all on the side of madmen" (256).

Perhaps most intriguing is her 1896 diary (or letter) turn on Faust's "Stay, thou art fair!"—a phrase Woolf will take up as well: "I have said to so many moments in life, 'Stay, thou art fair!' . . . Only they never stayed. And you have as much chance of finding the same moment again as the same mortal. Joy is a host of happinesses, each quite unlike all the rest. A thud behind me. Only the lily falling to bits. I did so want her to stay till to-morrow, so that the St. T———s might see her. But she won't stay. She is fair" (231). Twenty-two years later, in her December 31, 1932, diary entry, Woolf echoes: "If one does not lie back & sum up & say to the moment, this very moment, stay you are so fair, what will be one's gain, dying? No: stay, this moment. No one ever says that enough. Always hurry. I am now going in, to see L. & say stay this moment" (D 4: 135).

Woolf writes of Mary Coleridge four times to Lady Cecil between December 1907 and August 1908—the year following Coleridge's 1907 death from acute appendicitis at age forty-six. In December 1907, Woolf thanks Lady Cecil for sending her the posthumous collection of Mary's *Poems, New and Old*. The poems, Virginia writes, "have great charm—but I think H. Newbolt has printed too many fragments dont you? Some read like rash experiments. But they are very interesting" (L #398, 1: 320–21). In April 1908, she tells Lady Cecil that Coleridge "has a curious magic for 2 or 3 lines, or even more; but it seems to fade very easily. I don't suppose she could have managed a long poem—but some of these are perfect" (L #405, 1: 324). In an August 1908 letter to Lady Cecil, she places Coleridge in the line of lasting writers. "Did I say that Mary Coleridges poems would fade?" she asks. "I meant only that they are very slight; some seem to me first rate, in that line; they say exactly what she meant. I dont know what happens to such things, but I expect one or two manage to go on, for hundreds of years, like those anonymous poems, which are so charming, in the Anthologies" (L #436, 1: 353).

Woolf finds a clear foremother in Coleridge's great-great niece. She meets a writer publishing in many forms who savors change and transformation: one who goes to bed Ophelia and gets up as Falstaff. She finds a kindred mind that faults woman's treatment in literature. That Woolf remembers Mary Coleridge and perhaps is fortified by her can be seen from her 1924 *Times Literary Supplement* review of Molly MacCarthy's memoir, *A Nineteenth-Century Childhood*. Woolf praises MacCarthy for catching the nineteenth-century world, including "Mary Coleridge reading Browning aloud" (E 3: 444).

7

The Diary Coalesces

"To coalesce" means to grow together or fuse. This happens to Woolf's diary from 1915 to 1918. In 1915, the now married diarist blends place and portrait, event and thought, into an engaging life diary mural. In 1917, she re-grounds herself after illness through her country Asheham House natural history diary; however, she quickly adds a city diary alongside this country diary. And as her experimental first diary stage comes to an intensive close, her diaries both reach out and coalesce. She reads the Goncourt brothers' collaborative *Journals* in 1917, which spur her to try a joint diary of her own with Leonard. In her first 1918 Hogarth House diary, she both extends individual diary days and merges them—and blends her country and city styles as well. We leave her in July 1918 ready to launch her mature, spare (modernist) diary style.

The diaries Woolf reads during this expansive and coalescing time could not be more fortuitous. The *Journals* of Mary (Seton) Berry, which Woolf likely reads in early 1916, present an even more fervent voice for women than Mary Coleridge's—and the whole kernel of *A Room of One's Own*. The diaries of the literary curate Stopford Brooke, reviewed in 1917, show Woolf a searching mind, a mind continually opening and unifying across his creative days. In the last year of her life, Woolf tries to remember Stopford Brooke and to write a history of English literature akin to his in her unfinished "Anon."

Virginia Woolf's 1915 Diary

"The day is rather like a leafless tree: there are all sorts of colours in it, if you look closely. But the outline is bare enough."
(January 29, 1915; D 1: 30)

A mysterious gap of more than five years yawns between Virginia Woolf's 1909 life diary and her next surviving diary—a daily diary begun January 1, 1915.

This longest hiatus in Woolf's forty-four-year diary history invites thought. Several scenarios seem possible. Diary books for 1910, 1911, 1912, and perhaps even for part of 1913 may have been kept but then lost in September 1940 when Hitler's bombs destroyed Woolf's London flat. She salvaged most of her diary books from the rubble, but did she retrieve them all? How dreadful to think of her diary as a literal casualty of war, and yet how easily this might have occurred.[1]

The discovery in 2002 of a heretofore unknown diary—Woolf's 1909 life diary—fuels a more hopeful thought. Perhaps Leonard Woolf possessed *other* diaries that might yet still emerge. His biographer, Victoria Glendinning, describes the deluge of papers and books that flooded Monk's House (317). Virginia's return to a London diary in 1909 after four years of travel diary kindles hope that she continued diary-keeping. Would a diarist who has been maintaining several kinds of diaries rather continuously since Christmas 1904 suddenly stop diarizing altogether from 1910 through 1914? On the other hand, she seems to revisit in her 1908 and 1909 diaries the form and diction of her 1903 diary; perhaps she had explored the diary form all she could by 1909 and turned to other work.

Time may clarify this five-year caesura. Intriguingly, Walter Scott, Fanny Burney, and Samuel Pepys appear at the 1915 diary rebirth. These lively British diarists, whom Woolf first read at ages fourteen and fifteen as she launched her own first diary, hover over the new diary, one is tempted to say, like smiling parents. Scott dominates. On January 2, the second day of her diary, Woolf records reading his *Guy Mannering*. The diary emerges, therefore, with Scott's prose. Her January 11 entry begins rather erotically: "Leonard was in his bath this morning, & I was lying in bed, wondering whether I should stretch out my hand for *Rob Roy*, when I heard a commotion next door" (*D* 1: 15). On January 19 she compares Scott to Dostoevsky, underscoring the elastic, easy style she craves: "[Dostoevsky] seems to me to have the same kind of vitality in him that Scott had; only Scott merely made superb ordinary people, & D. creates wonders, with very subtle brains, & fearful sufferings. Perhaps the likeness to Scott partly consists in the loose, free & easy, style of the translation" (*D* 1: 23). Six days later, Leonard delights her on her thirty-third birthday with a three-volume first edition of Scott's novel *The Abbot*. Scott thus hovers in the background across these days. Woolf also recalls with joy the female diarist she calls "the mother of English fiction." On January 10, she describes a visit from Walter Lamb, who recounts his audience with King George V. The King's "style of talk reminds me of George 3rd in Fanny Burney's diary—," Woolf notes, "&

so one must bless Walter for something" (*D* 1: 14). She closes her January 27 entry with this nod to Pepys: "Home & finished Pope, & so to bed" (*D* 1: 29).

Thirty-six entries comprise Woolf's 1915 diary which covers the forty-six days from January 1 to February 15. This diary book lacks a cover today, but it is large: nine inches wide and eleven-and-a-quarter inches long. The volume's pages are white with blue lines, her ink also blue. That she takes pains with this new large diary can be sensed from the gummed labels she employs to mark each day; in fact, she even types the day of the week and the date on the first eleven labels before gluing them to the page.[2] She maintains a daily diary from January 1 through February 2. A ten-day gap then occurs, and when she returns she inserts her final three entries (for February 13, 14, and 15) on different paper: narrower and longer unlined sheets.

Woolf appears to reread her 1915 diary as she creates it—or at least the previous entry before starting the next. This reveals her interest in her diary and her wish, perhaps, for textual continuity. Her January 6 entry describes her ambivalence regarding a party that night at Vanessa's. The January 7 entry begins "No—we didn't go to the Gordon Sqre party," as if her entries converse with each other (*D* 1: 10). Her January 11 entry opens with an amused description of a minor fire in their lodgings set by Lizzy, the hapless maid. The next day's entry begins dryly: "Today did not begin with a fire" (*D* 1: 16). Diary entries thus link and narratives begin and unfold.

The 1915 diary is the first diary by Virginia *Woolf* rather than Virginia Stephen. The Woolfs had been married more than two years by January 1, 1915, although Virginia's illness and resulting rest-home stays in 1913 and 1914 caused their occasional separation. The daily 1915 diary discloses marital intimacy, particularly Woolf's pleasure in the nighttime dressing gown ease she had linked with writing in her 1903 diary. On January 6, as she ponders Vanessa's party, she writes: "On the third & final hand, the evenings reading by the fire here—reading Michelet & The Idiot, & smoking & talking to L. in what stands for slippers & dressing gown—are heavenly too. And as he won't urge me to go, I know very well that I shant. Besides, there is vanity: I have no clothes to go in" (*D* 1: 10). Woolf looks back on her single life in her January 15 entry: "We are dining early, & going to a Hall—an unheard of dissipation—though there was a time when I went out to operas, evening concerts &c, at least three times a week—And I know we shall both feel, when its over, 'really a good read would have been better'" (*D* 1: 19).

Morning intimacy reigns as well as evening. "We wrote this morning" repeats across the diary (*D* 1: 20, 4, 7, 17, 30, 33). That Woolf's rapport with her husband includes writing her diary in his presence is seen in this January 18 entry in which their intimacy interrupts the diary: "as I began this page, L. stated that he had determined to resign his commission to write a pamphlet about Arbitration—& now I shall stop this diary & discuss that piece of folly with him" (D 1: 22).

Leonard showers Virginia with gifts and treats on her thirty-third birthday, January 25; in fact, she writes, he "crept into my bed, with a little parcel, which was a beautiful green purse. And he brought up breakfast" (D 1: 28). As noted, some readers accuse Woolf of diary reserve; however, she reports marital discord on January 31, laments it, and seeks to understand it—although she refrains from rehearsing details. "O dear! We quarreled almost all the morning!" she exclaims. "& it was a lovely morning, & now gone to Hades for ever, branded with the marks of our ill humour. Which began it? Which carried it on? God knows. This I will say: I explode: & L. smoulders. However, quite suddenly we made it up, (but the morning was wasted)" (D 1: 31). Thirteen days later all seems well. After a ten-day diary gap, she writes February 13, "I met L. at Spikings & we had tea, & were very happy" (D 1: 34).

House hunting increases their intimacy (and commitment to each other) during the six weeks preserved in this diary. The search for more permanent housing becomes one of the diary's key storylines. In October 1914, the Woolfs had taken lodgings at 17 The Green, Richmond-on-Thames. Household catastrophes at The Green, running in tandem with the serious house search, become a comic diary motif. By January 22, Woolf is calling number 17 "this House of Trouble" (D 1: 25). Fourteen of the thirty-six entries document the vigorous search that leads to Hogarth House. On January 6, Woolf inspects chambers at Gray's Inn, and the next day she seeks rooms in Bloomsbury at Brunswick and Mecklenburgh Squares. Hogarth House (in the London suburb of Richmond) is mentioned on January 8, but they explore houses in Westminster and Wimbledon as well.

Over tea on her birthday, January 25, they resolve to take Hogarth House "if we can get it," and on January 30 she boasts "I have a nose for a house, & that was a perfect house, if ever there was one" (D 1: 28, 31). On February 1, she ends her entry with an exclamation: "it seems quite likely at this moment that we shall get Hogarth! I wish it were tomorrow. I am certain it is the best house to take" (D 1: 32–33). She replies with her next entry: "Well, it is tomorrow; & we are certainly nearer to Hogarth than we were. We have done little else & thought of little else all day, so it is as well we have some profit—" (D 1: 33). Her words here parallel her 1897 description of Stella's death: "That is all we have thought of since; & it is impossible to write of" (*PA* 115). The 1915 diary stops abruptly with the two-sentence entry ending with a dash—and it does not resume for ten days. The page following the halted February 2 entry is titled "The House," and Woolf underlines the title. However, this entry also stops abruptly after only two words: "The cause [?]." Both items suggest "The House" plays a role in the diary breach.

Three passages in the 1915 diary function as arresting counterpoint to the Hogarth commitment. On January 6, Woolf confides to her diary, "I could wander about the dusky streets in Holborn & Bloomsbury for hours. The things one sees—& guesses at—the tumult & riot & busyness of it all—Crowded streets are the only places, too, that ever make me what-in-the-case of another-one-might-call think" (*D* 1: 9). On January 28, after deciding for Hogarth on her birthday three days before, she suggests that London is more serious than Richmond—a portentous remark. "I decided to go to London, for the sake of hearing the Strand roar, which I think one does want, after a day or two of Richmond," she writes, launching a theme that will unfold across her diary until she leaves Richmond for London in 1924. "Somehow, one can't take Richmond seriously. One has always come here for an outing, I suppose; & that is part of its charm, but one wants serious life sometimes" (*D* 1: 29–30). Removed now to the Richmond suburb—hardly the same as "country" refreshment—Woolf finds creative nourishment in London *streets* if not in London lodgings. "Then I had tea, & rambled down to Charing Cross in the dark," unfolds her final 1915 diary entry, "making up phrases & incidents to write about" (*D* 1: 35).

Search for a suitable home supplies dramatic tension across the 1915 diary. The diary's most striking features, however, beyond its engaging narrative links, are its range, speed, and assurance. This diary differs from the previous diaries Woolf has kept, as if by age thirty-two she has absorbed the best of Scott, Burney, and Pepys (and the other diaries she now has read) and will explore the diary form anew. The diary's opening exudes confidence. "To start this diary rightly, it should begin on the last day of the old year, when, at breakfast, I received a letter from Mrs Hallett," she begins, launching the work with dramatic servant affairs and a novelistic scene (*D* 1: 3). The first entry moves swiftly through a range of topics: Lily, the wayward Asheham servant; Mrs. Waterlow's unjust chimney sweep bill; a visit to the Co-ops in the rain; and the sinking of the British warship *Formidable*. On this first day of 1915, Woolf seems immersed in the wash of daily life: servants, bills, organizations, and the news of war. Her last extant diary, the 1909 life diary, consisted of six essay-entries on separate, titled topics. The 1909 Florence travel diary similarly focused more on individual portraits than on events—or even places. With the 1915 diary, Woolf blends people and place, thoughts and events. We find a rich and various life diary, one ranging swiftly from corns to kings (*D* 1: 14, 19, 31).

Woolf frames her second entry as a specimen day. It showcases the loose and easy, swift-moving and wide-ranging life writing that characterizes the 1915 diary—and most of Woolf's diaries to come:

> This is the kind of day which if it were possible to choose an altogether average sample of our life, I should select. We breakfast; I interview Mrs Le Grys [their landlady]. She complains of the huge Belgian appetites, & their preference for food fried in butter. "They never *give* one anything" she remarked. The Count, taking Xmas dinner with them, insisted, after Pork & Turkey, that he wanted a third meat. Therefore Mrs Le G. hopes that the war will soon be over. If they eat thus in their exile, how must they eat at home, she wonders? After this, L. & I both settle down to our scribbling. He finishes his Folk Story review, & I do about 4 pages of poor Effie's story [*Night and Day*]; we lunch; & read the papers, agree that there is no news. I read Guy Mannering upstairs for 20 minutes; & then we take Max [their dog] for a walk. Halfway up the Bridge, we found ourselves cut off by the river, which rose visibly, with a little ebb & flow, like the pulse of a heart. Indeed, the road we had come along was crossed, after 5 minutes, by a stream several inches deep. One of the queer things about the suburbs is that the vilest little red villas are always let, & that not one of them has an open window, or an uncurtained window. I expect that people take a pride in their curtains, & there is great rivalry among neighbours. One house had curtains of yellow silk, striped with lace insertion. The rooms inside must be in semi-darkness; & I suppose rank with the smell of meat & human beings. I believe that being curtained is a mark of respectability—Sophie [their cook] used to insist upon it. And then I did my marketing. Saturday night is the great buying night; & some counters are besieged by three rows of women. I always choose the empty shops, where I suppose, one pays ½ [d] a lb. more. And then we had tea, & honey & cream; & now L. is typewriting his article; & we shall read all the evening & go to bed. (*D* 1: 4–5)

The entry moves swiftly from household affairs to writing and reading, and then to the outer world of nature and the suburbs, both carefully observed (and considered). In fact, the diarist projects herself into curtained rooms. A character, Mrs Le Grys, appears (she will become a familiar figure); her conversation is captured (using Fanny Burney's italics); and the war enters the diary in the form of daily domestic dis-ease. We notice Woolf's interest in women— "Saturday night is the great buying night"—and Woolf the public historian. We sense her curiosity regarding curtains as a social symbol and see her writing with her mind as well as her eye. The poet, too, is felt in the poignant image of the Thames, its "little ebb & flow, like the pulse of a heart." And all in a light and easy manner that belies the range of private and public, natural and cultural worlds conjoined.

Twice before Woolf tried a daily diary: in 1897 and 1905. Each of these diaries was so small—the brown leather 1897 diary only three-and-a-half inches wide and five-and-a-half inches long; the gray paper-covered 1904–5 diary four-and-a-half inches wide and five-and-three-quarter inches long—that they discouraged diary expansion. The large 1915 daily diary starts narratives—and unfolds them—creating interest and delight. Lily, the transgressing Asheham House servant (appearing in entries January 1, 4, 6, 7, and 15), is followed by Lizzy, the hopeless Richmond maid who breaks plates and sets the house afire (January 11, 12, 14, 22, 26, 30). "We were woken this morning (I see this is going to become a stock phrase like 'Once upon a Time' in a Faery story)," Woolf cracks in her January 14 entry that recounts Lizzy's latest blaze (D 1: 17). Lizzy, in turn, gives way to Maud, brain "full of illusions," January 29 and 30 (D 1: 30–31). We savor the jousts with the complaining Waterlows who have rented Asheham House from Virginia (January 1, 4, 5, 6, 7, 8, 14) and learn of Marjorie Strachey's love for Josiah Wedgwood—an affair treated sympathetically and seriously by Woolf (January 17, 20, 23). The war threads its way through it all, always there, obliquely met or addressed directly (January 1, 2, 3, 4, 5, 6, 7, 11, 12, 13, 14, 15, 16, 17, 18, 20, 21, 23, 24, 25, 26, 28; February 1, 14).[3]

The 1915 diary thus starts several stories and begins to create a world. Swift brushstrokes take the place of lengthy portraits, the diarist allowing her likenesses to accrete across time. Walter Lamb, like the servant Lizzy, becomes a recurring comic figure "shining in his alabastrine baldness like a marble fountain" (D 1: 34). Fresh similes like this amuse us and also animate the scene. John Maynard Keynes "is like quicksilver on a sloping board—a little inhuman, but very kindly, as inhuman people are" (D 1: 24). Molly MacCarthy is "incoherent, inattentive, & fragmentary as usual; like a little grey moth among machines" (D 1: 27). Beatrice Webb is "like an industrious spider at the table; spinning her webs (a pun!—) incessantly," while Flora, the youngest of Leonard's sisters, "will keep lively till a great old age, like a man playing with five billiard balls" (D 1: 26, 6). Similes allow Woolf to define, animate, and enlarge her subjects. "Shall

I say 'nothing happened today' as we used to do in our diaries, when they were beginning to die?" she asks January 29, and then answers: "It wouldn't be true. The day is rather like a leafless tree: there are all sorts of colours in it, if you look closely. But the outline is bare enough" (D 1: 30). "*There are all sorts of colours in it*" exactly sums up the 1915 diary.

Questions, as well as similes, enlarge the diary entries. "Does the weather prompt suicide?" Woolf wonders January 5 (D 1: 7). "Shall I say 'nothing happened today' . . . ? It wouldn't be true" (D 1: 30). Most of the diary's questions concern people, revealing Woolf's great curiosity regarding human beings—and human nature. "What is the truth?" she wonders in her first entry, of the servant Lily's contentious behavior—the same question she raised in 1909 regarding Mrs. Annie Loeb: "What was the truth of the matter . . . ?" (D 1: 3; CH 14). "Lizzy left, carrying a brown paper parcel & whistling loudly," Woolf writes January 28, "—I wonder where she has gone?" (D 1: 30). Woolf's quarrel with Leonard leads to questions: "Which began it? Which carried it on?"—questions with the rhythm of "Where do they come from, & whither are they bound?" from the 1905 Cornwall diary (D 1: 31; PA 296).

The 1915 diary serves as a reading notebook and a writer's diary too. Woolf uses her January 19 entry to envision future prose, a diary practice she will follow for the rest of her life. "I shall write a book of 'Eccentrics,'" she boldly declares (D 1: 23). She predicts public praise and private censure for her forthcoming first novel, *The Voyage Out*. Anticipating reader response will become another diary rite. She records an incident February 1 that will launch *Mrs. Dalloway*: "In St James Street there was a terrific explosion; people came running out of Clubs; stopped still & gazed about them. But there was no Zeppelin or aeroplane—only, I suppose, a very large tyre burst" (D 1: 32).

Woolf comments astutely on her own and others' writing. Comparing herself to Leonard, she hints not only that she possesses more self-confidence as a writer than he but also that her writerly *self-consciousness* preserves her from deep despair. On January 18 she attributes much of Leonard's melancholy "to sheer lack of self confidence in his power of writing; as if he mightn't be a writer, after all; & being a practical man, his melancholy sinks far deeper than the half assumed melancholy of self conscious people like Lytton, & Sir Leslie & myself" (D 1: 23). Her writerly critique of Leonard's novel, *The Wise Virgins*, intrigues. She finds it "a remarkable book; very bad in parts; first rate in others. A writer's book, I think, because only a writer perhaps can see why the good parts are so very good, & why the very bad parts aren't very bad" (D 1: 32). We wish she would say more.

Quentin Bell suspects that Woolf's 1915 diary "was at this time intended partly as a sedative, a way of proving to herself how normal she now was" (2: 23–24). Why the daily 1915 diary abruptly pauses February 2—and ends completely with the February 15 entry—remains a tantalizing question. We know Woolf becomes ill in late February, a first sign of the long illness soon to follow. Olivier Bell suggests that Woolf's anxiety regarding the soon-to-appear *The Voyage Out* "may well have been the cause of her renewed insanity" (D 1: 3). Woolf's one diary reference to this novel expresses apprehension, even dissatisfaction, with the work set to be published March 15: "everyone, so I predict will assure me [that the novel] is the most brilliant thing they've ever read; & privately condemn, as indeed it deserves to be condemned" (D 1: 29). That she says nothing more may in itself suggest unspeakable concern.

Although more prosaic, the weather may have been the real culprit, bringing on her illness. "Does the weather prompt suicide?" she asked as early as January 5 (D 1: 7). She begins her February 13 entry—after a ten-day interval—with these words: "There was a great downpour this morning. I am sure however many years I keep this diary, I shall never find a winter to beat this. It seems to have lost all self-control" (D 1: 33).

If the diary harbors any sign of Woolf's approaching illness, it resides in these weather remarks and also in the motif of aversion that crosses the diary, as if Woolf begins to recoil from the world. At a Queen's Hall concert January 3, appeals to patriotism via the national anthem (and a hymn) cause Woolf to identify an "entire absence of emotion in myself & everyone else" (D 1: 5). Community feeling is muddled, she suggests, by "intervening greatcoats & fur coats"—that is, by economic differences. "I begin to loathe my kind," she then writes, "principally from looking at their faces in the tube" (D 1: 5). On January 5, she "dislike[s] the sight of women shopping. They take it so seriously," and on January 9, she pens her famous thrust at mental disability when she sees and describes a long line of "imbeciles." "It was perfectly horrible," she writes. "They should certainly be killed" (D 1: 8, 13).

Four days later, wealth and class privilege again evoke rebuke. Of the "fashionable ladies" at Day's Library in Mayfair "who want to be told what to read," Woolf declares: "A more despicable set of creatures I never saw. They come in furred like seals & scented like civets, condescend to pull a few novels about on the counter, & then demand languidly whether there is *anything* amusing? . . . The West End of London fills me with aversion; I look into motor cars & see the fat grandees inside, like portly jewels in satin cases" (D 1: 17). She goes to the London Library January 21 but finds it little better: "a stale culture smoked place, which I detest" (*D* 1: 25). On January 28, she admires a beautiful woman on the bus but then reprises her "loathe my kind" view of January 3: "About one person in a fortnight seems to me nice—most are nothing at all" (*D* 1: 30).

Positive moments, however, alternate with these flashes of aversion. On January 16, Woolf describes a walk along the river with their dog, Max, a trek accented by a stolen bone, a bloody dog fight, and her loss of suspenders. She then declares surprisingly: "I thought how happy I was, without any of the excitements which, once, seemed to me to constitute happiness. L. & I argued for some time about this. . . . My writing now delights me solely because I love writing & dont, honestly, care a hang what anyone says. What seas of horror one dives through in order to pick up these pearls—however they are worth it" (*D* 1: 20).

When Thomas Hardy writes back to her, she exclaims with pleasure on January 22, and part of her birthday joy three days later comes from reading her father's prose: "I have been very happy reading father on Pope, which is very witty & bright—without a single dead sentence in it. In fact I dont know when I have enjoyed a birthday so much—not since I was a child anyhow. Sitting at tea we decided three things: in the first place to take Hogarth, if we can get it; in the second, to buy a Printing press; in the third to buy a Bull dog, probably called John. I am very much excited at the idea of all three—particularly the press" (*D* 1: 28).

Woolf resumes her diary February 13 to report that she and Leonard are "very happy," and her final 1915 entry begins with praise of her landlady Mrs Le Grys ("the best tempered woman in England"), finds shop women "often very charming," pictures herself "rambl[ing] down to Charing Cross in the dark, making up phrases & incidents to write about," and ends in full exhibit of her shopping success: "I bought a ten & elevenpenny blue dress, in which I sit at this moment" (*D* 1: 34, 35).

Woolf never sustained a daily diary. She was a *periodic diarist*, not a daily diarist, and that in itself may explain the 1915 diary's demise. Whatever the causes of its abrupt stop in mid-February, the diary conveys every sign Woolf thought her diary a "life" that would persist. On January 14 she calls "We were woken this morning" a stock phrase she anticipates using regularly in her diary, a phrase akin to "Once upon a Time" (*D* 1: 17). The next day she declares "I'd give a lot to turn over 30 pages or so, & find written down what happens to us" regarding Hogarth House, a declaration that treats the diary as an ongoing family tome (*D* 1: 19). On January 29, she rejects the phrase "nothing happened today," a phrase she recalls appearing "in our diaries when they were beginning to die," and as late as February 13, her vision of her diary as an ongoing "life" can be seen in her assertion that "I am sure however many years I keep this diary, I shall never find a winter to beat this" (*D* 1: 30, 33).

The 1915 diary supplies our first glimpse of Virginia Woolf the full-blown diarist, the Woolf employing Scott's (and Pepys's) "loose, free & easy" style to pass from inner to outer worlds and from the sinking of the *Formidable* to the sacking of Lizzy the maid. Narratives start; people swiftly appear; threads of a rich tapestry are taken up and brandished with amused attention. A world comes alive—as in a novel. One suspects Woolf does not know at this moment what she has started. Nevertheless, she has created an elastic style able to accommodate observations of nature and human nature, the war and its omnipresence, life in a Richmond boarding house in January and February 1915, and a portrait of a marriage of writers and of what an inquisitive artist reads, writes, and thinks.

Mary Berry's *Journals*

"Memoirs of Miss Berry?" unmarried Virginia Stephen inquired of Lytton Strachey February 16, 1912. "I expect they'd do splendidly: and I'll take immense care not to spot them" (*L* #605, 1: 491). She directs him to send "Miss Berry" to Burley, Cambridge Park, Twickenham—Jean Thomas's nursing home, where Dr. Savage has consigned her for a fortnight's care. Did Strachey mail the three-volume *Extracts of the Journals and Correspondence of Miss Berry from the Year 1783 to 1852* as a rest home cure? He might have thought them good medicine, for Berry's story touched on Virginia's own. Berry lost her mother at age three or four, adored her artist sister, and was herself a writer who, despite a broken engagement, lifelong headaches and melancholy, managed to live to be ninety and to pen work in many forms—including a diary.[4] The Berry sisters are buried in Twickenham Cemetery, the inscription at their gravesite: "They were lovely and pleasant in their lives, and in their death they were not divided" (3: 517).

In the *Journals* Berry describes her mother's death (giving birth to a third daughter) as an "irreparable loss," and recounts this story, which might have struck a chord with Woolf: "my mother, on hearing some one say . . . that I was a fine child, and that they hoped I should be handsome, said, that all she prayed to Heaven for her child was, that it might receive a *vigorous understanding*. This prayer of a mother of eighteen, for her first-born, a daughter, struck me when I first heard it, and has impressed on my mind ever since all I must have lost in such a parent" (1: 5).

Perhaps, however, Strachey sent the volumes later, for we know from Woolf's February 28, 1916 letter to him that "Miss Berry shall be sent off at once" (*L* #745, 2: 82). I will treat Berry's *Journals* here, for at least we know Woolf possessed them in February 1916.[5] It seems less certain she would retain Strachey's volumes across four years and many moves. She likely read—or reread—the *Journals* during her 1915 illness and recovery.

Berry's *Journals* were never "written for display," her able, handpicked editor, Lady Theresa Lewis, notes. They remained unpublished until 1865, thirteen years after Berry's death. They elaborate and corroborate Lady Charlotte Bury's subversive *Diary of a Lady-in-Waiting* which Woolf reviewed in 1908. The Berry sisters admired Lady Charlotte and were close friends as well with Lady Charlotte Lindsay, the *other* lady-in-waiting to the ill-starred Princess Caroline of Wales. In 1820, Lady Lindsay becomes a reluctant grilled witness in, now *Queen*, Caroline's sensational trial before the House of Lords. Editor Lewis includes Lady Lindsay's "Journal of the Queen's Trial" sent to the Berrys in Rome, providing Woolf with yet another woman's diary (3: 235–60).

In short, the three-volume *Journals* of Mary Berry transported Woolf to a world she knew well from earlier diaries.[6] Berry was denied formal education, so she taught herself Latin by age eleven and at age thirty-five began studying Greek with a tutor recommended by Charles Burney, Fanny's brother. Berry paints an admiring diary portrait of Fanny Burney in 1812, ending, "We did not talk much about France; but with her intelligence there was a great deal she could tell, and much she could not, having a husband and a French establishment, to which she was to return after the winter" (2: 508).

In 1808, Berry dines with Walter Scott and enjoys a long talk with him the next day at Bothwell, the birthplace of Berry's and Scott's mutual friend Joanna Baillie. The *Journals* preserve this scene of Berry reading Baillie's tragedy *The Family Legend* to Woolf's diary father: "It had a vast effect upon Walter Scott, and one that was very pleasing, from the evident feeling of one poet for another" (2: 381). Berry's journal world includes yet another diarist Woolf has read, Lady Elizabeth Holland, as well as that now ubiquitous diary figure Samuel Whitbread, the possible model for Hugh Whitbread in *Mrs. Dalloway*. In 1814, Princess Caroline has Lady Charlotte Campbell read to Berry her replies to the Queen's request that she not attend two forthcoming royal drawing rooms. "They were good, but too long, and sometimes marked by Whitbread's want of taste, who dictated them," Berry confides to her journal (3: 25). An 1808 entry reports the death in Spain of Sir John Moore, Lady Hester Stanhope's love, and an 1812 letter from Keppel Craven offered Woolf this further view of

Lady Hester in Constantinople. "You must not imagine that I am deck'd out in Oriental finery, like Lady Hester Stanhope," Craven admonishes. "I preserve my independence and European over-alls. She displays hers by Turkish trowsers, and rides *à la Mameluke* on a fine Arabian given her by the Pacha of Cairo, with an alarming number of pistols in her girdle" (2: 522).

Berry's *Journals and Correspondence* offered Woolf nothing new in diary *form*—merely further proof that a periodic diary could well convey a life. The volumes' editor serves the *reader* perhaps—although not Mary Berry—by allowing Horace Walpole's lively letters to dominate the first of the three volumes. The Berrys met Walpole by accident in 1788 when they took a house on Twickenham Common, becoming thereby his neighbor at Strawberry Hill. He was seventy-one at the time and Mary Berry twenty-five, but he doted on the sisters for the final nine years of his life, calling them his "twin wives" and even signing one of his letters "Horace Fondlewives" (1: 178). The Berrys began to visit Walpole on Sunday evenings, and editor Lewis writes that "The intimacy with Mr. Walpole now determined the acquaintances, the friendships, and often the place of residence of the Miss Berrys. His friends became their friends, his neighbours their neighbours. They formed an integral part of the society collected round this oracle of literature, wit, and taste."[7]

A year after they meet, Walpole begins to search for a permanent house for the Berrys. They take possession of Little Strawberry Hill in November 1791. Walpole secures tickets for them for the Warren Hastings trial, agonizes when they fail to write promptly, suffers when Mary cuts her nose in Italy, and regularly fears for her health. When he dies in 1797, he bequeaths Little Strawberry Hill to the sisters—along with a box of manuscripts for them and their father with the instruction that Mr. Berry undertake a new edition of his works, adding all the papers in the box. Editor Lewis includes a letter from Mary Berry to a friend explaining that in making her father his editor and the sculptor Anne Damer his executrix, "Lord Orford caused his papers being secured to *her* eye *and mine*, and made me his editor without the necessary publicity attached to the name" (2: 21). Her father, of course, had the credit.[8] Berry's editor makes clear that "Notwithstanding the frequent professions of equal attachment to both sisters, it is easy to see throughout the correspondence that Miss Berry herself was [Walpole's] first object" and "it was admitted by those best entitled to know, that at one time Miss Berry was conscious that the choice [of marrying him] was in her power; but she clung to his friendship too warmly and too sincerely, not to sedulously guard him from the expression of any feeling she could not fully return" (2: 20).

More than three-fifths of volume one of Berry's *Journals and Correspondence* is given over to the Prince of Letter Writers' playful, witty, and always engaging correspondence with the sisters Berry. Mary Berry began her journal at age twenty with the first of her European travels. Her editor rightly judges that her first travel journals "savour . . . too much of the guide-book," a trap Woolf repeatedly sought to avoid in her 1906 Greek and Turkish travel diaries at age twenty-four (1: 14).

Fortunately Berry and her journal command the second and third volumes of the work. The second volume opens with Walpole's death in 1797 and the death in 1796 of Berry's hopes of marriage to the highly suitable General Charles O'Hara. Berry had known O'Hara from at least 1784 when he is mentioned in her journal as accompanying their party to the Terni Falls. She describes him in 1796 as "the most perfect specimen I ever saw, of the soldier and courtier of the last age," as "universally popular," and as "the gayest and most agreeable person in the company" (2: 2). Editor Lewis reports that Berry "loved him with that warm and generous enthusiasm that invests its object with every human quality deemed necessary to perfection, and to the latest years of her life she firmly believed that her union with him would have given increased elevation to her own character, would have called forth the best feelings of her heart, and secured her happiness in this world" (2: 2).

Their ill-starred love reads like Jane Austen's *Emma* and *Persuasion* combined. In April 1795, O'Hara proposes and the two become engaged. Like Emma Woodhouse and Mr. Knightley, they worry how to convey (and enjoy) their happiness without causing pain to her surrogate father, seventy-eight-year-old Horace Walpole. Seven months later, General O'Hara quits England to become Governor of Gibraltar. "He proposed an immediate marriage, in order that Miss Berry might accompany him," Lady Lewis explains, "but she conceived it her duty to decline this offer out of consideration for others" (2: 3). The others, of course, were her sister, Agnes, her docile father, Mr. Berry— and perhaps Horace Walpole. Rather like Anne Elliot in *Persuasion*, Berry persuades herself to postpone her happiness. "In submitting to this absence," she writes, "I *think* I am doing right. I am sure I am consulting the peace and happiness of those about me, and *not my own*" (2: 3). But she is thirty-three when she makes this sacrifice—not Anne Elliot's nineteen. General O'Hara never returns from Spain. Their engagement is broken off in April 1796, and he dies in Gibraltar in 1802.

Berry's journal profits from these losses. With Walpole dead and General O'Hara lost and then dead, Berry gradually abandons hope of public success and begins a more intimate diary. As often happened with Woolf a century later, another's diary spurs Berry's recommitment to journal-keeping, and the revived journal presages the start of other, more public, literary works. "I am going in future to write a journal—the entertainment I have received from those of my friend here [Henry Greathead] has set me upon it," Berry writes at age forty-three.

And yet why begin a journal when more, *much* more, than half one's probable life is past, "and all the life of life" certainly gone for ever! I have hitherto avoided it, because I felt ashamed of the use, or rather the no-use, I made of my time—of the miserable minute duties and vexations which at once occupied and corroded my mind—of the manner in which I have let life slip by me, and missed its present enjoyments, by always aiming at and acting for some indefinite future.

But now that *no future* remains for me, perhaps I may be encouraged to make the most of the present by marking its rapid passage . . . (2: 318)

Forty-seven years of journal-writing follow this declaration, the pages a parade of famous figures and events. Berry finds the Irish playwright Richard Sheridan "completely drunk" at Lady Caroline Lamb's home in 1808 and dines with harelipped Thomas Malthus in 1811 (2: 346, 475). That year she visits William Blake's studio with Agnes. "He sketches in every style, and always well," she tells her journal. "I never saw a more perfect amateur" (2: 486).

She sees Tallyrand and the Duke of Wellington in Paris in 1816, and the Duke confides to her that "at the time the [Waterloo] armistice was concluded [with Napoleon] . . . they were hardly themselves masters of their own troops, or able to control their intentions, and were dreading that some unforeseen event might have discovered this dangerous secret" (3: 79). She hears violinist Nicolò Paganini play in Genoa in 1817, meets the English painter Charles Eastlake in Rome in 1820, and is an early admirer of historian Thomas Macaulay, whose conversational powers she describes as "yet greater than his House of Commons eloquence" (3: 140, 262, 414). Residing in Paris in 1820 at the time of the Duc de Berri's assassination, she provides a minute by minute record of the end of this heir to the French throne (3: 201–15). Fourteen years later, at age seventy-one, she preserves her visit to the French royal family at Fontainebleau (3: 425).

That the greatest minds of several nations were drawn to Mary Berry is shown by her relationship with the Italian sculptor Antonio Canova which unfolds in the later volumes. Canova sends Berry engravings of his Venus in 1816 and of his Cupid and Psyche as well. He scolds her for failing to come to Rome in 1817 and sees her daily when she finally arrives. Unlike Walpole, Canova is only seven years her senior, and when he dies unexpectedly in 1822, she confides to the Duchess of Devonshire: "you know what reason I had to be vain of his early, his continued, his unshaken attachment to me; and of what great pleasure I had proposed to myself at Rome in seeing him as usual every day, and my vanity anticipated the pleasure he would express at finding me here again. I will add no more, except a feeling of gratitude for having known and having been loved by such a mind as his" (3: 324). When she leaves Rome in 1823, she records in her journal, "I found time to give one parting glance, *quite alone*, to the genius of Canova" (3: 339).

Such scenes and portraits may have charmed Woolf; however, Berry's views on women (and women writers) may have riveted her more. Berry's editor prepares the reader for this topic in the first pages of the *Journals'* "Introduction." Berry's mind, Lady Lewis reports:

constantly soared above the sphere in which it could act; she longed to be useful, she longed to influence the welfare of her fellow-creatures, she longed to be great; she was fired with ambition in the best sense of that term; but there was no career. . . . [T]o the ambitious woman, in this country at least, there is rarely the power of earning distinction but as a reflection of the stronger, greater light of man. . . . She estimated very highly the intellectual powers of women. . . . [S]he saw with pain that as an isolated being the highest position she could attain in society was that of being considered, an "agreeable woman of the world."[9]

In her early years Berry notices gender boundaries. During her first trip to the continent at age twenty, she tells her journal that at Liege "Every priest openly keeps a mistress," and in Rome "no women are admitted upon the stage" (1: 20, 65). She and Agnes fail to see the remains of the Amphitheatre Castrense, she records, for "as we were women, they would not let us in to see it" (1: 95). In 1794, at age thirty-one, Berry thinks to take up Fanny Burney's role of court attendant. She writes to Walpole that "Much as attendance on princes and places at court are laughed at and abused (by those who can't obtain them), so desirable do I think any sort or shadow of occupation for women, that I should think any situation, that did not require constant attendance, a very agreeable thing" (1: 447). Berry reads Mary Wollstonecraft's "Thoughts on the Education of Daughters" in 1799 and writes that: "Our education (if education it can be called) is nearly ended by the time that our minds begin to open and to be really eager for information. . . . The wrongs or the neglect which women of superior intellect almost universally receive from men, are revenged by the various evils which men almost as universally suffer from the weakness, the folly, the meanness of those whom they commonly prefer in the character of their wives and friends" (2: 313, 314).

Berry reveres her good friend, the sculptor Anne Damer, and her own first published works—after the directed new edition of Horace Walpole—bring forth women's prose. In 1810, Berry edits the letters of Madame du Deffand and, in 1815, the letters of Rachael, Lady Russell. "The biographers of those who have been distinguished in the active paths of life, who have directed the councils or fought the battles of nations, have, perhaps an easier task than those who engage to satisfy the curiosity sometimes excited by persons whose situation, circumstances, or sex, have confined them to private life," Berry writes in the brief biography attached to Lady Russell's letters (and quoted in the "Introduction" to Berry's *Journals*). "To the biographers of public characters, the pages of history and the archives of the state furnish many of the documents required; while those of private individuals have to collect every particular from accidental materials, from combining and comparing letters, and otherwise insignificant papers, never intended to convey any part of the information sought in them" (1: xxii–xxiii).

At age seventy-seven in 1840, Berry publishes her commentary on the life and writings of the Russian Princess Dashkoff who, at eighteen, headed the revolution that placed Catherine the Great on the throne. Berry writes that Princess Dashkoff's memoirs: "give an account of one of the most extraordinary human minds that ever animated a female form. . . . the thoughtful, serious habit of mind into which she fell; her eagerness for reading, and especially such reading as called forth thought (how like myself at the same age!)" (3: 466, 467).

Berry did more, however, than publish women's prose and celebrate their minds. She insisted on women's equality and spoke of women's legacy. At age forty-eight, she writes of Oxford and Cambridge to the poet and playwright Joanna Baillie:

a little spark of sexual vanity creeps in with the wonder one cannot help feeling at *men* enjoying such advantages and doing so little and women labouring under such disadvantages doing so much. This, my dear Joanna, regards *you* more than any other female now living. Go on then and prove to them, that poetry, at least, is as independent of sex as of rule; that it is a spark of ethereal fire kindled on earth once in an Age, which Shakespeare alone has described, and with which you are enlightened. (2: 403)

This passage lays the way to *A Room of One's Own*: its Oxbridge opening, its contrast of male and female "advantages," its Judith Shakespeare, its notion of the "incandescent mind." In 1813 Berry seeks out Maria Edgeworth and tells her journal that the writer "received with much warmth what I said of . . . all the obligations that I felt in common with all our sex towards one of her genius" (2: 534).

Yet Berry's *Journals* disclose as well the boundaries women writers faced. Even Baillie, whose poetry Berry encourages, condemns parts of Berry's *A Comparative View of Social Life in England and France*. Baillie writes to Berry in 1828:

There is another thing which I could have wished otherwise [in the book], . . . the account given of Voltaire's mistress, Madame de Châtelet, rather offends as to that delicacy which is expected in the writings of a woman. The mention too of Lady W. Montague's poem on Lady Murray's disagreeable adventure, though very justly reprobated by you, falls a little under the same condemnation; and these I notice because they have been felt by others whose judgment and feelings I respect . . . (3: 371)

Berry vigorously defends herself: "On the charge of 'offending the delicacy which is expected in the writings of a woman,' . . . I have only to say that, if women treat of *human* nature and *human* life in *history* and not in *fiction* (which perhaps they had better not do), human nature and human life are often indelicate; and if such passages in them are treated *always* with the gravity and the reprobation they deserve, it is all a sensible woman can do, and (not writing for children) all she can think necessary" (3: 372).

Berry's editor, who believes the status of women writers improved by 1865, underscores the difficulties Berry and other women writers faced. She prints the positive reviews of Berry's 1810 Letters of Madame du Deffand, but then adds: "it is clear that comments were passed upon her undertaking in the society in which she lived, which justified her view of the desire shown at that time to check all literary efforts in women" (2: 470). Lewis then quotes as illustration this passage from a Monk Lewis letter included in Lady Charlotte Bury's *Diary of a Lady-in-Waiting*: "You know, of course, that they [Madame du Deffand's letters] were edited by your friend Miss Berry, who has also written the preface, the life, and the notes, all of which are most outrageously abused by many persons, though, in my opinion, without any just grounds" (2: 470). Berry's editor then adds Lady Charlotte's note to this letter: "It would be difficult to account for this outrageous abuse were it not an established fact that all women who meddle with literature, especially those in the higher ranks of life, place themselves in a pillory, at which every impertinent idler conceives he has a right to throw his rotten eggs." Berry might have resumed public writing even sooner than 1810, editor Lewis implies. As early as 1805 she "conceived the idea of engaging herself in some regular employment that from its very labour would have given repose to the over-activity of her mind; but it is also clear that the plan did not receive the sanction of those friends whose opinion she valued, and that it was consequently abandoned" (2: 296).

Several references beyond the Oxbridge scene of a Shakespearean sister lead me to believe Woolf read Berry's *Journals* later (in 1915 or 1916) rather than earlier (in 1912). Woolf credits Samuel Johnson as the source of her "common reader" title, and Brenda Silver dates the first *Common Reader* reading notebooks to January 1918; however, Joanna Baillie also used the phrase in an 1837 letter to Mary Berry: "I have endeavoured to set in array, for the use of common readers, all the texts of the New Testament bearing on a certain point of faith" (3: 453). Berry dines several times with Lord Byron and the Princess of Wales, and she worries in her 1812 journal that "his head begins to be turned by all the adoration of the world, especially the women" (2: 497). In her August 7, 1918 diary, Woolf finds it amusing "how easily I can imagine the effect [Byron] had upon women" (*D* 1: 179–80). Perhaps she imagined easily because she had pictured it before in Berry's *Journals*. Similarly, Woolf reports thinking on the meaning of the word "liberty" in her April 1918 diary (*D* 1: 138). Berry's *Journals* may have spurred this line of thought, too, for Berry gives over several pages of her journal to the 1820 debates on liberty in the French Chambre des Députés, outlining the three positions taken, and she writes in an 1841 letter: "I have read every word of Mazzini, and agree entirely with him in his views of what civil liberty ought to be, and with most of his statements of the absence of it in Italy" (3: 217–21, 474).

Berry's complex relationship with Madame de Staël likewise hauntingly prefigures Woolf's equally complicated friendship with Katherine Mansfield which begins to unfold in Woolf's 1917 diary. When Berry is twenty-one, she first meets sixteen-year-old Anne Necker in Lausanne. She does not, at first, approve of the young Swiss, observing that "the young English there, to her utter surprise, much neglect . . . her from the boldness of her manners" (1:

134). Berry visits the now married Madame de Staël in her "excessively dirty *cabinet*" in Paris in 1802 and waxes hot and cold on de Staël's novel *Delphine* (2: 145). Happily, the two writers come to know each other better in 1813 when de Staël lives in Richmond and then in London. They meet in London society and begin to visit each other's homes, often several times a week. "Madame de Staël . . . came, talked, questioned, and went away again like a flash of lightning, or rather like a torrent," is a typical Berry journal entry (2: 536). When de Staël leaves for Paris in May 1814 after almost a year of close confidence, Berry writes Damer: "I parted with Madame de Staël, *non sans attendrissement de ma part,* late on Saturday evening. . . . I own I much regret her absence. She had a frankness with me, and a power of exciting my mind. Now she is gone, while *I* am regretting *her,* she will never think more of *me* till we meet again. I know her well, with all her faults, ridicules, and littlenesses, and yet she is a very superior creature" (3: 13).

Editor Lewis intervenes here with a letter that shows de Staël "appreciated Miss Berry more than she was inclined to believe," de Staël telling a friend that "she had loved [Berry] the best, and thought [her] by *far* the cleverest woman in England" (3: 13). When Berry hears of Madame de Staël's illness in 1817, she writes a friend: "Amidst all the numerous host of her admirers, lovers, and friends, I believe few will more sincerely regret her than myself. . . . They say she is leaving this world with much regret. I should like to tell her how willing I should be to die for her" (3: 119–20). Berry writes de Staël herself: "Give me the hope, however distant, of seeing you somewhere; of having the happiness of finding myself with you in Italy, or in Switzerland, or at Paris. Tell me where you pass next autumn or winter, and I shall try to be with you. . . . Adieu! Keep well: and live to enlighten, to raise, and to interest all who can appreciate you; to be the glory of your own sex, and the worthy rival of the other" (3: 121–22). De Staël dies in Paris on Bastille Day 1817. A friend writes Berry that in her final week "M. de Montmorency was by her bedside, and she disputed with him the great question of liberty as formerly" (3: 139). Berry then writes to Lady Hardwicke, "I shall think the world less interesting without her"—almost precisely the words Woolf will use at Mansfield's death (3: 139).

One last sign of a 1915–16 reading relates again to *A Room of One's Own*. Mary Berry's mother bore "the ancient name of Seton" (1: 2). Mary was, then, through her mother, Mary Seton Berry. She was born in her grandmother Seton's home and lived there for two years with her parents and her mother's three unmarried sisters. Horace Walpole regularly refers to the "Seton women" in the letters included in the text Woolf read. In *A Room of One's*

Own, Woolf may offer veiled tribute to the Mary Seton Berry whose *Journals* she read in her thirties. Mary Seton Berry, diarist, historian, playwright, and woman of letters.[10]

Virginia Woolf's Asheham House Natural History Diary: 1917–1918

"Fields full of clover. Wasps beginning to bother. Bees swarming round the attic chimney yesterday; but we dare not look for honey."

(August 7, 1918; CM 31–32)

Nearly two-and-a-half years fall between Virginia Woolf's 1915 life diary and the very different diary she begins on the Sussex downs August 3, 1917: the Asheham House natural history diary. Olivier Bell believes Woolf forgot her 1915 diary during her illness and move to Hogarth House (*D* 1: 39). The Asheham diary that rises from this interval represents a new diary experiment altogether. That the diary pulse sounds in the country by this point hardly surprises. Seven of Woolf's first ten diary books begin outside of town.[11] Woolf observes and identifies with nature; then her voice sounds. As she explains to Saxon Sydney-Turner January 16, 1917, "[Asheham House] is a place that makes me feel completely natural—which, whether one is anxious or not, always makes life easier" (*L* # 814, 2: 135).

She pens 143 entries in the sturdy, burgundy-spined, colorfully covered diary kept at Asheham House from August 3, 1917 through October 6, 1918.[12] In *number* of entries, this diary ranks second only to Woolf's first diary as a fifteen-year-old with its 309 entries. However, in number of *word*s it sinks considerably, for its entries are as brief, terse, and narrowly focused as the previous 1915 entries had been expansive and varied. The small size of the Asheham diary—four inches wide and six-and-a-quarter inches long—may have invited compression. The Asheham diary is half the size of the 1915 diary and half the size of the 1917 Hogarth House diary that soon follows as its larger companion. Despite its small size this diary merits our eye, both for its experimental form and for showing the importance of diary-writing to Woolf in 1917 and 1918, for on seventeen days she actually makes entries in *both* the country and London diaries: the Asheham House natural history diary and the Hogarth House diary. As biographer Hermione Lee suggests: "The most vigorous rush of her energies went into her diary, which she began to keep again in August 1917" (374).

A staccato style characterizes the Asheham diary: short sentences, begun often with verbs (the subject omitted), with a singular focus on the physical world. Typical is the diary's opening entry: "Came to Asheham. Walked out from Lewes. Stopped raining for the first time since Sunday. Men mending the wall & roof at Asheham. Will has dug up the bed in front, leaving only one dahlia. Bees in attic chim[n]ey" (D 1: 39). The unsignaled shift from herself to the weather between sentences two and three—one first thinks *she* has "stopped raining"—hints at the interpenetration with nature she seeks. To name is to embrace.

Asheham House is being "mended"—it has bees in the attic chimney—and the diarist herself is mending, the diary playing a part. One is tempted, at first glance, to view these stripped-down entries as the prose of recovery, as Woolf trying to grasp and ground her world through nature description. "I am to be allowed to write, and gradually return to the world," she writes to Duncan Grant November 15, 1915, almost nine months after falling ill (L #736, 2: 71). "I suppose I am happy merely because it is so pleasant to be well again, and allowed to write for a little every day," she writes Katherine Cox February 12, 1916 (L #741, 2: 78).

Was Woolf rationing her words in the Asheham diary—or were they rationed for her? Were complex sentences out of reach? The letters say otherwise. Woolf's *letter* prose is as witty and complex as always from at least September 1915 on. Therefore something beyond rationed prose is in play with the laconic Asheham diary. Woolf is experimenting—trying out a natural history diary. The Woolfs' first printing press arrives in April 1917, and in the summer Woolf publishes her innovative story "The Mark on the Wall." Experiment, in short, is in the air. When Clive Bell praises her story, Woolf declares to him ten days before the Asheham diary starts, "Its an absorbing thing (I mean writing is) and its high time we found some new shapes, don't you think so? . . . why don't you try a few experiments" (L #852, 2: 167). Two days later, she writes to David Garnett: "Novels are frightfully clumsy and overpowering of course. . . . I daresay one ought to invent a completely new form" (L #853, 2: 167).

Observation provides the form and substance of the Asheham House diary. Woolf seems to limit the diary solely to what her eyes see (and ears hear). She begins a September 1917 entry in Pepsian fashion, "To the post at Southease," but then quickly ends the record: "A fine day, but nothing particular to be noticed" (D 1: 48). On March 31, 1918, she writes, "Nothing particular to be seen," and on September 20, "Nothing to notice" (CM 30, 34). The focus on "field notes" eliminates much from the Asheham diary. Narratives vanish, along with witty portraits. Language is stripped of figure. Only six similes appear in the entire diary, and very mild ones at that. A lone metaphor intrudes: "Clouds brewed over the sea" (*D* 1: 48). Nowhere can be found a Walter Lamb of the 1915 diary "shining in his alabastrine baldness like a marble fountain," and how we long for the leaves to color this bare outline of Katherine Mansfield's visit, including their walk together on the downs: "Met K. M.—her train very late" (August 18, 1917); "K. M. & I walked on M.'s walk" (August 21, 1917); "K. M. went after lunch, in the fly from the Ram" (August 22, 1917; *D* 1: 34, 43, 44). "Glad to be alone," Woolf writes the day after Mansfield departs—the only emotion registered in the whole Asheham diary (*D* 1: 44). Books and writing recede in this nature diary (along with people, tropes, and feeling). Only two references to Woolf's reading appear, and only one to her writing, the bare "reviewed 2 books" (*CM* 29).

If much is excluded from the 1917–18 Asheham diary, what remains stands out in high relief. The Asheham diary showcases threads of Woolf's diary fabric often overlooked in the more variegated life tapestry of her 1915 and later diaries. Foremost is Woolf the natural historian. If Henry David Thoreau's journal today is justly praised as a natural history diary, Woolf's diary also merits notice for its careful record of the natural world. Her Asheham diary records first sightings. "Heather growing on the top, making it look purple: never seen it there before," she writes August 23, 1917 (*D* 1: 45). On April 4, 1918: "Coming back found the first cowslip on the bank, not quite out but almost" (*CM* 31).

She makes current records, but she also compares her observations to other sightings, creating a diachronic map of the Sussex downs. "Into the hollow after tea & found the same caterpillar—dark brown with 3 purple spots on either side of the head—that we found last year," she records August 4, 1918 (*CM* 31). On September 30 she notes that "Leaves are hardly falling yet, & not nearly as withered as this time last year" (*CM* 35). And she analyzes as well as records. "[T]he rings of horse mushrooms seem to put an end to the others," she suggests August 14, 1917 (*D* 1: 42). "Trees have suddenly turned brown & shriveled on their exposed sides, though still green in shelter; as if dried up by very hot sun," she observes August 30 (*D* 1: 46). Rooks swarm through the Asheham diary. Pursuit of mushrooms becomes every bit as energetic as the search for houses in the 1915 diary. Woolf's concern for scientific accuracy can be seen in this March 26, 1918 report: "I heard what I thought was the first half of cuckoo, but the book says its too early" (*CM* 30).

If she writes as a natural historian in the Asheham House diary, she emerges as a public historian as well, another under-prized diary thread. Woolf's interest in ordinary human life and human labor extends almost as far back as her love for natural history. At Warboys in 1899, the seventeen-year-old preserved the women and children toiling in the Huntingdonshire harvest. At twenty-one in 1903, she penned the essay-entry "The Wilton Carpet Factory." At age twenty-five, in her scene-making 1907 Playden diary, she sought to imagine the life of a Sussex boy laborer, and the next year at Wells she paid tribute to the dormitory matron Mrs. Wall. Ten years later, again in Sussex, observations of daily life mingle with those of the natural world. The harvest once more is described (and preserved). "A great deal of the corn has to be cut by hand. Men still working & women too at 7," Woolf notes August 20, 1917 (D 1: 44). Two days later: "Two mowing machines, with 3 horses each, cutting the corn in the field across the road. Cutting round & round: finished last patch about 5. Corn already cut & standing on the fields across the river" (D 1: 44). A year later, she records "Men cutting corn in spite of Sunday" and men cutting corn by hand till 9 p.m. (CM 32, 33).

The Asheham diary preserves for historians, not only how corn harvesting was done in Sussex in 1917 and 1918 but also the prices of local produce. Woolf knew she was preserving for later use—her own or others'—the availability and cost of food during the war. The following entry reveals how upper-middle-class Britons put together a Christmas dinner in 1917 Sussex: "No milk to be had either from Gunn or Killicks. We got a certain amount from Bottens. 7d a quart. Had to make up with Nestles & Ideal Milk. Eggs 5d each. Had to buy dried eggs. Turkey 2/6 lb: so did not buy one. Bought a chicken which cost 6/- from Mrs Attfield. Able to get 4 lbs sugar from Coops. . . . Run Honey 1/- a lb in Lewes" (CM 29).

The Lewes market comes to life: "Calves wrapped in sacking lying on platform" (D 1: 42). We long to learn more of the sheep tragedy. "Gunn very angry about the lambs. They & the ewes have died in large numbers; makes a loss on them," she writes March 24, 1918 (CM 30). Her April 3 entry again figures the cost rather than the cause of the sheeps' demise: "Gunn has lost £100 by the sheep here. Eggs 4d" (CM 31). Woolf preserves local language as well as local labor. "Mrs G[eall] calls a fine morning either a brewing day or a hop-picking day," she notes in September 1918 (CM 35).

The war invades Sussex just as it touched the Richmond suburbs in 1915, and once more Woolf depicts it in its daily dis-ease. The very regularity of encounter (and ordinary people's forced accommodation to it) gives the war its particular horror in this diary. The Silver Queens, airships used to spot submarines, were stationed at Polegate, near Eastbourne, Olivier Bell explains (D

1: 44n21). Whenever she sees one, Woolf records it in her diary. "Five Silver Queens over the sea round Newhaven" she writes September 21, 1917 (*D* 1: 52). A month earlier: "Saw the Silver Queen over the down, going towards Brighton & coming back again. A great many aeroplanes passed over the house" (*D* 1: 44). "Aeroplanes" often mean gunfire and raids; these, too, are duly noted. Each of the years captures a tense drama. "Aeroplanes over the house early, which may mean another raid," Woolf writes September 29, 1917 (*D* 1: 54). The next day Vanessa and Roger Fry "heard guns over London & saw lights last night. Another raid" (*D* 1: 54). The next day Woolf meets Fry "Anxious about raids. Another last night between 7 & 8" (*D* 1: 54). She hears firing the next day, October 2, 1917, and her next day's entry relates the war to weather: "Not such a fine day. Wind rose, & grew cloudy. However, the raids will be stopped" (*D* 1: 55). Rationing appears in 1918, and the March 24 entry reports the following alarming news: "No guns heard, save in the Channel apparently, though the fighting is so heavy, & the news this (Monday) morning very bad" (*CM* 30).

Closer than the overhead planes and Silver Queens, however, are the German prisoners of war living among them. They become part of the harvest scene, their work observed. "Passed German prisoners, cutting wheat with hooks," Woolf writes August 11, 1917 (*D* 1: 41). "German prisoners now working for Hoper," she notes seventeen days later; "work very well, if given tea at 4.30, wh[ich]. they insist upon, & will then work an extra hour" (*D* 1: 46). In September 1917 she observes "German prisoners stacking corn at the back of the house. They whistle a great deal, much more complete tunes than our work men. A great brown jug for their tea" (*D* 1: 49). Woolf seems to be seeking here to understand the German prisoners and to note national differences. She records three tries to connect. On September 19, 1917: "Stayed talking [in Rodmell] about the war 'Whats it *for?*' . . . Met German prisoners on the road. D[esmond]. said Guten Tag, & they all answered. Sentry said nothing" (*D* 1: 51–52). Almost a year later she reports Adrian speaking German to one of the prisoners, and one of her last Asheham diary entries confesses: "To post at Southease. Always meet Germans coming back. When alone, I smile at the tall German" (*CM* 33, 34).

The Asheham diary offers Woolf's field notes for 1917 and 1918: notes of nature and notes of war. It shows her curiosity about the natural world and human labor and foregrounds the natural historian and public historian present in all her diaries but never better exposed. If all Woolf's diaries were as terse and narrowly reined as this, her diary readership would not be as large as it is, and Quentin Bell likely would not have called her diary one of the great diaries of the world. Yet even these field notes were of use. On August 4, 1917, the second day of the Asheham diary, Woolf refers to the signalman at Southease and Rodmell Halt, a man named Thomas Pargiter whose last name she will give the central family in the novel she will call *The Years*. Her October 2, 1917 entry preserves this telling teatime visit from Vanessa's boys, Julian and Quentin: "we gave them 2 of L's heads of deer which they liked very much" (*D* 1: 54). These skulls—at least one of them—"may perhaps be rediscovered in *To the Lighthouse*," Olivier Bell delicately suggests (*D* 1: 54n1).

The Asheham House diary soon gives birth to the 1917 Hogarth House diary, which returns to, and even expands, the rich range of the 1915 diary. Was the country diary a needed precursor? Does it mark Woolf's renewed grasp of the physical world? Whatever its role, the Asheham diary testifies to Woolf's drive to experiment, and it anticipates these words from her next-to-last 1941 diary entry: "Haddock & sausage meat. I think it is true that one gains a certain hold on sausage & haddock by writing them down" (*D* 5: 358).

Virginia Woolf's 1917–1918 Collaborative Hogarth House Diary

"The diary habit has come to life..."

(January 3, 1918; *D* 1: 95)

Sixty-seven days after launching her terse Asheham House natural history diary, Virginia Woolf provides it a companion: the splendid Hogarth House diary begun October 8, 1917. This book might be called the collaborative diary, for here, more than in any other diary, Woolf strives for a communal journal. Her high spirits and her collaborative goal emerge in the diary's opening:

This attempt at a diary is begun on the impulse given by the discovery in a wooden box in my cupboard of an old volume, kept in 1915, & still able to make us laugh at Walter Lamb. This therefore will follow that plan—written after tea, written indiscreetly, & by the way I note here that L[eonard]. has promised to add his page when he has something to say. His modesty is to be overcome. We planned today to get him an autumn outfit in clothes, & to stock me with paper & pens. This is the happiest day that exists for me. (*D* 1: 55)

Walter Lamb looms tellingly as this first Hogarth diary comes to life. Woolf links Lamb with Fanny Burney's journals in her 1915 diary—Burney, the mother spirit of Woolf's diary, Burney who wrote a diary shared with others. That Woolf recognized Lamb's import can be seen in her October 20, 1917 entry: "Going out for a walk, we ran into a smooth, sleek provincial looking man at the pillar box, our Walter—sent by Heaven for the baptism of this book I think" (*D* 1: 64). Female spirits have blessed (and authorized) Woolf's diaries in the past: Lady Katherine Thynne in 1903; Jane Carlyle in 1909—and now once more the comic diary portraitist Fanny Burney channeled through Walter Lamb.[13]

The 1915 diary made "us laugh at Walter Lamb"—not made *me* laugh—Woolf declares, revealing she views her diary as a shared work. The collaborative impulse should be seen as foundational to Woolf, for this 1917 diary opening at age thirty-five parallels the start of her first surviving diary at age fourteen: "We have all started to keep a record of the new year—Nessa, Adrian and I" (*PA* 5).

If the 1915 diary recorded Woolf's marital happiness, by 1917 Leonard seems even more esteemed. "A dull life without him!" she exclaims in her October 18, 1917 entry (*D* 1: 62). "In order to keep as much in L.'s company as I could," she confesses ten days later, "I determined to go to Staines with him" (*D* 1: 68). Leonard's absence unsettles her, for on December 10 she writes, "Today was a string of meetings for L. Out to lunch, to Philip [Woolf, his brother, wounded in the war], to another meeting & not back till 8.30; I pacing the room in some anxiety till I heard him" (*D* 1: 90). In her important November 2 entry, she seeks to explain her sense that he complements her; in fact, that he provides an essential part. On October 29, Leonard leaves for Manchester to give a lecture on international government. In his absence, Virginia travels to Asheham House with Saxon Sydney-Turner and also visits Vanessa at nearby Charleston; however, her November 2 entry calls these days failed distractions:

distractions, so as not to think how strange & solitary I was. Not solitary in the literal sense of course. First I spent 2 days with Saxon. . . .

But I was glad to come home, & feel my real life coming back again—I mean life here with L. Solitary is not quite the right word; one's personality seems to echo out across space, when he's not there to enclose all one's vibrations. This is not very intelligibly written; but the feeling itself is a strange one—as if marriage were a completing of the instrument, & the sound of one alone penetrates as if it were a violin robbed of its orchestra or piano. (*D* 1: 69, 70)

Once more we see Woolf's view of life as plural rather than single.[14] In her next entry, marking Leonard's return, she reports "divine contentment at being once more harmonious."[15] Music offers a rich trope for Woolf's collaborative ideal. She is "harmonious" with Leonard and engages in a happy "duet" with Clive Bell November 23, 1917. Her dissatisfaction with printing apprentices Alix Sargant-Florence and Barbara Hiles rests on their faulty harmony. On October 15, Woolf describes Sargant-Florence as being "as low in tone as a coal cellar," while Hiles wants variety in this December 11 entry: "I own that I sounded the very depths of boredom with Barbara . . . my evening fretted away without sensation, save of one standing under the drip of a water spout" (*D* 1: 60, 90). Woolf *lives* the close of her 1925 novel *Mrs. Dalloway* in this 1917 diary entry celebrating Leonard's return: "I woke 5 minutes before 7, & lay listening, but heard nothing, & was about, at 8 o'clock to flatten out all my expectations when I heard L. at the door & there he was!" (*D* 1: 70). *Mrs. Dalloway* ends with these sentences: "It is Clarissa, he said. For there she was."

A collaborative diary may have seemed a natural extension of the printing press partnership, literal text-making in tandem begun earlier that year. Even without Leonard's voice, Woolf's Hogarth diary entries converse with each other, the practice of the 1915 diary. Her second entry, October 9, speculates, "perhaps I shall have a raid to describe tomorrow" (*D* 1: 57). The next day's entry airily replies: "No air raid; no further disturbance by our country's needs" (*D* 1: 57). This third entry looks toward a dinner that evening with Katherine Mansfield "when many delicate things fall to be discussed" (*D* 1: 58). (They were to print Mansfield's "Prelude.") The next day's entry confirms: "The dinner last night went off: the delicate things were discussed" (*D* 1: 58). Once more entries link and stories start.

The printing press inspired experiment: "The Mark on the Wall," the Asheham House natural history diary in progress, and now the collaborative Hogarth House diary. Woolf's October 21 entry describes her lunch with Lytton Strachey, his completion of *Eminent Victorians* (itself a bold new life-writing trail), and his efforts to "leave London, & live 'for ever' in the country" (*D* 1: 64). "It seems a good thing that one's friends should try experiments," Woolf tells her diary. "Poor old Goldie [Goldsworthy Lowes Dickinson] is evidently beyond that stage. . . . no time for experiments, not enough curiosity perhaps . . ." (*D* 1: 64).

Woolf bursts with curiosity. She will take time to innovate. She takes the elastic form of her 1915 diary and plays with its expansion.[16] Events that might have been *reported* in the 1915 diary are *re-created* as *scenes* replete with dialogue in the new collaborative diary. A poignant view of Alix Sargant-Florence, who quits the Hogarth Press after one afternoon's work, materializes in this October 19 diary scene:

She has a kind of independence & lack of concern for appearances which I admire. But as we walked up & down Dover Street she seemed on the verge of rolling up the usual veil of laughter & gossip & revealing her sepulchral despair—poor woman.

Where are you going now Alix?

I really dont know.

Well that sounds dismal! Dont you look forward to say eleven tomorrow morning?

I merely wish it didn't exist that's all!

So I left her, hatless, aimless, unattached, wandering in Piccadilly. (*D* 1: 63)

This October scene of an "unattached" woman, one in "sepulchral despair," a woman unable to find life in collaborative printing, takes on special resonance in light of Woolf's November 2 description of her own solitary anguish when lacking the thickening wall of others.

In contrast to this sober scene, when Woolf visits Leonard's family October 28, she treats the event as a comic play:

Pink arm chairs were drawn up round a crowded but not luxurious tea table; a multiplicity of little plates, minute knives, people told to help themselves. . . . & soon Alice, Flora, Clara & Sylvia all appeared—malice suggested the whole of Kensington High Street poured into a room. The normality of it all impressed me. Nothing beautiful; nothing definite; most strange why nature has produced this type in such abundance. Then, the servant said "Mr Sturgeon"; Flora cried "I will go" dashed from the room; everyone said Oh! Ah! How Splendid!, as if on the stage, which indeed the whole scene might have been. We went, after the 2nd act . . . (*D* 1: 68)

Again the dry comic twist at the end. This scene makes its way into Woolf's novel in progress, the 1919 *Night and Day*.

Most notably, however, Woolf takes the swift brush strokes of her 1915 diary portraits and thickens them, creating richer, deeper characters. "[N]othing is more fascinating than a live person; always changing, resisting & yeilding [*sic*] against one's forecast," she observes in her December 7 entry (*D* 1: 85). The collaborative diary heralds the start of Woolf the exquisite diary portraitist. In this diary's forty-six entries, she introduces portraits of the major figures in her Bloomsbury circle as if consciously setting the stage for future diary scenes. Duncan Grant, and particularly her sister Vanessa, receive admiring portraits. "They are very large in effect, these painters; very little self-conscious; they have smooth broad spaces in their minds where I am all prickles & promontories," Woolf writes November 2. "Nevertheless to my thinking few people have a more vigorous grasp or a more direct pounce than Nessa" (*D* 1: 69).

Two portraits of Clive Bell appear, the second reinforcing this first on October 27:

> Clive came & was I thought, very pleasant, easy garrulous; starting a great many hares & chasing them smartly, & letting off his little tributes to himself quite inoffensively. He is so brisk & well kept mentally that I like an evening of him. L. immensely good tempered & urbane into the bargain. We gossiped; spun swiftly from thing to thing—Characters, French books, the Mansfield intrigue, & so on. He wears his chestnut suit; combs his hair back to hide the bald spot, but didn't hitch his trousers so much as usual—in short, he was at his best. (*D* 1: 67–68)

Woolf admires in Bell the very traits that mark her diary, a diary brisk, well kept mentally, spinning swiftly from thing to thing—Characters, French books, the Mansfield intrigue, and so on. Her second portrait, November 23, confirms their collaboration: "Clive came in, & we chattered away—he & I in duet for the most part—till 10:30."[17]

Woolf appears to have learned from William Allingham's diary the trick of rapid-fire adjectives to form a swift, yet vivid, diary portrait. "Emphie [Case] spirited, discursive, inconsecutive as usual," Woolf writes October 24 (*D* 1: 66). Aldous Huxley "infinitely long & lean, with one opaque white eye" (*D* 1: 62). These swift lines have the rhythm of Allingham's "Mr. Charles Darwin himself,—tall, yellow, sickly, very quiet" (184). But Woolf adds *reflection* to these swift outer descriptors. "I want to sink deeper and deeper, away from the surface, with its hard separate facts," she had written in her July 1917 story "The Mark on the Wall." "How readily our thoughts swarm upon a new object, lifting it a little way, as ants carry a blade of straw so feverishly, and then leave it" (*SF* 79, 77). In the 1917 collaborative diary she lets her thoughts "swarm" upon her portraits, and her reflections add depth and dimension. She follows her December 7 reproduction of Marney Vaughan's talk with a splendid portrait of Lytton Strachey within a teatime scene. "He is one of the most supple of our friends," she begins, and then lets her thoughts swarm:

I don't mean passionate or masterful or original, but the person whose mind seems softest to impressions, least starched by any formality or impediment. There is his great gift of expression of course, never (to me) at its best in writing; but making him in some respects the most sympathetic & understanding friend to talk to. Moreover, he has become, or now shows it more fully, curiously gentle, sweet tempered, considerate; & if one adds his peculiar flavour of mind, his wit & infinite intelligence— not brain but intelligence—he is a figure not to be replaced by any other combination. (D 1: 89)

She then reproduces *their* talk, and ends with hope of collaboration: "we laughed; remarked on our wish for an intimate correspondent; but how to overcome the difficulties? Should we attempt it? Perhaps" (D 1: 89–90).

If this first Hogarth House diary should be remembered for its singular portraits and collaborative goals, it also claims our interest for its deeper gaze at war. In the 1915 diary and the 1917–18 Asheham House diary, the war hovers over the house and enters the pantry. Woolf records the war's reach, yet largely observes it from a distance. The Great War becomes personal in the 1917 Hogarth diary. The volume's second entry, October 9, begins with the "horrid shock" of Leonard's summons again to soldier and their anguish and the energy they must redirect to resist the call (D 1: 56). Within two months, two of Leonard's brothers become casualties of war, Cecil dead and Philip wounded. Woolf does more now than simply record air raids and other war intrusions; she begins to analyze and criticize. In her October 14 entry, the Kingston examination site reminds her of Cambridge: "a great square, surrounded by barrack buildings . . . . A disagreeable impression of control & senseless determination" (D 1: 59). When they visit Philip Woolf in the hospital December 14, she writes, "A feeling of the uselessness of it all, breaking these people & mending them again, was in the air, I thought" (D 1: 92).

She notes war's inversion of natural response. Londoners now *flee* the city when the moon is full, and she begins to long for *bad* weather instead of good: "With time one would naturally welcome wet & wind . . . because one thinks of them as safety against the raid. So today I hardly grumbled, though it was heavy rain, cold, dark, inhuman, primeval weather" (D 1: 66). We value these war thoughts, as we do the diary's cultural observations on servants and on poverty. "Bert is wounded, & Nellie [their servant] has gone to Liz," Woolf writes October 22. "She felt it her duty & also her right—which shows how the servant is bettering her state in this generation" (*D* 1: 65). Woolf does not seem troubled by this class advance. After a row with Lottie (another servant) on December 13, she offers this tentative probe: "The poor have no chance; no manners or self control to protect themselves with; we have a monopoly of all the generous feelings—(I daresay this isn't quite true; but there's some meaning [in] it. Poverty degrades, as Gissing said)" (*D* 1: 91).

Across this diary's forty-six entries Woolf grapples with her failure to sustain a daily diary. Lapses trouble her at first. After four consecutive entries October 8 to October 11, a two-day gap appears and Woolf begins her October 14 entry: "That [break] . . . seems to show the signs of death already spreading in this book. I have excuses though" (*D* 1: 58). Daily entries follow for October 14–28; however, her October 23 entry hints that one or more of these days may have been recalled at some later date. "Another lapse in this book, I must confess," she admits, but then adds, "but, if I do it against my humour I shall begin to loathe it; so the one chance of life it has is to submit to lapses uncomplainingly" (*D* 1: 65). In both these entries, she treats her diary as a human "life"—and a pliant, vulnerable life at that, one awaiting death at the swing of a mood (a telling glimpse of Woolf's worldview, and also of a diary's lure). In November she hits on a strategy to address diary misses: the *combined entry*, that is, one entry for several dates.

Questions of identity and right climate weave through this diary. Describing an October 22 talk with Margaret Llewelyn Davies and Leonard about the current Co-operative Congress, Woolf confesses that "I get an occasional swinge of the tail which reminds me of the extremely insignificant position I have in this important world. I get a little depressed, a little anxious to find fault—a question of not being in the right atmosphere. L. I suppose feels the same about Gordon Sqre" (*D* 1: 65).

Bloomsbury continues to draw her, to offer more stimulus than Richmond. Her November 22 entry describes a Bloomsbury dinner with Roger Fry and Clive Bell, an evening rich in talk on literature, art, and aesthetics: "I said one could, & certainly did, write with phrases, not only words; but that didn't help things on much. Roger asked me if I founded my writing upon texture or upon structure; I connected structure with plot, & therefore said 'texture.' Then we discussed the meaning of structure & texture in painting & in writing. . . . This went on till I made myself go precisely at 10. . . . I liked it all very much (the talk I mean). . . . [T]he atmosphere puts ideas into one's head" (*D* 1: 80). Fifteen days later, Bloomsbury again supplies the climate she seeks. "I ended my afternoon in one of the great soft chairs at Gordon Square," she notes. "[S]o much alive, so full of information of the latest kind; real interest in every sort of art; & in people too. I rather expect L. to disagree with all this. I judge by the amount of animation of brain produced in myself, & sense of thoughts all liberated" (*D* 1: 86). London liberates and animates in the collaborative diary, while the country continues to consolidate and crystallize as shown in her final diary entry January 3, 1918: "one's faculties are so oddly clarified [at Asheham House] that the page detaches itself in its true meaning & lies as if illumined, before one's eyes; seen whole & truly not in jerks & spasms as so often in London" (*D* 1: 94–95).

Bloomsbury and the search for proper atmosphere interrupt Woolf's diary in November 1917. She opens her November 10 entry, following a three-day gap, with this explanation:

Another melancholy fact is that I've let all these days pass—two of them, Wednesday & Thursday because I was out late, the third Friday because I was too gloomy, & we were both too argumentative, to make writing possible. However, to deal with the dissipations first, though I dont admit they were the cause of the gloom. Nessa was up, & I had a Bloomsbury afternoon. . . . This was the prelude to a party on Thursday, to which I went, through the wet & the dirt, a very long expedition for 2 hours of life, though I enjoyed it. The usual people were there, the usual sensation of being in a familiar but stimulating atmosphere. . . . And now we see how the gloom came about. L. was testy, dispiriting, & tepid. We slept. I woke to a sense of failure & hard treatment [she had left once more promptly at 10 p.m.]. This persisted, one wave breaking over another, all day long. We walked on the river bank in a cold wind, under a grey sky. Both agreed that life seen without illusion is a ghastly affair. Illusions wouldn't come back. However they returned about 8.30, in front of the fire, & were going merrily till bedtime, when some antics ended the day. (*D* 1: 72, 73)

The last words represent one of Woolf's few diary references to sex. What seems clear is that the multiple voices of the London orchestra vie in this 1917 diary with Woolf's Richmond duet with Leonard. Both are collaborations, and Woolf works hard in the Hogarth House diary to achieve her Richmond duet.

Her keen interest in collaboration at this moment helps to explain her surprising observation November 22: "Ottoline keeps [a diary] by the way, devoted however to her 'inner life'; which made me reflect that I haven't an inner life" (*D* 1: 79). No *inner life*? What can this possibly mean? It means that "life" for Woolf at this moment cannot be neatly divided between inner and outer "realities." Her "vibrations" are both inner and outer, in concert with others and modulating so swiftly, perhaps, that inner and outer interpenetrate. She seeks, not the singular "inner," but the collaborative whole.[18]

Woolf never achieves the collaborative diary with Leonard she pictures at this diary's start, a double-voiced diary inspired, perhaps, by the Goncourt brothers' *Journals* she is reading at this time. She never overcomes Leonard's "modesty." He makes only one contribution to *this* collaborative diary—she presses him to continue in her 1918 diaries—and it is a subversive entry at that. "I rashly said that I would occasionally write a page here & now V. calls on me to redeem my word, & as it will take me from reading Joseph Chamberlain's speeches, I dont see why I shouldn't," Leonard begins more than a month into the collaborative diary:

> We went to the Webbs for luncheon & there too were Mr & Mrs Tawny [*sic*]. I had met her but not him. Before they came, the Webbs told us that he was an idealist. Now that I've met him the only thing which I can add with certainty is that he is an idealist with black teeth. One of the worst Webb meals to which we have been. . . . Mrs W. began to talk almost at once about the Reconstruction Committee which she is on. She talked incessantly & ever tenth word was "committee." She has apparently suc- ceeded in inventing a committee for babies, a committee for lunatics, a committee for the sick, a committee for the disabled, & a committee for the dead; but the scheme or the Cosmos is not complete because she has so far failed to invent a Committee for the Able-bodied & unemployed. However she still has hopes. (*D* 1: 74)

One senses Leonard aims for, and achieves, a bit of humor with this offering; however, his assault on committees ends *this* collaborative diary—at least in terms of his active role. In fairness, Leonard was less of a diary experimenter than Virginia, for at the time he was maintaining his own spare diary, as he continued to do throughout his life. Still and all, is there not something a bit hostile in his entry's subject and attack?

Woolf's collaborative goals fail repeatedly as this diary draws to a close. Wal- ter Lamb reappears in her final entry January 3, 1918, but now to refuse col- laboration. He "wouldn't shoot at those rabbits [the royal family] again for my diversion," Woolf laments of their failed duet (*D* 1: 93). On one hand, one senses her joy that "The diary habit has come to life at Charleston. Bunny [Da- vid Garnett] sat up late on the Old Year's night writing, & Duncan came back with a ledger, bought in Lambs Conduit Street" (*D* 1: 95). Will the diary close, then, with the diary spirit alive—and even contagious? Only partly so. "The sad thing is that we daren't trust each other to read our books," Woolf continues. "[T]hey lie, like vast consciences, in our most secret drawers" (D 1: 95).

Unlike Fanny Burney and her circle, the Bloomsburies do not share their diaries with each other. By 1917 Woolf knows of many diary communities less inhibited than her own. Besides the trusting Burneys and collaborating brothers Goncourt, she knows that Emerson and his brilliant Aunt Mary not only shared but also critiqued each other's journals. She knows Mary Berry read Henry Greathead's diary and received Lady Charlotte Lindsay's "Journal of the Queen's Trial." In November 1917, she reads and reviews the diary of the literary clergyman Stopford Brooke, who read his diary to his children. Despite her lament at Bloomsbury diary reserve, we have here Woolf's view of diaries as "vast consciences"—an apt description of her diary.

Although the communal spirit falters and Leonard disappoints her wish to produce a genuine Goncourtian collaborative diary, Virginia works hard to make her Hogarth diary as multi-voiced as possible. Her entries converse with each other. She creates diary scenes with dialogue and captures Marny Vaughan's voice in an extended entry.[19] That Woolf thinks of the 1917 collaborative diary as an artistic whole can be sensed from the diary's close. Walter Lamb reappears, and she writes "The End" following a final scene that further brings the diary to a full-circle close. The scene: an evening duet with Leonard. If he will not provide his own voice, she will supply it:

> So we come to an end of the year, & any attempt to sum it up is beyond me, or even to cast a final glance at the evening paper, with news from Russia, which has just come in and drawn L. to remark
> "A very interesting state of things—"
> "And what's going to happen?"
> "No human being can foretell that." (D 1: 95)

The 1917–18 collaborative Hogarth diary represents another diary experiment and an expansion of Woolf's 1915 diary style. Rising from the foundation of the Asheham House natural history diary—and continuing with it—this diary radiates good humor and collaborative good will. "We both make big or fairly big cheques monthly by reviewing," Woolf confides to her diary October 16, and perhaps this economic well-being enhances her bonhomie (D 1: 60). Her diary portraits convey positive likenesses more than negative; in the collaborative spirit, she seems as eager to report others' writing as her own. Despite the failure of the collaborative diary with Leonard, through her own efforts she crafts a diary ratifying her boast to Lady Ottoline Morrell: a diary that becomes "a never exhausted fount" (D 1: 79).

The *Journals* of Edmond and Jules de Goncourt

Virginia Woolf likely reads the Goncourt brothers' palpitating *Journals* right before (or in concert with) her own 1917–18 collaborative diary. Biographer Michael Holroyd writes that during the spring of 1918 Lytton Strachey read for the first time Charles Greville's *Memoirs* (a voluminous diary Strachey will later edit) "and the six volumes of the Goncourts' *Journals*, which Virginia had put him on to" (415). I believe Woolf read these *Journals* before January 3, 1918 because of an uncanny diary parallel. In their first month of diary-keeping, Edmond and Jules de Goncourt write this entry December 21, 1851: "On the way home it occurred to us to write, for the Théâtre-Francais, a review of the year in the form of a dialogue between a man and a woman sitting beside the fire during the last hour of the old year. We wrote the little thing and christened it *New Year's Eve*" (Galantière 3). As just shown, Woolf pens a similar fireside scene to end 1917 and her first Hogarth House diary. Furthermore, her October 27, 1917 entry reports talk of "French books" with Clive Bell, and on October 8 she starts a collaborative diary (with Leonard) (D 1: 67).

The Goncourts' lively *Journals* offered much to emulate and inspire. Like Woolf's diary, their journal comes to life in concert with other prose and becomes a sublime parallel companion to their published fiction and nonfiction. Like Woolf's diaries, the *Journals* may have aided the brothers' impressive productivity, and they have been called more than once the Goncourts' greatest work. English translator and editor Lewis Galantière reports that on December 2, 1851, the day the brothers' novel *En 18* appeared, "they first took themselves seriously as men of letters—and started their diaries" (vi).

Expurgated until 1956, the *Journals* were periodic in the form Woolf read and written at high speed. They offered a form, in short, much like her own 1917 collaborative diary. In a "Foreword" to the *Journals'* first published version, Edmond de Goncourt begs reader tolerance of their method: "in our insistence that each still-warm remembrance shall be instinct with life in this work hastily set down on paper and sometimes not reread, the reader will find our syntax of the moment and our occasional *passportless* word, just as they came to us. We have invariably preferred those phrases and expressions which least blunted and *academised* the vividness of our sensations and the independence of our ideas" (Galantière xii).

The *Journals* "may be said to have been written by my brother at the dictation of us both," Edmond continues (Galantière xii). In this respect, the Goncourts' *Journals* differ from Woolf's attempt at a dual-voiced diary written in *two* hands rather than one. Nevertheless, the brothers' harmony likely appealed. According to Galantière, the Goncourts could "indulge in the diaries their special taste for the instantaneous" (x). They were born experimenters, a trait Woolf prizes always but particularly at this time. In 1857, French historian Jean-Francois Barrière criticized the first volume of the Goncourts' *Intimate Portraits of the XVIIIth Century*, scolding them for devoting their talent "to excessively small subjects" (Galantière 43). "[H]istory that is new and original, that departs from the conventional forms of historiography," they lament in their *Journal*, "will never earn us one twentieth of what we could gain by a fat, messy compilation of the known and the oft-repeated" (Galantière 43). Three years later, when the publisher Lévy rejects their novel *Sister Philomène*, they console themselves by noting that "it occurs to us that if our novel was anybody's novel, a flat, pedestrian job, the novel anyone might write, and which the public has already read a score of times, it would be accepted out of hand. Oh, one pays for the luxury of wanting to create something new!" (Galantière 99).

The Goncourts inspire a new school of writers—the Académie Goncourt—that includes Émile Zola, Alphonse Daudet, and the proletarian novelist Jules Vallès. Jules, the younger brother, dies in 1870, but Edmond carries their work forward, including the diary.[20] In 1895, when three hundred attend a banquet to honor Edmond, Georg Brandes telegrams from Copenhagen: "All the Scandinavian writers will be with me to-day when I exclaim, 'Glory to the Master Initiator!'" (Galantière ix).

The Goncourts' *Journals* spur Woolf to experiment and to collaborate. She shares their "intimate preoccupation with art" (Galantière 137). "I believe that since the beginning of time there have never been men so absorbed, so swallowed up, in a concern for art and letters as we are," they tell their 1862 diary (Galantière 109–10). In 1865, they own to but one consuming interest: "*the passion for the study of reality.* . . . life itself, with its entrails still warm and its tripe still palpitating" (Galantière 200).

Edmond's contemporaries described him as "soldierly" in bearing, while his beloved brother Jules, eight years younger, is repeatedly dubbed a "pretty boy," a *joli garcon* (Galantière v). The brothers write of the painters and engravers of the eighteenth century, innovate, in fact, a series of picture albums that continue to be admired. They paint lively diary portraits of their contemporaries as well. While Woolf learned diary portraiture from Fanny Burney's droll hand—and from other diarists she read, particularly Scott, Boswell, and William Allingham—the Goncourts' precisely observed and vibrant portraits correspond with her emergence as a sure diary portraitist.

Galantière describes the brothers' sensibility as "infinitely exquisite and responsive": "They were excited by the shapes and colours of the external world, and this excitation was, with the years, disciplined by an intensive and deliberate training in exact observation. Since they were at the same time remarkably intuitive, it was natural that they should not merely paint a man or draw a house front, but be impelled to divine a character and imagine a household" (vi–vii).

In introducing the *Journals* to the reading public, Edmond mentions portraits immediately after collaboration:

In this day-to-day autobiography appear those people whom the accidents of life threw into the path of our existence. We have portrayed these men and women exactly as they appeared on a given day and at a given hour, reverting to them in the course of our journal, displaying them later under different aspects, accordingly as they showed themselves altered and modified. Least of all have we been concerned to emulate those compilers of memoirs who paint their historic figures all of a piece, in a single unrelieved light; or paint them in colours grown chill and damp with the recession in time of their meeting. In a word, our ambition has been to show meandering humanity in its *momentary reality*. (Galantière xi)

Edmond elaborates their goals in a footnote to an 1869 entry that probes Princess Mathilde's rage at literary critic Charles Augustin Sainte-Beuve: "We have simply been stung by the bee of analysis, by the urge to probe deeply into the psychology of a very complex personality, exactly as a naturalist, in love with science, might dissect and redissect an animal whose anatomy had seemed to him to have been inaccurately or incompletely defined by his colleagues" (Galantière 271).

Portraits for the Goncourts require talk and gesture as well as physique and psychology. Edmond warns us that:

what we have tried to do is to bring our contemporaries to life, for posterity, to paint them in their living, animated resemblances. We have employed to this end the vivid stenography of conversation, the physiological surprise that springs from gesture, the record of these swiftly passing moments of emotion in which a personality reveals itself, those *impoderabilia* which lend intensity to a human being, and, finally, a little of that feverishness which is characteristic of the heady life of Paris. (Galantière xii)

Paris and the Goncourts' literary set come to life in the Goncourts' *Journals*, and Woolf follows their model in her 1917 collaborative diary's portraits of London and the Bloomsbury set. The Goncourts' *Journals* capture the famous fortnightly Magny dinners, a spur, perhaps, for Woolf's November 22, 1917 preservation of her Bloomsbury dinner with Roger Fry and Clive Bell, with its fascinating talk on texture versus structure in prose and art. The Goncourts recount "a great noisy argument" about metaphors between Gustave Flaubert and Georges Feydeau (Galantière 45). At another dinner Flaubert confesses his virginity, and in 1860 the brothers describe Flaubert reading *Salammbô* to them "in his moving, sonorous voice that cradles you in a sound like a bronze murmur" (Galantière 176, 101). We find a Flaubert haunted by the Marquis de Sade, a Flaubert dubbed "a glutton for depravity and a collector of it," and a Flaubert kept by a little vanity from being perfectly sincere (Galantière 65, 199). We meet Ivan Turgenieff ("an attractive colossus, a gentle, white-haired giant"), Charles Baudelaire ("a man ready for the guillotine"), Sainte-Beuve asking to make their "intellectual acquaintance" with his little stammer and "immense and gossipy memory," Sainte-Beauve the "malicious monkey" and "horrible poisoner of eulogies" who makes himself earrings of cherry clusters at a Magny dinner (Galantière 143, 53, 104, 130, 224, 257, 179, 155).

Alongside is Théophile Gautier with his "galloping muse"; Gautier "that stylist in a red waistcoat," "the sultan of the epithet," rotten with modernity, repeating lovingly "*The idea is born of the form,*" a phrase Flaubert pronounced to him that January 3, 1857 morning (Galantière 276, 46, 112, 179, 39). We see Dumas the elder with "the tiny eye of a hippopotamus" (191); Joseph Renan describing his god as an oyster, "an oyster on a grand scale, mind you!" (228); Hippolyte Taine, "the incarnation in flesh and blood of modern criticism, a criticism at once very learned, very ingenious, and very often erroneous beyond imagining" (143). We meet historian Jules Michelet, near death, "this great somnambulist of the past, this original conversationalist . . . crossing his frockcoat over his abdomen in a tight gesture and smiling at us with his death's-head teeth and bright eyes, a tomtit of a man with the look of an irritable old *rentier*, his cheeks swept by long white hair" (171).

The Goncourts' *Journals* do more, of course, than preserve a literary scene. They create a world. The diary opens with a scene and dialogue about Louis

Napoleon Bonaparte's coup d'état. Across the years, the *Journals* describe the Moulin-Rouge and the Closerie des Lilas: "the only dance hall where one can still see in the flesh the little Parisian mouse Gavarni loved to draw. There you hear real laughter, genuine gaiety, and a hubbub in which women ask passersby for the hairpins they may need, while the music of the band is sung in happy chorus by the dancers and the students who, by way of tips, shake hands with the waiters when they leave" (Galantière 158).

The brothers seek even more immediacy for their scenes than Woolf does for hers. "We are at the Porte-Saint-Martin Theatre in Saint-Victor's box," begins a typical entry which goes on to describe the play between the acts. "But the play is not on stage," they write; "it is in the house" (Galantière 76, 77). The Goncourts turn to play form for at least one Magny dinner scene—a feat seen regularly in Fanny Burney's diaries and tried by Woolf in December 1917. As Galantière astutely remarks, "[T]he Goncourts painted a whole world in their diaries. Town and country, café and theatre, drawing room and street scene, out front and backstage, *femme entretenue* [mistress] and imperial princess, academician and bohemian—it is a society under the Second Empire . . . not merely a literary circle" (Galantière x).

Women figure in this world, but only on the fringes of the Magny literary clique. On one hand, the Goncourts dismiss most women in their journals, for they disrupt their intimacy. "For the first time in our life a woman has separated us for thirty hours," they cry in horror in an 1859 entry. "That woman is Mme de Châteauroux, who has persuaded one of us to go to Rouen to copy out a bundle of intimate letters written by her to Richelieu" (Galantière 73–74). Only for their art will they (briefly) separate and mix with women. "Men like ourselves," they explain in 1857: "require a woman with little breeding, small education, gay and natural in spirit, to charm and please us as would an agreeable animal to which we might become attached. But if a mistress had a veneer of breeding, or of art, or of literature, and wanted to talk on an equal footing with us about our thoughts and our feeling for beauty; if she were ambitious to become the companion of our taste or of the book gestating within us, she would become for us as unbearable as a piano out of tune—and very soon antipathetic" (Galantière 47).

They call Princess Mathilde Bonaparte, who leads "the true salon of the nineteenth century," "the perfect type of modern woman"; however, she bankrolls the Magny authors and is shown complaining "prettily and wittily about the extraordinary level to which woman has sunk" (Galantière 136). George Sand receives only grudging respect as a successful fellow author. In the June 22, 1863,

Magny dinner report crafted as a play, the Goncourts quote Renan as declaring "Madame Sand . . . the greatest artist of our time and the truest talent," but then they write "*General Protest*" (Galantière 153). However, a September 1863 entry preserves Gautier's priceless description of his visit with Sand at Nohant, her daily schedule, and the revelation that: "One day she finished a novel at one o'clock in the morning . . . and immediately started another. Turning out copy is a natural function with Madame Sand" (Galantière 163).

The Goncourts distrusted women, as shown in their fascinating treatment of Rose, their servant of twenty-five years. Men played no part in the Goncourts' upbringing, Galantière notes. *Journal* entries describe Rose's final illness and their care of her in her last days. When she dies, they celebrate her in their August 16, 1862 entry; however, five days later they report discoveries about her life that cause them (and the reader) to wonder if they ever knew Rose at all. She drank and kept men, they report: had pregnancies and miscarriages: "Poor creature! We have forgiven her, and we even feel deep commiseration on learning of all that she went through. But for the rest of our lives we shall be suspicious of all womankind, from the lowest to the highest. We are seized with horror at the thought of the duplicity of woman's nature, the powerful faculty, the science, the consummate genius, for lying that informs all a woman's being" (Galantière 127). Another 1862 entry records Gautier's declaration that "women are on the way out. Today, as we stand here, a woman is no more than a bit of venereal gymnastics, dished up with a touch of sentimentality. And that's all" (Galantière 112).

Yet women make up part of "meandering humanity" (Galantière xi). They offer warm entrails and palpitating tripe. The same Goncourts who dismiss and distrust women praise the *Memoirs* of Mme de La Rochejaquelein, translated by Walter Scott, and themselves write a volume titled *Women of the XVIII Century*. They recognize the irony of their own approach-avoidance. "It is very strange that it should be we . . . who keep women at the greatest distance, who should have undertaken the most serious and profound psychological study of the modern woman," they write in 1864 (Galantière 183). Woolf may have noted Michelet's advice to the Goncourts, preserved in an 1863 entry: "You, gentlemen, you who are observers, there is a history which you have not written and will one day write; it is the history of the personal maid. . . . The part played by female domestics in our history is strange and important, gentlemen. Menservants, now, have been less significant in our history" (Galantière 169, 170). Woolf will call for a similar history in her 1938 *Three Guineas* and supply a bit of it in *Flush*.

Ironically, the Goncourts widened the literary compass while cleaving to their own narrows. They admit their divorce from nature as well as from women. Were these estrangements one and the same? In an 1862 entry, nature (and the country) seem to threaten the brothers' own acts of creation. "Nature is for me an enemy. The country is to me a mortuary," they declare. "This green earth seems to me a great expectant cemetery" (Galantière 121). An 1857 entry sheds further light on their unease. The Goncourts seem overwhelmed by nature's range and power, its fecundity signaling only their demise. "What an insipid thing the country is and how little company it affords a militant thought!" they exclaim: "This calm, this silence, this immobility; these great trees with their leaves lank in the heat like the webbed feet of the palmiped! Women, children, and solicitors' clerks are made happy by it. But does not a thinking man feel uneasy in the country as if in the presence of the enemy, the work of God that will eat him up in the end and make of his brain a fertilizer for all this vegetation? You escape from these ideas amongst the stones of the city" (Galantière 48).

In 1868 they sell off their ancestral farms at Les Gouttes, "this chief nuisance in our life" (Galantière 261). Nature is best aestheticized; that is, placed under their control. "At this point I shall make a strange confession," they write as early as 1856. "[L]ooking at a canvas by a good landscape painter, I feel myself more in the country than when I stand in the middle of a field or a wood" (Galantière 34).

Woolf, of course, holds the opposite view of nature. Nature anchors her—even authorizes her voice. Despite this important difference, she shares temperamental affinities with the Goncourts as well as kindred notions of art. She, too, possesses an acute sensibility and grapples with melancholy. Galantière describes the Goncourts as "extravagantly neurasthenic, constantly subject to megrims, thrown into frenzies of incapacity and self-pity by noises, insomnia, indigestion" (Galantière v). (In such light Woolf seems practically stoic.) In 1859 they write of "Despondency, the blackest, deepest, most intense despondency—and we sink into it with a certain bitter, raging satisfaction" (Galantière 69). They see its literary potential. They had written in 1855 that "Nobody has yet expressed in literature the contemporary French melancholia, not a *suiciding* melancholia, . . . a sadness which is not without sweetness and in which there is a light smile of irony" (Galantière 23).

The brothers insist, as Woolf will, on the link between body and art. Admiring the vitality of that "healthy genius" Victor Hugo, they yet ask, "if a writer is to render the delicacies, the exquisite melancholies, the rare and delicious phantasies, of the vibrant cord of the heart and the soul, is it not necessary that he be, as Heine was, somewhat crucified, physically?" (Galantière 142). The next year, Taine offers a model for *Mrs. Dalloway's* Dr. Bradshaw in his pious denunciation of hypochondria. "Taine deplored this ailment peculiar to our profession," the brothers report. "He urged that it be fought with all the weapons of hygiene and right thinking, and fought methodically. Retort as we will that our talent, perhaps, exists only at the cost of this nervous condition, he still insists that we react against those moods of flabbiness and indolence which seem to him the sign of the centuries moving down the slope of civilization" (Galantière 176).

The Goncourts, like Woolf, suffer "brainfag" at a work's end (Galantière 189). They are acutely sensitive to criticism, like Woolf and Fanny Burney. Like Woolf, they write a writers' diary, offering, in 1857, this salute to the craft: "our harsh and horrible struggle against anonymity, those stations of indifference and abuse, an audience sought and ever slipping through our fingers, a future towards which we marched resigned but often in despair, the fight of our impatient and feverish will against time and our elders, one of the great privileges of literature" (Galantière 44). Surely Woolf felt kinship with some of that passage and with the following 1862 description of their writing process: "you stretch the cords of your brain to the breaking point over a single concentration. . . . grope like this, in the night of the imagination, for the soul of a book. . . . Finally the first contours, the vague *fizzing* of our novel made its appearance this evening. It happened while we were walking behind the house in the narrow path caught between the high garden walls" (Galantière 122).

Woolf does not seek a fully Goncourtian collaborative diary: "the two of us in profile, bound by a single pen" (Galantière 203). Rather she wants two pens and (at least) two voices. Furthermore, she does not think Leonard's view and voice identical to her own, nor does she see theirs as a "dual personality" as the Goncourts routinely do. Nevertheless, the Goncourts' *Journals* reinforce her drive to experiment and spur her to begin painting portraits "*ad vivum*" of her literary set (Galantiére xiii). Historians' neglect of female domestics enters her mind, and she reads a condescending attack on illness which she will give to her character Dr. Bradshaw in *Mrs. Dalloway* soon to come. She also follows the Goncourt brothers in buying a great many memoirs, autobiographies, collections of letters, and diaries, "all human documents—the charnel house of truth."[21] Although Woolf does not achieve in 1917 quite the collaborative diary she seeks, the Goncourt brothers' *Journals* propel her toward portraiture and the psychological novel—and show her vividly that "I" might become "we."

Stopford Brooke's Diary

The literary curate Stopford Brooke and *his* beloved brother "were at one in the love of literature and the arts"; however, they wrote no joint diary like the Goncourts (Jacks 1: 41). Instead, Brooke reads his diary aloud to amuse his children and leaves it open for them to read when they wish. He therefore offers Virginia Woolf another form of shared diary in November 1917. Brooke died in 1916. Woolf reviews for the November 29, 1917 *Times Literary Supplement* the *Life and Letters of Stopford Brooke* edited by Brooke's son-in-law (and former assistant) Lawrence Pearsall Jacks. The two volumes should have been called the life, letters, *and diary* of Stopford Brooke, for Jacks includes excerpts from the notebooks and diaries Brooke kept across seventy years.

Brooke's long-lived and revered mother also keeps a diary—"a very sacred document"—and she regularly gifts him diary books to further *his* diary-keeping.[22] In his youth in the 1830s and 1840s, the family talk revolves around literature, and particularly Walter Scott. "My father waked us every morning with snatches from the *Lay*, from *Marmion*, and the *Lady of the Lake*, and the day was haunted with their charm," Brooke writes. "We learnt for ourselves more than half of [Scott's] poems" (1: 22–23). Brooke was "passionately devoted" to Scott's work (1: 250). In 1908 he reads Scott's diary "with the most loving appreciation of his beautiful nature" and recommends it to Sir George Henschel.[23]

Woolf shares with Brooke more than deep love for Scott and Scott's diary. Brooke suffered illness as a child, his life repeatedly in peril. His quicksilver, perhaps even bipolar, mind also resembles hers. Across his life he is subject to violent affinities and repulsions. At age twenty-five he marries a wealthy woman with London ties, yet even on his honeymoon he writes his brother that "Sometimes I am immensely happy—at other times I am as downcast and ennuyé as I ever have been, but with my character I shall be for ever subject to these continued alterations of feeling" (1: 109). Jacks observes that "It was good for him that early in life his nature, which was subject to rapid changes of mood, should be wedded to another so calm and deep. It was good for him that he found in his wife an independent character, not blinded by his genius" (1: 114). Standing at a reading desk one morning, "a dark terror suddenly overwhelmed him," Jacks reports, and "for months afterwards he was haunted by the fear of its return" (1: 100).

Brooke, in short, was a complex, multisided person—a Christian, Greek, and Goth—who loved change with all his soul (1: 8, 303). Like Woolf, Brooke read "as much in one hour as most men get through in five" and, like her, he composed as he walked down Oxford Street (1: 93; 2: 610). He anticipates her London movements, taking a curacy at St. Mary Abbots in Kensington following his marriage (where he lives next door to Holman Hunt), then moving to Bedford Chapel in Bloomsbury in 1876.

Like Woolf, Brooke carries on a love-hate affair with London across his life, shaped, in part, by water's strong pull.[24] "I always feel that my proper centre is London, and I will always keep before me the *duty* of returning to it," Brooke writes from Berlin to his brother in 1862 (1: 144). To his diary, however, Brooke confides this repeated question: "Why do I live in London when I hate it so deeply and could so easily escape?" (2: 587). Jacks believes that "London was the center of [Brooke's] family life, from which it was impossible to tear himself away, and of all his artistic and humanitarian interests. . . . [I]t was precisely this mingling of love and hatred which made his life in London so fruitful in creative work" (2: 587–88). Nevertheless, he spends his final years in Surrey, building a home "on a high hill top whence the eye ranged over a wide landscape as far as the Sussex South Downs beyond which lay the sea" (2: 637). Within London, the isle of swans in the Serpentine draws him and becomes a favorite spot of repose; in fact, Brooke and his daughter, Evelyn, might have crossed paths with Woolf in Kensington Gardens from 1882 to 1916, the thirty-four years their lives overlapped.

Did Woolf see that Brooke anticipated her intellectual as well as geographical moves? Brooke founded the famous Bedford Chapel Debating Society in Bloomsbury where all the questions of the day were sounded by George Bernard Shaw, Sidney Webb, and other Fabians. He "was in close sympathy with the ideals of Socialism," Jacks writes (1: 319), and long before Woolf's Morley College years, Brooke gives his time to a Club for Working Girls that he founds. In the 1860s Brooke adopts John Stuart Mill's views on the political status of women, and when it comes to religion he declares that "female preaching . . . is a great want in our Church" (1: 116, 126). The lot of poor women, particularly, incites Brooke to rail at the economic system. A March 1, 1916 diary entry, written in the final month of his life, exclaims: "What a curse the society of Kings and Princes is to men and even more to women!" (2: 671). Brooke saw the tyranny of fathers as well as of kings and princes and suggested to Mrs. Crackanthorpe in 1896 that:

> Among your studies in selfishness write one on the aged parents who sacrifice their daughters on the shrine of their illnesses, or what they call their love. Call it *The Moloch Father*, for the fathers are much worse than

the mothers. They will not let their daughters leave home; they call them back after a fortnight if they do let them go: they keep them always in attendance: they claim their whole life: and the poor girls are thirty or forty before death releases them from a tyrant who has done all in the name of paternal love and duty. . . . Write this article and write it sternly. (2: 524–25)

Brooke's diary discloses a spirit tuned to gender difference. Jacks reports that Brooke hung a copy of the Mona Lisa outside his study and would often pause and say, "that face reminds me how little I know about a woman's soul" (1: 279). At age sixty-six, Brooke muses in his diary: "I sometimes wonder what women are made of. At any rate, the clay is very, very rarely uniform. But again I say we know nothing about them and they know nothing about us, which is one of the funniest things in this funny universe" (2: 504).

Brooke also writes in his diary of the horrors of war. His April 16, 1904 entry offers this view of the Russo-Japanese conflict, which he calls "Admiral Togo's games": "Games indeed! 700 souls, most of them good and honest, and taken away from the daily work of the world, blotted out in two minutes, because Russia would not be fair to the Japanese! And because the scientific manufacturers want to make money. I would forbid, on pain of death, the invention and making of annihilating munitions of war" (2: 568).

In the midst of World War I, Brooke celebrates art over war in a letter to the artist printer Thomas Cobden-Sanderson, whose own *Journals* Woolf will read and review in 1926. Cobden-Sanderson prints Goethe in 1915 in one of his beautiful editions, an act of political courage Brooke admires. "Literature, in the midst of the foolish wars, stands by itself in its own world, and its voices are eternal," Brooke writes the fellow diarist. "A single lyric of Goethe's or Shakespeare's or Dante's, is of more importance and of more endurance in the memory and thought of humanity than all the wars of all the world" (2: 679). Woolf might have recalled these words—we know she sought to recall Stopford Brooke—as she wrote her final work *Between the Acts*.

Brooke wrote a periodic diary—as did Woolf. Jacks confesses that he does not know "for what purpose Brooke kept his diaries, nor, indeed, whether he had any definite purpose at all beyond the desire to express himself in this manner" (2: 501). The simplest view, Jacks suggests, is that he wrote "these records because he enjoyed writing them—the motive of the artist. Their discontinuous character is in keeping with this supposition. . . . Illness sometimes accounts for the gaps: on the other hand, there are long portions which were written during illness, and owe no little of their interest to that very fact" (2: 502).

Brooke kept teenage diaries and Trinity College diaries; travel diaries of Switzerland, Italy, and Germany; and Kensington notebooks. In fact, he kept diaries across most of his eighty-three years. He wrote a wide-ranging and various diary. That it is simultaneously a writer's diary is suggested in Jacks' description of the Kensington notebooks of the 1860s:

He is evidently hard at work on the Life of [F. W.] Robertson. There are first sketches of Robertson's character, and the progressive developments of these into fuller details. There are important passages written and erased and then rewritten, three or four times. There are plans for treating the particular aspects of Robertson's work. . . . There are sketches in crayon of scenery in Switzerland or Italy, some of them, I think, of great merit. Many pages are filled with closely written notes on the art galleries of Italy. Every notable picture is carefully described and studied, and some are reproduced in rough sketches, and the peculiar manner of each artist defined and distinguished. Mingled with these are experiments in verse, translations of Heine, aphorisms in many languages, the striking sayings of friends, witty stories, and illustrations grave and gay.

In one of these note-books I find a list of books to be read forthwith. There are sixty-two of them. (1: 141, 142)

Despite its great range, by far the largest portion of Brooke's diary recorded his impressions of nature, Jacks reports, and reveals "an astonishing versatility of descriptive power, always fresh, individual and distinct" (2: 501). "Throughout the many hundreds of pages in the diaries that record his communion with nature," Jacks observes in wonder, "he hardly ever repeats himself" (1: 229).

Brooke thus was another experimenter. Like Woolf, he assayed a variety of genres in his public prose and expanded the boundaries of traditional forms. He was constantly writing verse, Jacks reports, and he wrote hymns, a lyrical drama ("Riquet of the Tuft"), sermons, biography, and literary history and criticism. "The Growth of the Novel," his first literary production at age twenty-three, might have interested Woolf, for Jacks reports that Brooke "appears to have read every English novel of note which had been written up to that time" (1: 47–48). His hugely popular 1875 *Primer of English Literature*, followed by his 1892 *History of Early English Literature* were precisely the sort of work Woolf liked to read— and, at the end of her life, sought to write. The Woolfs' library, in fact, contained *two* editions of Brooke's *English Literature from AD 670 to AD 1832* (D 5: 322n11).

Brooke read Woolf's father, Leslie Stephen, and critiqued his essays in his diaries.[25] Like Virginia's father, Brooke repudiated the church. When he finally makes the break, in 1880, Jacks reports that "The freedom that he won was freedom for the unrestricted expression of his own personality, and his whole nature rushed forward in a fresh outburst of prophetic fire and creative imagination" (2: 354). Rather than leave the church for literature, however, as Leslie Stephen had done, Brooke sought to expand the church by opening it to literature. According to Jacks, his 1872 Sunday lectures on "The Theology of English Poets," "mark a distinct turning point in the history of English preaching, and may be justly described as the work of a daring pioneer" (1: 248).

Brooke's range and ceaseless invention impressed Woolf in 1917. Moreover, his 1865 description of Turner's etching "Lost Sailor" might have supplied the central image for one of her most famous works. Brooke writes to his wife that right over the lost sailor:

in the distance—on the cliff—seen through a wild light of foam there stands the lighthouse—its saving gleam has shone in vain for the victim of the waters. It is the one touch of fine imagination which adds to the picture an infinity of human thoughts, pity, despair—all the past story of the ship which had struggled all the night against its destiny.... And there he lies now—drowned in sight of shore. Everything else, in the room, of Turner's sinks into insignificance before this one print. (1: 186–87)

Woolf clearly admired the *Life and Letters* [and Diaries] *of Stopford Brooke*. In her review, she treats the two-volume work as exceptional life writing:

For this biography has one quality at least which makes it very unlike the usual biography. It has the quality of growth. It is the record of the things that change rather than of the things that happen.... To our thinking, the result is a book not of revelations or confessions in the usual sense, but of spiritual development which carries the art of biography a step further in the most interesting direction now open to it—that of psychology.... We have spoken of growth and change, but the goal is always towards some synthesis in which views generally found antagonistic are harmonised. (*E* 2: 183–84, 186)

The traits she admires in Jacks' and Brooke's texts coincide with her own aesthetic goals: interest in change, in psychology, in the synthesis of "infinite discords" ("views generally found antagonistic"), as she noted as early as her 1908

Italian diary (*PA* 393). Is she thinking of herself as well as of Brooke when she writes that "The little circle of the great must be enlarged to include some of those who have spent themselves upon many things rather than concentrated upon a single one" (*E* 2: 183)? Once more she rejects single or final answers— as she did in 1910 when praising diarist Meryon's rich portrait of Lady Hester Stanhope—for she declares that the reader "will be wise . . . not to attempt to sum up Stopford Brooke as this, that, or the other until he has read to the end, when the desire for such definitions may have left him" (*E* 2: 183).

Stopford Brooke lived to be eighty-three, and his final stage as a diarist (like that of Fanny Burney) makes us lament that Woolf's life and diaries end at age fifty-nine. "No one can read the diaries of Brooke's old age without being constantly reminded of the conversations of [Dr.] Johnson," Jacks declares. "There is the same abounding sanity, the same glorified common sense, the same resolute facing of the fact, the same scorn for hollow phrases and cant, the same independence, the same unconcern for petty consistencies, and above all the same tenderness" (2: 588). Brooke never loses the wish to experiment. "[A] second harvest was to follow [an illness at age sixty-three]," Jacks writes, "a long period of self-recollection, in which he gathered up the fruits of his experience, and expressed them in new forms" (2: 471). At seventy-five Brooke writes in his diary: "I now resolve to rewrite all those ten lectures [on Shakespeare's plays] into another shape and style" (2: 595).

Ten years earlier, alone in Germany at age sixty-five, he begins a mystical commune in his diary with the literal wellsprings of Homburg. He invents and talks with three lively "water sprites," the "genii" of the Homburg wells. Brooke believed in their presence, Jacks stresses; it is these encounters that Brooke reads aloud to his daughters' delight. "It represents a return to the primitive worship of Nature," Jacks explains (2: 563–64). "The partition between the visible and the invisible worlds was for him exceedingly thin, and he could pass from the one to the other in a flash."[26] Woolf praises this diary expansion:

We have not space to go into the details of this strange dream world, or of Mr Jacks's most interesting analysis of it. We call it strange because the expression of that state with anything like Brooke's degree of fullness is so rare; but we cannot help thinking that the experience in one shape or another is common enough, especially among those who are in the habit of putting their mental experiences into words. For the most part a moral objection of some sort tends to deny this side of the mind expression, and thus starves it of life. (*E* 2: 187)

Brooke's "fancies" may have reminded her of those in Mary Coleridge's *Leaves* which she equally admired. Art, wrote Brooke in 1913, "is Nature trying to make herself known to Man" (2: 627). His earlier sermon on the "Development of Christ through the Influence of Nature" reveals his central aim, Jacks declares, of "effecting a synthesis between Nature and Spirit, art and religion" (1: 205).

Woolf shared with Stopford Brooke a "passion for self-expression" (*E* 2: 184). He modeled for her lifelong artistic experiments as well as spiritual and intellectual expansion. "But it is extremely rare to find a mind open enough to widen year by year so that there is room for each different plant to come to flower," she writes admiringly in her 1917 review, using a flower trope she soon will use for her own diary as well (*E* 2: 184). "The whole story of his life is the story of a mind kept open in part by a powerful instinct of self-expression, and in part also by the tendency which became stronger and stronger in him against morality 'save as the expression of love'" (*E* 2: 187).

Poignantly, Woolf seeks, but fails to recall, Stopford Brooke in the final seven months of her life. Her September 17, 1940 diary entry moves swiftly from the war to her prose:

No invasion. High wind. Yesterday in the Pub. Library I took down a book of Peter Lucas's criticism. This turned me against writing my book [Anon]. London Library atmosphere effused. Turned me against all lit crit; these so clever, so airless, so fleshless ingenuities & attempts to prove—that T. S. Eliot, for example is a worse critic than F. L. L[ucas]. Is all lit. crit that kind of exhausted air?—book dust, London Library, air. . . . Would one say the same of the Common Reader? I dipped for 5 minutes & put the book back depressed. The man asked What do you want Mrs Woolf? I said a history of English literature. But was so sickened, I cdn't look. There were so many. Nor cd I remember the name of Stopford Brooke. (*D* 5: 321–22)

That Woolf cannot recall this energizing critic and diarist at this moment of disgust and despair—like her inability to summon Fanny Burney—might be seen as sign of her coming illness. Brooke modeled experiment in 1917. He exalted the figure of the lighthouse and attempted the fusion of dissonant forms. He also supplied her with an image for her next-to-last diary entry. Brooke writes to J. R. Green in 1876: "There is never anything lost by hanging out our colours and letting them blow in the wind" (1: 297). On March 8, 1941, Woolf will declare, "I will go down with my colours flying" (*D* 5: 358).

Virginia Woolf's 1918 Coalescing Hogarth House Diary: January 4–July 23

"to take up the pen directly upon coming back from Asheham shows I hope that this book is now a natural growth of mine—a rather dishevelled, rambling plant, running a yard of green stalk for every flower. The metaphor comes from Asheham."

(May 28, 1918; D 1: 150)

If a collaborative mood inspires the first (1917) Hogarth House diary, a drive to consolidate marks the second. Woolf's intensive diary-keeping at this moment invites thought. *Three* Hogarth House diary books preserve Woolf's 1918 days: the first for January 4 through July 23; the second, July 27 through November 12; and even a third, November 15 through January 24, 1919, lodged in her reading notebook when her second diary book is full. The Asheham House natural history diary lives on as well across most of the year; however, as the above epigraph hints, town and country diaries start to merge.

Diary entries merge as well. The 1917 Hogarth House diary closes like a novel with a year-end scene by the fire and the words "The End." Woolf links her new diary to this finale and reveals she thinks diary *openings* of equal import. "There's no reason after all why one should expect special events for the first page of a new book; still one does," she begins, "& so I may count three facts of different importance; our first use of the [19]17 Club; talk of peace; & the breaking of my tortoiseshell spectacles" (D 1: 99). Her words reveal the range of the diary to come: it will embrace public events and private, the great and the small. The 1917 Club endorsed the ideals of the Russian Revolution, the topic of the 1917 diary's final fireside chat. In this first 1918 entry Virginia echoes Leonard's words. Asked to predict Russia's future, Leonard declared, "No human being can foretell that" (D 1: 95). Of "talk of peace," Virginia insists in the new diary, "What it now amounts to, one doesn't even like to guess" (D 1: 99).

Socialists, intellectuals, and artists met in Soho at the new 1917 Club. "The 17 Club is a success," Woolf proclaims in this first diary entry. "We met Alix [Sargant-Florence], settled in, already an habitué by the fire; together with a knot of very youthful revolutionaries. . . . The rooms are light, bear traces of Omega, & are less formal than usual" (D 1: 99). This fireside scene connects with the one before. The Club offers another site for the communal spirit and for experiments of all sorts. Woolf's visits to this socialist enclave throughout this diary are of a piece with the experiments also afoot in the diary itself. Seventy-two dated entries supply the superficial form for the 201 days covered in this first 1918 diary—an entry every two to three days, one might think. However, that number and the dates themselves prove deceptive, for Woolf experiments in this diary with ways both to extend and to link her days.

The diary begins with entries on nine consecutive days. However, as usual, Woolf does not sustain a daily diary. In late 1917, she tried to compensate for gaps with various combined-entry headings: "Saturday 3, Sunday 4, Monday 5 November" and "Sunday, Monday, Tuesday, & Wednesday; Wednesday being the 12th of December." In this first 1918 Hogarth diary, she tries out other ways to retrieve her missing days. An obvious tack is to embed absent days in the day she resumes the diary. Her January 23 offering begins: "I see I've forgotten yesterday; but it was uneventful. L. went up to a meeting, Barbara [Hiles] was left in control of the Press, & I took a walk by myself" (*D* 1: 111). She shifts then to the current day, and thus records the (ostensibly) missing day.

An odder method is to add days at the end of existing entries rather than to start a new entry heading as one might expect. The closing paragraph of her "Thursday 4 July" entry clearly is written the following day. It begins "Today, Friday, L. printed off the last of Prelude." She employs both ways to expand single entries in her Tuesday, July 16 offering. She begins by recalling July 13, 14, and 15, and, after recording her life on July 16, adds "On Wednesday 17th we glued 50 copies of Prelude" (*D* 1: 168).

She even tries a third way of joining her days. Her "Monday 28 January" entry ends with two words: "Next morning,"; she then writes the next day's heading, "Tuesday 29 January," and continues the sentence: "the after effects of the raid were swept aside by Barbara," followed by a scene with dialogue in which Barbara announces her engagement (*D* 1: 116). Diary *dates* lose authority under such an accordion scheme; markers dematerialize as days expand and fuse. We see here Woolf the constant diary experimenter. Perhaps these trials were needed steps toward her mature diary style: one unaffected by diary misses. Furthermore, she does more in this coalescing Hogarth House diary than just extend and link her *days*. She fuses Asheham and Hogarth diary *styles* as well, achieving again her favored "country in London" state.

Her collaborative mood persists across this first 1918 diary. Although Leonard's activities "are beyond counting now," Virginia writes, he finds time on May 1 for one last contribution to her diary: an entry preserving a more important Webb dinner than the last, one spent discussing the war, the League of Nations, and U.S. President Woodrow Wilson's Fourteen Points (*D* 1: 152, 145–46). The 1918 diary thus continues to be—however sparely—a two-voiced Goncourtian endeavor, and it now boasts 1917 Club scenes to match the Goncourts' Magny dinners.

This first 1918 diary also marks the first *journal* mention of the Bloomsbury Group as both an entity and cultural force. Bold moves have raised Bloomsbury's profile in the past year: the Hogarth Press; Lytton Strachey's *Eminent Victorians*; Roger's, Vanessa's, and Duncan's continuing Omega art; and Maynard Keynes' work in the British Treasury. On January 9, Woolf reports that their printing apprentice, Barbara Hiles, "won't take [Nick Bagenal] to see her Bloomsbury friends. Bloomsbury, I think, will have one more corpse to its credit; for poor B.'s attainments aren't such as to give her a very secure footing there" (*D* 1: 103). Five days later Woolf records a talk with Clive Bell, Fredegond and Gerald Shove, and Leonard "chiefly about the hypnotism exerted by Bloomsbury over the younger generation. . . . In fact the dominion that 'Bloomsbury' exercises over the sane & insane alike seems to be sufficient to turn the brains of the most robust" (*D* 1: 105–6). "Happily," she reflects, "I'm 'Bloomsbury' myself, & thus immune; but I'm not altogether ignorant of what they mean. & its a hypnotism very difficult to shake off, because there's some foundation for it. Oddly, though, Maynard seems to be the chief fount of the magic spirit" (*D* 1: 106). Woolf here sees the emerging aura of her social circle, acknowledges some merit to the group's artistic and intellectual sway, yet mocks it all as well in an entry a week later. Barbara has brought Nick to see them after all, she writes, noting "there are signs of his deep admiration for the great Bloomsbury group" (*D* 1: 110).

Women emerge, alongside Bloomsbury and the 1917 Club, as a major diary topic. This first 1918 Hogarth diary reveals Woolf's posture at this time. She attends to both public and private acts affecting women and she ponders behaviors; however, she keeps a critical distance from movements—a fact that might surprise those for whom Woolf *is* the women's movement. Her stance, however, is not unusual for an artist. A week into her new diary, Woolf commands her page "for the sake of recording that the Lords have passed the Suffrage Bill," giving British women over age thirty the right to vote (*D* 1: 104). "I dont feel much more important—perhaps slightly so," she confesses, taking her own pulse at this historic moment.

Three weeks later, when suffragette leader Pippa Strachey comes to call, Pippa makes it clear she considers Virginia totally outside of women's "campaign for equality," a view Woolf herself underscores on May 28 (*D* 1: 118, 151). Her March 9 critique of a suffrage rally suggests she finds gender rallies too narrow for either nature or the greatest art: "It was a very fine afternoon & through a glass door one could see the day light—a difficult light for speakers to speak down. . . . [T]he audience almost wholly women, as the speakers were too. The pure essence of either sex is a little disheartening. . . . I watched Mrs Pethick Lawrence rising & falling on her toes, as if half her legs were made of rubber, throwing out her arms, opening her hands, & thought very badly of this form of art" (D 1: 124–25).

Woolf shows more compassion for smaller-scale women's activism, for the women who attend the monthly Richmond branch meetings of the Women's Co-operative Guild she hosts in her home. When her brother, Adrian, speaks on peace to the Guild July 10, she reports that "The women were more stirred than usual, though their reasoning isn't very very strong; & they are of course ignorant. But they would all have peace tomorrow, on any terms, & abuse our government for leading us on after a plan of its own" (D 1: 165).

Women continue to be linked to the country (and to nature) in the 1918 Hogarth diary. When Ermengard Maitland visits April 26, Woolf describes her with positive tropes used also for the diary. "As L. remarked these country women get a slow bovine manner, rather refreshing to my taste," Woolf declares. "She breeds prize bulls, plays a double bass in the evening, & writes improper stories for children. She seems to have settled into a corner absolutely fitted for her, where she exists pleasantly, having a Quaker faith now to round her off. I got the impression of some large garden flower comfortably shoving its roots about & well planted in the soil—say a Stock, or a holly-hock" (D 1: 143). Woolf's diary has become just that: a "rather dishevelled, rambling plant, running a yard of green stalk for every flower" (D 1: 150).

Hampstead also thrives in this diary as London's surrogate "country." When she takes the bus and tube to Hampstead for tea with Margaret Llewelyn Davies May 3, Woolf finds 1918 Hampstead "the heart of the woman's republic" (D 1: 147). Yet twenty-five days later, when Lilian Harris reads a paper to the Guild "in a thoroughly co-operative spirit," Woolf again underlines her distance. "I think I should take exception to their maternal care of the women's souls, if I were connected with the movement," she writes, implying she is not connected with it. "But I see the terrible temptation of thinking oneself in the right, & wishing to guide & influence" (D 1: 151).

An unusual note sounds in this 1918 diary that reveals more of Woolf the restless innovator. Although only thirty-five at the diary's start, Woolf appears in this diary preternaturally obsessed with age. In her fiction she is creating elderly Mr. and Mrs. Hilbery; however, she never relates her many diary notes on age to the novel. Rather, her apprehensions seem utterly personal. Her age-edginess begins January 24, the day before her thirty-sixth birthday. "The last day of being 35," she discloses. "One trembles to write the years that come after it: all tinged with the shadow of 40" (*D* 1: 112). Impressions of age tint most of her diary portraits. When Pippa Strachey visits on February 3, Woolf makes the arresting observation that "age consists not in having a different point of view, but in having the same point of view, faded. Goldie shows this too" (*D* 1: 118). Harry Stephen—who will supply traits for Peter Walsh in Woolf's 1925 novel *Mrs. Dalloway*—"alluded several times to his great age. He is 58," she records on May 28 (*D* 1: 150). She links these "seniors" together in her vivid June 24 portrait of Margaret Llewelyn Davies as "a fine specimen of the public woman" (*D* 1: 159). The description ends in speculation: "I sometimes guess that she thinks her work less good than it should have been. Or it may be only the terrific shadow of old age, in to which no one, not Roger or Goldie or any of them, can enter without a shudder" (*D* 1: 159).

At thirty-five Woolf feels the shadow of age and gives a shudder. She vacillates in this first 1918 Hogarth diary between treating herself (mockingly) as "elderly" or as on the threshold of middle age. The "youthful revolutionaries" at the 1917 Club perhaps draw her mind to age (*D* 1: 99). "I was amused at the repetition of certain old scenes from my own past," she writes January 9 of the young men and pipe-smoking women she meets at the Club, "—the obvious excitement, & sense of being the latest & best (though not outwardly the most lovely) of God's works, of having things to say for the first time in history; there was all this, & the young men so wonderful in the eyes of the young women, & young women so desirable in the eyes of the young men, though this was not perceptible to me sitting elderly upon my sofa" (*D* 1: 103). When she finds Hilton Young at the Club in March, she recalls his marriage proposal eight years before but primarily thinks of age: "But we are elderly now. . . . I found myself pitying him for the very first time. I suppose he's more than 40, & after all, he wished for something which he's done without" (*D* 1: 130).

In June she views Ray Strachey's lecture to the Women's Co-operative Guild again through the lens of age: "How strange it is to see one's friends taking their fixed shape! How one can foretell middle age for them" (*D* 1: 155). It is the "fixed shape" she associates with age that makes Woolf pause and shudder. This relates to her writing as well. "I was asked to write a book in a series—Makers of the 19th Century," she writes March 2, "but after deliberation refused, nor did it at any moment seem possible. But I write this down partly to give an official look to this diary, & partly because it marks a middle aged condition" (*D* 1: 119–20). A series book would hardly be original, would be hard-pressed to be experimental. In 1918 Woolf links age to success—and fixity.

When Lytton Strachey visits her at Asheham House, she tells her diary that she suspects "he is now inclined to question whether Eminent Victorians, 4 in number, & requiring 4 years for their production, are quite enough to show for his age, & pretensions" (*D* 1: 131). Is she wondering the same about herself and her single novel? Her concern once more involves fixity. "Are we growing old?" she asks her diary of Lytton and herself. "Are our habits setting in like the Trade Winds?" (*D* 1: 132). Writing June 24 of her friend Katherine Cox, who has been offered a post at Newnham College, she observes: "So we all step into the ranks of the middle aged, the responsible people, the burden bearers. It makes me a little melancholy. Failure would keep us young at any rate" (*D* 1: 160). And unfixed, she might add. Three weeks later, Woolf writes to Vanessa of their sister-in-law, Karin Stephen, "Age too will harden her" (*L* #951, 2: 261); harden her into grooves.

Woolf herself finds new "grooves" in this diary—new forms and subjects, including approaches to the war. Philip Woolf "is back with his wound once more broken out, owing to lack of care at Fowey," she writes January 21, and Nick Bagenal "dangerously wounded" March 30, and Alfred North Whitehead's son dead (*D* 1: 111, 133, 135). However, her primary focus in *this* diary is on the increasing deprivations of war as well as on the hopeful "talk of peace," the latter deemed the most important of the three events that launch her 1918 diary. However, peace is like a wave: it "comes to the surface with a kind of tremor of hope once in 3 months; then subsides; then swells again" (*D* 1: 99).

"Everything is skimped now," she writes in her diary's second entry: "Most of the butchers shops are shut; the only open shop was besieged. You can't buy chocolates, or toffee; flowers cost so much that I have to pick leaves instead. We have [ration] cards for most foods. The only abundant shop windows are the drapers. Other shops parade tins, or cardboard boxes, doubtless empty. (This is an attempt at the concise, historic style.) Suddenly one has come to notice the war everywhere" (*D* 1: 100). She records food riots and strikes in east London in her January 21 diary entry and a new bill in April that "rakes in all the elder generations" to serve the war (*D* 1: 110, 137).

She continues to analyze (as well as to record) the costs of war. "The more one sees of the effects on young men who should be happy the more one detests the whole thing," she writes March 7—a remark laying the foundation for her heartbreaking *Mrs. Dalloway* character Septimus Smith (*D* 1: 123). Women suffer too. When Barbara Hiles' Nick is wounded, Woolf writes April 6 that "the state of waiting for telegrams & letters, without any certainty when they'll come, & this baby in prospect, must be as fair a combination of torture as human beings can invent for each other" (D 1: 133). But worse follows: women carrying death instead of life. In June, Woolf is appalled to learn of women's role in air raids. "Women's bodies were found in the wrecked aeroplanes," she writes June 7. "They are smaller & lighter, & thus leave more room for bombs. Perhaps its sentimental, but the thought seems to me to add a particular touch of horror" (D 1: 153). Nature, thus, remains inverted by war, and Woolf notes sarcastically, "Happily the weather is turned cloudy; spring blotted out, but one must sacrifice spring to the war" (D 1: 128).

The National Gallery hides its "precious pictures" in the subways while it publicly celebrates "the glory of war" with a "life size portrait of Lord Kitchener, & almost life size battle scenes" (D 1: 138, 168). Roger Fry's response is to translate the Greek anti-war play *Lysistrata* and seek to produce it. Bloomsbury replies with revolutionary art. In June, Woolf poses Mozart's *Magic Flute* as a counter to war's animality. "I went to the Magic Flute," she tells her diary, "& thought rather better of humanity for having that in them" (D 1: 153–54).

The Hogarth Press—as well as the Hogarth diary—provides Woolf with a means to counter war with lasting art.[27] Woolf brags in her January 25 birthday entry that Mansfield's "Prelude" will be done in five weeks (D 1: 113). In fact, it requires the whole seven months that comprise the diary. Some delay stems from the March printing of Cecil Woolf's poems: preservation in art of this brother lost to war. In April, Woolf is delighted to tell her diary of a letter from Harriet Weaver "asking whether we would consider printing Joyce's new novel [*Ulysses*], which no other printer will do, owing presumably to its sentiments. . . . She is to come here, though we can hardly tackle a book. I like this dipping into the great bran pie" (D 1: 136). When they send off Mansfield's "Prelude" on July 10, Woolf is surprised (and pleased) by its "professional look," and when she reads the story over July 12 she finds it possessing "the living power, the detached existence of a work of art" (D 1: 165, 167).

Woolf begins to sense in this coalescing diary that her journal serves her in vital ways. In April, she acknowledges that diary-writing soothes her; in fact, that her diary functions as a reservoir for her overflowing thoughts, as a private backwater to exercise her restless mind. "There is an awkward moment between coming back from London & dinner which is the salvation of this book," she writes April 8. "For some reason one can't settle to read, & yet writing seems the proper channel for the unsettled irritable condition one is generally in. Perhaps this condition is intensified by tea at the 17 Club, particularly if one happens to meet Roger [Fry] in the Charing Cross Road, in his wideawake hat with four or five yellow French books under his arm" (*D* 1: 134). Fry makes her "bristle all over with ideas, questions, possibilities which couldn't develope in the Charing Cross Rd" (*D* 1: 134). But she can spill them over into her reservoir diary. London continues to stimulate her while her diary serves as a soothing retreat, one sheltering her vibrations yet letting them sound.

Five days into the 1918 diary she treats her journal as a repository for random scenes. She recalls finding unusable pens at the Registry Office and another day a fish bag left on a bus seat: "Its odd, considering their triviality, how these little scenes come up again & again at odd moments: are thought of, re-enacted, & disappear. Odd too how one thinks by help of pictures of surroundings. . . . I'd give a good deal to know something of psychology."[28] The diary functions here as a writer's diary: a place to preserve odd scraps and scenes for future use and to nurture the scene-making gift.

Woolf articulates a related journal function in her April 18 entry. "To mark their place" she will call this (for her) foundational diary impulse. This revealing entry discloses her wish to preserve the life around her, perhaps as practice for her professional prose, but also for itself—and we see her despair at lost moments. "There is a grave defect in the scheme of this book which decrees that it must be written after tea," she begins and then employs tea as a trope to describe her diary process:

> When people come to tea I cant say to them, "Now wait a minute while I write an account of you." They go, & its too late to begin. And thus, at the very time that I'm brewing thoughts & descriptions meant for this page I have the heartbreaking sensation that . . . they're spilt upon the floor. Indeed its difficult to mop them up again. And at this moment the mere length of my list of unrecorded visitors frights me from beginning. Judge Wadhams, Hamilton Holt, Harriet Weaver, Ka, Roger, Nessa, Maynard, Shepherd, Goldie, not to mention the Guild & Alix & Bryn & Noel, (who may be called the 17 Club:) all these have accumulated since Sunday; & each deserves something to mark their place, & I did mark it at the time. But how recover the impression of Wadhams & Holt? (*D* 1: 139)

Life is like tea: it must be brewed (like her diary), but it can be spilled and lost should inadequate care be paid. That Woolf believes "each deserves something to mark their place" says much about her diary motive—in fact, about her writing goals as a whole—and explains her drive to add on days, to let no life slip through her hand.

Seven weeks later, she blames the fine weather for an eight-day diary gap and clearly laments the unmarked life. Nevertheless, she completes the Josiah Wedgwood/Marjorie Strachey love story in this entry—the one begun in her 1915 diary—and we sense from this and from her earlier effort to recapture her lost February days that she considers her 1918 diary as preserving "a whole current of life" (*D* 1: 119).

But the "life," the "current," must be *fresh* for diary prose. Woolf's January 18 entry describes "Another skip, partly due to my writing a long letter to Nessa, which drained up some of the things I should have said here" (*D* 1: 106). However, she asserts, "I like this better than letter writing," signaling the favored place her diary now holds (*D* 1: 106). Her important May 28 entry that declares her Hogarth diary "now a natural growth of mine" also laments brewed but unpoured diary tea: "let me recall Janet, Desmond, Katherine Mansfield & Lilian; there were others,—yes, there was Harry Stephen & Clive. Each left with me a page full of comments, but useless now partly I think from my habit of telling these incidents over to people, & once told, I don't want to retell them, the telling leaves a groove in my mind which gives a hardness to the memory, stereotypes it, makes it a little dull" (*D* 1: 150). This passage sheds light on Woolf the tireless innovator—in her diary and other prose. Repetition bores her. Past grooves harden and type life which loses its essential flux.

Woolf's first 1918 Hogarth diary overflows with scenes and vibrant portraits. Earlier narratives end and new ones start, most prominently the Saxon-Barbara-Nick triangle. Only ten days into her new diary, Woolf senses the possibilities. "Its matter for a comedy," she writes January 14 of Bloomsbury and the younger set. "Indeed I see the plots of many comedies brewing just now among our friends. There's the comedy of Alix & Bunny [Garnett]; of James [Strachey] & Anonyma; & the tragic-comedy of the two cockatoos [Clive Bell and Mary Hutchinson]" (*D* 1: 106). The plots are brewing and she will steep them in her diary. Walter Lamb makes his comic cameo April 13, causing Leonard to yawn "without concealment" and Virginia to yawn "with an attempt at concealment" (*D* 1: 138). When Desmond MacCarthy comes in his naval uniform to spend the night and takes to reading Joyce's *Ulysses* manuscript aloud and imitating the cat's meow, Leonard escapes to bed; "& though capable of spending a night in this manner," Woolf tells her diary drolly, "I had compunction, & decoyed Desmond upstairs, collecting books as we went" (*D* 1: 145). When she attempts an affectionate portrait of Leonard's mother July 16, Virginia declares she "should need a chapter" to achieve her desired effect "& rather hope one of these days to take one" (*D* 1: 167).

Woolf's whole long May 28 entry consists of one portrait after another: Clive, Vanessa, and Roger; Katherine Mansfield ("marmoreal, as usual" but looking "ghastly ill"); Janet Case and Lilian Harris; Harry Stephen who "still takes out an enormous pocket knife, & slowly half opens the blade, & shuts it," Harry the model for Peter Walsh in *Mrs. Dalloway*, portrayed in this entry as "An undoubted failure, but that has a freshening effect upon people" (*D* 1: 150, 151). An earlier entry supplies a portrait of Miss Matthaei, perhaps the model for another *Mrs. Dalloway* character, Miss Kilman:

> She has to earn her living. "I must tell you one thing, she said, when the talk was over, my father was a German. I find it makes a good deal of difference—it is a distinct hindrance commercially." L. agreed that it was. She is a lanky gawky unattractive woman, about 35, with a complexion that blotches red & shiny suddenly; dressed in her best, which was inconceivably stiff & ugly. But she has a quick mind, & is an enthusiast; said she loved writing. (*D* 1: 135–36)

Lively similes and metaphors animate these diary portraits. Robert Trevelyan, the historian, reminds her of "the man with the pointed stick, who picks up scraps of paper. So Bob collects every scrap of gossip within reach—& even stretches after those that are still beyond his reach" (*D* 1: 169). Publishers— both Leonard's and her own—emerge as loathsome dogs in this diary. Williams & Norgate put off publishing Leonard's book on the Co-operative Movement; however, in March, with Allen & Unwin now interested, Virginia writes that "the way is open, & instead of dealing with a surly unwilling spiteful mangy exasperating cur, he can make his own terms—which he's doing this afternoon with Allen & Unwin" (*D* 1: 124). The next day she worries that "Williams will still try to keep his paw upon the manuscript" (*D* 1: 124). Nine days later, when her own publisher, her half-brother Gerald Duckworth, comes to call, the metaphor shifts only slightly: "Gerald's likeness to a pampered overfed pug dog has much increased. . . . His commercial view of every possible subject depressed me, especially when I thought of my novel destined to be pawed & snored over by him" (*D* 1: 129).

They are gearing up, of course, to publish their own books. The Hogarth Press expands and consolidates across this 1918 Hogarth diary[29] and so does Woolf's prose of all kinds—including the diary. Olivier Bell notes that 1918 and

1919 are Woolf's most prolific years as a journalist (*AML* 28). In an interesting March 12 entry that Woolf took time to revise, she writes:

> I may say that I'm "rejected by the Times." To rub this sore point sorer, L. has 2 books [to review] from the Nation. Its the second week of my rejection; & it has the result of making me write my novel [*Night and Day*] at an astonishing rate. If I continue dismissed, I shall finish within a month or two. It becomes very absorbing. We both notice that lately we've written at a terrific pace: L. 40,000 words & as yet hasn't touched the book itself; I'm well past 100,000— (*D* 1: 127)

She revises this entry to reduce its melodrama. Her fourth sentence first opened "If I'm forever dismissed" which she changes to the less operatic "If I continue dismissed." Two days later, however, her "dismissal is revoked": "A large book on Pepys arrived, which I spent the evening reading" (*D* 1: 128).

Pepys' spirit, along with the Goncourts,' hovers over this 1918 Hogarth diary. In her April 4 *Times Literary Supplement* review of *Occasional Papers Read by Members at Meetings of the Samuel Pepys Club*, Woolf celebrates diaries as one path to lasting fame. "The number of those who read themselves asleep at night with Pepys and awake at day with Pepys must be great," she begins her review, suggesting a wide audience for vivid diaries (*E* 2: 233). Pepys is a "fertile" source, she declares, perhaps disclosing more than she knows (*E* 2: 236). She concedes that "He has little consciousness of dream or mystery, of conflict or perplexity"—traits she values (*E* 2: 235). However, he compensates with insatiable curiosity; his "quick and varied sensibility"; his "lively, candid, unhypocritical nature"; and the "unstudied ease" of his language—all traits her own diary shares (*E* 2: 235, 234). Woolf calls Pepys's diary "the store house of his most private self, the echo of life's sweetest sounds, without which life itself would become thinner and more prosaic"—a description that reflects some of her own beliefs and diary goals (*E* 2: 236). Pepys's unstudied, easy language "can deal with a day's outing or a merrymaking or a brother's funeral so that we latecomers are still in time to make one of the party," she writes of the distinctive collaborative pull of diaries (*E* 2: 235). "Indeed, the very fact that he kept a diary seems to make him one of ourselves" (*E* 2: 235).

Was this her hope for her own diary 250 years to come: that it would make her one of ourselves? Whatever her wish, the first 1918 Hogarth House diary conveys an "echo" of sweet life and, in so doing, thickens and elevates her days. This diary both expands *and* coalesces. The Hogarth and Asheham diary styles join, and Woolf's days are "melted into each other like snowballs roasting in the sun," as she writes in her March 2 entry (*D* 1: 120). Portraits proliferate and scenes abound. Seeds are sown for *Mrs. Dalloway* six years in the future along with an experience she will give her current heroine Katharine Hilbery in *Night and Day*: becoming lost in the streets of London. Woolf begins to see the varied ways her diary serves her. Pen strokes soothe her. Her diary becomes a private reservoir, both for storage of portraits and scenes and for exercise of her restless, curious mind. Her diary "marks their place" and preserves a "whole current of life." Most important, the Hogarth diary has become now "a natural growth" for Woolf, extending its roots and starting to flower into her mature, spare modernist diary style.

Epilogue

irginia Woolf leaves a trail in her first dozen diaries that shows how she comes to be the writer we know. Her diaries disclose (when carefully studied) a clear path of development no biographer yet has shown. The diaries reveal the young writer's early fascination with *change*. At seventeen she offers her aesthetic of changing light ("different shades & degrees of light—melting and mixing infinitely") in her dashingly experimental 1899 Warboys diary (*PA* 156). In her pivotal 1903 diary at age twenty-one, she turns consciously from London and the male literary tradition to embrace nature (linked to women) and the unconscious, an essential move repeated often across her early diaries. Her choice of the "outsider" role at age twenty-one positions her to become the writer we know. However, her simultaneous drive to find her own "Country In London" reveals the difficult synthesis she sought: country *and* London, nature *and* culture, unconscious *and* conscious, female *and* male. Her persistent move from culture to nature and her drive to merge the two are among her most significant diary acts.

The ghostly, haunted 1905 Cornwall diary marks her growing trust in her unconscious, "the inward sea," and her continued pursuit of empty, untrammeled spaces her imagination could fill. Curiosity enters the diary in 1906 (at age twenty-four) and, in concert with the increasingly trusted unconscious, leads to unwilled spontaneous invention and the first sign of Woolf's "scene-making" gift in her 1907 Playden diary.

Woolf's Continental travel diary of 1906 to 1909 shows her determined march toward a view, voice, and style of her own. She turns again and again from "guidebook prose" and from Western notions of the East to favor her own eye, mind, and prose. Drawn to Prosper Mérimée's "unknown woman," she imagines in the longest entry in her Greek diary a woman with "a rare mind, & perhaps, a rare nature"—a woman much like herself (*PA* 342). In her 1908 Italian diary, she reacts against the still silent beauty of a Perugino painting and offers her own enlarged (and modernist-tending) aesthetic: life in *motion*, beauty in "infinite discords," a "whole made of shivering fragments" (*PA* 393). Her 1909 diaries mark another artistic crossroads. She seeks finer discriminations in thought and greater subtlety and "indefiniteness" in her descriptions; she rejects timidity and determines to make her words blaze.

From 1915 to mid-1918, when this volume ends, Woolf's various diary forms and styles begin finally to fuse. In her six-week 1915 diary at age thirty-two, the now married Woolf weaves place and portrait, thought and event into a richly colored life diary that starts stories and creates a world. With her 1917–18 Asheham House natural history diary, she re-grounds herself, writes herself back from illness in the country and through her diary. Tellingly, however, she soon adds a London diary to her country diary and, in her most intensive year of diary-keeping, writes in *both* diaries on seventeen days. As my volume ends, country and London diary styles join in the first 1918 Hogarth diary, and Woolf's days are "melted into each other like snowballs roasting in the sun" (*D* 1: 120).

The hallmark of Woolf's first two decades as a diarist is her constant diary experiment. That her diary was from the first "ever . . . scornful of stated rules!" helped her to stretch and explore (*PA* 134). From the start to the end of her life, Woolf draws on *others'* diaries to aid her as she pursues her own path. Sir Walter Scott and Fanny Burney parent her and set her in diary motion. Others' diaries both refresh and fortify her. They suggest new ways to live and to see. Fellow writers Fanny Burney, Mary Coleridge, and Mary (Seton) Berry attend to women and their treatment across their diaries, providing Woolf a way of seeing she will follow throughout her days. Their diaries and others' supply matter for the compost heap she can transmute into art. They give her access to what she calls the natural human voice. In fact, they offer the concert of human voices that she eagerly joins. The very diversity and individuality inherent in diaries propel Woolf toward her own individuality and are part of the great appeal of diaries. By their very existence diaries mean *life*—life regularly renewed and often life become immortal.

In her *next* 1918 diary, her thirteenth diary book, Woolf will call the "elastic shape" and the "springy random haphazard galloping" style of Lord Byron's great poem *Don Juan* the format she long has sought for her diary and other prose (*D* 1: 181). A November 1918 Hampstead dispute with her women supporters will call forth a new audience and purpose for her diary and the start of her mature spare modernist diary style.

Notes

Introduction

1. "A Woman Writer's Diary: Virginia Woolf Revisited," 57, 58–59.

2. In 1924, Lady Anne Clifford's diary became a fifth diary Woolf regularly revisited.

3. Panthea Reid explores the jealousy and the sisterly rivalry of brush versus pen in *Art and Affection: A Life of Virginia Woolf*.

Chapter 1. Early Diary Influences

1. Writing at breakneck speed, Woolf often left out apostrophes. All quotations from her diaries and letters will reproduce her text.

2. In her 1939 memoir "A Sketch of the Past," Woolf recalls youthful ecstatic feelings related to Stella's engagement which suggest she had more positive thoughts at some point. That she does not share them with her 1897 diary suggests both that the "ecstatic moment" came before 1897 (in late 1896 perhaps) and also that the diary in 1897 functioned primarily as a defensive tool, a site of resistance.

3. Lockhart 8: 108. Scott's two diary volumes were larger than Virginia's, however: nine inches by eight inches.

4. Leslie Stephen owned Thomas Moore's *The Life, Letters and Journals of Lord Byron*, edited by Scott; therefore, it is possible, even likely, that Woolf read Byron's diary as well as Scott's, although she never specifically mentions doing so in her diaries, letters, or reading notebooks.

5. "A Scottish wedding should be seen at a distance," Scott writes, "—the gay band of dancers just distinguished amid the elderly group of the spectators—the glass held high, and the distant cheers as it is swallowed, should be only a sketch, not a finished Dutch picture, when it becomes brutal and boorish" (Lockhart 8: 323).

6. "Here is a day's task before you—the siege of Toulon," Scott writes in 1826 of his work on *Buonapart*. "Call you that a task? d—m me, I'll write it as fast as Boney carried it on" (Lockhart 8: 326).

7. Thomas Carlyle declared, in fact, that "No fresher paintings of Nature can be found than Scott's" (74).

8. Harriet Blodgett, historian and anthologist of English women's diaries, insists that "Reticence has been characteristic of Englishwomen's secular diary-keeping since the inception of the practice in the late 16th century when the earliest extant true diarist in English, Lady Margaret Hoby (1571–1633), made a habit of discreet silence in the diary she kept from 1599 to 1605" ("A Woman Writer's Diary" 64). Hermione Lee reminds us that Leslie Stephen also exhibited "a fierce stoicism which she [Woolf] would develop herself" (71). Woolf's diary invites a reconsideration of diary candor.

9. In *To the Lighthouse*, Woolf has Charles Tansley report over dinner that "One of his uncles kept the light on some rock or other off the Scottish coast" (92). Scott's 1814 diary of his voyage on the Lighthouse Yacht to Scottish lighthouses (reprinted in Lockhart's *Memoirs*) includes these suggestive passages: "As the keepers' families live here, they are apprized each morning by a signal that *all is well*. If this signal be not made, a tender sails for the rock directly" (3: 138). Lockhart adds a footnote to report that when asked to inscribe his name in the lighthouse album, Scott "penned immediately the following lines: PHAROS LOQUITUR Far in the bosom of the deep, / O'er these wild shelves my watch I keep; / A ruddy gem of changeful light, / Bound on the dusky brow of night, / The seaman bids my luster hail, / And scorns to strike his timorous sail" (3: 137).

10. Burney's mother died when she was ten. Annie Raine Ellis, the editor of the two-volume *Early Diary of Frances Burney* (1892), writes that when Fanny was told of her mother's death, "the agony of Frances's grief was so great . . . that Mrs. Shields declared that she had never met with a child of such intense and acute feelings" (1: xlv–xlvi). Dr. Burney was a widower with six children when he married a widow with three children. They had two children together. The doctor's income was a good one, "but it depended upon his health, which had once before failed," a situation parallel to Leslie Stephen's (*Early Diary* 1: 3). Fanny served as Dr. Burney's amanuensis to the detriment of her own writing. On February 26, 1897, Virginia tells her diary: "I began to do some shorthand for father" (PA 43). Across her diaries Fanny extols her sister Susanna as "the person most dear to me upon earth!" an affection parallel to Virginia's feelings for her sister, Vanessa (*Diary and Letters of Madame D'Arblay* 1: 404). "From our earliest moments . . . *we wanted nothing but each other.* . . . She was the soul of my soul!" Burney wrote at Susanna's death (*Diary and Letters of Madame D'Arblay* 3: 190).

11. Fanny, Susanna, and their half-sister, Maria Allen, sent journal-letters to each other, and brother James shared his diary with them—and with Mr. Samuel Crisp—as well. Fanny's husband, General d'Arblay, also kept a diary.

12. The *Oxford English Dictionary* records the first usage of the term "fidgets" in 1674 and cites Burney's diary usage among eighteenth-century sources. Woolf biographer Hermione Lee suggests Virginia borrowed the term from her father (72).

13. According to Ellis, Samuel Crisp was a collateral relative of the Sir Nicholas Crisp mentioned in Pepys's and Evelyn's diaries (*Early Diary* 1: xxix). Macaulay casts Mr. Crisp as a Johnsonian "common reader" for Burney: "Men like him have their

proper place, and it is a most important one, in the Commonwealth of Letters. It is by the judgment of such men that the rank of authors is finally determined" (*Diary and Letters of Madame D'Arblay* 1: xix).

14. *Early Diary* 2: 212. Woolf ends the first paragraph of her 1939 memoir: "So without stopping to choose my way, in the sure and certain knowledge that it will find itself—or if not it will not matter—I begin: my first memory" (*MOB* 64).

15. *Early Diary* 2: 41. A year earlier he wrote her: "Send a minute Journal of every thing, and never mind their being trifles,—trifles well-dressed, are excellent food, and your cookery is [with me] of established reputation" (*Early Diary* 1: 313).

16. *Early Diary* 1: 22. According to Macaulay, Dr. Burney sent two of Fanny's sisters to a seminary in Paris; however, he kept Fanny at home for fear she would be too susceptible to Catholicism. One of her sisters taught Fanny to write (*Diary and Letters of Madame D'Arblay* 1: xv).

17. In fact, one wonders if Woolf had Dr. Burney's sabotage in mind when she wrote on her father's birthday in 1928: "He would have been 96, yes, today; & could have been 96, like other people one has known; but mercifully was not. His life would have entirely ended mine. What would have happened? No writing, no books" (*D* 3: 208). Dr. Burney not only squelched Burney's comedy but editor Ellis also suggests that Fanny's extended early service as his amanuensis resulted often in her lacking time "to make her diary complete, and [she] carried 'Evelina' about in her head, long before she could write it down in patches, on scraps of paper, which she at last copied by slow degrees" (*Early Diary* 1: 224n1). Lorna Clark suggests that if Burney's plays had been staged when written, they "might well have altered the course of theatrical history" (283).

18. *CR* 2: 239. "But we tire of rubbish-reading in the long run," Woolf asserts, however, in the next line, suggesting she valued diary reading and writing primarily "to refresh and exercise [her] own creative powers."

19. Ellis reports that Burney added passages of praise for her father and Mr. Crisp (1: viii). In 1967, long after Woolf's death, scholar Joyce Hemlow noted the many relatives and final editor who further curtailed and rearranged *The Diaries and Letters of Madame D'Arblay* after her death. Hemlow's twelve-volume *The Journals and Letters of Fanny Burney* (1972–84) heroically seeks to restore the original texts. Lars Troide, Stewart Cooke, and Betty Rizzo are doing the same in multiple volumes with *The Early Journals and Letters of Frances Burney*.

20. Burney's first "Addressed to a Certain Miss Nobody" is dated March 27, 1768; her first diary entry, May 30, 1768; and her next, September 3, 1768.

21. Even when Woolf returned to "Mrs. Thrale," herself a diarist, in the last two months of her life, it was to Mr. Clifford's Mrs. Thrale—not Fanny Burney's Mrs. Thrale and Mrs. Piozzi.

22. A mere quarter of the manuscript was printed in this first edition (Latham & Matthews 1: lxxxiv).

23. Lockhart notes that Pepys's diary was published in Edinburgh in July 1825 and was the only book Scott took with him to Ireland. "I never observed him more delighted with any book whatsoever," Lockhart writes. "He had ever afterwards many of its queer turns and phrases on his lips" (8: 107). On January 15, 1826, Scott made this intriguing slip in his own diary: "Meantime, I will correct that curious fellow Pepys' Diary. I mean the article I have made of it for the Quarterly" (Lockhart 8:196). Scott's lengthy *Quarterly Review* tribute was reprinted in Scott's *Miscellaneous Prose*, a work Virginia also may have read.

24. *E* 1: 349. This detail can be found in Pepys's May 1, 1667, entry (Wheatley 6: 282–83).

25. Drew Patrick Shannon argues in his 2007 dissertation that Virginia's description of the Queen's Jubilee parade in her first diary is influenced by Pepys's account of the Great Fire, and that her persistent effort to record public events can be traced to Pepys's influence (149).

26. "Has Nobody any curiosity to read an account of this frolic?" Burney asks at seventeen, soliciting her own report. "I am sure Nobody has, and Nobody will I satisfy by writing one. I am so good natured as to prevent Nobody's wishes" (*Early Diary* 1: 70).

Chapter 2. The Experimenter

1. The question mark in brackets signals editorial uncertainty regarding the word "preaching."

2. *PA* 160n8. In his *Charleston Magazine* review of *A Passionate Apprentice*, Andrew McNiellie writes that "For deciphering the dark, crabbed script of the 'Warboys Journal' alone, [Leaska] deserves some kind of medal" (44).

3. *PA* 138. She reprises this sentiment in her 1908 Italian journal, hoping her diary will "suggest finished pictures to the eye" (*PA* 384).

4. *PA* 161–62. Her sense of literary inadequacy in 1899 can be noted in a June 13, 1899 letter to Emma Vaughan even before her Warboys diary. She writes, "Would that I could utter / The thoughts that arise in me. / (as the poet says)" (*L* #25, 1: 26).

5. Joanne Campbell Tidwell sees Woolf as "moving towards a more 'masculine' voice" in her Warboys diary: "The self is vague and undefined, but she is attempting the early stages of an autobiographical self by using the male model before her in newspapers and essays" (18).

Chapter 3. Choosing the Outsider Role

1. *PA* 418. On September 27, 1900, Virginia reported to her cousin, Emma Vaughan, that the Warboys Rectory was "almost burnt to the ground" along with sixteen cottages, a brewery, and a cycle manufactory (*L* #33, 1: 37).

2. *PA* 171, 172. One thinks of Katharine Hilbery's passion for astronomy in Woolf's 1919 novel *Night and Day.*

3. The other two London entries are "An Expedition to Hampton Court" and "Earls Court."

4. Woolf biographer Hermione Lee calls Woolf's novels "the most pastoral city novels ever written" (415).

5. Sadly part of this entry has been lost: cut out.

6. *PA* 193. "Romsey Abbey" strikes the diarist similarly: "a rubbish heap of Saints heads, & pious stone"; like Wilton Hall, she finds it "a jumble of styles" profaned by its restorers (*PA* 203, 202).

7. The five critical essays are "Wilton—From Outside The Walls," "Wilton From Inside," "Salisbury Cathedral," "An Evening Service," and "Romsey Abbey."

8. For more on the importance of walking to Woolf, see Rachel Bowlby's "Walking, Women and Writing: Virginia Woolf as *Flâneuse.*" Biographer Hermione Lee writes that "The rhythm of walking gets into [Woolf's] sentences" (427).

9. *PA* 192. Thirty-six years later, in the 1939 "A Sketch of the Past," Woolf writes that the sound of "the waves breaking" is "the most important of all [her] memories" (*MOB* 64).

10. *PA* 166–67. Virginia used the word "suck" in her essay on "Salisbury Cathedral": "So much ancient stone however fairly piled, & however rich with the bodies of Saints & famous men, seems to suck the vitality of its humble neighbours" (*PA* 193). Betty Kushen notes that Virginia's mother told her a story of a mother who waltzed her child round the room until it died (134). In *The Voyage Out*, the dancers are "swept off" into the "great swirling pool" (157).

11. *PA* 177. This diary is six-and-a-quarter inches wide and eight-and-seven-eighth inches long, its white pages numbered in the upper right hand corner.

12. Disagreement exists between Mitchell Leaska, the editor of the first seven journals, and Nigel Nicolson and Joanne Trautmann, the editors of Woolf's letters, regarding the precise entries Virginia sent to Dickinson. Leaska suggests that six early entries may have been sent to Dickinson: "Thoughts Upon Social Success," "A Garden Dance," "An Expedition to Hampton Court," "An Artistic Party," "The Country In London," and "Earl's Court." Noting that these entries appear out of sequence in the journal, Leaska suggests that "one probable explanation is that AVS wrote them initially on separate sheets and sent them to Violet Dickinson for criticism, only copying them into her journal, heedless of chronology, when they were later returned" (*PA* 167n4). Nicolson and Trautmann suggest that Virginia's statement "I shall send you my manuscripts to read" in a letter to Dickinson they date October/November 1903 may refer to "the short descriptive essays (on such subjects as Wilton, Stonehenge, 'Country Reading,' and 'The Talk of Sheep') which Virginia wrote before, during, and after her holiday at Salisbury" (*L* 1: 103n2).

13. Frederick Pottle, who edited the new edition, pointed out that the previous

version "remained one of the most indiscreet books ever given to the world (did it not bring its author to the verge of a duel?)" ("Preface" xiii). The edition I quote from here was edited by Robert Carruthers and published in 1852 and 1860.

14. *E* 1: 251. Note the similarity to Fanny Burney's description of her listening powers.

Chapter 4. Professional Writer

1. In a May 1905 letter to Violet Dickinson, Virginia writes: "I . . . describe myself as a 'journalist who wants to read history' and so I do feel a professional Lady" (*L* #227, 1: 190).

Chapter 5. Embracing the Unconscious

1. This diary is more spacious than her small last diary. The Cornwall diary is six inches wide and nine-and-a-half inches long.

2. In the opening entry, Virginia personifies Cornwall as "our mistress": "These trifles testified to the scrupulous exactitude of our observation, & proved how accurately we had known our mistress" (*PA* 283).

3. *PA* 286. In a letter to Emma Vaughan dated September 17, 1905, Virginia offers a similar assessment: "You can't think how people strip themselves of their coverings at the sea and appear as nature made them" (*L* #249, 1: 207).

4. Seven months later, Madge's diary remains on Virginia's mind, for she asks in a letter whether Madge is "writing a great work—on the lines I once laid down?" (*L* #395, 1: 318).

5. In her sixth entry, for instance, she describes her walk to the village of Feizor as "dreamlike" and Feizor itself as a "wizard like name" (*PA* 305).

6. Thoby and Adrian Stephen stay only two days before returning to London; however, Virginia and Vanessa entertain George Duckworth, Hester Ritchie, and Emma Vaughan during their nearly month-long stay (*PA* 309n1).

7. *SF* 43. Wives' names are omitted in the Martyn family tree, a further sign of women's devaluation (*SF* 42).

8. That her mother treats her with respect is seen in her giving Joan Sir Amyas's proposal to read for herself, "that you may consider whether this exchange seems to you a fair one" (*SF* 50).

9. *SF* 59. Virginia's Florence diary entry in 1909 offers a similar ecstatic link of country and prose: "Walking on San Miniato the other evening, it occurred to me that the thing was running into classic prose before my eyes. I positively saw the long smooth sentence running like a ribbon along the road" (*PA* 396–97).

10. See French diary theorist Philippe Lejeune's marvelous essay "How Do Diaries End?" in *On Diary*, 187–200.

11. Virginia also learned of the death of Frederick Maitland, her father's close friend and biographer, at the New Forest. See *L* #330, 1: 270.

12. Tellingly, in her letter to Dickinson describing the excursion she offers what will become one of her most persistent images for unconscious composition: the desk. "I am going to walk round my desk and then take out certain manuscripts which lie there like wine, sweetening as they grow old" (*L #369*, 1: 299).

13. As a fifteen-year-old, she observed, "One ought to be a poet if one lives in the country—& one is? what" (*PA* 119). The country again evokes questions in parallel 1905 Cornwall and 1906 Blo' Norton diary passages. "Where do they come from, & whither are they bound?" she asks of the Cornwall ships/birds in 1905, while of the Norfolk carriage she inquires, "you watch it pass & disappear & wonder where it comes from & whither it goes, & who is the lady inside" (*PA* 296, 312). However, in none of these early entries does she seek to *answer* her queries.

14. In her 1939 memoir "A Sketch of the Past," Woolf declared that "whatever the reason may be, I find that scene making is my natural way of marking the past. A scene always comes to the top; arranged; representative. . . . [I]n floods reality; that is a scene . . . that is a proof of their 'reality.' Is this liability of mine to scene receiving the origin of my writing impulse? . . . Obviously I have developed the faculty, because in all the writing I have done (novels, criticism, biography) I almost always have to find a scene; either when I am writing about a person, I must find a representative scene in their lives; or when I am writing about a book, I must find the scene in their poems or novels" (*MOB* 142).

15. *PA* 368–69. Does the dead postman signal the end of communication with the public world—or even of male communication?

16. Woolf reads James's *The American Scene* during the holiday (*L #377*, 1: 304). On November 6, 1907, she writes to Madge Vaughan, "We spent the summer, which seems a long time ago, in Rye, and saw a great deal of Henry James" (*L #395*, 1: 318).

17. Emerson invited Allingham to see him during his 1872 London visit and offered to make a selection of Allingham's poems for America—a generous offer his growing infirmity prevented (222).

18. On December 27, 1867, Allingham records Tennyson's view of "Poe on metres—he knows nothing about them" (168).

19. Allingham finally married at age fifty.

20. Regrettably the expurgated diary portions were destroyed (Warner 66).

21. In "Behind the Bars," her December 12, 1919, *Athenaeum* review of *The Life and Letters of Lady Dorothy Nevill*, Woolf projects the scene: "Wolterton Hall, in Norfolk, was full of carving and mantelpieces, and there were rare trees in the garden, and a large and famous lawn. No novelist could wish a more charming and even romantic environment in which to set the story of two little girls, growing up, wild yet secluded, reading Bossuet with their governess, and riding out on their ponies at the head of the tenantry on polling day" (*CR* 1: 197).

22. Pawlowski 299, 288. Pawlowski suggests that Woolf blended the traditions of "scrapbooking and commonplacing to create a new form as eyewitness to history" (312).

23. Lady Nevill kept the silkworms in her home and they "occasionally [would] stray about and get up people's trousers, much to their inconvenience and horror" (242). When she tried an outdoor silkworm "farm" instead, the tits ate the worms (243–44). Sonya Rudiokoff points to this link in the *Virginia Woolf Miscellany* 28 (Spring 1987): 4–5.

24. 1: 92. I use "Lady Charlotte," for the diarist did not meet the Reverend Bury until many years after this diary's close.

25. 1: 209, 401. Lady Charlotte's *Diary* offers more than seventy of Princess Caroline's letters, written in her amusing Germanized English. The volume reveals that Sir William Gell and Keppel Craven, equerry and chamberlain, respectively, to the Princess, call the bickering royals the "Thompsons" in letters to Lady Charlotte and make fun of the German Princess's English. In late 1817, for instance, Gell thanks Lady Charlotte for sending him extracts of "The Thompson correspondence" and writes: "I am happy to see 'we' have lost none of our powers of writing; '*dat*' would be a great pity; and trust some day that all those invaluable specimens of her epistolary genius will be gathered together, and printed, and set forth, as models for letter-writing to posterity" (2: 185). Lady Bury's *Diary* does just that.

26. Whoever prepared the *Diary* for 1838 publication sought to conceal the diarist's identity. Diary passages referring to the novel may have been omitted to prevent identification.

27. Biographer Hermione Lee suggests that Woolf caricatures Walter Lamb in Hugh Whitbread (243); however, she may be reprising Samuel Whitbread as well.

28. That Virginia's attitude toward the "male" was known is disclosed in Vanessa's letter to Virginia August 21, 1908. Vanessa and Clive Bell are visiting Scotland during Virginia's Manorbier stay, and after reporting her horror at a walk with Clive during which he killed three rabbits, Vanessa writes: "There is an atmosphere of undiluted male here. How you would hate it!" (*Selected Letters of Vanessa Bell* 70).

Chapter 6. The Problem of Description

1. Note the unknown woman of the portrait in Woolf's final novel *Between the Acts* (68).

2. 1: 159. The Earl of Ilchester's 1909 edition of Lady Holland's *Journal* omits passages Lady Elizabeth copied into her diary from the books she "devoured," but it includes authors and titles and her evaluations.

3. As Virginia notes in her review, Sussex appears forever associated with Sir Godfrey and her unhappy marriage (*E* 1: 231).

4. *E* 1: 237. "[A] hard woman perhaps, but undoubtedly a strong and courageous one," are the review's last words (*E* 1: 238).

5. *PA* 399. Woolf's portrait of Meynell here as a timid, transfixed hare offers a clear instance of her projection of her own conflicts into her diary portraits, for Maggie

Humm writes that Meynell "had defended Mary Wollstonecraft's writings, encouraged the Royal Academy to include more women artists, and bravely praised Degas's *L'Absinthe*, as early as 1882, as well as being as voluminous a writer as Woolf" (6). However, perhaps Woolf did not know this in 1909.

6. *CH* 3. She said the same about the New Forest in her Christmas 1906 travel diary entry.

7. Joanne Campbell Tidwell agrees with those who criticize the 1909 life diary. She calls Virginia's voice "less confident," a voice that "tends to be cruel and insensitive" and the whole diary's tone "harsh and bitter" (24, 25).

8. In the manuscript, the entry is dated February 29; however, Bradshaw notes that there was no February 29 in 1909. Therefore, the date probably was March 1 (*CH* 20n1).

9. Hampstead boasted the offices of the Women's Co-operative Guild.

10. *CH* 14. This food recoil may also signal impending illness. Quentin Bell mentions Woolf's "aversion to food" during her 1913 and 1914 illness (2: 12). At Mrs. Woolf's death in July 1939, Woolf offers an echoing line about her own Jewish mother-in-law: "Still she was somebody: sitting on her high backed chair with the pink cushion, . . . a cigar always for Leonard, & plates of cakes which she pressed us to eat" (*D* 5: 223).

11. Roundell 24; *Travels of Lady Hester Stanhope* 1: 55. Virginia's 1906 Greek diary suggests she shared diarist Charles Meryon's response to Greece. Lady Hester's physician wrote: "My bosom beat with emotion as I now trod, for the first time, the soil of a people, in studying whose language and habits the chief part of fifteen years of my early life had been—I still think wisely—expended" (*Travels* 1: 27).

12. Lady Charlotte Bury, in fact, appears in Dr. Meryon's diaries. The doctor reads Lady Bury's novel *Memoirs of a Peeress* to Lady Hester in 1838, and the volume so pleases Lady Hester that she declares, "If I were rich enough, I would invite Lady Charlotte here—and she would come, for she has children, and would like to show them the East. How pleasant it would be for me to have such a companion for two or three hours a day! What a beautiful woman she was!" (*Memoirs* 3: 185). Lady Hester likely forgot at this moment that she fled Mount Lebanon for Antioch in 1816 to avoid entertaining Princess Caroline of Wales during *her* tour of the Levant, and that she had roundly criticized and mocked this woman Lady Charlotte served and sought to defend—behavior preserved, however, in Dr. Meryon's diaries (*Travels* 3: 307–9; *Memoirs* 1: 308). Once more Woolf's diary worlds intertwine.

13. Dr. Meryon's diary style seems modeled on Boswell's *Journal of a Tour to the Hebrides with Samuel Johnson*. "It is necessary that I should introduce my readers to this person, who played a very conspicuous part in Lady Hester Stanhope's establishment," he writes in his first diary (*Memoirs* 1: 268). In his second, he ventures, "In order to render intelligible to the reader many passages which have occurred, and will occur again, in Lady Hester's conversations, . . . it may not be amiss to give a brief outline of her system of astrology" (*Memoirs* 2: 251). In his third diary, he again

begins a section in perfect Boswellian style: "As the Druze insurrection has excited considerable attention in Europe, and as the origin of it is but imperfectly known, I may be excused for making a short digression from my diary in order to…" (*Memoirs* 3: 67). The conscientious doctor also laments his diary lapses. "Why had I not written down more for these last three days? I said to myself, when I saw the scantiness of my memorandums: alas!" he writes in 1838 (*Memoirs* 3: 170).

14. Besides her own, Lady Hester also contrived her oldest brother's escape to the continent from their oppressive patriarchal home (Roundell 5).

15. *Memoirs* 1: 85–86. In 1812, in fact, Lady Hester writes to a friend from Damascus: "Like Doctor Pangloss, I always try to think that everything is for the best; if I had not been shipwrecked, I should have seen nothing here; if I had been born a man instead of a woman, I could not have entered all the harems as I have done" (*Travels* 2: 40).

16. Her defense of Lady Hester may have been fueled by her previous diary reading as well as by this *DNB* jibe, for eighteen months earlier she had read writer Monk Lewis's gossipy sneer at Lady Hester in Lady Charlotte Bury's *Diary of a Lady-in-Waiting*: "I hear that Lady [Hester Stanhope] is living at Constantinople with young [Michael] B[ruce], avowedly as his *chère amie*; and that she says nobody was ever so handsome, nor so clever, and that his is in short, and *is to be*, one of the first characters in these kingdoms. I wish him joy of his conquest, and had rather *he* than *I*" (1: 75).

17. Part II, 166. Joan Haslip, however, in her 1936 *Lady Hester Stanhope: A Biography*, calls the doctor's diary "painstaking and unimaginative" (146).

18. She also reads Emerson's essays "The Conduct of Life" and "Society and Solitude" (*RN* 151).

19. 1: 232. On March 21, 1821, Emerson offered "a neat, concise and *pithy* comparison of country and city life" to the Pythologian Society (1: 48).

20. In her letter, Woolf follows her lament at the memoir's thin portrait by saying, "But I didn't know her. From her poems, one expected something—I dont know what" (*L* #525, 1: 426).

21. Mary Coleridge exhibited other interests akin to Woolf's. Coleridge was drawn to painting as well as writing. Virginia also learned from *Gathered Leaves* that at her death in 1907 Coleridge left a medieval romance unfinished on her writing table.

Chapter 7. The Diary Coalesces

1. Describing "The Monks House Library" in 1973, George Spater writes that "one must conclude that many books of Virginia Stephen had been previously disposed of or lost in the Blitz" (64). Woolf makes no mention of lost diaries, however.

2. After *typing* the first eleven labels, she shifts to pen and ink for the remaining label dates.

3. In *Virginia Woolf and the Great War*, Karen L. Levenback seeks to show that the

Great War was "a constant presence" in Woolf's writing (8). These 1915 diary entries support that view.

4. Berry wrote a two-volume *Comparative View of Social Life in England and France from the Restoration of Charles II to the Present*, a play, and edited volumes of French and English letters.

5. The editors of Woolf's *Letters*, Nigel Nicolson and Joanne Trautmann, indicate that Woolf refers here to Berry's three-volume *Journals and Correspondence* (*L* 2; 82n1)

6. The *Journals'* editor, in fact, directs the reader several times to Lady Bury's *Diary of a Lady-in-Waiting* and once to Fanny Burney's diaries (2: 170n*; 470n*; 535n+; 3: 33n*).

7. 1: 160. Walpole loathed Dr. Johnson and in his letters to Berry speaks slightingly of the dictionary maker and those diarists surrounding him: James Boswell, Hester Thrale—and even Fanny Burney (1: 305, 412, 414, 488).

8. In 1937 W. S. Lewis and A. Dayle Wallace criticized Berry's editorial work on Walpole's letters: "No letter which passed through the hands of Mary Berry remained the same. She inked out paragraphs, suppressed proper names, and wrote her notes wherever there was room for them. Her object was to improve the letters by deleting what she considered to be their less brilliant passages—the passages which are today, as often as not, of the greatest interest—for the Walpolian orchestra must play *fortissimo* or not at all" (*Horace Walpole's Correspondence* 1: xix).

9. 1: xvi. This theme of denied calling sounds across Berry's journals. "[M]y sex and situation condemning me to perfect insignificance, and precluding all possibility of my ever taking an active part," she writes in 1797 at the age of thirty-five (2: 22). In Rome on her sixtieth birthday she exclaims in her journal: "Thirty-nine years have passed since I was here on the anniversary of this day, when I had reached my twenty-first year. What regrets I felt then at having been born a woman, and deprived of the life and position which, as a man, I might have had in this world!" (3: 332).

10. "O for the power of involving myself in fiction," Berry once exclaims, "and throwing aside (for the time at least) all the dull realities of life!" (2: 314). As several commentators have noted, the old Scottish "Ballad of the Queen Marys" is the more obvious, yet not necessarily the only, source of Woolf's Mary Beton, Mary Seton, and Mary Carmichael (Hussey 12–13). In *Mrs. Dalloway*, Clarissa's admirable love is Sally Seton.

11. They include the 1899 Warboys diary, the 1903 diary (begun at St. Albans), the 1904–5 daily diary (begun at the New Forest), the 1905 Cornwall diary, the 1906–8 Great Britain travel diary (begun at Giggleswick), and the 1906–9 Continental travel diary (begun in Greece). Of her first ten diaries, only Woolf's first (1897) diary, her brief 1909 life diary, and her 1915 diary begin in London.

12. The solid burgundy of the spine extends three-quarters of an inch onto the front and back covers, which have a lighter red background on which are traced waving lines of gray, white, and green.

13. In her January 10, 1915, diary entry, Woolf wrote of Lamb's account of King George V: "His style of talk reminds me of George 3rd in Fanny Burney's diary—& so one must bless Walter for something" (*D* 1: 14).

14. The synesthetic word "echo" will become an important image in Woolf's diary. In her haunting June 27, 1940, entry chosen by composer Dominick Argento for his song cycle "From the Diary of Virginia Woolf," Woolf projects a similar scenario: "the war—our waiting while the knives sharpen for the operation—has taken away the outer wall of security. No echo comes back. I have no surroundings. I have so little sense of a public that I forget about Roger [her biography *Roger Fry*] coming or not coming out. Those familiar circumvolutions—those standards—which have for so many years given back an echo & so thickened my identity are all wide & wild as the desert now" (*D* 5: 299).

15. *D* 1: 70. Leonard Woolf expressed similar thoughts in his November 1, 1917, letter from Manchester: "I shall never leave you again, I think, partly because you want a Stewart Goose to look after you & partly because life is so intolerable without you. I keep on thinking this morning that it's only today & to-morrow now before I see you again. We'll go & fetch poor old Tinker from the vet in the afternoon & walk by the river & then we'll come back to tea & sit over the fire & talk" (*Letters of Leonard Woolf* 219).

16. The 1917 collaborative Hogarth House diary is much larger than its Asheham House diary companion—it is seven inches wide and nine inches long—but it is two inches shorter in length than the even larger 1915 diary. However, in other physical respects the 1917 diary resembles the smaller Asheham House diary. Its sturdy red spine spills over one inch onto the diary's front and back covers; the rest of the cover is blue-gray marble, the membranes on this blue-gray background brown mixed with white.

17. *D* 1: 81. Woolf's ease with Bell likely stems from the fact that Leonard has thoroughly replaced him in importance, for Woolf acknowledges in her December 7, 1917, entry that "Clive starts his topics—lavishing admiration & notice upon Nessa, which doesn't make me jealous as once it did, when the swing of that pendulum carried so much of my fortune with it: at any rate of my comfort" (*D* 1: 86). Woolf has been accused of diary reserve; however, her diary contains this and many other unflinching confessions.

18. Joanne Campbell Tidwell asserts that Woolf's remark that she has "no inner life" is disingenuous: "her inner life is well recorded in the pages of the diary" (50).

19. So interested was Woolf in this diary ventriloquism that two days later she sent a longer "sketch" of her duet with Vaughan, structured in dramatic form, to Vanessa as a "thank offering for the loan of your picture; and if you think it a fair exchange, we might do traffic on these lines" (*L* #894, 2: 199).

20. Edmond Goncourt shared Fanny Burney's need to find consolation following a loved one's death by commemorating the death in a diary. Edmond writes: "When my brother died I considered that our literary work was ended and I determined to

seal the journal as of the twentieth of January 1870, where his hand had written its last lines. But then I was seized by the bitter desire to recount to myself the final months and the death of my beloved brother" (Galantière xii). His sentence continues: "and almost immediately thereafter the tragic occurrences of the Siege of Paris and the Commune impelled me to continue this journal" (xii). In this way the collaborative journal became a single one.

21. Galantière 235. On October 24, 1864, the Goncourts write that "Since Balzac, the novel has nothing in common with what our fathers understood by 'novel.' The novel of today is written with the help of documents narrated or taken from nature" (Galantière 190).

22. 1: v. "A thousand thanks for your accustomed cadeau," he writes December 28, 1868, at age thirty-six. "I remember the time I used to jot down in them sonnets to my mistress' eyebrow in Kingstown. I have one or two at home full of snatches of poetry written to half a dozen young ladies—and now I am a father, four bouncing children!" (1: 161).

23. 2: 618. "I am happy to think that as you read about the nature of the man, you thought of me," Brooke wrote to Henschell of Lockhart's *Life of Scott*, "but between me and Sir Walter Scott—even in nature—there is all the difference between a mountain lake, and the great Ocean. Do read the Diary" (2: 618).

24. He resembles his fellow Irish poet and diarist William Allingham in that regard. Brooke's very name perhaps shaped him for, according to Jacks, "at all periods of his life, [he] was a haunter of streams and a lover of running waters" (1: 2).

25. "Leslie Stephen's Essays are too cold, but he realizes this and tries to avoid it," Brooke tells his diary February 15, 1908. "He recognizes the need of warmth and works for it, but his nature is too strong for him. Yet all he says is carefully thought and well supported; and whenever good thinking is all that is to be applied in criticism, few better or more interesting criticisms have been written" (2: 598). The day before, Brooke writes: "Read Leslie Stephen on Kingsley—a good essay, but not enough in sympathy with Kingsley's type to be quite fair. He tries hard for fairness, and says many wise and just things of K., but it is plain that K. irritates L. S. And I don't wonder. K. screams often when he ought to speak" (2: 597).

26. 2: 591. Three months before his death, Brooke writes a friend: "I don't feel yet as if dying were possible, but I know it comes. I hope I shall like it, but I have enjoyed living very much, and I am very fond of this gracious Surface and all its doings. Anyway, it is well to be close to the heart of Mother Earth and to hear the beating of her heart" (2: 684).

27. That the Press aimed to be experimental and to challenge the status quo can be seen from letters Woolf writes during this diary's time frame. She writes to Violet Dickinson, for instance, January 14, 1918: "We are hard at work printing a long story by a woman called Katherine Mansfield. . . . It's very good I think; but the publisher wouldn't take it" (*L* #902, 2: 209).

28. *D* 1: 102. In her January 21 entry, she declares her interest in joining the British Society for the Study of Sex Psychology (*D* 1: 110).

29. In a February 25, 1918, letter to Vanessa, Woolf confides that she and Leonard are thinking of bringing their little press to the country, and on June 10, 1918, she writes to Violet Dickinson: "We are just bargaining for a new press, which we shall put in the basement" (*L* #909, 2: 219; #941, 2: 249).

Works Consulted

Primary Sources

Boswell, James. *The Journal of a Tour to the Hebrides with Samuel Johnson, LL.D.* Ed. Robert Carruthers. London: Office of the National Illustrated Library, 1852.

Boswell's Journal of a Tour to the Hebrides with Samuel Johnson, LL.D. Pub. from the original ms. Ed. Frederick A. Pottle and Charles H. Bennett. New York: Viking Press, 1936.

The Diary and Letters of Madame D'Arblay (Frances Burney). With notes by W. C. Ward and essay by Lord MacCaulay. 3 vols. London: Frederick Warne, 1892.

The Diary of a Lady-in-Waiting: Being the Diary Illustrative of the Times of George the Fourth interspersed with Original Letters from the Late Queen Caroline and from other Distinguished Persons. Ed. A. Francis Steuart. 2 vols. London: John Lane, 1908.

The Diary of Samuel Pepys. Ed. Robert Latham and William Matthews. 11 vols. Berkeley: University of California Press, 1970.

The Diary of Samuel Pepys. Ed. Henry B. Wheatley. 8 vols. London: G. Bell, 1962. First published in 10 vols., 1893–99.

The Early Diary of Frances Burney, 1768–1778. Ed. Annie Raine Ellis. 2 vols. London: G. Bell and Sons, 1913.

Extracts of the Journals and Correspondence of Miss Berry from the Year 1783 to 1852. Ed. Lady Theresa Lewis. 3 vols. London: Longmans, Green, 1865.

Extracts from the Letters and Journals of William Cory. Selected and arranged by Francis Warre Cornish. Oxford: Horace Hart, 1897.

The Famous Miss Burney: The Diaries and Letters of Fanny Burney. Ed. Barbara G. Schrank and David J. Supino. New York: John Day, 1976.

Gathered Leaves from the Prose of Mary E. Coleridge. With a memoir by Edith Sichel. London: Constable, 1910.

The Goncourt Journals 1851–1870. Ed. and tr. Lewis Galantière. Garden City, N.Y.: Doubleday, Doran, 1937.

Jacks, Lawrence Pearsall. *Life and Letters of Stopford Brooke.* 2 vols. New York: Charles Scribner's, 1917.

The Journal of Elizabeth Lady Holland (1791–1811). Ed. Earl of Ilchester. 2 vols. London: Longmans, Green, 1908.

The Journal of Sir Walter Scott. Ed. W.E.K. Anderson. Oxford: Clarendon Press, 1972.

The Journal of Sir Walter Scott 1825–32. Ed. David Douglas. Edinburgh: Douglas & Foulis, Printed from the stereotype plates made for the edition of 1891, with a few inaccuracies corrected.

The Journal of Sir Walter Scott 1825–26. Ed. J. G. Tait. Edinburgh: Oliver and Boyd, 1939.

The Journal of Sir Walter Scott 1827–28. Ed. J. G. Tait. Edinburgh: Oliver and Boyd, 1941.

The Journal of Sir Walter Scott 1829–32. Ed. J. G. Trait and W. M. Parker. Edinburgh: Oliver and Boyd, 1946.

The Journals and Letters of Fanny Burney (Madame D'Arblay). Ed. Joyce Hemlow with Curtis D. Cecil and Althea Douglas. 12 vols. Oxford: Clarendon Press, 1972.

The Journals and Miscellaneous Notebooks of Ralph Waldo Emerson. Ed. William H. Gilman et al. Vol. 4. Cambridge, Mass.: Harvard University Press, 1964.

The Journals and Miscellaneous Notebooks of Ralph Waldo Emerson. Ed. A. W. Plumstead and Harrison Hayford. Vol. 7. Cambridge, Mass.: Harvard University Press, 1969.

Journals of Ralph Waldo Emerson [1820–1824]. Ed. Edward Waldo Emerson and Waldo Emerson Forbes. Boston: Houghton Mifflin, 1909.

Journals of Ralph Waldo Emerson [1824–1832]. Ed. Edward Waldo Emerson and Waldo Emerson Forbes. Boston: Houghton Mifflin, 1909.

Lockhart, John G. *Memoirs of the Life of Sir Walter Scott*. 10 vols. Edinburgh: Robert Cadell, 1839.

Meryon, Charles. *Memoirs of the Lady Hester Stanhope, As Related By Herself In Conversations With Her Physician*. 3 vols. London: Henry Colburn, 1845.

———. *Travels of Lady Hester Stanhope: Forming the Completion of Her Memoirs Narrated by Her Physician*. 3 vols. London: Henry Colburn, 1846.

Moore, Thomas. *The Life, Letters and Journals of Lord Byron*. London: John Murray, 1866.

Nevill, Dorothy. *Leaves from the Note-Books of Lady Dorothy Nevill*. Ed. Ralph Nevill. London: Macmillan, 1907.

Silver, Brenda. *Virginia Woolf's Reading Notebooks*. Princeton: Princeton University Press, 1983.

William Allingham: A Diary. Ed. H. Allingham and D. Radford. London: Macmillan, 1907.

Woolf, Virginia. *Carlyle's House and Other Sketches*. Ed. David Bradshaw. Foreword by Doris Lessing. London: Hesperus Press, 2003.

———. *The Common Reader*. New York: Harcourt Brace Jovanovich, 1925.

———. *The Complete Shorter Fiction of Virginia Woolf*. Ed. Susan Dick. New York: Harcourt Brace Jovanovich, 1985.

———. *The Diary of Virginia Woolf.* Ed. Anne Olivier Bell. 5 vols. New York: Harcourt Brace, 1977–84.

———. *The Essays of Virginia Woolf.* Ed. Andrew McNeillie and Stuart N. Clarke. 6 vols. New York: Harcourt Brace, 1986–2011.

———. *Granite & Rainbow: Essays.* New York: Harcourt Brace, Jovanovich, 1958.

———. *The Letters of Virginia Woolf.* Ed. Nigel Nicolson and Joanne Trautmann. 6 vols. New York: Harcourt Brace, 1975–80.

———. *A Moment's Liberty: The Shorter Diary.* Abr. and ed. Anne Olivier Bell. Intro. Quentin Bell. New York: Harcourt Brace, 1990.

———. *Moments of Being.* Ed. and Intro. Jeanne Schulkind. 2nd ed. New York: Harcourt Brace, 1985.

———. *A Passionate Apprentice: The Early Journals 1897–1909.* Ed. and Intro. Mitchell A. Leaska. New York: Harcourt Brace Jovanovich, 1990.

———. *A Room of One's Own.* New York: Harcourt Brace Jovanovich, 1929.

———. *The Second Common Reader.* New York: Harcourt Brace Jovanovich, 1932.

———. *Three Guineas.* New York: Harcourt Brace Jovanovich, 1938.

———. *To the Lighthouse.* New York: Harcourt Brace Jovanovich, 1927.

———. *The Voyage Out.* New York: Harcourt Brace Jovanovich, 1920.

———. *A Writer's Diary: Being Extracts from the Diary of Virginia Woolf.* Ed. Leonard Woolf. Afterword Louise Bogan and Josephine Schaefer. New York: New American Library, 1968.

Secondary Sources

Argento, Dominick. *From the Diary of Virginia Woolf.* Nashville: Gasparo, 1989.

Auden, W. H. "A Consciousness of Reality." Rev. of *A Writer's Diary*, by Virginia Woolf. *The New Yorker* 6 Mar. 1954: 99–104.

Bell, Anne Olivier. *Editing Virginia Woolf's Diary.* London: Bloomsbury Workshop, 1990.

Bell, Quentin. *Virginia Woolf: A Biography.* 2 vols. New York: Harcourt, Brace, Jovanovich, 1972.

Blodgett, Harriet. *"Capacious Hold-All": An Anthology of Englishwomen's Diary Writings.* Charlottesville: University Press of Virginia, 1991.

———. *Centuries of Female Days: English Women's Private Diaries.* New Brunswick, N.J.: Rutgers University Press: 1988.

———. "A Woman Writer's Diary: Virginia Woolf Revisited." *Prose Studies: History, Theory, Criticism* 12.1 (May 1989): 57–71.

Bowlby, Rachel. "Walking, Women and Writing: Virginia Woolf as *Flâneuse.*" *New Feminist Discourses: Critical Essays on Theories and Texts.* Ed. Isobel Armstrong. London: Routledge, 1992. 26–47.

Burrow, Colin. "Shower of Firedrops." Rev. of *Samuel Pepys: The Unequalled Self*, by Claire Tomalin. *London Review of Books* 14 Nov. 2002: 11–12.

Carlyle, Thomas. "Sir Walter Scott." *Critical and Miscellaneous Essays*. Vol. 4. New York: Charles Scribner's, 1901. 22–87.

Clark, Lorna. "The Diarist as Novelist: Narrative Strategies in the Journals and Letters of Frances Burney." *English Studies in Canada* 27 (2001): 283–302.

Cottam, Rachel. "Secret Scratching: The Diary and its Writing." Diss. University of Sussex, 1996.

Dalsimer, Katherine. *Virginia Woolf: Becoming a Writer*. New Haven: Yale University Press, 2001.

DeSalvo, Louise A. "1897: Virginia Woolf at Fifteen." *Virginia Woolf: A Feminist Slant*. Ed. Jane Marcus. Lincoln: University of Nebraska Press, 1983. 78–108.

———. "Shakespeare's *Other* Sister." *New Feminist Essays on Virginia Woolf*. Ed. Jane Marcus. Lincoln: University of Nebraska Press, 1981. 61–81.

———. *Virginia Woolf: The Impact of Childhood Sexual Abuse on Her Life and Work*. New York: Ballantine Books, 1989.

Froula, Christine. "Virginia Woolf as Shakespeare's Sister: Chapters in a Woman Writer's Autobiography." *Women's Re-Visions of Shakespeare: On the Response Of Dickinson, Woolf, Rich, H. D., George Eliot, and Others*. Ed. Marianne Novy. Urbana: University of Illinois Press, 1990: 123–41.

Glendinning, Victoria. *Leonard Woolf: A Biography*. New York: Free Press, 2006.

Godden, Rumer. "Virginia Woolf, Critical and Creative, Always the Dedicated Writer." Rev. of *A Writer's Diary*. *New York Herald Tribune Book Review* 21 Feb. 1954: 1.

Gristwood, Sarah. *Recording Angels: The Secret World of Women's Diaries*. London: HARRAP, 1988.

Haslip, Joan. *Lady Hester Stanhope: A Biography*. New York: Frederick A. Stokes, 1936.

Hemlow, Joyce. "Letters and Journals of Fanny Burney: Establishing the Text." *Editing Eighteenth-Century Texts. Papers given at the Editorial Conference, University of Toronto, October 1967*. Toronto: University of Toronto Press, 1968. 25–43.

Hewitt, David, ed. *Scott on Himself: A Selection of the Autobiographical Writings of Sir Walter Scott*. Edinburgh: Scottish Academic Press, 1981.

Holroyd, Michael. *Lytton Strachey: The New Biography*. New York: Farrar, Straus and Giroux, 1994.

Humm, Maggie, ed. *The Edinburgh Companion to Virginia Woolf and the Arts*. Edinburgh: Edinburgh University Press, 2010.

Jackson, Anna. "Towards a Poetics of the Diary." Diss. University of Oxford, 2000.

Johnson, Samuel. "Milton." *The Lives of the Poets*. Ed. John H. Middendorf. New Haven: Yale University Pres, 2010. 99–205.

Kushen, Betty. *Virginia Woolf and the Nature of Communion*. West Orange, N.J.: Raynor Press, 1983.

Lee, Hermione. *Virginia Woolf.* New York: Knopf, 1997.

Lejeune, Philippe. *On Diary.* Ed. Jeremy D. Popkin and Julie Rak. Trans. Katherine Durnin. Manoa: University of Hawai'i Press, 2009.

Letters of Leonard Woolf. Ed. Frederic Spotts. London: Bloomsbury, 1992.

Levenbeck, Karen L. *Virginia Woolf and the Great War.* Syracuse: Syracuse University Press, 1999.

Mallon, Thomas. *A Book of One's Own.* New York: Ticknor & Fields, 1984.

Marburg, Clara. *Mr. Pepys and Mr. Evelyn.* Philadelphia: University of Pennsylvania Press, 1935.

McNeillie, Andrew. Personal interview. 15 June 2001.

———. Rev. of *A Passionate Apprentice: The Early Journals of Virginia Woolf,* ed. Mitchell Leaska. *The Charleston Magazine* 2 (Autumn/Winter 1990): 42–44.

Patten, John A. *Sir Walter Scott: A Character Study.* London: James Clarke, 1932.

Pawlowski, Merry M. "Virginia Woolf and Scrapbooking." *The Edinburgh Companion to Virginia Woolf and the Arts.* Ed. Maggie Humm. Edinburgh: Edinburgh University Press, 2010. 298–313.

Podnieks, Elizabeth. *Daily Modernism: The Literary Diaries of Virginia Woolf, Antonia White, Elizabeth Smart, and Anaïs Nin.* Montreal: McGill-Queens University Press, 2000.

Poole, Roger. Rev. of *Virginia Woolf: The Impact of Childhood Sexual Abuse on Her Life and Work,* by Louise DeSalvo; *Who Killed Virginia Woolf? A Psychobiography,* by Alma Halben Bond; *Virginia Woolf: A Study of the Short Fiction,* by Dean R. Baldwin; and *Virginia Woolf: Strategist of Language,* by William A. Evans. *Modern Fiction Studies* 37.2 (Summer 1991): 300–305.

Rosenwald, Lawrence. *Emerson and the Art of the Diary.* New York: Oxford University Press, 1988.

Roundell, Mrs. Charles. *Lady Hester Stanhope.* London: John Murray, 1909.

Selected Letters of Vanessa Bell. Ed. Regina Marler. New York: Pantheon, 1993.

Sellers, Susan. "Virginia Woolf's diaries and letters." *The Cambridge Companion to Virginia Woolf.* Ed. Sue Roe and Susan Sellers. Cambridge: Cambridge University Press, 2000. 109–26.

Shannon, Drew Patrick. "The Deep Old Desk: The Diary of Virginia Woolf." Diss. University of Cincinnati, 2007.

Simons, Judy. *Diaries and Journals of Literary Women from Fanny Burney to Virginia Woolf.* Iowa City: University of Iowa Press, 1990.

Spater, George. "The Monks House Library." *Virginia Woolf Quarterly* 1.3 (Spring 1973): 60–65.

Stephen, Leslie. *Studies of a Biographer.* Vol. 4. New York: Putnam, 1907.

Strachey, Lytton. "Lady Hester Stanhope." *The Atheaeum* 4 Apr. 1919: 131–33; 11 Apr. 1919: 166–67.

Tait, J. G. *The Missing Tenth of Sir Walter Scott's Journal.* Edinburgh: Oliver and Boyd, 1936.

Tidwell, Joanne Campbell. *Politics and Aesthetics in The Diary of Virginia Woolf.* New York: Routledge, 2008.

Tomalin, Claire. *Samuel Pepys: The Unequalled Self.* New York: Knopf, 2003.

Warner, Alan. *William Allingham.* Lewisburg, Penn.: Bucknell University Press, 1975.

Willy, Margaret. *English Diarists: Evelyn & Pepys.* London: Longmans, Green, 1963.

Index

Berry, Mr., 175, 176. *See also* Berry, Mary

Birrell, Augustine, 72

Blake, William, 110, 162, 177

Blodgett, Harriet, 1, 12, 24, 228n8

Blo' Norton Hall, 87, 89–90, 91, 122

Bloomsbury, 89, 166, 167, 207

Bloomsbury Group, 1, 8, 56, 191–92, 194–95, 197, 201, 205, 215, 219, 221

Bolton Abbey, 39

Bonaparte, Louis Napoleon, 201–2

Bossuet, Jacques-Bénigne, 233n21

Boswell, James: William Allingham's diaries and, 105, 106; curiosity of, 71; diaries of, 3, 4, 7, 67, 68, 147–48, 151, 153, 200; *Journal of a Tour to Corsica*, 72; *Journal of a Tour to the Hebrides with Samuel Johnson*, 3, 54, 67–74, 109, 235–36n13; Samuel Pepys and, 3; retentive memory of, 21, 70, 71, 72, 73, 74, 106; vitality of, 71; Horace Walpole and, 237n7

Botten, Jasper, 186

Bowlby, Rachel, 231n8

Boxall, Nelly, 193–94

Bradley, Katharine ("Michael Field"): diary of, 3, 6. *See also* Cooper, Edith

Bradshaw, David, 136, 138, 139, 140, 141, 142, 143, 145, 235n8

Brandes, Georg, 199

British Society for the Study of Sex Psychology, 240n28

Brooke, Evelyn, 207. *See also* Brooke, Stopford

Brooke, Rupert, 141

Brooke, Stopford: diary of, 163, 197, 206–12, 239n22; London and, 207; nature and, 207, 209, 211–12, 239nn24,26; reading and, 206, 209, 210; Sir Walter Scott and, 206, 239n23; Leslie Stephen and, 210, 239n25; *To the Lighthouse* and, 210; war and, 208; water and, 207, 211, 239n24; women and, 207–8; writings of, 209

Brougham, Henry, 113

Brown, John (American abolitionist), 105. *See also* Allingham, William; Emerson, Ralph Waldo

Brown, John (servant to Queen Victoria), 106

Browne, Sir Thomas, 161

Browning, Elizabeth Barrett, 134

Browning, Robert, 107, 133, 159, 162

Bruce, Michael, 236n16

Burke, Edmund, 29, 36, 69

Burney, Dr. Charles, 21, 28, 31, 107, 110, 229n19; harms Fanny's writing, 19, 25, 26, 228n10, 229nn16,17; portraits and, 23

Burney, Frances (Fanny and Madame d'Arblay), 61, 111, 178; attention to women, 11, 24–29, 116, 226; Mary Berry's journals and, 174, 237n6; Lady Charlotte Bury's diary and, 110, 114; Mary Coleridge and, 158; William Johnson Cory and, 38; diary of, 3, 7, 11, 14, 19–31, 34, 41, 46, 48, 53, 67, 71, 73, 106, 116, 151, 153, 160, 164, 167, 169, 188–89, 197, 202, 211, 212, 226, 229nn20,21, 230n26, 232n14, 238n13; dress and, 24; education of, 25, 229n16; family similarities to Woolf, 11, 19–21, 228nn10,11; "fidgets" and, 4, 19–20, 26, 228n12; Edmond Goncourt's journal and, 238–39n20; horse trope and, 26, 28–29, 155; "Miss Nobody" and, 19, 24, 25, 30, 31, 34, 160, 229n20, 230n26; passion for books of, 20, 158; Samuel Pepys and, 3, 31, 32, 33, 34; portraiture in, 22–23, 41, 189, 199–200; retentive memory of, 21–22, 41, 106, 232n14; in *A Room of One's Own*, 27–29; Mr. Seaton and, 22; sensitivity to criticism of, 20, 26, 205; shyness of, 4, 19, 20, 25, 158; spontaneous invention of, 21, 26; Horace Walpole and, 237n7; war and, 26–27; Woolf's "Dr. Burney's Evening Party," 3, 19, 20, 21, 25, 28, 29, 32; Woolf's "Fanny Burney's Half-Sister," 3, 19, 28; Woolf's *Three Guineas* and, 26–27

Burney, James, 228n11

Burney, Susanna, 19, 22, 25, 31, 228nn10,11

Burrow, Colin, 33

Bury, Lady Charlotte, 235n12; Mary Berry's journal and, 174, 180–81, 237n6; diary of, 4, 81, 109–14, 131, 147, 149, 174, 180–81, 234nn24,25,26,27, 236n16

Byron, George Gordon, Lord, 107, 110, 147, 181, 226; diary of, 15, 31, 227n4

Cabot, James Eliot, 155

Cambridge, Richard Owen, 26

Special thanks to

The Henry W. and Albert A. Berg Collection of English and American Literature
The New York Public Library
Astor, Lenox and Tilden Foundations

Excerpts from *The Goncourt Journals 1851–1870* by Edmond de Goncourt and Jules de Goncourt, edited by Lewis Galantiere. Text copyright © 1937. Reprinted courtesy of Random House.

Excerpts from *Carlyle's House and Other Sketches* by Virginia Woolf. Reprinted by permission of The Society of Authors as the Literary Representative of the Estate of Virginia Woolf.

U.S. print rights

Excerpts from *The Essays of Virginia Woolf, Volume I: 1904–1912*, edited by Andrew McNellie. Text copyright © 1986 by Quentin Bell and Angelica Garnett. Reprinted by permission of Houghton Mifflin Harcourt Publishing Company. All rights reserved.

Excerpts from *The Essays of Virginia Woolf, Volume II: 1912–1918*, edited by Andrew McNellie. Text copyright © 1987 by Quentin Bell and Angelica Garnett. Reprinted by permission of Houghton Mifflin Harcourt Publishing Company. All rights reserved.

Excerpts from *The Complete Shorter Fiction of Virginia Woolf*, edited by Susan Dick. Copyright © 1985 by Quentin Bell and Angelica Garnett. Reprinted by permission of Houghton Mifflin Harcourt Publishing Company. All rights reserved.

Excerpts from *The Letters of Virginia Woolf, Volume I: 1888–1912*, edited by Nigel Nicolson and Joanne Trautmann. Letters copyright © 1975 by Quentin Bell and Angelica Garnett. Reprinted by permission of Houghton Mifflin Harcourt Publishing Company. All rights reserved.

Excerpts from *The Diary of Virginia Woolf, Volume I: 1915–1919*, edited by Anne Olivier Bell. Diary copyright © 1977 by Quentin Bell and Angelica Garnett. Reprinted by permission of Houghton Mifflin Harcourt Publishing Company. All rights reserved.

Excerpts from *A Passionate Apprentice: The Early Journals 1897–1909*, edited by Mitchell Leaska. Text copyright © 1990 by Quentin Bell and Angelica Garnett. Reprinted by permission of Houghton Mifflin Harcourt Publishing Company. All rights reserved.

World, excluding U.S., print rights

Excerpts from *A Passionate Apprentice: The Early Journals 1897–1909* by Virginia Woolf. Published by Hogarth Press. Reprinted by permission of The Random House Group Limited.

Barbara Lounsberry has devoted her life to the study and practice of artful nonfiction in its many forms. She has worked closely with literary journalism pioneer Gay Talese, with whom she edited *Writing Creative Nonfiction: The Literature of Reality*. Her own books include *The Art of Fact: Contemporary Artists of Nonfiction, The Writer in You*, and *The Tales We Tell: Perspectives on the Short Story* (coedited with Susan Lohafer).

Lounsberry served as the nonfiction editor for *The North American Review*, the oldest literary magazine in the United States, from 2000 to 2003 and was a contributing editor to *Keep it Real: Everything You Need to Know About Researching and Writing Creative Nonfiction*. Lounsberry serves on the Board of Directors of the Norman Mailer Society, and she has published book chapters and essays on the nonfiction of Mailer, Talese, Ernest Hemingway, John McPhee, Joan Didion, Tom Wolfe, Patricia Hampl, Lewis Thomas, Virginia Woolf, and others.

A PhD in English from the University of Iowa, Lounsberry regularly taught seminars on "Virginia Woolf" and on "Literary Nonfiction" at the University of Northern Iowa before retiring to write full time in 2006.